Celtic Astrology
from the Druids
to the Middle Ages

Celtic Astrology from the Druids to the Middle Ages

M.G. Boutet

Foreword by David Frawley

McFarland & Company, Inc., Publishers
Jefferson, North Carolina

Originally published in French as
*Les Druides et l'astrologie: Origine et fondements de l'astrologie
celto-druidique de la préhistoire au Moyen Âge*

LIBRARY OF CONGRESS CATALOGUING-IN-PUBLICATION DATA

Names: Boutet, Michel-Gerald, author.
Title: Celtic astrology from the Druids to the Middle Ages /
M.G. Boutet ; foreword by David Frawley.
Other titles: Druides et l'astrologie. English
Description: Jefferson, North Carolina : McFarland & Company, Inc.,
Publishers, 2017. | Includes bibliographical references and index.
Identifiers: LCCN 2017022902 | ISBN 9781476670041
(softcover : acid free paper) ∞
Subjects: LCSH: Astrology, Celtic—History. | Druids and Druidism.
Classification: LCC BF1714.C44 B6813 2017 | DDC 133.5/93916—dc23
LC record available at https://lccn.loc.gov/2017022902

BRITISH LIBRARY CATALOGUING DATA ARE AVAILABLE

ISBN (print) 978-1-4766-7004-1
ISBN (ebook) 978-1-4766-2869-1

© 2017 Michel Gérald Boutet. All rights reserved

*No part of this book may be reproduced or transmitted in any form
or by any means, electronic or mechanical, including photocopying
or recording, or by any information storage and retrieval system,
without permission in writing from the publisher.*

Front cover: Celtic Tetradrachm of the Danube Valley from
the 2nd or 1st century BCE. Left: the head of Aries, right:
a horse (Pegasus) topped by the Northern Crown and below it,
the sun disk. The rake symbol represents the constellation of
the Boar (Little Dipper). Drawn by the author.

Printed in the United States of America

*McFarland & Company, Inc., Publishers
Box 611, Jefferson, North Carolina 28640
www.mcfarlandpub.com*

To the memory of the late Joseph Monard.

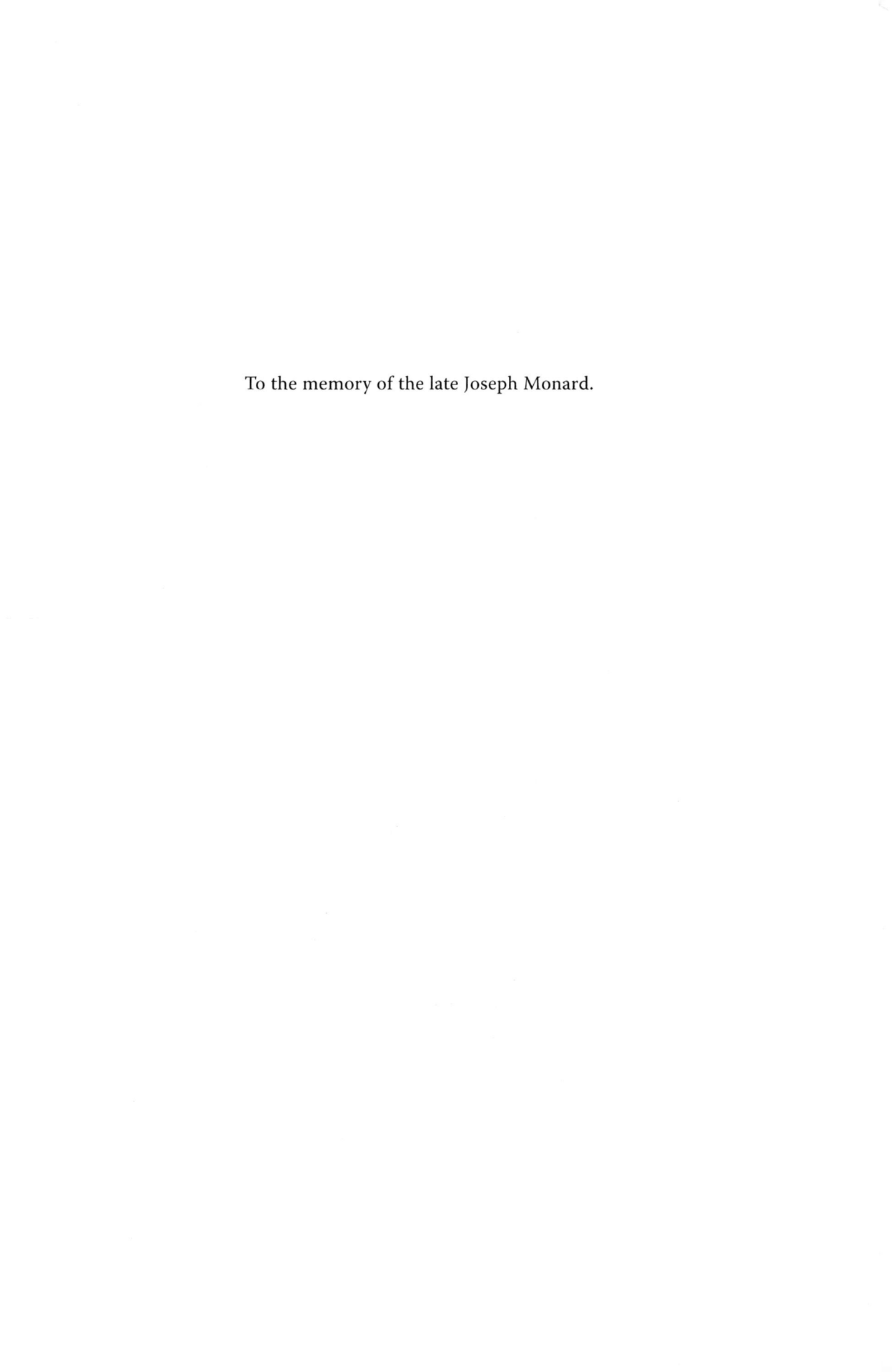

Contents

ACKNOWLEDGMENTS	viii
FOREWORD BY DAVID FRAWLEY	1
PREFACE	7
INTRODUCTION	9
I: On the Origins of Twelve-Sign Astrology	17
II: The Indo-European Bases of Astrology	31
III: Astrology of the Druids	44
IV: The Luminaries	67
V: The Planets	86
VI: The Stars	95
VII: The Astral Cusps	119
VIII: The Astral Houses	134
IX: The Lunar Mansions	154
X: Signs of the Zodiac	169
XI: Planetary Yokes and Cosmic Forces	187
XII: Themes and Predictions	203
XIII: Medical Astrology	210
APPENDIX: ADDITIONAL DATA AND CELTIC NOMENCLATURE	227
CHAPTER NOTES	239
BIBLIOGRAPHY	245
INDEX	249

Acknowledgments

First and foremost, my thanks go to Joseph Monard who guided me all along in this research as he revised the early manuscripts. Much of the information used for this study in the fields of linguistics, astronomy and calendar research are from the many letters and monographs that he so generously shared with me. My acknowledgments to Alain Le Goff, editor of *Ialon Kad Nemeton*, the Druidical studies journal, who most kindly gave me his advice and shared his thoughts. My thanks also go to Marcus Brown of the Royal Irish Academy for the photocopies of the *Book of Ballymote*, the astronomical and medical tract (Ms. B. II. 1) from the academy's manuscript catalogue. The contribution of the Vedic scholar and astrologer David Frawley is acknowledged. Also very useful were the rare books on Hindu astrology that were given to me by my friend, the astrologer Michèle Généreux. Last but not least, to my wife Paule, who supported and assisted me.

Foreword by David Frawley

Culture of the Aryas

The pre–Christian Europeans and the peoples of ancient India and Iran, as well as many related groups in Central Asia, Anatolia and the Near East shared a common culture that has been called Indo-European or Aryan. Arya was originally a term of nobility among various groups and was applied to the aristocrats and the elite of the culture. It was most used for great kings and sages who exhibited high standards of conduct, valor and wisdom, and who worked hard to spread this exalted culture throughout the world for the benefit of all people.

The Irish had their Arya princes and Arya gave the country its name, Ire-land, Arya-land. The Irish culture sustained perhaps the greatest historical and cultural legacy of Western Europe. Persian kings like Cyrus proclaimed themselves Arya and their land as the land of the Aryans, Iran. They challenged the hegemony of Mesopotamian despots and even freed the Jews from their Babylonian captivity. Western Afghanistan was also called Ariana or the realm of the Aryas. North India from sea to sea was called Arya-Varta, the land of the Aryas by the great law-giver and legendary first man or first king, Manu. Lord Buddha gave the name Arya Dharma, or the Arya Way of Truth, to his religion that today we call Buddhism.

This Arya tradition encompassed much of Asia and Europe. It included the most of the pre–Christian peoples of Europe including not only the Celts and Greeks but also the Romans, Germans, Slavic and Baltic peoples. In Asia it included the Hittites, Mittani, Kassites, Parthians, Armenians, Scythians and Tocharians, as well as most of the peoples of India. They shared a common culture that crossed over several ethnic groups and endured for thousands of years.

We should remember the noble and spiritual basis for Arya and remove from it the distortions that came by way of Nazi Germany and its fascist and German nationalist distortions. We should remember that fascism as such was born in Italy and had the tacit support of the Church, which also never officially challenged the Nazis. This church support was extended to Franco as well as to many petty dictators of South and Central America, as part of a century old alliance of authoritarian religious and political rulers.

The Arya heritage reflects one of the oldest and most profound legacies of the human race, which is not a tradition of tyranny but one of spiritual knowledge and respect for the earth. It has given us not only the great spiritual teachings of India—the Hindu, Buddhist and Jain—but the great wisdom traditions of ancient Europe as well, whose profundity we are just beginning to rediscover today. Much of the beauty and wisdom of European folklore comes from this tradition, including the older traditions of the Norse sagas, the German ring stories and Lithuanian mythology.

The Indo-Europeans are generally identified today by linguistic affinities, by the similar languages that they spoke. But these reflect a deeper cultural affinity. They had common words not only for basic human relationships, like mother and father, brother and sister, but also for concepts of class and kingship, for names of God and the word Divine itself. In fact, the Indo-European reflect more a culture than a simple linguistic grouping, as mere linguistic connections, which few ancients were aware of, cannot serve to unite people. It was their cultural practices like fire worship or similar bardic traditions that sustained their affinities.

There has been an attempt to identify the Indo-Europeans in terms of ethnicity, but this has often been naive. After all, culture is much more complex than similar body types. Great cultures reflect a diversity of peoples, customs and trades. Nineteenth century European scholars, reflecting their colonial and missionary prejudices, defined the Aryan in terms of a northern European ethnicity—blond hair and blue eyes. Naturally, it was difficult to explain how India, a land of dark skinned people, could have the oldest records of Aryan culture through its Vedic literature, or how Arya land was the name of Iran, which also lacks such northern European ethnic types. So an invasion/migration of European ethnic types into India and Iran was invented to explain how such things could occur. The invaders, after imparting their culture and language on the land, then got absorbed into the indigenous population, leaving little impact on the ethnicity of the peoples, so the theory went.

That the oldest Indian records of Aryan culture, like the *Rig Veda*, and India's own historical records, the Puranas, know of no such invasion, was ignored or made into a poor historical sense on the part of these non–European peoples. Even the Iranians place their origins in the east, not in the west. We should note that in the vast plains of Eastern Europe and Central Asia the population has always been a mix of northern European ethnic types, not all of whom spoke Indo-European languages like the Finns and Hungarians today, along with various Turkish, Mongolian and Iranian peoples. Racial or ethnic purity was not as important a concept for ancient peoples as it was for nineteenth century European scholars, living in the age of racism.

New archaeological evidence from Europe to India is pushing back the advent of the Aryas into all these regions. The civilization of India, including the great cities of Mohenjodaro and Harappa, now appears to be part of an older Vedic Sarasvati culture that existed before 3000 BCE, with the great majority of ancient ruins on the Sarasvati River of Vedic fame that dried up by 1900 BCE. Ancient India now shows an indigenous culture of the region going back to 7000 BCE (the Mehrgarh site). The advent of the Aryas into Europe and the Mediterranean is now also placed well before 2000 BCE, if not before 3000 BCE. The diffusion of Arya culture, therefore, occurred at an earlier era and came in various waves. Even when the Celts came to Europe they already found Indo-Europeans cultural groups already in existence there.

The Need for a New Paradigm of Civilization

The model of civilization as first invented in Mesopotamia and then transferred and developed further in Greece is the dominant model of Western civilization. It uncritically follows the Christian model, with Christianity coming out of a Judaic basis, which in turn derived from Mesopotamia, and then moving west and becoming the dominant religious and cultural force of Greece and Rome.

Today we are now in a post-colonial era in which Euro-centric and Christian-centric views are being questioned, and often rightfully rejected, of which the Aryan invasion/migration is one of the most important. We must recognize the greatness of non–European civilizations like India and China, which through most of history were ahead of their contemporary European culture, including in terms of science and technology. We must also recognize the greatness of pre–Christian religions of Europe, not only Celtic, Greek and Roman, but also Germanic, Baltic and Slavic, which were quite advanced in various ways and interconnected. We have to face the living greatness of non–Christian traditions like Hinduism and Buddhism, with their powerful yogic and meditation paths, which have so far survived the missionary onslaught, though not without damage.

Such groups, pejoratively called pagans or barbarians, had a sophistication of philosophy, mysticism and spirituality that dwarfs Western creedal religions that mainly follow a hypnotism of belief, not any profound thinking or enquiry. Such so-called pagan groups had a tolerance that missionary cults have hardly ever approached. In fact it was the Greco-Roman pagan tradition that gave the modern world the basis for science, humanism and democracy. It was not the theocratic, authoritarian and divisive beliefs of dominant Biblical religions. The Biblical God appears not like a democrat, but like an oriental despot, demanding blind allegiance and threatening great suffering. If the world has progressed today it is not because of the spread of missionary religions but, rather, the resurgence of earlier and more tolerant attitudes, attitudes that they would call pagan.

At the two ends of the great Arya world stand the Celts and their Druids and the Hindus and their Rishis, reflecting much of what is noblest in the Arya tradition, and between the two were many related groups of similar sophistication. The Druid or Rishi is the true Arya, a person of great learning, contemplation, awareness of nature, and connection with the Divine not on the level of belief but that of consciousness. Both Druid and Rishi traditions were connected on many levels and reflect the same legacy of a spiritual and enlightened humanity.

The Arya traditions—whether of Europe or Asia—had advanced cultures in several key areas. They had deep mystical philosophies such as we see in the Hindu Upanishads, in Iranian mysticism, in Greek Gnosticism and in Druidical systems. They had strong natural medicine teachings using herbs and elixirs such as we find in Ayurveda today, in old Greek medicine, and in the remnants of European herbalism that survived through the Christian era. They had detailed systems of astronomy and astrology, along with sophisticated calendars for linking our human time with the eternal. They understood the directional and earth forces, which we see in the orientation of their towns, temples and monuments.

The Modern Revival of Ancient European Traditions

As we move out of the colonial and missionary age with its Euro-centric and Biblical centered view of humanity, we are once more discovering the importance of other civilizations. We must recognize the importance of India and China as prime centers of civilization that seldom looked to the West for anything before the last few centuries. We must also recognize the pre–Christian culture of Europe, not only the Greeks, but also the Celts, Germans, Slavs and Baltic peoples. These groups are strongly going after their ancestral Dharma today, and have worthy traditions of high philosophy, yoga and mysticism that we are just beginning to recognize. In them we find traces of an older heritage that had affinities with Asia, particularly India.

The ancient Europeans had more in common with Indian or even Native American traditions than with later European Christianity. Our own European ancestors were more like such native peoples than we would think. They were the first victims of the religious intolerance and imperialism of exclusive beliefs. As we begin to appreciate indigenous traditions throughout the world, we must consider our own as well.

Today there is a new awakening in the pre–Christian European or pagan traditions that is part of the general planetary movement toward a new spirituality and universality. The very creeds that missionary beliefs sought to eradicate through centuries of oppression are coming forth again with new life and vigor. It appears that Europe was never entirely converted to Christianity. Scandinavia held out until the eleventh century and Lithuania until the fourteenth century, with pockets lasting yet longer. The old ways continued, sometimes in secret, sometimes in Christian garb, often as mere folk practices, and today can emerge again as spiritual paths as the authority of religious dogma disappears.

Yet much of the New Age Native awakening remains trapped in fantasy and emotion, not real spirituality. The New Age movement has little real scholarship of the older traditions and seldom has a deep intuitive connection to them. New Age teachers take a few native terms and remake them in the image of their own more modern beliefs, coloring them with current political correctness or even adorning them with science fiction forms—and adding a good dose of modern commercialism to them as well. The result is that in spite of this large and growing movement the deeper spiritual tradition has yet to come forth. Our image of the Druids is part Hollywood and part New Age but seldom really grounded in the real venerable tradition.

On the other hand, there is also a large academic study of these older traditions. This, however, remains mired in academic and semantic concerns, looking at them more as fossil pieces or at best a kind of folklore culture of Europe, something quaint but hardly serious. Apart from preserving old texts it has little ability to open their secrets.

This is the importance of the work of Boutet. He represents a genuine scholar with an excellent knowledge of the Celtic languages and traditions, as well as the greater situation in ancient Europe. He does not project naive New Age ideas into his work but grounds it solidly in what the tradition really teaches. At the same time he is no dry academic. He approaches the tradition as a living teaching, embodied in the cosmic mind and not just a relic of old books. He remarkably balances both a scholarly and a spiritual vision. Notably he understands the greater Aryan picture, including India and does not approach the Celts in isolation or the Europeans by themselves.

Druidical Astrology

The current book deals with the Indo-European bases of astrology, particularly the Druidic and Celtic aspect of older Arya astrology, which is one of its most important Arya ways of knowledge (Arya Vidyas). Astrology was in fact the science of cosmology and showed how the ancients understood time and space as a field of consciousness and karma. On this foundation Boutet weaves a fascinating and well-documented study of astrology and all of its implications, both externally and internally, astronomically and mystically.

The stars are the most natural mirrors of the soul. A culture's astrology shows its soul orientation and the key to its spiritual vision. The ancient Gods and Goddesses were, if not astrological manifestations, at least having astrological counterparts. In this way astrology comprehends and contains the essence of all the other ways of knowledge and culture.

Naturally, astrology as a science was shared to some extent by all ancient peoples. Much later, European astrology uses the model of Greek astrology that contains many Babylonian and Egyptian elements. But there was an earlier system of Celtic astrology and there were early Indo-European astrologies, with their own relationships with Middle Eastern systems and their own independent forms.

Boutet explains and explores all these variant systems of ancient astrology, including such poorly understood systems as those of the Hittites and Sumerians, and shows their underlying coherence, as well as their historical development through the Middle Ages. He shows us many keys to ancient constellations, calendars, deities and rituals, revealing the world-view and culture behind them.

Another issue is who invented the zodiac or system of the twelve signs that we remarkably find with similar names and divisions from India to Greece and Ireland. Generally, Babylonia is made the home of this knowledge and Greece was made its main recipient and developer. The actual situation is much more complicated, as no culture existed in isolation. It is probable that the Aryas had more to do with the original formation of the zodiac than we might think. The Celts had terms for the zodiac that are pre–Greek and also not Babylonian either. India also had a tradition of animal signs for the heavens going back to the earliest era, connected to a wheel of heaven divided into twelve parts. Babylonia was a small state compared to the greater Indic culture that traded with it. If ideas and cultures went in one direction, it was more likely from India to Babylonia than the other way around.

Astrology was always part of various occult and spiritual sciences and with them was based upon a system of five elements and three qualities. Boutet unfolds the Druidical understanding of the elements with depth and clarity, showing the Druidical mind and its characteristic preoccupations much like that of the elemental speculations of the ancient Hindus and Greeks.

The idea of star beings as our ancestors and star worlds as our place of origins is found in many ancient mythologies. Whether this is a fact of space travel or a connection on the level of the cosmic mind, or both, is an interesting speculation. In fact it could be both. Boutet unfolds this knowledge as well, showing how the ancients were quite aware of the greater universe in which they lived and in which the Earth is just one inhabitable sphere, not the center of the universe as in Biblical thought. In the Vedic view we all return to the stars after death according to our karma, reflecting also our return to our place of origins in the cosmic mind. The stars are the world of heaven, which is realm of the expansion of consciousness, not a glorified realm of bodily pleasures. Boutet shows how the soul sojourns in the realms of the planets and what qualities it can learn from them, as the individual human being seeks its integration into the cosmic being, the supreme Purusha.

He discusses the signs of the zodiac in the broadest sense and reveals an entire range of animal symbolism, of which the present animal signs for the zodiac, like the ram and the bull, are but one variety, if not a simplification. In discussing the houses Boutet shows a Celtic view that regarded Libra as the analogue for the first house, not Aries, Scorpio as an analogue for the second house, not Taurus and so on. Several Vedic astrologers have noted the same idea to me. This affords a new view on the houses that can bring in many important new insights. In this context he introduces new tools of astrological interpretation for astrologers to explore that could revolutionize the practice of astrology. He also discusses the lunar mansions in Celtic lore, which parallel the Nakshatras of Vedic thought, giving to a new slant to them as well.

On the predictive side of Druidic astrology Boutet discusses the yogas or combinations that bring about certain results in the chart, which parallel those found in Vedic astrology. His discussion of color in the astrological context reminds one of the importance of gems and colors as remedial measures in the Vedic system. He moves into tree signs and omens, much like the Brihat Samhita of the great Vedic astrologer Varaha Mihira, showing the spiritual and occult meaning of such symbols. Similarly, he tackles stars, meteors and comets, long seen as messengers from the heavens indicating important changes in the world.

His discussion of Druidic medical astrology provides a good introduction to Druidic medicine and its Greek and Ayurvedic counterparts. In this context he introduces the yogic or spiritual practices of the Druids with their Vedic equivalents, including an interesting discussion of the chakras and their astrological equivalents, including various Celtic mantras. He shows the universality of the yogic path in the Arya wisdom traditions that has great relevance to all true spiritual seekers.

The book contains a wealth of sacred lore that can afford the reader many hours of deep contemplation. It is bound to aid not only in a true revival of the Celtic soul but of our planetary connection to the ancient sages. The book probably contains the most authentic presentation of Druidic astrology from both scholarly and spiritual angles and is a foundational work in this field. Druidical Astrology should be carefully studied by all students of astrology, by all those interested in Celtic lore and by all those interested in East-West connections. Boutet is like an ancient Druid taking birth in the modern world to teach those who really want to understand the older wisdom. Let us hope that readers will have the acumen to be able to study and appreciate his in-depth presentation that reflects not only years, but lifetimes of serious study.

David Frawley (Pandit Vamadeva Shastri) is the president of the American Council of Vedic Astrology (ACVA) and the author of several books, including Astrology of the Seers *and* Yoga and Ayurveda.

Preface

Why Another Book on Celtic Astrology?

Simply because this isn't just another book on Celtic astrology but rather an in-depth research on what was, or must have been, the views of the ancient Druids on cosmology and astrology. Our present understanding of what was Celtic Astrology is based mainly on the speculations of modern authors such as Robert Graves, et alia, and thus suffers many misconceptions. To my knowledge, no other book has thoroughly expounded this difficult subject. Many prefer to add on to the wild imaginings of these authors, or to the contrary, choose to avoid the subject altogether. Serious scholars rarely bring the discussion beyond the known commentaries of classical Greek and Roman authors. Although this safe intellectual stand is commendable, it unfortunately doesn't yield much progress. Then again, the sheer mention of the subject of astrology is sure to attract ridicule and misunderstanding. My interest on the subject started more than two decades ago when I was introduced to the presence of astronomical and astrological symbols found in ancient Rock Art. I wasn't interested by the conclusions of Art historians claiming that abstract symbols escape interpretation or that the keys to their interpretation are hopelessly lost. My gut feeling was that if one was able to put himself in the shoes of an ancient seer, one had the way to penetrate his cosmic vision. I am not concerned with what astrology may mean to contemporary horoscope readers, but what it meant to those in the past. I take the Carlos Castaneda approach. If one is to understand the productions of a Shaman one must think like a Shaman.

As moderns, we have the tendency to underestimate the state of science professed by the ancients. Nothing was arbitrary for them. Everything belonged to an ordered system. And the reality of this system was permeated with ideological views that belonged more to the mythic than to the mundane. The Celtic Druids maintained a sacred language comparable to the Sanskrit of the Vedic Brahmans and this shows clearly in the few examples we have in the old Gallic language. Indeed, a fundamental artifact for the comprehension of ancient Celtic astronomy is the *Coligny Calendar* discovered in France.

The material that follows consists of collected data from the known commentaries found in manuscript sources from Antiquity to the medieval ages. This carefully collected material was then compared with cosmological and astronomical lore found in the existing and surviving Celtic cultures. Also used were the vast data bases of the other past and present Indo-European peoples. For this analysis, the methodology of compared myths and languages as devised by Georges Dumézil was put to use. Also used was Ewin's Panofsky's iconographical methodology for images in Art.

Specific Nomenclature

Astronym—astronomical term, designation for a heavenly body, star, constellation or astral object.
Decan—a ten degrees division of the zodiacal circle.
Mythonym—mythological term, usually the name of a god, hero or legendary figure.

Introduction

The Two Druids, 19th century engraving after a bas-relief from Autun, Burgundy, France. Reproduction from the original by Thiroux for Bernard de Montfaucon, in *Antiquitas explanatione et schematibus illustrata*, vol. ii, 1719, p. 436.

Although star divining was practiced within the shamanic Stone Age cultures of Eurasia and beyond, the twelve sign Zodiac, falsely attributed to the Chaldeans, finds its beginning in the proto–Indo-European culture. The zodiacal system, as a divining art, then reached a higher level of sophistication as it was coupled with mythological motifs and the early naked eye astronomical science of these early Indo-Europeans. Indeed, the celestial movements of the heavenly bodies found their explanation in cosmological tales in which the mythological players performed in the theatre of the stars.

Many attempts have been made at restoring or reconstructing the ancient Celtic Zodiac. These models are for the most part, hypothetical, when not completely fabricated. Not surprisingly, these tree Zodiacs bear very little resemblance to both Western and Eastern Astrology. This being that most of the "re-constructionists" have worked from assumptions picking-up from those proposed by Robert Graves who seems to have confused the lunar-based Almanac with the solar-based Zodiac.

Certainly, the Almanac is lunar and the Zodiac, solar, but nevertheless, these are two different systems, the first is based on the yearly lunar cycle of 354.3 days comprising of approximately 12 lunations and the second, is based on the solar cycle of 365.6 days. An important consideration is that the Moon visits the zodiacal constellations in but one month only while the Sun takes a full year to complete the same course. The cosmic workings of the luminaries around the ecliptic and the zodiacal belt were organized in a neat system. This conceptual model was adopted (and slightly adapted) by the main agricultural civilizations of Eurasia and Northern Africa with little variation from culture to culture. The earliest Zodiac was probably of 8 constellations. But because of the discrepancy in the time and space the sun had to travel between constellations, a twelve house astral course was imposed. Therefore, what is the reasoning behind these very different Zodiacs proposed by our modern Celtic astrologers? Since these authors often fail to give their references, it becomes almost impossible to verify their claims. In short, all we have to go by is their only word, or again, desperately try to follow the paper trail. And once we do follow this bread crumb trail leading to the original Tom Thumb, we inevitably stumble on one heck of a storyteller, Robert Graves, the Goose that laid the Golden Egg, the one who started it all in the first place. Therefore, to fully understand the origins of this Celtic Tree Zodiac and its workings, one must inevitably start with Robert Graves.

Robert Graves, seeing the impossibility of the Zodiac as being a "perpetual calendar," erroneously thought that the Beth-Luis-Nion letter sequence could not reconcile the equinoxes and solstices with the twelve zodiacal constellations. He believed that the Zodiac emerged from the thirteen month lunar calendar and suspected that the dual Gemini constellation was fused into one sign in order to harmonize the lunar-solar cycles. His hypothesized tree order starts on Christmas Eve in December on the 24th; which is an impossibility since the Celtic lunar-solar year commenced earlier in mid–Fall around October–November moon. Also impossible are his fixed dates, we now know from archaeological data collected on the Coligny plates from France that the Druids had reconciled, in a most ingenious way, the discrepancies between the two cycles. Monthly dates followed the Moon phases with the zodiacal months overlapping. Corrections were made by indexing the shorter lunar cycle with the longer solar cycle and adding an extra month every two and three years following a five years turn-around. Thus, there were no fixed dates in the druidical scheme, just floating or moving dates. Here is a quick recall for the reader's sake:

> **The Sidereal Month** is defined as the mean time of the Moon's revolution in its orbit from one constellation back to the same constellation again (the zodiacal constellations here defined as lunar mansions) in precisely 27 days, 7 hours, 43 minutes, 11.5 seconds of mean time.
> **The Sidereal Year** is defined as the mean time in which the earth completes one revolution in its orbit around the Sun measured with respect to the zodiacal constellations as fixed stars (i.e. from the vernal point and back, from Aries and back to it again): in precisely 365 days, 6 hours, 9 minutes, and 9.54 seconds of solar time.

Indexing Cycles

Difficulty arises as one tries to combine the lunar cycles with the solar year. In fact, the average Moon year of twelve months is of 354.3669 days compared to the average 365.2422 days of the solar cycle. The task was to combine these two years into one synchronous year but still keeping tract with seasonal changes. The solution was found in the intercalary month and year, which introduces every third year a thirteenth month called Santarana (Santaros\-a\-on "aside"). This technique of inserting an extra month is qualified as embolismic for "clotting" or leap month. Apart from the use of an additional leap month there was the possibly of adding an extra day in July thus complicating things further. The first leap month was called Ciallosbuis Sonnocingos which means, "check-up of the Sun's course," and it returns every five years while the second, Mens in Dueixtionu, inserted between October and November, also runs every five years, but at the beginning of each lustrum. Mens in Dueixtionu means "month in duplication," and is found abridged as MIDX in the Coligny Calendar.

DURATION OF THE PLANETARY CYCLES

- Moon: 19.00011 years, lunation on the same zodiacal degree for one Metonic cycle;
- Sun: 33.00004 years, for return to the same zodiacal position, same time of the day

Positions of the Sun and Moon in the Zodiac[1]

Sun in:	Full Moon in:	Last Quarter in:	New Moon in:	First Quarter in:
Libra	Aries	Cancer	Libra	Capricorn
Scorpio	Taurus	Leo	Scorpio	Aquarius
Sagittarius	Gemini	Virgo	Sagittarius	Pisces
Capricorn	Cancer	Libra	Capricorn	Aries
Aquarius	Leo	Scorpio	Aquarius	Taurus
Pisces	Virgo	Sagittarius	Pisces	Gemini
Aries	Libra	Capricorn	Aries	Cancer
Taurus	Scorpio	Aquarius	Taurus	Leo
Gemini	Sagittarius	Pisces	Gemini	Virgo
Cancer	Capricorn	Aries	Cancer	Libra
Leo	Aquarius	Taurus	Leo	Scorpio
Virgo	Pisces	Gemini	Virgo	Sagittarius

Under the assumption that the Celtic alphabet derived from the Greek and Roman ones, Graves then went through great pains in trying to explain the tree order through the Classical myths. But where he really went wrong was when he took poetical license for the literary truth. Ironically, his muse, the White Goddess, took him down the wrong path. One wonders which Celtic white goddess he was referring to, was it Branwen (< Branna-uinda), the white raven of fallen heroes, or was it Gwenhwyfar (Irish Finnabhair < Soibra-uinda), the white specter, the White Lady, a haunting of the past?

Robert Graves' Tree Calendar

B Birch: December 24	L Service tree: January 21	N Ash February 18
F Alder: March 18	S Willow: April 15	S (Z) Prune tree: April 15
H Whitethorn: May 15	D Oak: June 10	T Holy: July 8
C Hazel: August 5	C (Q) Apple: August 5	M Vine: September 2
G Ivy: September 30	NG Reed: October 28	R Elder: November 25
I Ivy: November 25	E Poplar: December 23	U Heather: December 23
O Furze: December 23	A Spruce: December 23	A Palm: December 24

Mother Nature, anthropomorphic tree, engraving by the Italian painter Pietro Ciafferi (1600–1654), also known as Lo Smargiasso, "the braggart."

Robert Graves' Tree Zodiac

Winter Solstice: A/I, Spruce/Yew		
Sagittarius: B/R, Birch/Elder	Capricorn: L, Service tree	Aquarius: N, Ash
Spring Equinox: O/E, Furze/Poplar		
Pisces: F, Alder	Aries: S, Willow	Taurus: H, White-thorn
Summer Solstice: U, Heather		
Gemini: D/T, Oak/Holy	Cancer: C, Hazel	Leo: Q, Apple
Fall Equinox: E/O, Poplar/Furze		
Virgo: M, Vine	Libra: G, Ivy	Scorpio: NG, Reed

Then again, much of this relies on modern interpretations derived from the book Ogygia by the seventeenth century bard Roderick O'Flaherty. O'Flaherty claimed that his information was gained from Duald MacFirbis, clan bard of the O'Briens. Credited scholars such as R.A.S. Macalister, not least, argue that the Ogham ascriptions given by O'Flaherty were "artificialities" having little to do with the original bearings (Nigel Pennick 1991). If these were late musings inspired from the Bardic tradition, then these had to be re-adaptations of the old medieval ascriptions. Since the Bardic schools were essentially Christian, it is very unlikely that the druidical ascriptions were carried on intact that long into the Christian era.

If you may pardon the pun, the Druids, as were the other sages of Antiquity such as the Mathematici, Rishis, Chaldeans and Magi, certainly not "lost in space." That they would confuse the 13 month lunar cycles with the 12 month zodiacal cycles, says much more on the lack of credibility of some of these contemporary astrologers than on the state of astral-science during late Antiquity. As fine observers of the skies, the Druids worked within the limits of "naked eye" astronomy. That is, they always worked from direct observation. For example, in Barddas the Isle of Britain, it is written that there were formerly fifteen planets. Which in reality means that the ancients knew five planets or "vagabond stars," besides the two luminaries, and that the tripling of five expresses a sacred notion well understood even by the Christian Bards. In short, according to the mythic plan, each of the five planets is also simultaneously in all of three worlds. This notion of multidimensional places was found in Celtic cosmology and referred to as Sid or Sidh. In Vedic astrology, we also find this concept expressed in the multiple worlds called Lokas, "places," seen as astral planes or heavenly planetary places or spiritual sojourns. Again, although worlds apart, there is agreement with the Indian and Celtic traditions!

We also know, that the Druids had such mastery of astrology or astronomy and natural sciences for which they were envied not only by the Romans and Greeks, but also by the other ancient peoples surrounding them, this included the Germanic and Thracian tribes along with the Etruscans who were quite astute sky gazers. Latin Classical authors are strong to mention that of all the peoples of the empire, the Gauls were the most receptive to astrology. Astrology was in those days a speculative science and a divining art which was not only widespread, but also very popular. Julius Caesar and later Pomponius Mela (ca. 43 CE), had noticed how much the Druids were very highly admired for their "speculations on the stars." There is also a mention by Ammian Marcellinus Jornandes (or Jordanis), a Goth scholar quoting from Cassiodorus (Flavius Magnus Aurelius Cassiodorus, ca. 490–583 CE), about the Getae, a Celticized Thraco-Dacian people of the Danube, which he confused with the Germanic Goths, on their knowledge of astronomy. In *The Origin and Deeds of the Goths*, Book XI, verses 68 to 78, he states that the Getae knew the course of the twelve signs of the zodiac as well as the planets passing through these signs and the entire astronomy. In chapter III, we will explore this in detail.

For the Druids, the order of the Cosmos or Multiverse reveals the presence of a higher state of being, a higher intelligence which is not defined by human standards. The terms recton or rexton defined this ancient Celtic notion of order. This monist conception of the universe implied that the Supreme Being, referred to as Guton Uxellimon, is both transcendent and immanent. This non-anthropomorphic, omnipresent, divinity could not be defined or named through the limited language of man. For these reasons, neutral terms were used to evoke this abstract entity. Theon, the neutral or collective Greek form of *theós*, "god," is also found in the Greek name Pantheon meaning "all the gods." It also appears in the name of the Mother Goddess Meter Theon, a title given to both the goddesses Rhea and Phrygian Cybele. In the old Greek translation of the Gospels, God the Father is respectfully referred to as Theon. The Hindus, also used the neuter case to designate the Brahman or Atman, the Soul of the Universe.

The following is a list of Old Celtic neuter case names used to evoke the Supreme Being:

Anatmon, "soul, breath";
Anmeneticon, "the unnamed";
Angegneticon, "the uncreated, not begotten";
Arimathes, "the primary good";
Dits Ater, "the father of disintegration";
Albiorixs, "the king of the sky";
Guton Uxellimon, "The Supreme Being."

The above list is similar to that the Vedic one with:

Brahman, "Soul of the Universe," who was also called Brihaspati, "Lord of prayer";
Prajapati, "Lord of creatures"; and Swayambhu, "The self-existing."

Druidical theology, not unlike the Hellenic and Vedic ones, speculated much on the nature of the gods and on the qualities of the soul. According to the concept of the expansion of spiritual beingness, seen as light projection, thus doexleucos, "projecting light," godly mind projections simultaneously emerge from the andoexleucos, non-manifesting light in various hypostases called uassoi "subordinates," in Old Celtic. Then, through the various stages of degradation, the essential nature of being occurs. It was called biotos and had the meaning of "living, alive."

In short, it is from the non-manifested Monad that come into being the personalized light-emitting gods and demi-gods along with the animated physical beings such as mortals. The gods of the Celtic pantheon did not appear all at once, but came in a succession. This succession is described in the myths where their genealogies are given. As will be mentioned in the following chapters concerning the planets, Caesar, in his *De Bello Gallico* or "Gallic War Commentaries," gave the ranking of the Gaulish gods as follows: Mercury, Jupiter, Mars, Apollo and Minerva.

Roman gods	*Gaulish*	*Welsh*	*Irish*
Mercury	Lugos/Lugus	Lleu	Lug/Lugh
Jupiter	Esus, Taranis, Teutates, Sucellos,	Bran, Mathonwy	Dagda, Ruad Rofessa, Eochaid Ollathir
Mars	Ogmios, Nodons	Owain, Nudd/Llud	Ogma, Nuada
Apollo	Belenos, Grannos, Maponos	Beli Mawr, Mabon	Oengus, Mac Òc, Diancecht
Minerva	Belisama, Brigantia/Brigindo, Epona, Nantosuelta, Rosmerta, Suliuia	Aranrhod, Branwen, Don, Morgan, Rhiannon	Boand, Bodb, Brigit, Danu, Etain, Macha, Medb, Morrigu/Morrigann etc.

To conclude, these comments from the classical authors contradict the so-called Celtic or Runic astrologies with thirteen or so extended signs that the contemporary Zodiac makers have so emphatically argued for. In the following chapter, we will see how this twelve constellation astrological model developed.

Map of Europe according to Strabo, ca. 7 BCE. Engraving by Philibert Mareschal, ca. 1598 CE.

I

On the Origins of Twelve-Sign Astrology

"If a bard were every poet that is on earth, on the brine and on the cultivated plain, on the sand and on the seas, and in the stars of astronomy, the giver with the gentle and ready hand being judge, More than they could I should wish, and also do, to relate the power and bounty of the Creator."—"A Blessing to the Happy Youth," *Black Book of Carmarthen XXIX*, translated by Skene

Sonnocingos, the Sun's path. Drawing by the author.

The zodiac was already very ancient when Hipparchus of Nicaea had catalogued the positions of some 1,022 stars and 49 constellations. By this time, the ancients were already in possession of a sky chart. They remembered that their ancestral homeland was situated in the stars of the northern skies. This is why the study of stars was very important to them. The ancient seers saw themselves as star children. Zodiacal constellations were a thing long familiar to the seers of European Antiquity. In 174 BCE,

Hipparchus identified a new star in the constellation of Scorpio. From then on, he was very eager to chart all the visible stars for he correctly suspected that the skies were not fixed and eternal. He became famous by discovering the 25,600 year cycle of the Earth's precession caused by the oscillation of the rotational axis. This oscillation affects the position of the celestial poles by causing a slow shift of the equinoxes. Then around 280 BCE, another Greek astronomer, Aratus of Soles, in *Phenomenons and Prognostics*, gave a very precise description of the skies for the practical use of navigators and farmers. Aratus, who was born in Cilicia, Asia Minor, sometime around 320 BCE, was drawing upon information from the work of Eudoxus (ca. 370 BCE). This study was the first true scientific work on astronomy. The old constellations identified by the ancients were generally those running along the ecliptic, that is, those referred to as the Zodiac and which serve to mark the passing of seasonal time. They also identified the circumpolar stars, Ursa Major, then called the Great Wain, including alpha Draconis, the Pole Star prior to 2500 BCE. On examination of the old Greek names found in the Zodiac, we can grasp the general pastoral theme; for example: Orion, the hunter, and his dog (Sirius), struck by the bow of Artemis (Scorpio).

The Dendera planisphere, a sky map found on the ceiling of the portico in the temple of Hathor and dedicated to Osiris, was generally thought to be one of the oldest representations of the Zodiac. French scholar Joseph Fourier (1768–1830 CE), believed that the sky chart dated back to 2500 BCE and was the oldest proof for the creation of twelve sign system in western astrology. Long kept at the Bibliothèque Nationale de Paris, and now preserved at the Louvre, the Dendera Zodiac was readily accessible for study by Egyptologists and historians of cosmic science and astronomy. Thus, it was first speculated that the artifact recorded celestial events dating from before 1800 BCE. But afterwards, further research revealed that Hathor's temple of Dendera was only erected during the late Greek Ptolemaic period and that the planisphere, showing Roman influence, was planed-out in the first century (50 BCE) and executed under emperor Tiberius (42 BCE–37 CE) sometime later. Therefore, the Dendera Zodiac was drawing upon classical Greek and Roman astronomical sources. Keeping this in mind, it was observed that the planisphere's uncharted skies, without zodiacal representations, run along the 36 degrees latitude and that the center of the band coincides with the position of the southern pole in 2500 BCE. This brings us right back to square one at the time when Exodus first mapped-out the skies! Also, traditionally argued is the notion that the Alexandrian Macedonian Greeks gave the 12 sign zodiacal scheme to the Vedic Indians.

The fact that this astrological tradition was contemporaneous with that of India was taken as a sure sign for cultural diffusion from Hellenic Bactria on to Vedic India. The idea of a common Indo-European origin for these cultures was not yet in the picture, let alone the existence of a very ancient cultural continuum from the Danube-Black Sea region on to the Sarasvati and Indus valleys.

The Vedic scholar and Jyotish astrologer, Dr. David Frawley, discovered through an exegesis of the Brahmanas, the Yajur and Atharva Vedas, that the vernal equinox was in the Krittikas (Pleiades; a sub-constellation of Taurus) and that the summer solstice (Ayana) was in Magha (early Leo) thus yielding a date of around 2500 BCE for the creation of the Vedic system. This, according to Frawley, proving that Vedic astronomical science was contemporaneous with that of the Harappan culture.

I: On the Origins of Twelve-Sign Astrology

Who copied who, was it Exodus who copied the pundits of India or were it the pundits who copied Exodus? In the ancient past, astrology was already one of the pillars of Vedic science as it was also for the Greeks, the Hittites, the Persians, and Celts even. That is, star-science was an integral subject matter in the curriculum of Indo-European philosophical teaching. Hints of the ancient traces for astrology in the hidden past of the Indo-European peoples may be found in the verses of the *Rig Veda*, but older still, may be the inscriptions from the Danube River which may date from as far as 8000 to 40000 BCE.

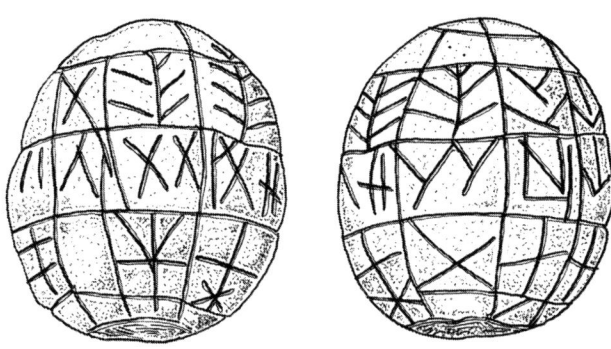

The Lepenski Vir planisphere. Author's drawing after Winn 1981.

Harald Haarmann in *Early Civilization and Literacy in Europe*, wrote that the *Lepenski Vir* round stone is no doubt the oldest example of the use of writing for oracular purposes. Although he could only speculate on the stone's use, Haarmann was certainly right about its relation to magic. All suggests that this stone ball was used for mystical and astrological purposes. The sphere does indeed remind us of a planisphere or celestial star chart. The tree symbols tend to confirm the antiquity of the Celtic tree symbols. That is, that the early Indo-Europeans saw star clusters as trees in a forest. More intriguing, is a stone amulet depicting the four areas of the Northern sky.

Each of these quarters seems to represent a section of the night sky starting with the scale and bow, the rake, usually representing the "Boar" (Ursa Major) on Gallic coinage, the bow and arrow (Sagitta?) and a delta with sun rays and lunar crescent (the three horned Bull in Hittite cuneiform) along with a "Tanit" goddess figure. The "Tanit" figure probably represents Hausōs Deiwa the Indo-European Dawn Goddess (Greek Hera?). An interesting icon is that of the scale or ladder which in early Indo-European culture symbolized the ascent to the stars. In Greek astromythology, Sagitta represents the arrow with

Clay amulet (dated ca. 5500 to 5300 BCE) discovered in 1961 at the Tărtăria site by archaeologist Nicolae Vlassa. Author's drawing.

which Hercules slew the eagle (Aquila) that fed upon the liver of Prometheus. The Boar star was akin to the Great Bear (Ursa Major) and identified with the god *Khrysaor*. The star of *Khrysaor* was later moved to the Sword, a sub-constellation of Orion, while Ursa Major assumed the name of *Kallisto*, the "bear." These stars which never set below the horizon were described as immortal. The constellation of Hercules was originally called *Engonasin* "the Kneeler" by the Greeks. In iconography, the hero *Engonasin* was generally depicted on his knees, holding a club and slaying a dragon. The dragon, called *Ladon*, was described as a hundred headed beast guarding the Garden of the Hesperides. *Hera*, the "Lady," the queen of Heaven, was the goddess who first set the stars in place.

Another early Indo-European artifact is the Nebra disc. The recently discovered Nebra disc star chart comes as a God-given gift fallen down from the skies. It was unearthed from Mittelberg hill, near Nebra in Saxony-Anhalt, by treasure-hunting looters and will be revealed to be the most unlikely object ever found. On it, are depicted the ecliptic, the solar orb surrounded by the lunar crescent in the shape of a nave, the seven stars of Taurus, the Pleiades, the Hyades and other bright stars which included Betelgeuse. Harder to believe still, was its age of almost 4000 years (1600 BCE). After having observed this incredible data, what did the specialists conclude? Simply that the Bronze Age Europeans of what is now Germany came under the influence of the Egyptians and that they had naively copied these cosmological motifs from an Egyptian artifact. Sillier still, was the idea that the disc was brought directly from Egypt. Needless to add, that before it was subjected to the scrutiny of the scientific analysis of chemist Heinrich Wunderlich and metallurgist Ernst Pernickaet, this was the accepted explanation. So then, what was the conclusion from the laboratory tests? Surprise! The object was made of gold and copper mined in Transylvania and in the Austrian Alps.... Conclusion, the object was European made.[1]

Incidentally, the Bronze Age culture in Europe begins and ends from around 1800 to 700 BCE. It was then followed by the Hallstatt culture (ca. 700 to ca. 450 BCE) which ended at the start of the La Tène Iron Age culture. At the time, on the other edge of the Indo-European world, science provided further evidence for more ancient astronomical knowledge from these people. Just recently, the Russian archaeologist Viktor Sarianidi discovered and unearthed the remains of an Indo-European civilization in the Kara-Kum desert of Turkmenistan (Ikshvaku sites), just east of the Caspian Sea in what was once Greek Bactria and Indo-Iranian Aryavarta. There, he found the remains of 150 fortified towns with splendid brick houses, granaries, royal palaces, gorgeous temples and astronomical observatories. Older than 4000 years (from around −2300 BCE), archaeologists were to discover seals bear-

Astronomical disc of Nebra, Mittelberg, 1600 BCE. Drawn by the author from a photograph in *National Geographic*, 2004.

ing an unknown script along with fruit presses for the extraction of the Soma along with animal figurines (the same as those in the Zodiac) and gold, silver and bronze jewelry with pottery in great number.

"A wheel with a twelve spoked rim and three hubs; what included this? Three hundred and sixty poles fixed as it is above without play."[2] This very ancient Vedic text is eloquent in many ways: the old Aryans had, at least since the 2nd millennium BCE, a map of the astral zodiacal band separated into 12 sections. The Greeks also document the same layout in the 5th century just about when the Chaldeans (from Babylon under Persian control) abandon their annual lunar astral signs of 17 to 18 in place of the accepted 12 zodiacal constellations. From this oldest Vedic account on the zodiacal constellations, it is clear for David Frawley that the old Aryan astronomers had not only cut the sky into 12 equal signs, but that they also developed a geometrical model using a 360 degree circle cut into 30 sections. Again, is found the underlying principle of conceptual tripartition discovered by the French scholar Georges Dumézil (1898–1986).

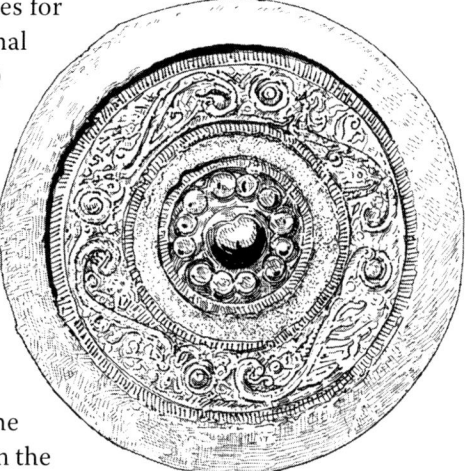

Indo-European bronze disc showing the twelve constellations of the Zodiac dating from the fourth millennium BCE. Koktepe archaeological site, plain of Zerafshan, north of Samarkand. Drawing by the author.

It is well documented that the old Vedic texts related astronomical facts and considerations prior to the said Chaldean origin for the 12 sign Zodiac. In short, this is what the texts relate:

- Calculations on the geometry of the circle;
- Calculations on the occurrence of eclipses;
- Measure of the circumference of the Earth;
- Speculations on the Earth's gravity;
- Speculations on the stellar nature of the sun;
- Determination of the number of observable planets.

The Indian astronomer Yajnavalkya (active before the 1st millennium BCE) proposed a cycle of 95 years which reconciled the lunar and solar cycles. Another treatise on astronomy, dating from 1350 BCE, is attributed to the Vedic sage Lagadha. Vedic tradition assigns to an Asura ("spirit master," from the Proto-Indo-European root hensu- "spirit") named Maya Danava the invention of astronomy and astrology in addition to geometry and sacred architecture.

Maya Danava, who lived in the Other-world of Talata in the heavens of Svarga, built at the request of the deva Šiva, a celestial Vimana. This Vimana was a flying vehicle which could travel to the stars down to Earth and back. These celestial adventures of Maya Danava are reminiscent to those of the Irish Mog Ruith, an avatar of the Wheel God. As it is stated in the Irish texts (Second Battle of Mag Tured): "The Túatha De

Danann were in the islands of the North of the World, learning druidical science and magic, wisdom and art. And they surpassed all the sages of the world in the arts of paganism." Then again, the *Sûrya Siddhânta* mentions that the sun god Surya said these words to Maya Danava:

> O Maya, hear attentively the excellent knowledge of the science of astronomy which the sun himself formerly taught to the great saints in each of the Yugas.
> I teach the same old science.... But the difference between the present and the ancient works is caused only by time, on account of the revolutions of the yugas.[3]

Both of these distant Indo-European traditions, the Celtic and the Vedic, assign a northern origin to the creation of the 12 constellation Zodiac which indicates that these cultures were drawing from a common source. This view is also shared by the classical thinkers of Greece and Italy as evidenced by Lucian's comments (ca. 120 to 180 CE) when he mentions that he did not believe in a Chaldean invention for astrology. Here are his exact words:

> The Babylonians also are acquainted with these matters; aye, if we believe them, they were so long before the others; but in my opinion, it was not till much later that astrology came to them. The Greeks however have what they know of it neither from the Ethiopians nor Egyptians: but Orpheus, Oeager's and Calliope's son, was the first that revealed somewhat of it to them; indeed not very clearly; because he was not intent upon the promulgation of the science itself, but, in conformity to his character, on applying it to his magical juggles and mysteries. Thus, for instance, the lyre of which he was the inventor, served him as the principal instrument of his mystical worship; but this lyre, which was furnished with seven strings, was to him a symbol betokening the harmony of the planets. This occult science it was, by which he charmed and controlled everything; he cared naught about the lyre of his own fabrication, and what is commonly understood by music: (astrology was the great lyre of Orpheus), and the respect of the Greeks for his occult science, was the reason of their allotting to him and his lyre a place in the sky, where a particular constellation still bears the name of Orpheus's lyre. The sculptors and painters usually represent Orpheus as singing and playing on his lyre, with a multitude of animals standing round, among whom are distinguished a man, a bull, a lion; in short, all the animals of the Zodiac. When you see this, remember what I say, and you will presently guess at what that singing and that lyre denote, and who the bull and the lion are, that stand listening to him; if you understand me, you will discern all these things in the sky.[4]

So then, why was the creation of the 12 sign Zodiac attributed to the Chaldeans? It was because of Peter Jensen, a German orientalist, who, in 1890, in a book entitled *Die Kosmologie der Babylonier*, first asserted that the Greek Zodiac and names of the constellations were borrowed from the Babylonians and the Chaldeans. The idea was then picked up by other Orientalists such as the linguist Fritz Hommel, the archaeologist Alfred Jeremias, and later on by the pan–Babylonist Franz Kugler in a study of 1907 (Sternkunde und Sterndienst in Babel) which he further developed in a 1927 article entitled *Orientation*.[5] According to the scholars of the time, the science of the stars, made by all high cultures, can only take origin in Mesopotamia, the "cradle of civilization."[6]

In fact, it was by about 420 BCE that the Chaldeans of Mesopotamia reformed their lunar calendar of 17 or 18 stellar regions and adopted the zodiacal model of 12 equal sections comprised of thirty degrees. At that time, Mesopotamia was under Persian rule. And this was well before the accession of King Cyrus the Great (559 to 530 BCE) to its throne. Therefore, at that time, Babylon was under the yoke of the royal

Persian Achaemenid capitals of Pasargadae, Persepolis and Susa. Here is a list of the Persian kings who called themselves "King of Babylon":

Persian Ruler	*Time of Reign*
Artaxerxes I	464–424 BCE
Xerxes II	424 BCE
Sogdianus	424 BCE
Darius II	423–405 BCE
Artaxerxes II	404–359 BCE
Artaxerxes III	358–338 BCE
Asses	337–336 BCE
Darius III	335–330 BCE
Alexander the Great	331 BCE

This being, prior to the reign of king Darius, the Third, when Alexander the Great of Macedonia took over Babylon and Persia in 331 BCE, there submitting Susa and Persepolis and there claiming the crown of Babylon.

In short, it appears that it was under the old yoke of the Persian kings and Greek Macedonian rulers that Babylon adopted the sky chart of the Indo-Europeans. Some scholars have also proposed that Indo-European mythology originated in the Fertile Crescent or in Sumer? But contrary to what the Orientalists of past centuries claimed, civilization was also passed down from many other venues. Henceforth, the astrological scheme of the 12 sign zodiacal belt was not invented in Babylon. Let us clarify:

- It is in these two Indo-European traditions, Greek and Indian, that we have the best evidence of the early stages of a solar zodiacal astrology of twelve signs running along the ecliptic.
- It is in these two traditions that we have the most similar Zodiacs.
- And it is in the verses of the *Rig Veda*, attributed to the Rishi Dirghatamas, that we have the best testimony for the 12 sign Zodiac in ancient times: "The wheel of law with twelve spokes does not decay as it revolves around heaven. Oh Agni, here your seven hundred twenty pair sons abide."[7]

The 360° circle is also mentioned in the hymns of the *Rig Veda*: "With four times ninety names, he (Vishnu) sets in motion moving forces like a turning wheel."[8] The *Rig Veda* document is explicit, and the entire mechanical workings of the cosmology for the Zodiac are there.

Many believed that the earliest evidence for the 12-part Zodiac was found on an Egyptian planisphere or world map called *Dendera Zodiac* by the Egyptologists. The artwork was long kept in the Bibliothèque Nationale but is now on display at the Louvre Museum in Paris. At most, this artwork dates back to around 50 BCE, that was, at the time of the reign of Cleopatra, the Egyptian Queen of the Alexandrian Greek Ptolemaic dynasty. This Egyptian-style Zodiac is Ptolemaic in its plan and is largely of Greek conception. The Greek Zodiac, as we know it, dates back to the fifth century BCE, just at about the time of the Athenian astronomers Meton and Euctemon (at about 432 to 439 BCE) who are said to have discovered the Metonic or Enneadecaeteris ("nine year period" in Greek) cycle. Greek astronomers used it as the basis for the development of a sidereal calendar called Parapegmata, a device used for keeping track of cyclical events, particularly the movement of stars.

The Roman sophist author Aelian (Claudius Aelianus, 175–235 CE) speaks of Meton who erected the pillars on which was marked the revolutions of the sun, there giving him credit for having discovered the cycle of the "great year" of 19 years. Aelian, in his *Various History*, mentions of a certain Oenopides who set up an astronomical table for the Olympics:

> Oenopides the Chian, an Astronomer, set up a brass Table at the Olympics, having written thereon the Astronomy of fifty nine years, affirming this to be the Great Year. Meton the Laconian, an Astronomer, erected Pillars on which he inscribed the Tropics of the Sun, and found out as he said the Great Year, which he affirmed to consist of nineteen years.[9]

Much earlier in 280 BCE, another Greek wise man, the poet Aratus of Soli (ca. 312–240 BCE), gave in his work entitled *Phaenomena*, "Appearances," a very accurate description of the heavens for orientation and prognostics to be used by navigators, travelers and farmers. Aratus, who was born in Cilicia, Asia Minor, drew much on the works of Eudoxus of Cnidus (written in 370 BCE, but which are unfortunately now lost).

Then, around 130 BCE, the Greek astronomer and geographer Hipparchus of Nicaea (ca. 190–120 BCE), working from observations recording over 169 years of astronomical events, discovered the phenomena of the precession of the equinoxes and accurately determined the duration of the tropical year. That is, that the equinoxes move at a rate of 1° every 71 years, therefore taking 2,148 years to move through a zodiacal constellation and approximately 26,000 years to complete a full cycle around the ecliptic. At that time, in the fifth century BCE, the vernal point was in Aries. At around year one of the Common Era (1 CE), the vernal equinox started in Pisces. Therefore, in 2147 BCE when the astrological tables were first established by the Indo-European astronomers, spring was in Aries and remained there until year 1 CE. Also, the oldest zodiacal records charting the skies show a blind spot just below the 36th latitude. Mesopotamia (just above the 30th) is well below that latitude, which means that the creators of the Zodiac were well above that latitude.

According to David Frawley, from his exegesis of the Yajur, Atharva Vedas and the Brahmanas, the Spring equinox was at the time of their creation in Krittikas (the Pleiades an asterism or cluster of Taurus) and the summer solstice was in Leo. The early Vedic material therefore dates from 2500 BCE. Which again, brings us right at the time the disc of Nebra from Bronze Age Europe. The Bull is also a central theme in Celtic imagery and is found on the Gundestrup Cauldron (dating from the 1st or 2nd century BCE). It is echoed by the familiar Old Irish tale of the Táin Bó Cuailnge, or "Cattle raid of Cooley" (manuscript of the 11th century recording more ancient oral lore). Evidently, spring was the highlight of the year for the Trans-Danubian agrarian peoples who had not yet measured, as later did the Greek astronomers, the subtle shift of the precession of the equinoxes, but nevertheless had felt the drift for the precise moment of the passage of the vernal point. Hittite scribes, also drawing upon ancient lore, when describing the passage of the vernal equinox, seem to hesitate between Bull and Aries.

Map of the Mediterranean Sea during the Bronze Age (circa 2500 BCE). Notice the line of the 36th latitude running just below continental Greece, the Aegean Islands and Anatolia in Asia Minor. At that time, this general area was populated by differentiated Indo-European cultures such as the Archaic Greeks, Minoans, Aegeans and Hittites of Asia Minor.

But then, according to the oldest Indo-European cosmological myths, order was gained from chaos. This underlying theme is found in most of the IE daughter cultures; and the Hittite tablets offer no exception:

> On the altar, the gods are put in order.
> In the barn, cattle were put in order.
> In the pen, the sheep are put in order.
> (1 + KUB XXIX)[10]

Hittite-Luwian Star Order

The Hittite of Anatolia, who were at the crosswords of Europe and Asia, kept a star chart at a very early time which they called "tablets of Doom"; Doom, most likely hinting at the dark skies of autumn night. All suggests that the Hittites, who began springtime in Pisces, seemed unaware on the precise time of passage of the sun at the equinox. What they used for the recognizance of the vernal passage was a very old strategy which was also practiced by Aryan astronomers (as outlined in the *Surya Siddhanta*). This scheme relied on marking the transit of the lunar ascending node in Pisces in the area of Zeta Piscium. These naked eye astronomers of old knew that this asterism marked the start of the zodiacal eras. Here is cosmological plot as described by the Hittite seers:

> The Great River (magically) tied the current. And inside, with the fish in position.... The waters he retained. High mountains, he tied, deep valleys, he tied, the prairie storm god, he tied. And

inside, the (pure) rushes, he tied. The ongoing eagle, he tied. Bearded snakes, coiled, he tied. Deer at the foot of the tree, he tied eye; the leopard in a remote place (lit.: "difficult place"), he tied, the wolf in a high place, he tried, the proud lion (...), he tied; the graceful antelope, he tied; and milk from the antelope, he drew. The throne of the holding deity, he held. And you Ištar (< Sittar, "star"), say this to Maliya, and repeat it to Maliya Pirwa, and then repeat it to Pirwa Kamrusepa. And afterwards, Kamrusepa harnessed his horses and went trotting to the Great River. And then, the Great River conjured Kamrusepa. And then from inside, she (Ištar) first conjured the fish in the water. The Great River and its current was unleashed again. The Fish (in position in the water, he retained)...

1. The Fish (Pisces) out of Hannahannas, the impetuous water mother of the gods.
2. Then the high mountains, Mount Imgarra (Aries). Hapantalis is the shepherd of the sun god, a sheep is sacrificed for Ziparwa. And for Wurun Katte, the god of war; and Wurusema, the solar goddess of Arinna. And the sun god, Estan.
3. In deep valleys is the prairie storm god Taru, the "tree" [Taru/Tarhunda/Teshub] with his godly items. Tella (Tilla) and Seris (Serisu), the sacred bulls are overlapped by the storm god (Taurus), Wawa "the bull" is sacrificed for Ziparwa.
4. The Rushes in Gemini: Telipinus and Telepinus, the gods of agriculture are the son and daughter of the god of the storm.
5. The eagle wing Kashky, the god of the moonbeam is the eagle (Cancer).
6. Bearded serpents: Hedamu, the snake lover of Ishtar and Illuyankas, the dragon. The Illuyankas or dragons (Lunar Nodes) are bound by a mortal hero (Ophiucus, the Serpent Bearer).
7. Deer tree Eya in Virgo: Kuruta (Kurunta), the Deer, fawn god of rural areas. Goddesses of fate are sitting under the hawthorn. Others, in the city of Apsu (Abzu) are the guardians of the tablets of Doom.
8. Parsana, is the leopard of lost places (Libra). Telepinus, the god of vegetation disappeared (fall season).
9. Next, the wolf from the heights (Scorpio). Urbarra, the wolf, wild and free, from outside the clan, the outlaw (The wolf begins twelve days or periods following the winter solstice sun or renewal).
10. The proud lion (here hinting at divine kingship?). The lion is the sacred animal of the Hebat (Hepit/Hepatu) goddess, goddess of lions.
11. The graceful antelope (Sagittarius): Imbaluris, the messenger of gods (Capricorn), went to the sea to praise Kumarbis as the worthy king of the gods.
12. The throne of the divine Holder (Aquarius): Halmasuit, the goddess guards the throne (of the sky) of Alalus, the King of Heaven (KUB VII 1 + 21).

Aries and Taurus are also mentioned in another tablet: "The king sacrificed for Ziparwa, a ram [Aries] and a bull [Taurus]" (37 KUB XXV):

I. "Leashed were the Bearded Serpents intertwined (Pisces)";
II. (KUB XXV 37) "The King sacrifices for Ziparwa";
5. A Ram (Aries);
6. A Bull (Taurus);For the Eya Tree a Ram and a Bull they slay for above.
III. (KUB XII 62) "to the True GiSh-RU, under which sleep the Newborn Lion and Deer of the Year;
7. Leashed was a Leopard in a Lost Land (Gemini);
8. Leashed was a Wolf in a High Place (Lepus);
9. Leashed was a proud Lion (Leo);
10. Leashed was a gracious Antelope and its milk (Sagittarius?);
11. Leashed was the Throne of the Tutelary divinity (Aquarius)";
IV. "And Ishtar (the Star) said this to Maliya, and Maliya repeated it to Pirwa; and Pirwa repeated it to Kamrusepa. And Kamrusepa saddled his horse and trotted away to the Great River (Milky Way).
12. The three World Horses: White Horse, Red Horse, and Black horse (Day, Dawn and Dusk, Night)";
V. "And she conjured Kamrusepa the Great River (Milky Way). And then in it, She conjured the Fish in the water first. The Great River and its current were unleashed."
VI. "The Fish were unleashed (Vernal Point)."[11]

Some would argue that the Hittites or Luwites, after the famous Trojan War, were influenced by the Greeks and that they borrowed from them their cosmological bestiary. Or again, that these Bronze Age Anatolians were impressed by the Lion Gate entrance of the citadel of Mycenae. The lion was an important symbol in Hittite culture and is found at many archaeological sites. Such gates were found in the Upper City of Hattusha dating from 1343 to 1200 BCE. In my mind, this argument is but a scholar's Trojan horse! Again, not unlike the Indians, the Myceneans were drawing from a common Indo-European source. This neatly explains the overall structural similarities between these related Zodiacs.

The Hittite Zodiac

1. Aries	The Ram
2. Taurus	The Bull
3. Gemini	The Rushes
4. Cancer	The Eagle
5. Leo	The Proud Lion
6. Virgo	The Deer
The Vernal Point	"Leashed was the Great River and its current"
7. Libra	The Leopard
8. Scorpio	The Wolf
9. Sagittarius	The Graceful Antelope
10. Capricorn	The Messenger of the Gods Riding a Sea Monster
11. Aquarius	The Throne of the Sky God
12. Pisces	The Bearded Serpents

The Hittite tablets were written in cuneiform and date from between the 16th and 13th centuries BCE. And concerning the antiquity of the Hittite tablets, David Frawley had this to say:

> We know that the Vedic literature is considerably older than the historical Hittites. The Hittites, Mittani and Kassites consisted mainly of non–Aryans of Asia Minor supervised by the aristocratic elite of Aryan Kshatriyas. Even the Assyrians had such rulers as evidenced by their purely Sanskrit names: Asurbanirpal (Asura Vanir Pal "Whoever protects the Word of the Asuras"; Asurnarsipal, Asura Nari Pal "Whoever protects the people of the Asuras") [David Frawley, letter dated 25 April 2000].

Frawley's reading of the Assyrian king's names as being Sanskrit or Old Aryan is in itself very interesting. As we have seen, Babylon had long been dominated by Persian warrior kings. And the Avesta, despite the Zoroastrian reform (ca. 600 BCE), does not at all contradict the cosmological scheme described in the Hittite tablets: "I invoke the Kara fish, who lives beneath waters in the bottom of the deep lakes. I invoke the ancient and sovereign Merezu, the most warlike of the creatures of the two Spirits. I invoke the seven bright Sru...."[12]

The Chaldeans had a very different sky chart prior to the Indo-European conquests. So, for the sake of sceptics who believe that the Chaldean scheme was tropic, therefore solar, here is the full Chaldean lunar astrological model of 18 divisions (also, please note that an annual lunar calendar is much shorter than that of a solar year, and even less so than a full course of the moon around the Zodiac which tales one month comprising of 27 or 28 days):

(1) MUL.MUL, "the hairbrush or comb," passing through the Hyades and Pleiades moon in Taurus.
(2) MUL.GUD.AN.NA, "the bull of Anu," the moon passes through Taurus.
(3) MUL.SIPA.ZI.AN.NA, "the cattle herder of Anu," he moon passes through Orion.
(4) MUL.SHU.GI, "the old man," the moon passes through Perseus.
(5) MUL.GAM ZUBI, "the wand," the moon through Auriga.
(6) MUL.MASH.TAB.BA.GAL.GAL "The Great Twins," the moon through Gemini.
(7) MUL.AL.LUL, "Procyon," the moon crosses the Little Dog (Canis Minor).
(8) MUL.UR.GU.LA "The lioness," the moon through Lion (Leo Major).
(9) MUL.AB.SIN, "the furrow," the moon crosses Spica in the constellation Virgo.
(10) MUL.ZI.BA.NI.TUM, "the scales of Heaven," the moon passes through Libra.
(11) MUL.GIR.TAB, "Scorpio," the moon crosses Scorpio.
(12) MUL.PA.BIL.SAG, "the grandfather," the moon passes through Sagittarius.
(13) MUL.SUHUR.MAS, "the goat-fish," the moon goes through Capricorn.
(14) MUL.GU.LA, "the tall one (giant)," The moon passes through Aquarius.
(15) MUL.ZIBBATI.MESH MUL.KUN.MESH, "the tails," the moon goes through Pisces.
(16) MUL.SIM.MAH, "the great swallow," the moon through Pegasus (Pisces and Epsilon Pegasi).
(17) MUL.A.NU.TI.TUM, "Anunitum," (a goddess compared to Andromeda), the moon passes through its center.
(18) MUL.LU.HUN.GA, "the hireling," the moon passes through Aries.[13]

According to an old Sumerian account entitled *Enmerkar and the Lord of Aratta*

[ca. 21st century BCE] the king of Uruk, Enmerkar, wanting to submit his rival the lord of the prosperous city of Aratta in Iran, had his emissary send him a quoted message. Following the advice of his sister Inanna, he also sent the messenger with a tribute of gold and silver. Unfortunately, after this long and perilous journey through the high mountains and deserts, the messenger forgot several parts from his long missive. After a series of trips to and fro and great misunderstandings between the two cities courts, Enmerkar decided to inscribe the message on a clay tablet in cuneiform code so that it could always be faithfully repeated.

This story deserves attention for several reasons: first, because it informs us on the relationship between the proto–Sumerians and the Indo-European peoples and the necessary spread of writing, and secondly, for cosmological reasons which we will further explore.

According to the archaeologist Colin Renfrew, Indo-European was spoken in Asia Minor as back as 7000 BCE. Thus, placing it in the proximity of the Elamite and Dravidian peoples of Sumer and the Indus Valley. David Frawley has pointed out to me (in a letter dated August 29, 1998) that Aratta (Ara-tta) was, according to the Mahabharata and other Vedic texts, the Sanskrit name of the ancestor of the Arattas, an Aryan people of the region of Pancanada or Punjab. The Arattas were a tribe from Central Asia called the Druhyus and whose ancestor was Yayati. Ara in Sanskrit, means "speed, the radius of a wheel," also taken for the radius of the Wheel of Time when not "metal, copper, brass or iron," when not one the names for the planets Mars or Saturn.

Furthermore, This name is etymologically linked to that of the Greek poet and astrologer Aratus, living in the third century BCE and who was in the service of King

Antigonas II Gonatas of Macedonia and to Antiochus I of Syria. Let's not forget that it was he who drew a map of the stars of the northern skies thus giving them some of their mythological names. Author of the reputed *Phaenomena*, Aratus of Soli (who flourished from about 315 to 245 BCE). Although the event related in the story of Enmerkar is at a much earlier date, there seems to be an underlying mythic pattern with the Iranian city of Aratta and the Greek Aratos. The name Ἄρατος, often defined as meaning the "Plowman" (from ἀροτριάω, arotriaó: "to plough"), is most likely from ἀρᾶσθαι "to pray." Aratos was also the name of a settlement (now in the Rhodope Prefecture) in the East Macedonia and Thrace region of Greece.

On Enmerkar and the Lord of Aratta, vs. 499 to 576:

> His speaking [...] Recite his omen to him. At that time, the lord [...], on the throne daises and on the chairs, the noble seed, [...] His speech was substantial, and its contents extensive. The messenger, whose mouth was heavy, was not able to repeat it. Because the messenger, whose mouth was tired, was not able to repeat it, the lord of Kulaba patted some clay and wrote the message as if on a tablet. Formerly, the writing of messages on clay was not established. Now, under that sun and on that day, it was indeed so. The lord of Kulaba inscribed the message like a tablet. It was just like that. The messenger was like a bird, flapping its wings; he raged forth like a wolf following a kid. He traversed five mountains, six mountains, seven mountains. He lifted his eyes as he approached Aratta. He stepped joyfully into the courtyard of Aratta, he made known the authority of his king. Openly he spoke out the words in his heart. The messenger transmitted the message to the lord of Aratta:
>
> "Your father, my master, has sent me to you; the lord of Unug, the lord of Kulaba, has sent me to you."
>
> "What is it to me what your master has spoken? What is it to me what he has said?"
>
> "This is what my master has spoken, this is what he has said. My king is like a huge mes tree, [...] son of Enlil; this tree has grown high, uniting heaven and earth; its crown reaches heaven, its trunk is set upon the earth. He who is made to shine forth in lordship and kingship, Enmerkar, the son of Utu, has given me a clay tablet. O lord of Aratta, after you have examined the clay tablet, after you have learned the content of the message, say whatever you will say to me, and I shall announce that message in the shrine E-ana as glad tidings to the scion of him with the glistening beard, whom his stalwart cow gave birth to in the mountains of the shining me, who was reared on the soil of Aratta, who was given suck at the udder of the good cow, who is suited for office in Kulaba, the mountain of great me, to Enmerkar, the son of Utu; I shall repeat it in his jipar (temple), fruitful as a flourishing mes tree (tree of life), to my king, the lord of Kulaba."
>
> After he had spoken thus to him, the lord of Aratta received his kiln-fired tablet from the messenger. The lord of Aratta looked at the tablet. The transmitted message was just nails, and his brow expressed anger. The lord of Aratta looked at his kiln-fired tablet. At that moment, the lord worthy of the crown of lordship, the son of Enlil, the god Ickur, thundering in heaven and earth, caused a raging storm, a great lion, in [...] He was making the mountains quake [...], he was convulsing the mountain range [...]; the awesome radiance [...] of his breast; he caused the mountain range to raise its voice in joy. On Aratta's parched flanks, in the midst of the mountains, wheat grew of its own accord, and chickpeas also grew of their own accord; they brought the wheat which grew of its own accord into the granary of [...] for the lord of Aratta, and heaped it up before him in the courtyard of Aratta. The lord of Aratta looked at the wheat. The messenger's eyes looked askance [...] The lord of Aratta called to the messenger: "Inana, the lady of all the lands, has not run away from the primacy of her city, Aratta, nor has she stolen it for Unug; she has not run away from her E-zagina, nor has she stolen it for the shrine E-ana; she has not run away from the mountain of the shining me, nor has she stolen it for brick-built Kulaba; she has not run away from the adorned bed, nor has she stolen it for the shining bed; she has not run away from the purification for the lord, nor has she stolen it for the lord of Unug, the lord of Kulaba. Inana, the lady of all the lands, has surrounded Aratta, on its right and left, for her like a rising flood."[14]

The Sumerian language, decoded in mid–19th century by Henry Rawlinson and Edward Hincks, is classified by linguists as an isolate belonging to no linguistic family, although some tie it to Caucasian and perhaps Dravidian. Sumerian was spoken from after the 4th millennium to after the 2nd millennium BCE when it was replaced by Akkadian, a Semitic language. At some time in the proto–Sumerian past, the culture was in proximity of Indo-European speakers as is shown in its vocabulary. Also, all indicates that the Sumerians probably borrowed the cuneiform script from the Aratta Aryans of Iran. The Sumerian Zodiac also shows 18 constellations visited by the moon, and is thought by many experts to be the prototype for the Chaldean and Greek Zodiacs. It is estimated to date from around 2000 BCE. The Sumerian and Chaldean charts were in fact designed for moon divining and were quite different from the Indo-European 12 sign models that charted the sun's course around the ecliptic. As mentioned above, since a lunar month is of 29.53 days, then after 12 lunar months, the lunar year, of 354 days, is in average 10 to 11 days short of the solar year. The 18 part moon chart of the Chaldeans and Sumerians worked on the moon's movement on a span of 360 solar days (18 constellation visits × 20 days). The moon does not orbit the sun the same way the earth does since it is tilted to about 5° on the ecliptic. Therefore, the moon spends half of the time slightly north and the other half slightly south of the ecliptic. It crosses the ecliptic twice a month. This downward and upward movement from the ecliptic gave slightly different apparent astral conjunctions from those of the sun. So for these cultures, Sumerian and Semitic (Assyrian, Ugaritic, Phoenician, Canaan and Hebrew), time keeping was basically lunar (Paul Couderc, 1945).

The Sumerian Zodiac

(1) The Hair Brush (Pleiades)
(2) The Bull of Anu (Taurus)
(3) Anu's True Shepherd (Orion)
(4) The Old Man (Perseus)
(5) Gamlu, The Sickle Sword or Harpé (Auriga)
(6) The Great Twins (Gemini)
(7) Al.Lil (Procyon or Cancer/Crab)
(8) The Lion or Lioness (Leo)
(9) Furrow (Spica)
(10) The Scale (Libra/Scales)
(11) The Scorpion (Scorpio)
(12) The Archer (Sagittarius)
(13) The Goat) fish (Capricorn)
(14) The Great Star or Giant (Aquarius)
(15) The Tails (Pisces/Fishes)
(16) The Great Swallow (Piscis SW with Epsilon Pegasi)
(17) The Goddess Anunitum (in Piscis to the North East and in the middle part of Andromeda)
(18) The Hireling (Aries/Ram).[15]

II

The Indo-European Bases of Astrology

"In the beginning the Golden Embryo arose. Once he was born, he was the one lord of creation. He held in place the earth and the sky."—*Rig Veda*, 10.121 vs. 1

Val Camonica Rock Art, Italian Alps, digitally drawn after a photograph from UNESCO.

Indo-European Religion—A Cosmic Ideology

It was in a very early age, possibly at the start of 8000 BCE, that the Indo-European culture was diffused over much of Southern central Eurasia. Even then, it had the solidity and unity that nowadays is still not suspected from outside of a small intellectual circle. When one considers the pre–Vedic phase of Indo-Aryan religion, admittedly, one turns to the Steppe culture, but it turns out a pre–Vedic culture was already found in the Indus Valley with the Harappa civilization which dates from as early as

4000 to 1700 BCE. It should also be noted that artifacts from Sumer do not yield dates prior to 4000 BCE. And as we have seen, if the Sumerian cuneiform writing is very close to that of Aryan Aratta, the Iranian pre–Avestic texts are sensibly older, but not as old as the Harappa hieroglyphs which are now regarded as pre–Sanskrit. The kingdom of Aratta on the Iranian Plateau was right between Sumer and Harappa (now in Pakistan) that is, to the south of the Black Sea where also flourished the Danubian civilization which begins at around 6250 BCE.

The dates for these dispersed Indo-European cultural areas are as follows: Vinça Lepenski Vir (Danube) culture, after 6500 BCE, Yamna Eastern European culture (Hungary) 4500 to 2500 BCE; Sredny Stog, Dnieper-Donets and Sarama cultures, domestication of the horse, from 4500 to 4000 BCE; the Yamna Kurgan builders culture, steppes expansion, and the Maykop culture in northern Caucasus 4000 to 3500 BCE; Harappa (Indus) culture, dating from circa 4000 BCE; Yamnaya culture expansion from 3600 to 2200 BCE; Anatolian and Jiroft-Aratta (Iranian Plateau) cultures, from before 3000 BCE; the Yamnaya Pontic steppe Kurgan Culture (South Caucasus), circa 3000 to 2500 BCE; and the Ikshvaku culture (Caspian Sea), circa 2300 BCE.

At some time around 3000 BCE, the Central European ancestors of the Hittites and Luwians cross the Bosporus into Anatolia where they become acquainted with cuneiform writing. With the Hittite tablets one discovers a highly coherent system of beliefs still present in the later forms of the Brahmanic Ṛta Dharma, Avestic Asha or Classical Greco-Roman devotion. This being that the Proto-Anatolian and Indo-Aryan branches were linguistically close when they separated from the main trunk.

Contrary to popular belief, the early Indo-Europeans had developed a priestly caste that was no longer at the pre–Indo-European level of shamanism and witchcraft. In fact, these priests were neither magicians nor shamans, but chaplains to a warlord and his people. Therefore, it is an error to speak of "Vedic, Celtic or even Germanic Shamans." We are not speaking here of an animistic world of anarchy and chaos where the individual human soul must negotiate with a greater animal spirit, but that of a world order in which humans and gods coexist, compete and cooperate, in accordance with a universal cosmic "World Order." Henceforth, we are truly in the presence of a world ruled by ritual law and social order, of harmony and structure, of mind and fate, a world timed as a clock and essentially cyclical in nature. Any breach in this ethic order spells moral depravity, chaos and degeneration.

Wisdom had it that man, the Just,[1] understood the laws of ritual order and that he acted in honor of the gods. This law of rite was called *ṛta* or *rita* in Sanskrit or *ritus* in Latin, *asha* in Avestic Persian and *litus* in Celtic. Keeping to ones dharma[2] was more than an oath; it is what distinguished the nobly-born[3] from the uncouth. And this is what bonded him to the higher realm of the immortals. In commemoration of this, the young nobleman (ario—"host, lord, master") at his coming of age, was given a white linen tunic and a threaded woolen strap or cordon to tie it.

Priestly order	white	flax
Warriors' order	red	hemp
Producers' order	Black, dun, blue-green	wool

One of the duties of the arios faithful was to tie and untie this cordon at least thrice daily that is, morning, noon and evening. In his service to the gods as a householder, the married man had many sacrificial duties to perform. These included keeping the sacred fire and preparing the *soma* or *amrita*.[4] For the Teutonic tribes it was "the heavenly beer of the gods" brewed with heavenly care. Soma is a plant which grows in former Sogdian, in what is now known as Turkestan, but was once the homeland of the Uttarakuru to which the early Cimmerians belonged. It also grows further north and is found on the mountain slopes of Kerman. Its botanical name is *Sarcostema Viminalis*. Shoots and stalks of Soma are mixed with curled milk, barley meal, or in India, mixed with nirvana or trinadhanya thought to be wild rice which fermented, produced a strong intoxicant considered nourishing and healthy. As a divine fortifier, it was seen as prolonging life.[5] One favorite saying of the Brahmans which just about sums the spirit of Indo-European religion was, "Who wishes to gain heaven must sacrifice." And even the concept of the Other-world, Heaven or Paradise, is linked to the notion of fate, seen mainly as the netherworld, the Fairyland of the European folktales. Does not the term "fairy" derive from Fata, the goddess of fate?

Gradually, around the third or second millennium in the northern steppes, shamanistic types of practice were almost abandoned for a highly regimented priesthood structured around an elite called Blagmena.[6] This second phase was highly codified and ritualistic with the focus on ceremonial and scriptural injunctions ordering sacrificial rites. After 1000 BCE, the steppes migrations of the Aryan Scythians and Proto-Thracic or Proto-Celtic Cimmerians and Tocharians[7] of Central Asia came into contact with the Turkish and Mongolian shamans, thus bringing Indo-European ritualism to the area. How was it that these people could influence such diverse, different and culturally marked societies?

This was possible only because the early Indo-European cultures were still related and that these people formed a highly mobile culture. Let us not forget that it was the elite, the travelling poet-seers and their aristocrats who were the main proponents for the spread of aryanic culture as a spiritual force.[8] The doctrines and concepts of Yoga, along with the Àtman (the spiritual self) and Dharma, Karma and reincarnation, were probably already articulated at the common level of Indo-European thought. At about this time examples of seated gods in lotus position were found in many areas, from the Indus valley on the Mohenjo-Daro tablets and on to Bulgaria on the Gundestrup Cauldron. As was the case for the Gaulish mummies of the Remoi found in d'Acy-Romance near Rethel in the Ardennes, all were found seated in the lotus position. These bodies were not incinerated and therefore could have either been aristocratic warriors or either noble holy men. In short, yogic practices were widespread and did not simply originate within some Dravidian ascetic practice as it was originally proposed by modern Western scholars.

Therefore, because of this fundamental mindset and common Indo-European cosmological and mythological world view, the state of affairs in the world of the gods necessarily affected those in the world of the mortals. Hence the hermetic maxim: "As above, so below!" This notion that the macrocosm is reflected in the microcosm was not only professed by the Greek philosophers but was also present as an underlying concept in the other Indo-European wisdom traditions.

French linguist Jean Haudry (born in 1934) has very well demonstrated that Indo-European thought was essentially cosmological. His observations are well summarized in a short article which he wrote for the *New Antaios Journal*.[9] The following excerpt sums it all in the chapter entitled "General Characteristics of Indo-European Religion, The Heavens and the Earth":

> "The Indo-European gods are called deywòs "those of the day-sky" (Haudry 1987 b: 28 f.), a term whose origins go back to a period in which the Day-sky, dyéw-pHtér-, was the first among the gods. Hittite Sius "Sun god" is his most archaic reflex, which retains his temporal character, the limitation of the day. He lost this primacy in those cases where he remained the sky (so the Vedic Dyaùh), whereas his name passed to the sovereign god in the case of the Greeks (Zeùs) and the Romans (Jupiter). To the deywos of day who inhabit the heavens are opposed the demons whose habitat is the Night-sky or Hell. This theology, initially linked with the revolving-sky-cosmology, is perpetuated in the various dualism which place gods and demons in opposition to one another, such as the Mazdeism of the Iranians. The earth-mother is, in the last state of this theology, the consort of the "sky," but in more ancient times she was the consort of a black Night-sky who was succeeded by the white Day-sky after the brief reign of a red Dawn- or Dusk-sky.

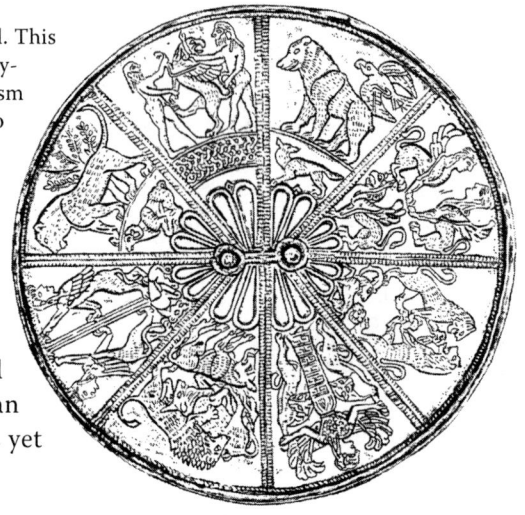

Prajapati, Lord of Beasts, Harappa Mohenjo-Daro, Indus Civilization. This seated figure coiffed with bull's horns is probably the oldest representation of the Ophiuchus constellation which anciently marked the starting point of the sun's course through the Zodiac following the Fall equinox.

Although, we can suspect that there could have existed a common Indo-European Zodiac, for the time being, no artifact has yet been uncovered in the archaeology digs.

It is nevertheless possible to reconstruct a prototype by comparing the oldest Indo-European models of the Zodiac. The earliest Zodiac is thought to have comprised of eight non-equal constellations with two other stellar signs added on in the final model. This assumption is

Hellenic-style Thracian-Cimmerian or Scythian Mirror (650–620 BCE) with cosmic and astrological symbols, from Kuban Valley at Kelermes in Russia bordering Ukraine and kept at the Hermitage Museum, St. Petersburg, Russia. Author's drawing from a photograph published in *Les dossiers de l'archéologie*.

corroborated by many examples found in Rock Art depicting four-spoked, six-spoked and eight-spoked wheels, but rarely twelve. It is also assumed that the early charts started at the fall equinox and not at the vernal equinox as was the practice later on. The oldest graphic example on an eightfold zodiacal chart was to be found in 1903 by a mine technician with no archaeological expertise, a certain D.G. Shultz, at the Kelermesskaya Stanitsa site in Russia. There, he hastily excavated four burial mounds where he found the mirror. This artifact is not only of great artistic merit, but also provides much detail on the cosmological considerations of the ancient late Kurgan culture.

The Kurgan Zodiac

Classical Constellations	Zodiacal Symbol or Theme
Pisces and Aries	A giant snow leopard, the World Tree in bloom over a ram with bonded legs
Vernal Equinox	Two winged sphinxes (North and South winds) holding the World Axis lying of the back of a slain wolf (end of winter)
Taurus	A lion (Hyades) devouring a bull (of days) over a wild boar (Ursa Minor)
Twins and Cancer	The Sky Goddess holding two panthers (spring and summer)
Leo and Virgo	Two opposing lions (Leo) over a goat and a ram's head
Libra and Scorpio	Opposing sphinxes (South and North winds) over a griffon
Sagittarius	An eagle (Aquila) flying over a bear (Ursa Major)
Capricorn	Two giants or heroes, young and old (days of the year), combating a griffon (winter solstice)

Greek, Vedic and Celtic Astrologies Compared

The Archaic Greek Order

Regarding the presumed ancient Greek order, this sequel starts at the fall equinox and not at the usual the spring vernal point as it is for Vedic, Classical, and contemporary western charts. Not that there is error here, as Frawley noted, simply that the older cosmological order of cyclical time started with the annual dark period. The Celts seem to have maintained this old practice much longer than the Greeks or Indians. Therefore, this Hellenic prototype also started in fall. Most of the Greeks calendars started in autumn and winter except for the Attic calendar, which started in summer.

DZÔDIAKOS KYKLOS,
"circle of little animals," the zodiacal cycle;

I—Ophiucos, Ophiuchus, that is, Asclepius and his snake begin the cycle of the twelve zodiacal constellations; symbol for the dark and cold areas.

1 **Krysopheros,** "the golden antler," or Chelae, "claws (of the scorpion)," or Zugos, "the Yoke," for Libra; Libra, "the Scale," is the later Latin name for this constellation which was formerly seen as the Scales of Astraia, the Greek goddess of Justice.
2 **Elaphos Kyroskerôs,** "the deer with golden antlers," or Skorpios, "the scorpion," for Scorpio; also Elaphos Kerynitis, "the deer of Ceryneia," or Elaphoi Krysokeroi, "the deer with golden antlers," who were sacrificed to Artemis, Apollo's sister.
3 **Toxotes,** "the archer," for Sagittarius); Kentauros, "the centaur," followed by Lukábas, the twelve day period after the winter solstice; also called Lúkeios, "the master of wolves."
4 **Khimaira,** "cold air," the Chimera of Capricorn; or Tragos, "the goat," for Capricornus; the Chimera was a half-lion, half-goat, half-serpent, monster.
5 **Hydrochoös,** "the water pourer," or water pot, for Aquarius; For the nymph Ganymede, Zeus's water carrier.
6 **Ikhthyes,** "the fishes," for Pisces; In mythology, there were large river fish attending the birth of Aphrodite. The Ikhthyokentauroi, were "sea centaurs," the poetic name for the stars of that constellation.
II—**Kórunthos,** "the cock-rooster"; Eoos, "the one of Dawn"; symbol for the clear and warm period.
7 **Krios,** "the ram," for Aries; Aries, "Mars"; Ares, the god of Mars. His chariot was driven by the goddess Aphrodite.
8 **Tauros,** "The bull" (Taurus); Tauros, also Khalkeos, "the brazen bull," a fire-breathing bull forged by Hephaestus.
9 **Dioskouroi,** "the twins"; for Gemini; Castor and Polydeukes (Castor and Pollux).
10 **Karkinos,** "The Crab" (Cancer);
11 **Léôn,** "the lion," for Leo; Léôn Nemeios, "the lion of Nemea," the mountain valley of Nemea in Argolis where the Nemean games were celebrated. Heracles killed the lion there which desolated the country. He made a cloak of his skin.
12 **Astraia** or Astraea, "the stellar one," for Virgo; The virgin goddess of justice; the name also connotes Astrape, "lightning."

The Vedic Order of Jyotisha

1 **Mesa,** "ram" (Aries);
2 **Vrsabha,** "bull" (Taurus);
3 **Mithuna,** "the pair" (Gemini);
4 **Karkataka,** Kartaka, Karka, "crab" (Cancer);
5 **Simha,** "lion" (Leo);
6 **Kanya,** "girl" (Virgin);
7 **Tula,** "scale" (Libra);
8 **Vrushchik,** "Scorpion" (Scorpio);
9 **Kamuka,** "flower," Dhanus, "bow"; as Dhanvin, "the archer" (Sagittarius);

10 **Ena** or **Mrga,** "the antelope"; as Makara, a mythical sea monster, or a dolphin, or a crocodile (Capricorn);
11 **Kumbha,** "the pot" (Aquarius);
12 **Matsya,** "the fish," also Jhasa, Timi, Mina (Pisces).

Puns on the Names (Çlesha in Sanskrit)

Dhanus/Dyanus, "archer"; connoting "mainland or island, dry land"; and "good";
Vrsika/Vrsiha, "scorpion"; connoting "scissors";
Makara, "sea monster, crocodile"; connoting "crier";
Mithuna, "pair, couple"; that is, a "couple as an interchangeable pair."

The Gundestrup Cauldron and the Celtic Astral Tradition

I—**Libra and Scorpio:** Caruos/Sidos, "deer"; opposite to Taurus on the zodiacal circle. Representation of a god grabbing two deer by the hind legs; that is, Cernunnos, the horned god or Natronouiros for Ophiuchus, "the serpent bearer."
1 **Libra:** Cantalon, "the (memorial) pillar."
2 **Scorpion:** Samonios/Semonios, "the sower."
3 **Sagittarius:** a wolf (uolcos in OClt); Duniomannos, the centaur.
4 **Capricorn:** Moritasgos, the child riding a sea monster (a sturgeon or dolphin) opposing a Lion; Riuones, "the rays."
5 **Aquarius:** Medua, "intoxication," the goddess of ritual drunkenness surrounded by her two male companions, one bearded and one beardless while holding her left breast or nipple; Anaxs, "the pot, the tumbler."
6 **Fish:** Snake on the head of a ram; a god grabbing two dragons as two monstrous wolves devour two men; Ogronios, a cold-blooded animal, or a reptile.
7 **Aries:** A young warrior with his sword jabs at a wolf; the chariot-driver goddess is flanked by two elephants (seen as giant boars), two griffins (winds) and a wolf; Cutios, Aries.
8 **Taurus:** Taruos a bull lying on a bobcat or a lynx; three bulls attacked by men armed with swords; Taruos Trigarannianom, "the bull with three cranes"; Gammos, "ox."
9 **Gemini:** A god grabbing two youths holding small boar piglets with a dog to his right shoulder and a winged horse by his left shoulder; Semiuesses, "the small springy pigs."
10 **Cancer:** A winged horse; Equoredioi, four riders on the run; each wearing a helmet with the effigies of: a feathered crest, bull horns, a wild boar and a bird (crow, hawk or eagle?); Equos, "the horse."
11 **Lion:** A god waving his arms flanked by two boxers and a rider on the run; an opposing lion with a child straddling a sea monster; two leaping lions; Elembos, "the fawn."

12 Virgo: Dexsiutera, "the righteousness"; the goddess holding a wren in her right hand and a young man lying in her left arm; a dog or wolf lies further; the hair of the goddess is combed by a lady; another maiden is sitting next to her right with a wolf leaping over it; two eagles fly over on both sides.

Comparative Table of the Indo-European Zodiacs

Classical Greco-Roman	Hittite	Vedic	Gaulish
Aries: Mars, Ram	Ram	Mesa, Ram	Cuti Prinnios, Ram
Taurus: Bull	Bull	Vrsabha, Bull	Giamoni Prinn., Sprouts
Gemini: Twins	Rushes, Reed	Mithuna, The Pair, Couple	Semiuisoni Prinn., Spirited
Cancer: Crab	Eagle	Kartata, Crab	Equi Prinn., Equalised, Horse
Leo: Lion	Lion	Simha, Lion	Elembiui Prinn., of Fawns
Virgo: Maiden	Deer by the tree of the maiden Eya	Kanya, Virgin, Maiden	Edrini Prinn., The Hot Flux
Libra : Scales	Leopard	Tula, Scales	Cantli Prinn., The Ring, Buckle
Scorpio: Scorpion	Wolf	Vrsika, Scorpion	Samoni Prinn., Of the Sower
Sagittarius: Archer	Antelope	Dhanus, Archer	Dumanni Prinn., Of darkness
Capricornius: Goat Fish, Goat	The Messenger	Ena, Mrga, Antelope/ Makara, Sea Monster, Dolphin, Crocodile	Riuri Prinn., Of Frost, of Rays
Aquarius: Water Carrier	Throne of the Sky God	Kumbha, Water Pot or Jar	Anaganti Prinn., Of Inaction, Calamitous
Pisces: Fishes	Serpents/Fish	Mîna, Fish	Ogroni Prinn., Cold blooded, Fish, Snakes

Common Zodiacal Designations

Many of the astral designations (astronyms) were gleaned from the different early zodiacal charts. There is a certain consensus surrounding the majority of the names for the majority of signs. The following lists show the great unity and subtle originality of the different astral charts.

Classical Zodiacal Twelve Signs: Aries; Taurus; Gemini; Cancer; Lion; Virgin; Scales; Scorpio; Sagittarius (the Centaur Archer); Capricorn; Aquarius; Pisces.

Vedic Zodiacal Signs: Ram; Bull; Pair/Twins; Crab; Lion; Maiden; Scales; Scorpion; Archer; Antelope/Sea Monster; Water Pot; Fish.

Luwian-Hittite Signs: Ram; Bull; Pair/Twins; Lion; Fish/Snakes.

Gallic List (Coligny Calendar) of the Astral Signs: Ram; Bull; Fish.

II: The Indo-European Bases of Astrology

For the sake of comparison the Gallic list from the Coligny calendar, having the shortest list of classical zodiacal symbols, seems to be the most archaic since it has, along with the Hittite Zodiac, maintained the stag or deer constellation of the Indo-Europeans. The Sumerian or Chaldean star charts seem to have contributed the astronyms which appear in the Classical and Vedic lists. To wit, the list of Sumerian-Chaldean lunar signs shared with the other Zodiacs: Bull; Gemini, Leo, Libra, Scorpio, Capricorn. Therefore, as can be observed, at least half of the Classical and Vedic names are present in this list.

Although Ophiuchus, with its two sub-constellations, Caput Serpentis and Cauda Serpentis (Head and Tail of the Snake), is one of the major constellations through which the sun passes on the ecliptic plane, it is not included as a zodiacal constellation. And this despite of the fact that the sun stays in this constellation four times longer than in Scorpio. Let's remember that in the remote past, Ophiuchus was considered as the first constellation of the Zodiac. In Scandinavian cosmology, Ophiuchus was called the "door of Valhalla," and Níðhöggr, the Snake found at the base of Yggdrasil, the World Tree (or Milky Way) was identifiable to Scorpio. Eikþyrnir, The Deer (along with 4 others), browses at the foot of the Yggdrasil tree. The ancient Greeks also shared the same cosmological theme. Elaphos Kyroskerôs, the "Deer with the Golden Horns," the Deer constellation, was the name for the stars grouping Libra and Scorpio. The archer's bow points to it. The brightest stars of this region of the sky form the deer's antlers.

In the Hittite Zodiac, Scorpio was represented by a wolf. For the Scandinavians, it were the stars of Sagittarius that were referred to as Fenrir the Wolf. This being that the constellation of the Wolf (Lupus) is now in Libra and Scorpio just west and east of the Centauri cluster. In Greeks myths, this animal was pierced by the spear of the centaur archer. In these cosmologies, the Wolf symbolically marks the revival period of the winter sun springing up in March. For the Greeks, the calendar month of Lukios, covered the period from February to March when not, from April to May.

To quote Aristotle, here is the outline of the traditional mythological plot:

> The wolf resembles the dog in regard to the time of conception and parturition, the number of the litter, and the blindness of the newborn young. The genders couple at one special period, and the female brings forth at the beginning of the summer. There is an account given of the parturition of the she-wolf that borders on the fabulous, to the effect that she confines her lying-in to within twelve particu-

Praying figures and mazes, rock art from Val Camonica, Italian Alps, dating between the 8th and 1st millennium BCE. Drawing by the author from a photograph by Elisabetta Roffia, UNESCO.

lar days of the year. And they give the reason for this in the form of a myth, viz. that when they transported Leto in so many days from the land of the Hyperboreans to the island of Delos, she assumed the form of a she-wolf to escape the anger of Here. Whether the account be correct or not has not yet been verified; I give it merely as it is currently told. There is no more of truth in the current statement that the she-wolf bears once and only once in her lifetime.[10]

In Rome, these twelve days were under the auspices of the twelve Luperci "those of the Wolf." Their institution was created before the time of Romulus and they are recruited from the great patrician families of the Quinctilli and the Fabii. Every year in February, they performed magic rituals for the protection of sheep against the wolves. The Lupercalia (Lupercalia) were fertility festivals in honor of the god Lupercus, an equivalent of the Greek god Apollo Lúkeios represented by a lynx. In Rome, Lupercus was also called Faunus. This is because Faunus was later likened to the Greek Pan. On the Celtic side, January had the Gaelic name Faoilteach for the time "of wolves," and the Gaelic name for the February feasts of Lupercalia was Imbolc. If Imbolc is thought to come from *im'bolg*, literally "in the bag," or "in the belly," referring to the pregnancy of ewes, this is because of a late medieval word play replacing the old pagan meaning by a Christianized one. That is, Imbolc is rather from the Old Celtic root ambi-uolca-ia for "lustrations," and connoting "from around the wolf-bitch." The wolf-bitch was, in Antiquity, synonymous with dog days, increase of heat and sexual activity. On the Gundestrup Cauldron, wolves and dogs are inseparable. Did not the Celts tend to confuse wild dogs from domesticated ones?

At the feast of Robigalia in April, the Romans sacrificed dogs to Robigus, the god of wheat rust. It was held just after the rising of the star Sirius, Canis Major and Canis Minor, which they called Canicula, "the little dog." Dogs were also killed during the dog days of September in honor of the youth fraternities. The Scandinavians also associated dog days with sexual heat; hence the names: Lokabrenna and Hudastjarna, the "Dog Star," for Sirius.

Capricorn was formerly represented by a sea monster, probably a sturgeon and then later replaced by a dolphin, or a goat-fish, when not simply by a goat. According to the *Vedanta*, the seven Rishis or sages of the North ascended to the stars of Makara (Capricorn) while the Devas, the highest celestial deities (Rudras Kumaras Adithyas, Gandharvas or Asuras), made their descent from there to Earth in order to teach humanity wisdom and to establish right and order. And, from the North skies came the seven cosmic rays affecting the seven planets or the seven worlds. The Gallic Riuros[11]

Praying figure accompanied by a pack of dogs. The dogs probably represent the heat of the dog days during the rise of Sirius in summer. In Val Camonica Rock Art, the dog figure is found depicted with a radiant sun orb. Engraving dating from the fifth millennium BCE. Author's drawing after a photograph from the Camunian Centre for Prehistoric Studies.

months, for "freezing," is also marked by these beams. The Romans called this winter constellation Capra, "goat," same as with the Scandinavians who called it Heidrun, also for "goat." Each evening, the udder of the goat Heidrun filled with mead a huge basin. By its horns, the goat is also the symbol for the heavenly waters of the moon, hence the pouring of Soma (Haoma in Indo-Iranian). The Hittite designation for Sagittarius was the "graceful Antelope," and "messenger," for Capricorn. On the Gundestrup Cauldron is featured a boy riding a sturgeon or dolphin. In Greek myths, Taras, was rescued from a shipwreck by a dolphin sent by his father the sea god Poseidon. The dolphin boy somewhat brings us closer to the god sent messenger of Hittite myth.

For Aquarius, the Hittite had Halmasuit, the "Holder of the god throne," for "Sovereignty." The idea of a pouring pot featured in the Vedic Zodiac is also present in other charts such as those of the Greeks and Romans. The Gallic (*Coligny calendar*) designation of Anacanti, for "calamitous," is also found on the Gaelic side with Fii from the *Book of Ballymote*, meaning "disastrous."

There is a general consensus for most of the charts to have the fish symbol for the Piscean constellation. However, it seems that snakes first represented Pisces as it was for the Hittite and Gallic Zodiacs. In the Hittite Zodiac, Pisces was called "Bearded Serpents," and in the Gallic (Coligny calendar), Ogronios stood for "of cold-blooded animals, snakes or fishes." Here, Gallic terminology hesitates between snakes and fishes.

In Vedic literature, Taurus is described as a being of fire, of heat, and referred to as "the Bull of days." As Lord of Heaven, the Maruts, his martial companions, are surrounded with fire and rain. In ancient art, the Bull of May was represented as a great white ox attacked and devoured by an oversized feline, most often a lion.

For the Greeks, it were the nymphs of Hyades who brought rain. In the *Avesta* of Zoroaster, the heavenly showers depended on the twin stars Sata-vaêsa (Aldebaran, alpha Tauri), and Tištriya (Sirius or Canis Major). The asterisms of Taurus, the Pleiades and the Hyades, were already figured on the Nebra disc (ca. 1600 BCE). The Pleiades, called "the Seven Sisters," embodied the Fate Fairy consorts of the "Seven Seers," of the Septentrion. The Scandinavians simply called them the Sjaustiarnar, "the seven stars." In their midst, is the boar Sæhrímnir who is devoured every day in order to be reborn again every night. The Boar Star then passes by the cauldron of Andrimnir. They appear in May, peaking until the harvest season only to appear again at sunset at the approach of winter in November. Hesiod believed that their influence was like that of the moon on agriculture. The Celts called the Pleiades Trigaranai, the "Three Cranes," thereby identifying these three bright stars to the old lady, the crane or the witch. The Scandinavians called them the "hens of Freya." Freya, who was the goddess of love and death, drove a chariot pulled by two cats. These cats were identifiable to the two bright stars of Hyades, also called the Cat Stars[12] by the Celts and other peoples of Antiquity. The Greeks maintained that the Hyades, the Pleiades, were the daughters of Atlas and the sisters of Hya, who cried rain storms. The pouring water god of Aquarius, was not only symbolically linked to the pitcher pot but also to pigs or boars.[13] Henceforth, the Hyades mourn the death of Hya who was gutted by a boar, and in other versions of the myth, he was attacked by a lion or a snake. This asterism or cluster of Taurus therefore marks the rainy season in November. The Romans called the V-shaped cluster of Hyades, Sucula, "the pig," while the Welsh called it Cath Palwg[14] "the mouse-catcher cat," and the Teutonic peoples, called it Litilaes Vulfaes Hrakón for "the mouth of the little wolf."

The Gemini, Castor and Pollux of the Greeks were called Mithuna, "the pair," by the Indians. The notion of pairs is also shared by the Scandinavians with Þlazis Augar "the eyes of Thiazi." That is, according to natural law, everything comes in pairs. The solar symbolism of the eye is here self-evident. And on the Eye in the Sun motif, the *Rig Veda* expresses it clearly:

> The father of the eye (the Sun), who is wise in his heart like butter (of offering) created these two worlds folded down. As soon as their extremities left in the east, at that time heaven and earth moved apart.[15]

And again, in the *Rig Veda*:

> The Moon was gendered from his mind, and from his eye the Sun had birth; Indra and Agni from his mouth were born, and Vāyu from his breath.[16]

The "rushes," or "reeds," of the Hittites most certainly connote water, a concept that goes back to the idea of the Greek rainy Hyades. The grass rods are indeed safe from water fires; here symbolically connoting the "heat of inner being." Indra, who takes refuge in a reed or lotus stem, is eventually found by Agni during for his quest for the many names of the god. Agni, the fire god, enters the stem and sets fire to the reed. And, according to Zoroastrian literature, it was also with the use of magic that Nôtarga created a cow that feeds for a year on harvested reed to give milk to nourish her three sons.

As regards to the race and genealogy of the Kayanians, there is this passage in the Persian Avesta:

> This too one says, "The glory of Faridoon had settled on the root of a reed, in the ocean Frakhvkart. Notarga having with sorcery transformed a cow into a goat, led her there. Having reaped the reeds there for a year, he gave them to the cow till the glory went over to the Cow. Having brought back the cow, he milked her milk and gave it to the three sons, such as Vamun, Shun, and Changranha, which he had. The glory went not to the sons but to Frana. Notarga wished to kill Frana; Frana went from under the father's sway by means of the glory, and made a vow, saying: "I will give my first child to Ushbam." Then Ushbam saved her from her father, and the first child she bore was Kay Apiveh whom she gave to Ushbam, and she went in a mingled state again with Ushbam, as Ushbam's companion.

But for the Celts, this asterism was represented by pigs or piglets. In the *Book of Ballymote* the sign for Gemini is marked by the word: Ruidzûig (ruidh sûig < roudos succoi, "the red pigs"). The Old Irish word for "pig," sug, also can be taken for "joy, laughter or happiness." On the Gundestrup Cauldron is shown a figure of a god clutching two young boars or holding small piglets. And on the Coligny calendar, is engraved the Gallic name Simiuisonios meaning "capricious breezes," or connoting Simiuesses/Semi-uesses, "little flighty pigs, or frisky, piglets."[17]

The Eagle or the "Wings of the Eagle" of Hittite cosmology differs much from the Crab found on other charts. Cancer, "the crab," was not the original Indo-European name for it and was probably borrowed from the Sumerians. Winged creatures more often appear in relation to sky deities, but not aquatic animals. On the Kelermes mirror, the Sky Goddess is represented with wings and a winged horse is found on the Gundestrup Cauldron. In Celtic cosmology, the horse symbolizes the adjustment of the dueling time cycles and equos, the name for horse, also marks the month of July on the Coligny calendar.

Although the lion was probably not the ancient name for Leo, it rapidly became widespread as the main astronym by the time of the Hittites and Cimmerians who placed it in this constellation. On the Gundestrup Cauldron, as on the Kelermes mirror, two opposing lions are figured while on the Coligny calendar Elembos, the "fawn," is marked in place of Leo. Besides Edrinos, "arbitrator," for the Celtic Gauls, the Virgin appears to be the unanimous symbolic figure for that zodiacal constellation. Interestingly, the Hittite names for this sign were Ea, the "fairy," and Aliya-, "deer."

III

Astrology of the Druids

"Next morning, at the dawn of day, they arose. And they took way along the sea coast, up towards Bryn Aryen. And at the top of Cevn Clydno they equipped themselves with horses, and went towards the Castle of Arianrod. And they changed their form, and pricked towards the gate in the semblance of two youths, but the aspect of Gwydion was more staid than that of the other. "Porter," said he, "go thou in and say that there are here bards from Glamorgan." And the porter went in. "The welcome of Heaven be unto them, let them in," said Arianrod."—Lady Charlotte Guest, *The Mabinogion*, Math the Son of Mathonwy, 1877

Assembly of the Druids, old book engraving by Charles Knight, England.

Druidical Astrology

Roman scholars have often reported that the Gauls, of all the empire's people, were the most receptive to astrology.[1] This pedagogical art and Druid-science was always on top of the agenda as an important subject matter in the curriculum of all the pagan schools of southern Gaul. And as Peter Berresford Ellis remarked, it is very surprising considering the classical sources that there is so little mention of it in the Celtic texts. Pomponius Mela[2] (ca. 43 CE) noticed the high regard given to the Druids who were held for their "speculations" on the stars."

Then there is this passage by Flavius Magnus Aurelius Cassidorus[3] (ca. 490–583 CE) concerning the Getae or Gets, an eastern Celticized Thraco-Dacian tribe, where he mentions them as being learned in moral and natural philosophy and well informed on the "course of the twelve signs of the Zodiac and the planets passing through them, including the whole science of astronomy." The Danube valley land of Dacia was also peopled by powerful Celtic tribes such as the Scordici and the Britolagai (Latin, Britogalli). The Celtic influence was the underlying civilizing factor in the transformation of the Dacian Getic culture. The Greeks knew them as the Γέται or Gètai.

In some Roman documents, the name for the Daci is spelled Dagae and that of the Getae is spelled Gaete. The etymology of Getae is most likely from the Indo-European stem guet- "to utter, to talk" (cf. Gaulish, gutu, Old Irish, guth "voice," Old Norse goði "priest" < gʰutjon- "calls, invokes, summons"). The Celts would certainly not have missed the pun of Getoi with Gettoi "big butted."

In his translation of Cassiodorus's text, Jornandes writes Gauthigoth in place of Getae. Many have confused the name with the northern Germanic Goths, but these are two distinct peoples.

A king of the Gets, Dromichætes,[4] who defeated the Macedonian king Demetrius I in 294 BCE, was most likely Celtic. The name of Diceneus,[5] the philosopher teacher of the Gets, also looks Celtic. In no other classical text do we get such a vivid picture of the teachings of astronomy and natural science in the ancient Celtic realm than from Pausanias:

> What made their salvation, their happiness, the fulfilment of their wishes, was that they understood the use of the rules given by their counsellor Diceneus, and that they sought by every means to apply these and put them to practice. Diceneus, seeing that the spirits obeyed him in all things and that this people was gifted of natural wit, taught them almost all of philosophy; since he was a master of this science.
>
> He introduced them to morals hoping to keep the away from barbaric mores; in revealing to them the laws of physic, he taught them to live according to those of nature under the regulation of they own laws handed down to this day by the writings of the Belagines[6]; through the lessons of logic, he trained them to reason better than the other nations: in showing the practice, he persuaded them to perform good deeds; in demonstrating the theory, he showed them the twelve signs of the Zodiac, the passing of the planets through these signs ; and all of astronomy; he instructed them on how the lunar disc waxes and wanes ; he showed them how the flaming orb of the sun surpasses in greatness the circumference of the earth; he exposed under which names and signs the three-hundred and forty-four stars pressing at the pole of the sky or distancing from it descend while moving from the orient to the occident.
>
> What was it not, may I ask, his will to bring essentially bellicose men to put down arms at time for four days in order to penetrate the teachings of philosophy!
>
> There, we could see one studying the positions of the sky, another the properties of the herbs

and fruits of the earth; another follow the waxing and waning of the moon; and the other observe the work of the sun and seek how, caught in the rotation of the sky, this heavenly body hastily attempts to reach the eastern shore is brought back towards the western shore.

Then after having been made aware of all of these phenomena, they took rest. Diceneus, thanks to his knowledge, having taught the Goth all these things and many others still, inspired them such great admiration to the point that he not only commanded men of modest rank, but also to the kings themselves.[7]

The Sicilian Greek, Strabo (64 BCE–24 CE), spoke of a Celtic Druid named Abaris[8] who was invited to Athens to discuss such matters with the Greek philosophers. At a time when astronomy and astrology were the same science, the Celts were, according to Cicero, Caesar, Pliny, Tacitus, and other classical writers, masters of astronomy."[9] The apparent silence of Druid astronomers after the days of Taliesin can only be explained by the success of Christian censorship on pagan science. Peter Berresford Ellis also had noticed, thanks to his vast understanding of the various insular texts, that parallels were found in both Celtic and Vedic cosmologies. He noticed that the ancient Celtic astrologers used similar systems as those of the Vedic astrologers. This system was based on the twenty seven lunar mansions called *nakshatras* in Sanskrit. His main argument was found in the motif of the circular palace of King Ailill which comprised of twenty-seven windows and through which he could observe his twenty-seven "Star Maidens." Berresford Ellis also noticed that Ailill had traits similar to those of the Hindu Soma god. More startling were the names of the mead goddesses,[10] the Old Irish Medba and the Sanskrit Madhavi.

As for Taliesin, "brilliant forehead," the name seems to be a Celticized early Welsh rendering of the Greek name Ptolemaios "war-like," from Πτολεμαος (*Ptolemaios*), from πόλεμος (*pólemos*), ("war"). Therefore, Taliesin was to the Welsh what Claudius Ptolemaeus (circa 100 to 170 CE) was to the Alexandrian Greeks.

The following is from a poem of Taliesin entitled *The Hostile Conspiracy*:

> I am learned in the principal sciences, and the reasoning of astrologers concerning veins and solvents, and the general nature of man (The Hostile Confederacy) [...] I am a wise man of the primal knowledge, I am an experienced astrologer, pronounce solutions, I speak to habitual sycophants, I continue to behold God.

From Geoffrey of Monmouth, more fragments of ancient Welsh astrology attributed to Merlin are to be found in the *Historia Regum Britanniae* (ca. 1134 CE). A 10th century text, the *Saltair na Rann* (Psalter of Quatrains), states that every educated Irishman knew the names of the signs of the zodiac in order, and the correct day and month when the sun entered the signs. And according to Cormac Mac Cuileannain (836–908 CE) in *Sanas Chormaic* (or Cormac Glossary), any well-informed person could throughout the year estimate the hour of the night by the positions of the moon and stars.

At the time of Strabo[11] astronomy and astrology were one and the same, that is, a divining art as well as a science. So, according to the classical authors, Cicero, Caesar, Pliny, Tacitus, Cassiodorus, Plutarch, and so on, the Druids were the undisputed masters of the natural arts and sciences of the sky. Plutarch, in *Moralia*, concerning the inhabitants of the island of Ogygia (Ireland), wrote:

> Here then the stranger was conveyed, as he said, and while he served the god became at his leisure acquainted with astronomy, in which he made as much progress as one can by practicing

geometry, and with the rest of philosophy by dealing with so much of it as is possible for the natural philosopher.[12]

Unfortunately, the comments gleaned here and there from the Greek and Roman writers is all too vague and sketchy to grasp what the astrology of the Druids really was like. However, one interesting detail in Plutarch's *Moralia*, is the mention concerning the wise of Ogygia who knew of the thirty years cycle of Saturn.

> Now when at intervals of thirty years the star of Cronus, which we call *Phenon* "Splendid" but they, our author said, call *Nycturus* "Night-watchman," enters the sign of the Bull, they, having spent a long time in preparation for the sacrifice and the expedition, choose by lot and send forth a sufficient number of envoys in a correspondingly sufficient number of ships, putting aboard a large retinue and the provisions necessary for men who are going to cross so much sea by oar and live such a long time in a foreign land.[13]

If we are to understand druidic astrology, this passage of Plutarch is all the more interesting. Firstly, he explains the manner by which these "holy men" grouped years into thirty year cycles and not centuries as did the Romans and secondly, he gives the Gaulish name for planet Saturn rendered in Greco-Latin as Nycturus (< Nucturos "Nightly"). To better grasp this astute computation, a revolution of Saturn around the sun is of 29 years, 165 days and 11.68 hours. This explains why the Druids counted their ages in 30 year cycles. The number thirty (or occasionally twenty-nine or twenty-eight days) is also the duration of a month. Again, Plutarch (in *Moralia*, mentions that when abroad in the land of Ogygia, he gained much in astronomy as much knowledge as can be acquired after a consuming investigation.

> Here then the stranger was conveyed, as he said, and while he served the god became at his leisure acquainted with astronomy, in which he made as much progress as one can by practicing geometry, and with the rest of philosophy by dealing with so much of it as is possible for the natural philosopher.[14]

This says much about the astronomical knowledge gained at the contact of the Hibernian astronomers, and contrary to what the experts say for a Chaldean origin. As found in the early sky charts of Greece, the 12 sign astrological model was created well above the 36th parallel. This contradicts the theory of a single Egyptian or Sumerian Chaldean origin. At these latitudes, well above the Aegean Sea at the 40th parallel, we find the Balkans and Black Sea. Also, there is a date for its invention: 2500 BCE, right at the time of the Bronze Age during the spread of the Danubian and Pontic peoples! This Indo-European origin best explains the parallels between the Greek and Vedic astrologies, which at the time were the two main civilizational poles of the ancient world. In fact, the Greek and Indian systems are so much alike that we are forced to conclude that both derive from a single prototype. Most evidently, this early 12 sign model evolved and was eventually refined in the local cultures through the speculations of the Greco-Latin mathematici, the Persian magi, the Vedic Rishis, or even Celtic Druids, among others. And as previously mentioned, Peter Berresford Ellis was the first to notice that the Irish texts described the 27 lunar mansions along the same mythological lines as those of the Vedic scriptures where they are called *Nakshatras*.

According to the Irish myths, king Ailill[15] had a circular palace in the shape of a wheel in which there was a large room with 12 windows and a small one with 27 windows, where he could admire its 27 "daughters of the stars." And in other Irish mythological tales, the god Lugh, King of the Tuatha Dé Danann, boasted to master all the sciences and arts of the Druids:

> Prompt and bold is Lugh with his long hand that beat warriors. He, the son of Eithe Imdhearg, daughter of Balor Bhailchbheimnech, granddaughter of Nuachrothach Neid, set mind to consider and look at length at the sea to observe the appearance and course of the stars, examine the sky, study the sun, in order to remember the planets, making sure that they should not set and remain in their twilight so that they remained longer, more lasting, prolonging the warriors' combat, so that the shape-shifting poly-technician distinguished the break of day or if his army was with him (...)? Or again, if it turned to his advantage. Hence he found that he had actual knowledge of the signal of daybreak or night's end [...]? [...] That day.[16]

In addition, we know from archaeology that the Gallo-Roman astrologers were interested in prediction techniques from the Egyptianized Ptolemaic Greeks. In an archaeological dig of 1967 at the site of a Gallo-Roman sanctuary at Grand, France, was found a diptych engraved with a detailed astrological chart (made around the second century CE). The signs of the Zodiac, along with the names of decans in old Coptic, were engraved in Greek characters on it. One of the panels is kept in the town of Épinal, France, at the Departmental Museum of Vosges, while the other is kept at the Museum of Antiquities in Saint-Germain-en-Laye.

And more recently at Chevroches, Nièvre, France, during excavations by the archaeological team lead by F. Devevey in 2001 to 2002, an astrological disc (dating from the fourth century CE) was discovered. It is inscribed with three lines bearing the Egyptian, Greek and Roman months along with the twelve signs of the Zodiac. The disk is now kept at the Chevroches Archaeological Museum of Dijon, France. Although these artifacts do not inform us on Celtic astrology, these archaeological finds nevertheless prove the importance astrology had in ancient Gaul. Unfortunately this information gap leaves us with the need to fine comb the voluminous corpus of Irish and Welsh texts. Starting with Welsh literature, we have the legendary Taliesin, the Claudius Ptolemaeus of the Old Britons, we presume.

In *The hostile Conspiracy*, one of the poems attributed to Taliesin and translated by W. F. Skene in 1858, it is declared: "From me no one shall know. The wise man of the primary sci-

Pictish stone probably depicting an astronomer or geographer holding a navigational instrument and knife. Drawing from the work of Richard R. Brash, *Inscribed Monuments of the Gaedhil of the British Isles*, George Bell and Sons, London, 1879.

ence, the astrologer reasoned, about wrath, about the resolvent, about the man describing windings." And in *Historia Regum Britanniae* (ca. 1134 CE) by Godfrey of Monmouth, there are other elements on Celtic cosmology, attributed to Merlin, not the least, found in old British literature. Then, concerning Irish literature, Berresford Ellis found in an introductory comment to a manuscript of a tenth century Culdee monk, the *Saltair na Rann,* or "Psalter of Quatrains," a passage insisting that any educated Irishman knew in order the twelve zodiacal signs and the correct day and month in which the sun entered each sign along with the seven planets:

> The conception of the universe in the first poem, with its ideas of the seven heavens, the colored and fettered winds, and the sun passing through the opening windows of the twelve divisions of the heavens, is curious; the earth, enclosed in the surrounding firmament, "like a shell around an egg," being regarded as the center of the universe.[17]

This quote probably explains another obscure passage found in the *Saltair na Rann* in one of poems on the twelve winds of the heavens, *The Creation of the Universe*:

> The twelve winds, Easterly and Westerly, Northerly and Southerly, the King who adjusted them, He holds them back, he fettered them with seven curbs.
> King who bestowed them according to their posts, around the world with many adjustments, each two winds of them about a separate curb, and one curb for the whole of them.
> King who arranged them in habitual harmony, according to their ways, without over-passing their limits; at one time, peaceful was the space, at another time, tempestuous.
> Measurements of the Universe. King who didst make clear the measure of the slope from the earth to the firmament, estimating it, clear the amount, along with the thickness of the earth-mass.
> He set the course of the seven Stars from the firmament to the earth,
> Saturn, Jupiter, Mercury, Mars, Sol, Venus, the very great Moon.[18]

Berresford Ellis also found in a work attributed to Cormac MacCuileannain (836–908 CE), the *Sanas Chormaic* or the "Glossary of Cormac," a line mentioning that a "well-educated person should be able to estimate the time of the night from the moon and the position of the stars." In *Cormac's Glossary* are also found old Gaelic names for many of the heavenly bodies, moon, sun, stars, etc.: "Retglu, f a 'star'; Esca, f 'moon'; Grian, f 'sun'; Fiie, i.e. the rising of the sun in (the) morning; Máirt i.e. Marte, from the god of battle of among the gentiles. Mars, was his name."[19] However, if some of the astronyms found in *Cormac's Glossary* are truly Gaelic, many of these names are Latin borrowings. To discover the original astronyms, we must turn to the *Book of Ballymote*, abbreviations 21 (*Lebhor Bhaile Mhota*: LBM, manuscript copy dating from 1390–1391 CE), wherein the Celtic symbols of constellations and zodiacal signs are found.

Finally, according to Joseph Monard, the names of the Gallic zodiacal constellations inscribed on the Coligny calendar, went as follows:

Cantli Prinnios, "cycle-settling," cantos ring (Libra/Scales);
Samoni Prinnios, "of the meeting, of the sower," (Scorpio/Scorpion);
Dumanni Prinnios, "darkening," (Sagittarius/Archer);
Riuri Prinnios, "of frost," (Capricorn/Goat Fish);
Anaganti Prinnios, "inactive," (Aquarius/Water-Bearer);
Ogroni Prinnios, "of cold, of snakes," (Pisces/Fish);
Cuti Prinnios, "fiery, ram," (Aries/Ram);

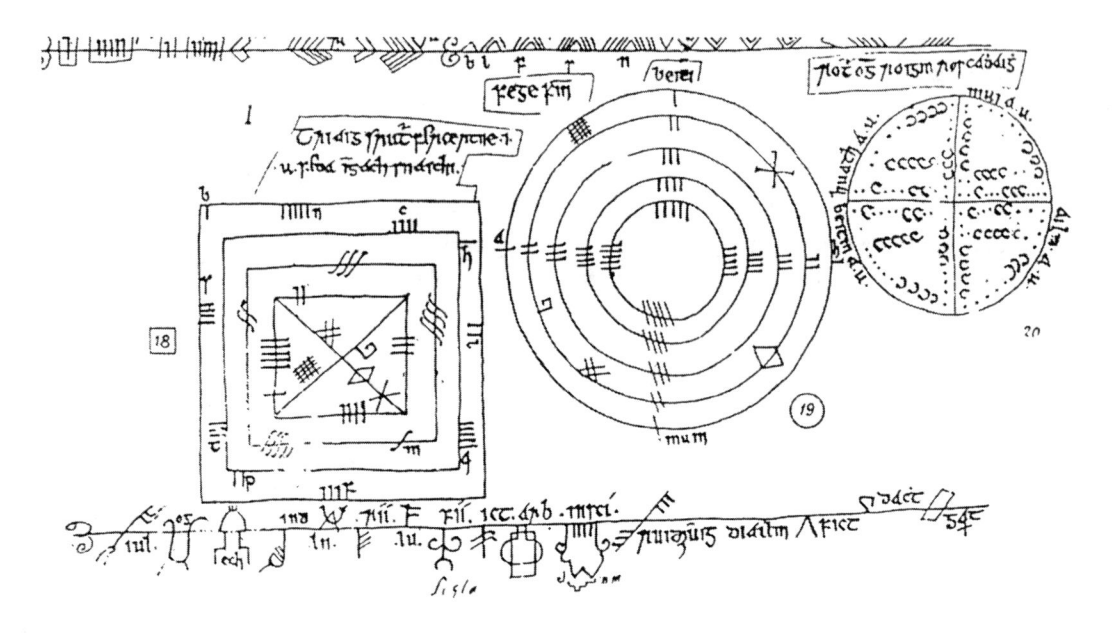

Gaelic astronomical abbreviations from the *Book of Ballymote* (from a photocopy of the Royal Irish Academy).

Giamoni Prinnios, "of shoots, of sprouts," (Taurus/Bull);
Simiuisonni Prinnios, "capriciously-breezed, vivacious, dashing," (Gemini/Twins);
Equi Prinnios, "balanced," (Cancer/Crab);
Elembiuii Prinnios, "of arbitration," and connotes, "hot flux," (Leo/Lion);
Edrini Prinnios, "of the arbitrator judge," (Virgo/Maiden).

A Celtiberian druid astrologer? Detail of a painted pottery sherd depicting a priest offering a libation during a religious sacrifice. The conical cap and the large white apron recall other examples found in Celtic art. In his left hand, he holds a drinking horn while in his right hand he caresses a gallinaceous bird perched on a cauldron. In ancient imagery, zigzag patterns most often represent water and sometimes peaks (hills and mountains). For the Celts, the constellation of Crater was represented by a cauldron. So, the rooster announcing daybreak can be one of the bird-messengers of the Sky-god. The Raven (Corvus) and the Horn (Triangle) are found over Hydra. It is therefore an allusion to the cycle of cosmic waters described in the various Indo-European cosmologies. Author's drawing from a copy taken from *Celtiberian Ideologies and Religion* by Gabriel Sopeña, E-Keltoi Museo Numantino, Soria (Sopeña 1995).

The Druid Astrologer

Talhayarn yssyd	Talhayarn is
Mwyhaf there sywedyd.	The greatest astrologer.
Pwy amgyfrawd gwyd	meditation of the woods.
O aches amot dyd.	Which is the eloquence according to day.

—*Book of Taliesin VII—Kyfyndawt Angar, The Hostile Conspiracy*

There is a quote on Claudius Ptolemaeus by Jim Tester that describes very well the competence of a good astrologer: "The astrologer, said Ptolemy, should so understand the movements of the heavenly bodies that he can know 'the place of any configuration.'"[20] As we know, men of science, throughout the period of Antiquity, made no distinction between astrology and astronomy, as either art or science, and used the general term *astrologia* to designate the two disciplines. It was in fact the Visigoth bishop Isidorus of Seville (560–636 CE) who, in the seventh century (*The Etymologies or Origins*), was the first to make the distinction between both terms. And indeed, in those times we were still far from the technological means of modern science. Therefore, the druid-astrologers of the ancient Celts went over the same ground as the Latin *mathematici* (philosophical Pythagorean astronomers), Avestan magi or Vedic Rishis did.

Also, as stated by Julius Caesar in *Gallic Wars* on Gallic astronomy and geography, the Druids, much like the Greeks, had calculated the distances between the Earth and the luminaries and understood Earth's rotundity. "They likewise discuss and impart to the youth many things respecting the stars and their motion, respecting the extent of the world and of our earth, respecting the nature of things, respecting the power and the majesty of the immortal gods."[21] Unfortunately, Caesar, who was drawing information directly from the Gallic Druid Diviciacus, does not give more detail on what were the names of the stars, the planets, let alone the nature of this science.

The science of astronomy has many names in various modern Celtic languages and at least seven Gaelic names for the astrologer can be noted: rollagedagh, "one who studies the stars," fisatóir, "one who studies the heavens," eastrolac, "one who studies the moon," fathach, "soothsayer (by the heavenly bodies)," n'éladoir, "soothsayer (by the sky)," realt-eolach, "knower of the stars," and réaltóir, "astrologer."[22]

Recently, astrologers have speculated much on the cosmological and astrological properties of the Germanic Runes and have proposed a similar underlying concept for the Irish Ogham. It is a proven historical fact that in the past the art of writing was linked to magic and cosmology. The scribe was not just a writer, an analyst, but also the "scribe of the gods." And these gods resided in the stars. Therefore, the astrologer was also a rune-master, that is, one who kept up the secret annals. Thus, the Gaelic scribe, the Ogham expert (Ogmodanos in Old Celtic), looked over the Ogham letters or fews (feda), that were represented by the trees of the heavenly forest, seen as constellations marked by zodiacal cusps. Also bear in mind that the astronomical observation of the ancients was essentially geocentric. The same conclusion can be made for the Celtic and Teutonic star-gazers.

The Sidereal Worlds

The ancient Indo-European seers saw the cosmos as a vast ocean surrounded by a ring of fire. These specific realms in the cosmos were strictly imaginary, mythical or mystical in nature. Imagined as invisible worlds, we should not confuse them with the *Sidhs*, which were seen as planetary godly places or residences similar to the Vedic Lokas. The Gaelic name Sidh is from the Old Celtic Sidos meaning "residence, tranquility."

In Vedic astrology, a Loka generally refers more specifically to a region of the sky, or the cosmos, world, earth, sky, atmosphere or any of the lower regions. These sites were classed as follows: the earth, the sky or firmament, the middle region, or place of rebirth, or place of truth, where reside the blessed mortals. The *Lokas* include seven worlds: *Bhu-loka*, the earth; *Bhuvar-loka*, the atmospheric space between the earth and the sun, where reside the Siddhas (enlightened ones) and their companions; *Svar-loka*, the heaven of Indra above or between the sun or the space between the sun and the North Star; Mahar-loka, the region above the North Star inhabited by Bhrigo and other wise men who survived the destruction of the last three lower worlds; Janar-loka, a place inhabited by the four Kumaras, the sons of Brahma, including Sanat Kumara and company; Tapar-loka, inhabited by the deified Vairagins; and finally, Satya-loka, or Brahma-loka, the abode of Brahma.

The Greeks and Romans also entertained similar notions concerning the "Soul of the World," and of the movement of the stars. Plutarch, quoting the Lampridius's catalogue, speaks of a loss of influence through the course (or curse) of comets. It would be nice to know more, but unfortunately, we can now only deplore the loss of Lampridius's work. Although these hypothetical or fabled domains were much debated by the ancient astrologers, stranger even, were their discussions on the music of the spheres.[23]

Macrobius, who was inspired by Porphyry, speaks at length of the Platonic idea of the cosmic concert emitted by the movements of the heavenly bodies. What follows is Macrobius's comment found in *Saturnalia* on Cicero who wrote about this "Heavenly symphony":

> The older orbs turn with an even greater impetuosity the wider they are and at the same time, they travel much heavier by the blast which is still at its starting point, as Cicero said, they move by making a chirping sound precisely because of their faster rotation. To the contrary, the lunar globe, being smaller, makes a deeper sound because of the wind that has turned, has reached the end of its course and is already weakened. It also rotates slower because of the impetuosity its narrow sphere in which is enclosed the penultimate orb.

This is but an example on how the astrologers of Antiquity debated on such esoteric notions as the music of the heavenly bodies. That heavenly bodies do emit audible vibrations, which we now know thanks to the means of our modern technological wizardry, but how on Earth did the ancients know about this? Needless to add that we are left to accept the ancients' belief in ethereal sounds manifested in mystical places. This passage from Macrobius better explains the same notion found in other related cultures such as those of the Celts; as described in Irish literature where emission and the audition of ethereal music from the faerie Sidhs resound. Therefore, it is conceivable that the Druids had maintained the same conceptions on the heavenly symphony of the higher spheres.

The Astrological Ogham

In 1937, R.A. Stewart Macalister declared in *The Secret Languages of Ireland* (p. 40) that the so-called Ogham (abbreviations 18 to 21 that appear in *The Book of Ballymote*) were not actually Ogham, but magical or semantic representations for the diviniz-

III: Astrology of the Druids

ing arts. One list, labeled sigla 21 in Latin, does hint at astronomical terms such as *am* for "totalized time" and *iul* for "July."

SIGLA 21:

(1) IUL.
(2) og
(3) ech
(4) ind
(5) ln./lii?
(6) rii. and
(7) lu.,
(8) fii.
(9) ict.
(10) arb.
(11) insci.
(12) ruidzûig diailm; fict; dact; gaxt/gact or gart?
(At the bottom of the list, a hook, stairs and the letters "am").

The following is a thorough linguistic analysis of the series with their corresponding etymologies and their symbols resembling conventional astrological signs.

The Ogham Words with Their Gaelic Meanings

Ogham Root Word	Dictionary Definition
IUL	Iul < Julii, "(month of) July"; for direction/orientation, course, track, guide, landmark, buoy (sea), namely, knowledge, learning, art, judgement, leader, commander, service, attention, etc.
Og	Og < og/óc (abbreviation ogham), "young boy, young man"; Ogh, a Gaelic name of the letter 'O'; Ogh, "virgin, pure, whole, honest."
Ech	Ech > each, "horse"; echu > aecuos, "equalized, balanced," that is, ech for "horse" and "equalized"; compare with personal name Eochaidh > iuocatus, "the clear/yew and combat."
Ind	Ind < ind- prefix, ind-os/-a/-on, adj. "end, penultimate," cf. English, "end."
ln./Lii./Li. Len	Len, "canvas (sail or curtain)"; linn, "age, century, race, family, descendants"; lii., or given as: 'le < i-le, the "marker, the number"; li. < liv/lif, "colour, tint, paint."
Rii.	Rii. > ri, "king, regent."
Lu.	Lu., "small," the first element is found in luachaman "leprechaun"; lû, "gain."
Fii.	Fii. < fia/fea < feannag, "carrion-crow, raven, rook, cock-raven."
Ict.	Ict. > icht, "offspring, children, protection"; ict for Greek chthys or Latin ichthus, ictus, "fish."
Arb.	Arb. > arba, "cart, chariot."

Acronym and Ogham	Dictionary Definition
Insci.	Insci./inscii > innsgin, "spirit, courage, vigor"; insgne, "speech, language."
Ruidzûig	Ruidzûig > ruidh/ruith, "red/wheel"; sûig > succos, "pig"; sug, "joy, laughter, happiness," or maybe ruid ruig, "red queen?"
Diailm	Di-ailm < di-, "negation," prefixed to ailm, the letter 'A,' implying an exit from the letter 'A.' Arb is the only notation starting with the A initial.
Fict	Fict > fecht, "time, turn, occasion, feat."
Dact	dact/dect > decht, "right."
Gaxt or gact	Gaxt > gact > cachd, "captive, young slave or servant"; cacht, "the world"; cacht, "exalted cry, shout," or a spelling mistake: gart/gort, "garden, enclosed yard, vineyard."
Hook and stairs	
Am	Am < ama < amannan, "time period," that is, time in general, past or present.

The notation *am*, to wit, "totalized annual time" corresponding to the sun's course through the 12 zodiacal constellations whose names are conveniently noted as acronyms starting with: Cancer, Leo, Virgo, Libra, Scorpio, Sagittarius, Capricorn, Aquarius, Pisces Aries Taurus Gemini. The *am* notation, abbreviated from amannan, and given in final note (along with the hook and staircase symbols), indicates that what preceded pertained to a total time period. It should be noted that this list begins and ends at the summer solstice in Gemini and Cancer. This was probably because of the heliacal rising of the constellation at the time of the summer solstice where the sun is at its peak. As recorded in the *Coligny calendar*, this period was also an adjustment period for the annual and monthly cycles. Some of the early Greek calendars also started at the summer solstice.

These abbreviations from the *Book of Ballymote*, recognized as acronyms by most Ogham scholars, seem at first incomprehensible.... But nevertheless, for those who have the patience to see beyond these truncated consonants, one can distinguish the tree from the forest. Similar abbreviations are also found on the Coligny calendar, therefore, helping us better understand what these obscure charades hint at. What follows are some of my etymological proposals for the LBM sigla starting with the *iul* siglum:

(1) **Iul,** "July," the list starts in July. The Gaelic name *Iul* for this month was from the Latin patrician name Iulius and could have been confused with the Gaelic iul, from the Celtic root Iuliuos meaning, "jubilant" or iiulucos, "jubilatory cry of victory," if not iiulon, "sung prayer, yodel." This shift in word meaning could be the work of a Christian copyist. Then also, it could be an inversion from iul to uil < uillos, "horse." This month was also under the patronage of the horse in the Gallic calends: Ecuos/Equos, "horse." Uil- also connotes uilia < euilia for "willingness, honesty." But then again, this month also had a Gaelic name: Iuchar > iecuurios, "(time) spawning." The other astronyms

were: equos, "horse," Partanos, "the reddish, the crab," or Legustros, "the crustacean."

(2) Og. : Og-, is the usual abbreviation in LBM Ogham for óg < ogos, "intact," which implies, "egg"; ogia, "virginity, purity, young"; ogiomu, "purity, freshness"; ogios, "young, youth"; *aghuist mins* from the Latin *mens Augusti*, "month of August"; aga/agica, "doe"; agliu, "deer"; aglo, "big game"; ago/agu, "fight" and "commitment"; agomaros/agontios, "driver, leader"; agos, "horned beast, steer"; agtos/asctos, "act, fact, action"; agtu, "manner, condition, condition"; Ogma, "champion"; ogmio, "magic link"; ogmo, "sudden decision, inhibition"; ognos, "lamb." Other astronyms: Elnbos/Elembos, "fawn"; Leuo, "lion."

(3) Ech < ecu, "cattle"; eqos, "horse"; ecco, "country priest"; ecuodecs, "perfectly fair," ex: exo, "start count," abbreviation for "starting a computation." Esoxs, "pike, salmon"; Gaelic name for the month of September: Sultuine > sultennos, the "lavish." Other astronyms: edrinos, "judge"; carca, "hen."

(4) Ind < indon, "end, extremity, ultimate"; indonesodion, "pending issue"; indouelicon, "ultimate ring or circle"; Indamia, "servant, follower." Month names: Deireadh Fómhair/anDàmhair < Damodàris, "rutting deer." Other astronyms: Cantlos, "loop"; Sidos, "deer" (Libra and Scorpio).

(5) Lii -Ln. < (A)ln- < alnos, "from beyond, noble"; (e)ln- < elnos, "roebuck"; elna, "prodigy, herd, flock"; elnô, verb "to go, to come"; olnos, "elm, ash"; ulnos, "fleece"; ln: < lengmen, lingmen, "on scene, on arrival"; lon, "momentum," lon, "blackbird"; lona, "female sheep"; slogmen, "gathering"; lii. < Lingonis, "jumper, dancer, go-getter"; lingmen, "jump, jump"; lenuos, "child"; (s)li- < sìoladair < siltarios, "sower." Name of month: Samhain < Samonios, "of the meeting, of the sower." Other astronyms: Samonion, "the gathering."

(6) Rii. < (A)rii < ariios, "free man, landowner"; ariomos, "farmer"; bogdarios, "archer"; rii- < riios, "free"; ridir, "rider, cavalier, knight"; rixio, "shape, appearance, form (representation)." Name of month: an Dúbhlachd < Dubilectos, "dark, covered." Other astronyms: Uarcustos, "archer."

(7) Lu. Lu- < lupos, "bar, wolffish"; (i)lu/(e)lu/(a)lu- < eluo, "gain, profit"; eluos, "herd"; eluen/oluen, "shower of sparks"; eluios, "whistling swan"; eluioi, "many" (this is the time of the swan song because at this time this constellation slips below the northwest horizon)"; eluinos, "owner"; lu- < lucius/lugius, "pike"; luuios, "guide, chief"; lucio, "personality, remarkable person"; ad/at-lu < attiluis, "sturgeon (that is to say a horned fish)." Name of month: an Faoilteach < Uailuticos, "of wolves." Please compare with the Gallic name Riuros for, "cold, frost." Other astronyms: Gabra, "goat"; Boccos, "goat"; Riuri Prinnios, "the constellation of frost."

(8) Fii. < -Uii < uiis < uisucios, "respectable"; uisucios/ueseceos, "male raven, chough"; uisucia, "female raven"; uecuos/uesacos, "crow"; uiscioch > udesciocos, "aqueous, watery"; Month name: an t-Uisceadoir > udesciodouor, "the pouring water"; uetsis > uisis, "young pig, piglet." Other astronyms: Anaganti Prinnios, "the constellation of inaction."

(9) Ict. < **Ict-** < **ictus,** a Latin borrowing from the Greek ikhtus, "fish" in wordplay with, ictis, "down at the bottom, bottom," and can be understood by the Latin term ictus for, "part, stroke, blow, shock, impairment"; (p)ict-/a/on, "careful"; iction, "strait, channel"; -ect < ectamos, "extreme"; ext-, "outside"; extincón, "abundance brilliance"; eictami, "utterance, scream"; iactis/iectis, "language"; iegtos, "frozen, frozen"; iacceto, "health"; iaccetos/iaccitaros, "healer." Month name: an Giblean < Gegdoblonacos, "time of goose fat." Other astronyms: Escoi "fish"; Ogroni Prinnios, the "constellation of cold-blooded animals, fish and reptiles."

(10) Arb. < **Arb-/aru-** < **aruos,** "plow"; aruon, "furrow, plowed field"; aruos/aruios, "attacking"; arubianos, "blushing"; aruerniiatis, "provider, supplier"; (c)arb > caruos/caruosidos, "deer"; caruts, "hero"; cairaxs, "ram"; tsiburnos, "ram"; Aedu, Aidu, "young Aries," called Aros in Old Celtic, the equivalent of Ares or Mars. Month name: an Márt, from Latin mens Martis, "month of Mars." Other astronyms: Cuti Prinnios the "constellation of Aries"; Putios/Qutios > Cutios, "Aries, Fiery, Ram."

(11) Insci, insci < **insqiia/eniscuia,** "discourse, speech"; in-sciatacos, "in-winged, winged"; tarbh-insci < insciatos taruos, "the winged bull," is also spelled indsci for an(d)- scia(tach) > sciatacos ander, "the winged cattle"; sciathon "shield (highly probable in this astrological context.)"; connoting inicia/inisia, "island." Other astronyms: Taruos, "bull"; Taruos Trigarannianom, "bull with three cranes"; Month name: an Ceitean < Cetonos, "the prime time." Giamoni Prinnios, "the constellation of germination."

(12) Ruidzûig > **roudiosuccones,** "the red pigs"; roudiosuccoi, "the red piglets," if not, ruidriug > roudia-rigu, "the red queen." Roudios has at least three meanings: "red, rough or loud," and "ruin, fall." Similarly, *suc-* can also connote: suca > suga/suba, "girl," and/or sucô/slucô, the verb "to knock, to strike." Month name: an t-Òg-mhios < mins Ogii, "month of the youth." Other astronymes: Cancstica, "mare"; Simiuisoni Prinnios, "the constellation of capricious breezes."

(13) Diailm < **di-Ailm,** "out from" the letter "A," for alamios, "pine"; alamos, "cattle, livestock, a head of cattle, wealth."

(14) Fict > **uict-/uect-** < **uecta, uegta,** "time, occasion, tour"; uecta, "feat, exploit."

(15) Dact < **dect** < **decht** < **dexsiua,** "right"; diexstagô, verb "to release (a halter), to unclip"; or punning with decton, "fire"; ditaca, "smoke"; digatma, "seamless area"; doagt, verb, "to go"; doaget, verb, "it is going."

(16) Gaxt-/gact- < **cact-** < **cacteto,** "taking, seizure"; cacto, "power"; cectos < cenctos < canctos, "applied strength, power"; adj. cantec-/os/a/on and cantic-os/-a/-on "girth"; also given as, gart-/gort- < gorta, "enclosure"; gorton, "closed garden."

(17) Am. > **ama** > **amannan** > **Ammania,** "duration, period, totalized time."

Compared Zodiacal Charts

Classic	Vedic	Gallic	Gaelic
Aries, Mars, Ram	Mesha, Ram	Cuti Prinnios, "constellation of the Ram, Aries";	Arb < Aru- < Aruos, "forward," punning with Aros (the equivalent of Ares or Mars) and/or Tsiburnos, "Aries"; month: An Giblean < Gegdoblonacos, "time of goose fat."
Taurus, Bull	Vrishabha, Bull	Giamoni Prinnios, "constellation of Germination";	Insci < in-sci-insqiia, "discourse"; in (d)sci < Sciatacos Ander, "winged cattle," or Insciatos Taruos, "winged bull"; Bealtaine < Belotennia, "bright lights."
Gemini, Twins	Mithuna, Pair	Simiuisoni Prinnios, "constellation of brisk breezes";	Ruidzûig/ruidsûig < rudio-succoi, "red pigs"; rudia riga, "red queen"; month: Meitheamh < mediosamosenos, "mid-summer weather."
Cancer, Crab	Kataka, Crab	Equi Prinnios Equos, "balanced constellation, the horse";	Iul < iuliuos, "jubilant"; uil-uillos, "horse"; Iuchar < Iecuurios, "spawn time."
Leo, Lion	Simha, Lion	Elembiui Prinnios, "constellation of the fawn"; Elembos, "fawn";	Og< og-/ag- < ago/agu, "fight," aga, "doe"; Lunasa < Lugi Naissatis, "commemoration of Lugh."
Virgo, Maiden	Kanya, Maiden	Edrini Prinnios, "constellation of the arbitrator"; Edrinos, "judge, arbitrator";	Ech < ec-/ eq- < ecuodecs, "perfectly fair"; ecco, "country priest"; ecu, "livestock"; ecuos/eqos "horse"; month: An t-Suiltine < sultennos, "lavish"
Libra, Scales	Thula, Scales	Cantli Prinnios, "constellation of the loop, ring, buckle"	Ind < ind-/end- < indon, "end"; Indouelicon, "ring or ultimate circle"; Indamia "servant," An Dàmhair < Damodàris, "person in rut, deer rut"
Scorpius, Scorpion	Vrishchika, Scorpion	Samoni Prinnios, "constellation of the sower, reunion, gathering";	Lii< -lii-, liio "outpourings, effusion"; lucios, "pike"; or Ln. < ln- > lingmen, "starting stage, on the scene"; .ln. < alnos, "the hereafter"; lingonis, "jumper, getter, dancer"; siltarios, "the sower"; Slogmen, "gathering"; Samhain < Samonios, "the sower of seeds, meeting."
Sagittarius, Archer	Dhanus, Archer	Dumanni Prinnios, "constellation of darkening," connoting: "of fumigation";	Rii < -rii -ariios, "free man, noble"; riios, "free"; ariomos, "plowman"; Bogdariios, "Archer"; Dubilectos < Dubhlachd, "dark, damp."
Capricornius, Goat-fish	Makara, "Sea Monster," dolphin or crocodile	Riuri Prinnios, "constellation of the Frost";	Lu < -lu- < lupos, "bar, wolf-fish," and/or lucius, lugius, "pike"; Attiluis, "Sturgeon, (goat-fish?)"; Faoilteach < Uailuticos, "of wolves."
Aquarius, Water-Bearer	Kumbha, Pot	Anaganti Prinnios, "constellation of inaction";	Fii < ui- < uiscias < udesciocos, "the Aqueous," and/or uisucios, "raven"; Na Féile Brighde < Ueilias Brigindonos, "Day of Brigitt."
Pisces, Fish	Mina, Fish	Ogroni Prinnios, "constellation of cooling, cold-blooded animals, fish and snakes";	Ict- < ictis, "down"; escoi, "fish"; month: An Gearran Gerro, "time of castration."

The Vedic "Seed" Syllables Compared to the Celtic "Key" Sounds

One of the particular aspects of common Indo-European cosmology is the notion of the primordial sacred utterance or vibration which ordered the Cosmos and set the world into place. In a Welsh manuscript is found the mention of a central character to this theme called Menw ap Teirgwaedd. We find him in the *Llyfr Coch Hergest* or *"*Red Book of Hergest,*"* a collection of Welsh mythic tales, compiled in 1382 CE and which are now kept at the library of the Oxford University. In 1877, Lady Charlotte Guest (1812–1895), collected and translated the tales in a book she retitled *The Mabinogion* or "tales of youth." Menw ap Teirgwaedd is figured in one of the tales entitled *Kilhwch and Olwen or the Twrch Trwyth*. The following was quoted from her book on p. 252:

> And after Yskithyrwyn Penbaedd was killed, Arthur and his host departed to Gelli Wic in Cornwall. And thence he sent Menw the son of Teirgwaedd to see if the precious things were between the two ears of Twrch Trwyth, since it were useless to encounter him if they were not there. Albeit it was certain where he was, for he had laid waste the third part of Ireland. And Menw went to seek for him, and he met with him in Ireland, in Esgeir Oervel. And Menw took the form of a bird; and he descended upon the top of his lair, and strove to snatch away one of the precious things from him, but he carried away nothing but one of his bristles. And the boar rose up angrily and shook himself so that some of his venom fell upon Menw, and he was never well from that day forward.

The underlying cosmological motif is here quite apparent. Here, Arthur is the Welsh version of the Old Gallic Artaios, "the bear-like," Twrch Trwyth (Twrch < Turcos, "boar," Trwyth < Tretios "boar") and Menw ap Teigwaedd (< Meneuos Trigutouatios, "the minded of the three utterances") holds the three cosmic rays from the Septentrion. This same motif is found in Greek myths with Arcturus "the bear watcher" watching over the path of bear cubs, the stars of Ursa Minor (Eburos, "the Boar" in Gaul).

The Welsh held the notion that their writing, the Coelbrenn was first created from three sun rays uttered by the primordial world giant called Einigan or Einiget (in J. William's *Barddas, on Symbols*, p. 33):

> Who was the first that made letters?
> Einigan the Giant, or, as he is also called, Einiget the Giant; that is, he took the three rays of light, which were used as a symbol by Menw, son of the Three Shouts, and employed them as the agents and instruments of speech, namely the three instruments B. G. D. and what are embosomed in them, the three being respectively invested with three agencies. Of the divisions and subdivisions he made four signs of place and voice, that the instruments might have room to utter their powers, and to exhibit their agencies. Hence were obtained thirteen letters, which were cut in form on wood and stone. After that, Einigan the Giant saw reason for other and different organs of voice and speech, and subjected the rays to other combinations, from which were made the signs L. and R. and S., whence there were sixteen signs.

The name Einigan or Einiget derives from the Old Celtic Anagantios or Anacantios, for "calamitous," which punned with Anagantios, "inactive," or with Incaitalis, "reed," and was the Celtic name for the month of February. Hence, morphologically connecting the name with 'Ncu, the "Ng" letter of the Ogham which stood for, "finality," and "fatality." The "Ng" symbol was also present in the Coelbrenn and Teutonic runes. In the runes, Ing or Ingwaz was also in relation to the theme of Life and Death. This shows that the cosmological three rays of light symbol was common to both the Celtic and Germanic peoples. It can also be found in the list of Vedic mantra seed sounds as: Nga for naga for, "snake," or for "not moving, inactive." Upon reflection, all of this seems much older than at first suspected, thus bringing us way back to the common Indo-European level. The Celts maintained that from the World Tree, the nuts of knowledge fell into the water of a pool where the Salmon of Wisdom resided. Hence, from this sacred hazel tree fall the seeds or nuts of innate knowledge expressed as "prime utterances."

Mantras or seed sounds are grouped in a pedagogical compendium called *bija mantra* in Sanskrit. The bija, "seeds," or "seed syllables," are the basis for qualified chant called mantra or saman in Sanskrit. The word *saman* has various meanings in Sanskrit, it can be taken to mean, "a breath, to live," or at second degree, "the terms of acquisition, possession, property, wealth and abundance." Or again, implying the sense of "peace, tranquility," and connoting the expression of kind words in order to gain an opponent through conciliation and negotiation. In this case, *saman* is the calming principle against opposition and is therefore the allegorical bearer of peace.

For the Celts, *samon*, meant "the meeting, the gathering," or "assembly," and puns with *semon*, "seed," and *semon*, "reverend." The Vedic term, *saman*, in the religious sense, came to designate a hymn, a sacred song or a praise. Some sacred verses are also called *saman*. In the *Rig Veda* (RV. × 90, 9), *saman* refers to the ability to produce sound, if not a tune, a song (either sacred or profane), and otherwise the buzzing of bees. It goes without saying that the "seed sounds" are also related to a yogic practice called Dvadazap-attraka. This yogic practice uses twelve syllables harmonizing with the signs of the Zodiac and annual months. It seems that the syllables from the Irish Ogham charts contained in the *Book of Ballymote* are the harmonic equivalents of these twelve-tone "seed vibrations" found in Vedic astrology. It should therefore not be an exaggeration to interpret these as elements of a druidical practice comparable to Yoga. To wit, iul, from *iiulon*, the "sacred song"; *og*, from *ogos*, "egg," the Ogham letter "O"; *insci*, from *insqiia/eniscuia* "speech, address"; *uii-*, for *uidues*, "woods," the astral "cusps," that is to say, *uidia/uidiia*, *uidtu*, "science, knowledge, awareness and understanding (of the seers)."

Also along these lines, is the parallel idea found with the Celtic *indon* and Vedic *antya* terms. The *ind-* acronym is from the Celtic root word *indon* meaning, "the end, the outcome," that is to say finality, the last cosmic sound and astral sign. And this concept is again found in Vedic astrology. The Sanskrit term *antya* has the same meaning: "in last place, right at the end," or "final order." It is also for the stars of Pisces and last sign of the Vedic Zodiac called Antyabha used to qualify Revati, the last of the Nakshtra lunar mansions.

And then, according to the traditions of the *Lebor Gabala Erren* (Book of the Taking of Ireland) and the *Auraicept na N-Éces* (The Scholars' Primer), the ancestors of the Irish were said to come from Scythia and were the descendants of a King Feinius Farsaid, a King of Scythia. This Feinius Farsaid and his son, Nel, went into Asia to work on the fabled Tower of Nimrod (Tower of Babel in biblical texts) and were thus present at the subsequent dispersal of the races after the destruction of the said tower. Feinius and his son, both learned in the new languages which resulted from this dispersal, eventually returned to Scythia where Feinius founded a great school of languages on the Scythian plain.

And to quote the Scholars' Primer:

> Query, well, then, whence are the Ogham vowels and consonants named? Not hard, Secundum alios quidem, it is from the school of Fenius Farsaidh, to wit, the school of poetry which Fenius

sent throughout the world to learn the languages. There were five and twenty that were the noblest of them so that it is their names that were put for the Bethe Luis Nin of the Ogham, both vowels and consonants; and there were four who were the noblest of these again, so that it is their names that were given to the seven principal vowels: 15.

It is Gaedel Glas who fashioned the Gaelic language out of the seventy-two languages: there are their names, Bithynian, Scythian, etc. Under—poeta cecinit- who of the school went to it thither? Not hard. Gaedel, son of Ether, son of Toe, son of Baracham, a Scythian Greek.

To what is this beginning? Not hard. To the selection that was selected in Gaelic since this is the beginning which was invented by Fenius after the coming of the school with the languages from abroad, every obscure sound that existed in every speech and in every language was put into Gaelic so that for this reason it is more comprehensive than any language. "Er" then is every beginning, for this was the beginning with the poets, which every obscure sound should come in the beginning, to wit, the Beithe Luis of the Ogham on account of obscurity.

Query, what is the reason why select language should be said of Gaelic?

Not hard. Because it was selected from any language; and for every obscure sound of every language a place was found in Gaelic owing to its comprehensiveness beyond every speech.

Query, how much did he bring of it? Not hard. The whole of it except what the poets added by way of obscuration after it had reached Fenius.

Query, what language of the seventy-two was published by Fenius first?

Not hard. The Irish language.... For it is he whom he preferred of his school, and whom he had reared from his youth, and it is he that was the youngest of the school, and on account of its comprehensiveness beyond every speech, and it was the first language that was brought from the Tower. Fenius had Hebrew, Greek, and Latin before he came from Scythia, and he had no need to establish them at the Tower, wherefore on that account it was published first.

The *Auraicept* maintains that Soim was the first thing to be written in Ogham and that "R" is for Graif. What is the meaning of this? First, Soim from Soimos < Soibos means "magic," "illusion," and Graif < Grauon, "writing." It couldn't be clearer, Ogham is magic writing! Og-uaim < Actusama "perfect alliteration," the Ogham, in accord with sound, comes from Ogma/Fenius, its prime inventor. And the learned are the prime agents who apply it to poetry. In the order of intellectual values, thought is superior to the spoken word, most often its imperfect expression. The spoken word is superior to writing, which kills it by fixing it forever. This fixing of word nevertheless binds it through magic. Graif (Grauon), writing, is superior to Delb (Delua), image, in that writing is the property of the learned, those initiated to the mysteries, while imagery is understood also by the ignorant and unlearned, therefore the initiated. As Eochra ecsi ecsi (< Axario Axscas "Key to writing [grooves])," writing forces reflection. Only meditation generates intelligence. Therefore, voice and sign, through mantra binding, are forever fixed in eternity. This is why the Ogham belongs to the god Ogma, Lord of Iugon (Yoke), magic, thought sounds, and martial arts. Therefore, the creator of the Ogham is Ogma (< Ogmios "Champion, Notcher") and Fenius (< Uenios "Host, Clan man"), is one of his aliases.

The Circle of Finn, *Book of Ballymote.*

The Circle of Finn

Finn was the god qualified as the "possessor wheels," and as you will see, this is not a euphemism. In the *Book of Ballymote*, there is this annotation over a bull's-eye labeled "Fege Fin," or "Feige Fion," and it is usually translated as "Finn's Window," or "Fionn's Track." He appears in the *Cycle of Finn mac Cumail* which narrates the battle of *Cath Fionntragha*, or "Battle of Ventry," in which he and his Fianna oppose Dáire Donn, the world-king.[24] Fionntragha was the battlefield overtaken by Dáire Donn[25] and the name meant "the fair track or range." Using his father's spear given to him by Fiacra, he saves the palace of the High King of Ireland at Tara threatened by the onslaught of a powerful demon. He is then reunited with Gráine, the sun goddess.

The sun shield and spear are the usual arms of the solar hero. In Greek myth, a golden shield falls from Helios's chariot, the sun god, onto the battlefield where it is picked up by an Apollonian hero. In Irish myth, the theme of the wheel brings us back to Mog Ruith's wheel called *roth rámach*, the "oared *wheel*" (from Ramaca Reta, literally, "the rowing wheel"), and which has two meanings or interpretations:

(1) As a cosmological symbol representing the contour of the ecliptic, a schematic model of the organization of the cosmos maintained by the Druids.
(2) As a divining instrument representing the macrocosm, a wheel, also called Tasgopeilas Reta, Tarabarra or Taratron in old Celtic and from which probably came the name Tarot for the French card game. The wheel of Fortune was called Kalachakra in Sanskrit. The medieval Wheel of Fortune was most likely a reminder of the zodiacal Circle. As for Taratron < Tarot, "auger," the name hints at late Antiquity drilled or inscribed divining lead plates called *tabulae defixionis in Latin* and talouaro or talouero in Old Celtic which means "threaded."

The Tasgopeilas Reta, "the powerful thinking wheel," or "wheel of divination," and "prayer wheel," by extension, referred to the zodiacal belt.

The Ogham abbreviations in the *Book of Ballymote* are given as follows:

"di- fict Ailm dact gaxt (or gart) from 'A' a right turn in circumference (in fenced plot or garden)."

A Ailm , B, Beth, H, Huath , Uath , M , Muin, Min, Th/Oi (r), Quinlan/Oir, Feorusoir, P/Ui, Peith, Pethbol/Uillean, O, I, Ohn; Ph/Ia, Phogos/Iphin, L, Luis D, Daur, Ch/Ea, Choad/Eashadh; G, Gort, Gart, U, Ur, N, Nuin, Nion, T, Tinne, Ng, Ngetal, E, Eadha, Eodha, F (V), Fearn C, Coll, St (Sd), Straif, I Ioho, Idho, Iubhar, S, Saille, Q, Quert, R, Ruis.

"Per alio" Ae/xi, Amancholl, that is to say, sentence or Mor-Xi.

"Ae , Amancholl, abalone mountain pine ogham, that is to say, the divine pine wood, which are derived the four Ifins or vineyards, #, per alios, the name of the branch"

And again, from the *Book of Ballymote*:

Ifin > Spiðna, "gooseberry."
Per alio "otherwise"; alio adv. "Elsewhere (with movement), to another place." So send the letter Ae elsewhere.... That is to say that sentence, Head, alias Amanchol (Ae/Xi-mor—the solar grid sign) is sent instead of Peith, pethbol/uilleann (w/ui = #, the lunar square) between Ohn and Iphin.

Ferchertne's Strand

The Ogham transcribers generally read this as meaning: "Triaig Srut fircertne. Iu fida ingach snaithi (snaschi?)." That is, "Traig Sruth Ferc(h)ertne iu (U preceded by c: cu-, Coig.?) Feda in gach snaithi."

Meaning, "The range or course of Ferchertne, to wit, five letters in each thread."

THE ETYMOLOGICAL STUDY FOR THE OLD IRISH TERMS

Triaig < triagi, genitive of triagos/treagos, "fork, three-pronged," if not tricarios, "triple power, triple strength"; corrected as traig by translators, that is, traig < tractos, "beach, strand, seafront, shore";

Strut < Srutu, "fast course, torrent";

Fircertne < Cerdonuiros, "skilled worker, technician";

.i. < in, "in," or eri for, "cause"; ei- < epi-, prefix with an idea of intention.

.u. < iuo, "order"; eu > aue, "too much, too little"; eu > neue, "or"; compare with Gaelic ua, preposition, "from, out of."

fida, feda < uida/uido < uidta, "knowledge, wisdom," in wordplay with uidu, "wood, tree," or "peg/cusp (in the astrological sense)."

Ingach < in-gach, in as with English, "in," and **gach** < gac < agac-, "every, all, everyone"; or, in < eni, "in, inside"; ina, "here, so"; cacto, "power"; cactio, "possess, enter"; cacteto, "taken, seized."

Snaith, "pull, pull hook," from the verb snatô, "to spin, to weave"; snatio, "swimming"; snatos, "cord"; or maybe snaschi < snasaich, "buff, made sleek, polishing, decorate, cutting, analyze, criticizing"; in wordplay with senicatis (gen. -eios), "ancient tradition," or "ancient monument."

Thus reading: "...Triaig srut fircertne i ... u fida ingach snaithi." "At triple power (...) because of Fircertne, directs knowledge (connoting wood) by the entry (or power), of the cord."

THE OGHAM WHEEL OF ROIGNE ROSCADACH

Rot og (m) roigni roscadaig, "Ogham wheel of Roigne Roscadach";
Beith a.u.–Huath a.u.–Muin a.u.–Ailm a.u.;
With C, Coll. ... C... cc ccc cccc.... ccccc in each quarter of the sun disc.

Astrology and Ogham

> "As a mighty tree in the forest, so in truth is man, his hairs are the leaves, his outer skin is the bark. From his skin flows forth blood, sap from the skin (of the tree); and thus from the wounded man comes forth blood, as from a tree that is struck."—*Brihad-Aranyaka Upanishads, Third Adhyaya,* verse 28

The Upanishads inform us that Manu is to be likened to a tree for it is said that the self, the Atman is ruled by the mechanisms of the Atmakaraka (principle main Lord) as found in the Ashtakavarga system of prediction. The Ashtakavarga (eight sources of energy or acmes) set the lots of fortune for Man's growth and development. All this modelled on the Bharata (Tree) or Maha Bharata (Great tree) which is to be likened to the Scandinavian Askr Yggdrasils. In Celtic society the terms *coilu* for "prediction," and *prennios*, "wood," set the divinatory mood to the mode of predicting with augural sticks. This very ancient system is described by many authors of Antiquity. And as Joseph Monard remarked to me in 1998, "These sticks were tossed into the air by the vate, in order to make a reading following the order of their fall, and interpret the omens through answers. This technique was known to the Bretons as the Prenn-denn, the Crannachar to the Gaelic tribes, and the Talamatia to the Cisalpine Gauls."

Again, the *Upanishads*[26] give us further details on the cosmographical aspects of this system: "These are the eight abodes (the earth, etc.), the eight worlds (fire, etc.), the eight gods (the immortal food, etc.), the eight persons (corporeal, etc.). He who after dividing and uniting these persons, went beyond (the *Samana*), that person, taught in the Upanishads, I now ask thee (to teach me). If thou shalt not explain him to me, thy head will fall. Sakalya did not know him, and his head fell, nay, thieves took away his bones, mistaking them for something else." This something else might very well be the omen sticks.

> The lumps of his flesh are (in the tree) the layers of wood, the fiber is strong like the tendons. The bones are the (hard) wood within, the marrow is made like the marrow of the tree. But while the tree, when felled, grows up again more young from the root, from that root, tell me, does a mortal grow up, after he has been felled by death? Do not say "from seed," for seed is produced from the living; but a tree, springing from a grain, clearly rises again after death. If a tree is pulled up with the root, it will not grow again; from that root then, tell me, does a mortal grow up, after he has been felled by death? Once born, he is not reborn; for who should create him again?

The explanation is quite clear; like the tree, unless man does not bear seeds, he cannot be reborn in the world of the living.

In de la Villemarqué's *Barzaz Breiz*, we read that there are three parts to the world: three beginnings and three ends, for man as well as the oak. In Vedic literature, the primordial man is dismembered and his body-parts spread across the cosmos. At the center, his genitals which seed the future world seen as a vast plain. The ancestor of the Gaels, Partholon, clears four plains, along with Magh Elta[27] each marking the four corners. Since the microcosm reflects the macrocosm, Ireland's four provinces are the allegories of the seasons and solar stations. Then comes Nemed and his people, the Nemedians, who clear twelve plains for each of the zodiacal constellations. Finally, Medb comes to clear the land turning it into a vast desolate field (27 lunar houses) with at its center, Medb's Tree. And, it is in her enclosed garden around her tree that evolve the zodiacal beasts.

In 2005, Joseph Monard wrote to me confirming that the Celts did see the constellations as trees: "The zodiacal constellations were imagined as "trees," called prinnioi, akin to prennes (tree) and it is probably for that reason that tree names were given to the constellations." The sun, the moon, and other heavenly bodies entering a constellation or star cluster, are therefore seen as light shafts entering the clearing of a forest. In other words, fedha < fida < uidu/uidus for, "wood," or "tree," in Gaelic expresses the same notion as that of the Old Brythonic, prennos, also for "wood," or "tree." This being that the Druids referred to astral cusps or "horns," as trees. From Irish and Welsh poetry, it appears that these star seers saw two cusps, in and out, where the Classical astrologers saw one per astral house. That is, for the Celtic astrologer, each constellation had a front door and a back door. In Classical astrology, a cusp is a mathematical point marking the entry of the sun in a house. However, for the Oghamic scheme not all fedhas represent zodiacal cusps. These are the forfedhas or over-fews which represent the five elements, space and other abstract ideas.

The four directions: -x-/+; the confines of space seen as circle or square: -o- /-◊-; the grid (dragon's head Ω): -#-; the spiral or hook (dragon's tail): -∂-; the double hashed grid for the sun's light: -##-. Therefore, forfedha have nothing artificial or improvised.

The forfedha as symbols of the five elements: Ch/Ea, xdonion, "chthonic, earth"; Th/Oi, tepnia > tennia, "fire"; P/Ui, (p)idsca/udesca, "water"; Ph/Ia, auela, "air, blast"; auentos > uentos, "wind"; auentia, "inspiration breath"; Xs/Ae, uxdulon, "high element, ether."

The forfedha (< uorbentioi, "completing, additional"),

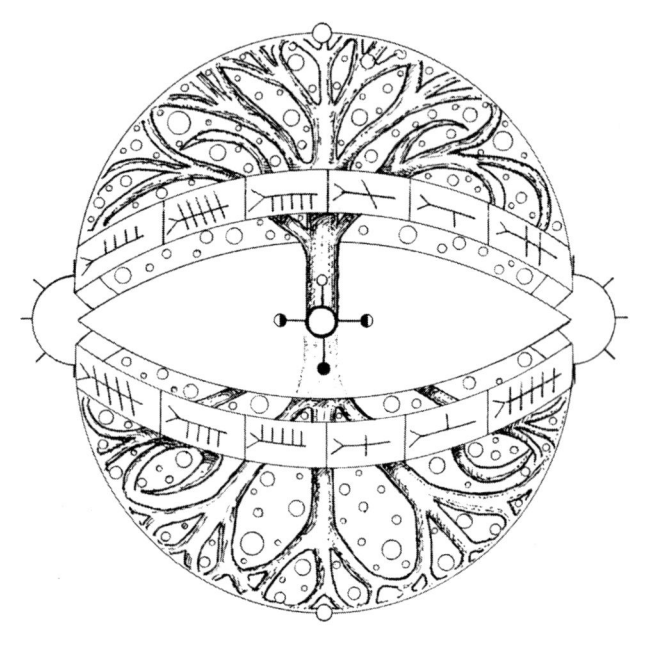

The world tree with symbols of Ogham. Author's drawing.

are in reference to ueruidoues, "the over-woods," implying a higher notion than the Zodiac. In addition to representing the five elements, the also represent greater cosmic considerations such as the movements of the sun, the moon and the nodes.

Etymological Run Up of the Fedha "Letters" in the Oghamic Directional Sun Wheel
(along with their esoteric meanings)[28]

A, Ailm < alamios, "pine"; alamos, "cattle herd, wealth, possessions";

B, Beth < betua, "birch"; betis, "road"; bitu, "(live) world"; bitus, "life."

H < Sq/Sp < Sc, Huath, uath < squiats, "hawthorn"; squertos, "thicket"; squetlon, "narrative, narrative history";

M, Muin, min < muinia, "bramble or vine"; muinos/moinos, "treasure"; muinon, "benefit."

P/Ui, Peith, pethbol < petios/quetios, "opulus"; Uillean < uillo, "honeysuckle"; uillos, "horse"; uilia, "willingness, honesty";

Ph <B/Sp/Ia < Fea < Phogos < bagos, "beech"; bagios, "boar"; bagacos, "fighter, warlike"; Iphin < spiðna, "gooseberry (mackerel)"; spina/sparna, "thorn."

III: Astrology of the Druids

O, I, Ohn < ocstino/acstino, "gorse"; acunos, "spice";

L, Luis < lusis, "rowan"; lugos, "brightness, splendor"; louxsnos, "light."

C > K < X > Ch/Ea, Choad < coiton/caiton, "thicket"; caitos, "woody bush"; coitos, "common"; Eashadh < esados/elto, eltos, "poplar (white)"; esa, "cascade";

D, Daur < daruos/deruos, "oak"; deruos/derbos, "safe, certain, proven."

T > Th/ Oi(r), Tharan < taranos, "green oak"; tarannos, "thunder"; tarandos, "reindeer"; thesmerion, "hibiscus"; Oir, Feorusoir < uorosorios, "charcoal"; uorrice, "goat willow"; uoros, "wise"; uornoctos, "bare, naked";

G, Gort, Gart < gortia, "ivy, thorny shrub"; gorton, "garden"; gorta, "famine."

U, Ur < uroica/broica, "heather"; ur/uron, "fire";

F < V < U, Fearn < uernos, "alder"; uernos, "good"; uiriona, "sincerity"; iaru, "truth."

T, Tinne < tennos, "holly"; tepnia > tennia, "fire (wood)";

Ng < Nc, Ngetal < ingaitalis < caitalis, "reed"; ancouo > ancu, "death (personified)"; anacantios, "disastrous."

E, Eadha, Eodha < idato, "aspen"; edemnos, "need"; iduna, "wisdom";

S, Saille < salicos/salixs, "willow"; suligu, "harmony"; sauelios, "sun"; sulisma, "look."

C, Coll < coslos, "hazel"; cailos, "pomp, favorable, auspicious";

St (Sd), Straif < sdragenos < dragenos, "barberry"; draco, "head, chief, war lord"; drangos, "ghost."

A Noble character with a large crescent-shaped felt hat receiving a libation from a bald maid with a staff and snake coming out from the crest of her head. Detail of a bronze plaque from Kuffarn Situla, Lower Austria. Author's drawing from a photograph at the Naturhistorisches Museum, Vienna, Austria.

I, Ioho, Idho < iuos; Iubhar < iburos/eburos, "yew"; iuos, "good, suitable, safe, sound"; eburos, "(old) boar, lone boar";

N, Nuin, Nion < onna, "ash"; ninatis, ninnatis > nenadis, "nettle"; nentios < nantios, "injury (war)."

Q, Quert < qerta, "apple"; qarios, "cauldron"; qartis, "party";

R, Ruis < ruscia, "elder"; roudios, "red, ruin."

Finally, there are many indications from Taliesin in the *Cad Godeu*, "The Battle of Trees," Book of Taliesin I, *Priv Cyfarch*, "The First Address of Taliesin," translated by Skene, that letters and cosmology were all part of the same esoteric language:

> "And before I desire the end of existence,
> and before the broken foam shall come upon my lips,
> and before I become connected with wooden boards,
> May there be festivals to my soul!
> Book-learning scarcely tells me
> of severe afflictions after death-bed;
> and such as have heard my bardic books
> they shall obtain the region of heaven, the best of all abodes."

IV

The Luminaries

Pleasant, the moon, a luminary in the heavens;
Also pleasant where there is a good rememberer.
Pleasant, summer, and slow long day;
  —Taliesin, *Aduvyneu Taliesin, The Pleasant Things of Taliesin*, Book of Taliesin IV

Gallic currency of the Triviri with three beams of light and the ecliptic. Drawing by the author.

Solar and Lunar Deities

The oldest Indo-European deities are directly related to light. As we have seen, the term deiwos, for god (literally, "One of light") designates these light beings that populate the sky. At the oldest level of Indo-European cosmology, the luminaries were at the base of the structuring foundation myths. This cosmological order was structured accordingly:

(1) Sun for day light, day sky and the colors white, blue and gold;
(2) Moon for night, night sky and darkness, the color black;
(3) Venus, the morning and evening star for dawn, dusk and the colors salmon pink, orange and red.

As evidenced by the earlier Latin tradition, the cult of Sol, the sun deified, is as old as the cult of Luna, the moon. For the Latin people, the goddess Luna was of less importance than the god Sol, while for the Celts, it was the opposite. Medb, the Queen of Heaven, completely overshadows Ailill, lesser in royal stature, but nevertheless, is very bright, diligent and rich in possession. The Greeks imagined Selene, daughter and sister of Helios Hyperion and Theia, as a most beautiful lady who appeared in the night sky riding in a silver chariot. Meanwhile, at night, Helios, the Sun, was carried away in his sleep in a moon crescent boat on the waves of the dark Ocean. And Venus, the goddess of dawn and dusk, was imagined in a silky white dress running on the celestial solar path before the bronze chariot of the sun prince Apollo, there scattering flowers along the way.

In Vedic literature, deities are classified according to their astral lineage into distinct competing houses. The Adityas are deities belonging to the solar dynasty, and Somavamza, under the auspices of King Soma or Chandra, belongs to the lunar dynasty. It seems that

Names and Genealogy of the Celtic Gods of the Solar and Lunar Dynasties

IRELAND	
Apollonian Dynasty (solar)	*Selene Dynasty (lunar)*
1. Bilé + Danu: 2. Dagda, Elcmar, Nechtar, Midir; 2. Dagda + Boand: 3. Brigitt, Aongus, the Mac Og, Dearg Bodb and Cermat.	**Lir's lineage:** 1. Lir: 2. Mannannàn Mac Lir; 1. Lir + Aobh: Fionnuala, Aedh, Fiacra, Conn; 2. Mannannàn + Fand: 3. Gaiar, Niamh, Cliodna. **Queen Medb's lineage:** 1. Queen Medb and King Ailill: 2. their 3 daughters: Aobh, Aoife, Arbha; 2. their 7 sons: Maine Mathramail, Maine Athramail, Maine Mogor, Maine Mingor, Maine Mo Epirt (also called Maine Milscothach), Maine Diligent and Maine Gaib uile. 2. Aoife + Cùchulainn: 3. Conlai.
WALES	
Apollonian Dynasty (solar)	*Selene Dynasty (lunar)*
1. Manogan, father of Beli Mawr; 2. Mathonwy, father of Don and Math. **Lineage of the goddess Don** 1. Beli + Don: 2. Gwydion, Arianrod, Gilvaethwy, Amaethon, Nudd, Penardun, Nynniaw; 2. Gwydion + Arianrod: 3. Nwyvre, Llew, Dylan.	1. Gods: Gwyn ap Nudd, Arawn pen Annwn, Llyr, Iweriadd, Penardun, Euroswydd. **Lineage of Llyr** 1. Llyr + Iwerdiadd: 2. Bran and Branwen; 1. Llyr + Penardun: 2. Manawydan. 2. Manawydan + Rhiannnon: 3. Pryderi, son of Pwyll pen Annwn and Rhiannon, foster son of Manawydan. 1. Euroswydd + Penardun: 2. Nissyen, Evnissien.

from the Celtic myths and from the interpretation of the many plural god names found in archaeological excavations in Gaul and in Britain of the Roman period that a similar classification was used. For example, the Suleviae, a group of sun goddesses, which may very well be Latinized manifestations or avatars of Suliuia. Or the many avatars of the Gallic Apollo known under the names of: Atepomarus, Belenus, Cunomaglus, Grannus, Maponus, Moritasgus, Vindonnus and Virotutis.

The Moon

Gallic coinage depicting Epona, the mare-goddess topped with the lunar crescent and solar disc or full moon. Author's drawing.

In Lunar Time

In their progression around the ecliptic and its zodiacal constellations, the two luminaries, sun and moon, do not take the same time since their cycles are not of equal duration. The almanac or monthly calendar is the lunar record of annual events, while for the sun it is the Zodiac.

Indexing the events of the lunar annual cycle and reconciling it with the longer solar cycle around the ecliptic was the difficult task of calendar makers. The term almanac comes from *almanachus*, a Latin term most likely borrowed from the Old Germanic *allmonaxta*, for "all moons," or "all of the moon's acts," in English. It is therefore not from the Spanish-Arabic *al-manakh* as it is often claimed in the etymological dictionaries. The Old Celtic name for it was *Amserolenmen* which literally meant, "Sequential time."

As previously mentioned, the many constellations of the Zodiac were compared to a forest of trees called Prinnioi. The lunar year was called Blidnis in Old Celtic and comprised of a 12 moons registry called Reuia. Again, poets were quick to make the usual puns with the words Reuia and Reuesia. In that, Reuia was for "lapse, time space" and Reuesia for "clearing or cleared space," here again the forest theme! Given that the Old Celtic vocabulary related to the moon was very rich and diverse, many other related "bardic" puns could be made. Since the moon had many alternative names, the list went as follows: Diuon, the moon as a heavenly body and diuon "light source" (adj. diuon-/os/a/on, "light emitting") and Deuon "God," this being that Deuonna or Diuonna was the name of the Moon Goddess.

In addition to other designations for the moon there was Luxna, a word attested by the Coligny calendar and Irish Luan. Luxsna, also has a similar etymology as that of the Latin Luna. Another synonym was Leucara (which evolved into Lugra, then Loer and Lloer in Breton and Welsh) and the name refers to its bright appearance. And on the Gaelic side, we have Éasca < Eidsciia meaning "in phases (pl. neutral)," and Gealach < Gelaca "clear." Given that the Old Celtic vocabulary related to the moon was very rich and diverse, many other related "bardic" puns could be made, as commented Monard in 1994. The moon's associated color was black, for night.

Indexing Cycles

The difficulty in keeping annual synchronized time arises when one tries to combine the lunar cycles with the solar year. In fact, the average lunar year of twelve months is of 354.3669 days compared to the average of 365 days, or more precisely 365.2422 days for the complete solar year. For the first calendar makers, the task was to combine these two years into a synchronous year, while still keeping track of the advent of seasonal changes. The solution was found which the introduction of an intercalary month inserted every three years as a full thirteenth month called *Santaranos mins,* or *Santaros mens,* for "special, embolismic month or month set apart." This special technique of inserting an extra embolismic ("clotting") month has the advantage of maintaining the two cycles synchronous. In addition to the use of an additional intercalary month, there was the insertion of an extra day in July which further complicated things. In this first cycle, an added mid-month luster reappeared every five years and was appropriately called *Ciallosbuis Sonnocingos for* "indexing of the sun path." It occurred during the spring equinox right between the months of March and April. The second embolismic month was called *Mens in dueixtionu* and was inserted at the beginning of the October and November lunation. It was set every five years. The term *mens* or *mins in dueixtionu* stood for "month in duplication" and was found inscribed on the Coligny calendar in abbreviated form as: MIDX.

One of the names found in the above list, Samonios, is related to the Gaelic month name Samhain. However, it is not known whether these Gallic names were primarily used by the other Celtic cultures. It is also likely that some of these terms were commonly known in Druidic times, but that Christian clerics censored them in favor of more neutral or popular agricultural designations. Eventually, under the Church's influence, Latin terms replaced the old Celtic ones. Another interesting Gaelic month name is *Mí Deireadh Fomhair* which refers to a class of mythological beings called the Fomoiri.[1] The Fomoiri, also spelled Fomhair, Fomore and Fomhoire, were akin to the Greek Telkhines, a class of primordial spirits. Their king was Balor[2] "of the evil eye."

The Coligny Calendar

Month Names	Number of Days for Month Halves	Codes for Month Length
SAMONIOS	15 + 15 = 30	Mat. < mata even, for 30 days
DUMANNIOS	15 + 14 = 29	Anm. < anmata uneven for 14 + 15 days
RIUROS	15 + 15 = 30	mata
ANAGANTIOS	15 + 14 = 29	anmata
OGRONIOS	15 + 15 = 30	mata
CUTIOS	15 + 15 = 30	mata
GIAMONIOS	15 + 14 = 29	anmata
SIMIUISONIOS	15 + 15 = 30	mata
EQUOS	15 + 14 = 29 or 15 + 15 = 30	anmata or mata
ELEMBIUOS	15 + 14 = 29	anmata
EDRINIOS	15 + 15 = 30	mata
CANTLOS	15 + 14 = 29	anmata

Names of the Month in the Surviving Celtic Languages

Month	Gaelic and Brythonic Names	Old Celtic Etymology and Definition
November	Irish: Mí na Samhna Erse: an t-Samhuinn	Month of Samhain < Samonios, "of the gathering, of the sower"
December	Irish: Mí na Nollag Erse: Dubhlachd Welsh: Mys Du Breton: Miz Du	From Latin natalis, natalicia, "nativity, birthing, Noel" Dubilectos, "dark, damp" Mins dubis, "dark month"
January	Irish: Mí Eanair Erse: Faoilteach Cornish: Kervardhu Breton: Kerzu	From Latin januarius, "of Janus," a Roman god Ualuticos, "of wolves" Couiros dubis, "frankly dark" Certos dubis, "all as dark"
February	Irish: Mí Feabhra Irish: Mí na Féile Brighde	From Latin februarius, "of purification" Mins uelias Brigindonos, "month of the feast of Brigitt," or "of Brigindo"
March	Irish: Mí Márta Erse: am Màrt Erse: an Gearran	From Latin martiae, "of Mars" Mins Gerronos, "shortened month, of castration"
April	Irish: Mí Aibreán Erse: an Giblean	From Latin aprilis, "bloom of buds" Mins Gegdoblonacos, "month of goose fat"
May	Irish: Mí na Bealtaine Manx: Boaldyn Erse: an Cèitean	Mins Belotennias, "month of bonfires (of Beltaine)" Belotennia, "of bonfires" Mins Centonos, "month of prime time"

Month	Gaelic and Brythonic Names	Old Celtic Etymology and Definition
June	Irish: Mí Meitheamh Manx: Mean souree Welsh: Mehefin Cornic: Metheven Breton: Mezheven Erse: an t-Òg-mhios	Mediosamosenos or Mediosamos, "mid-time festival" Mins Ogii, "month of youths"
July	Irish: Mí Iúil Erse: Iuchar/an t-Iuchar Welsh: Gorffenhaf Cornish: Gortheren Breton: Gourzheren	from Latin Julius, "Jules" Iecuurios, "fresh time" Gortus-somareti, "heat of summertime"
August	Irish: Mí Lùnasa Erse: Lùnasdal Manx: Luanistyn	Lugi Naissatios Samosenos, "(month) of Lug's commemoration"
September	Irish: *Mí Meán Fomhair* Welsh: Medi Erse: an t-Sultine Cornish: Gwyngala Breton: Gwengolo	Mens minos Uomorii, "month of the little monster" Meðon, "to reap" Sultennos, "plantish" Uindos Golouos, "splendid, white light"
October	Irish: Mí Deireadh Fomhair Erse: an Dàmhair Welsh: Hydref Cornish: Hedra Breton: Here	Mins deruedon Uomorii, "month of the (giant) monster's end" Mins Damodãris, "month of deer rut, of deer belling" Sutrebos, "autumnal"

The Lunar Nodes

Ancient Boiian Celtic coin from Bohemia, dating to circa 2nd and 1st centuries BCE, and showing the horned-serpent or dragon. Author's drawing from an old book engraving.

The lunar nodes are the intersection points on the ecliptic which are crossed by the orbits of the sun and the moon. These two points of intersection are strictly conceptual and do not correspond to any tangible physical reality such as that observed with the visible stars, both fixed and moving such as, the planets, comets and asteroids. A complete nodal cycle is completed every 18 years and 5 months. The expression *North Node* means that the moon is on its upward path coming from the south and moving on to the north at the ecliptic intersection. Likewise, when the moon reaches its peak, it then dips downward and crosses the *South Node*. Each of these mathematical points is found

IV: The Luminaries 73

exactly to the opposite of the other on the ecliptic. In order to better predict eclipses, the ancient astrologers were quick to notice the moon's movements passing over and under the sun's orbital path. The line connecting the two nodes is called "axis of the dragon."

In former ages, those able to correctly predict eclipses were highly regarded, not only by the superstitious, but by the court rulers who saw in these ominous events signs of times to come. The presence of a wandering star in this part of the sky was not only regarded as an occult phenomena, but as an omen. In light of this, the lunar nodes were seen as the seat of eclipses and indicators of future events. In Vedic astrology, the nodes were even counted as planets. This was not the case for classical Greco-Roman astrology.

The Celts however, unlike their southern neighbors, were in agreement with the Indian Jyotisha (astrologers). Celtic mythology also speaks of cosmic and astral phenomena in relation to dragons. The best example that comes to mind is the episode found in the Arthurian cycles where King Uther Pendragon has Merlin explain to him the causes of his difficulties. Merlin there explains that the British monarch is confronted with dueling dragons, one white (Saxons) and one red (Welsh). The white dragon, for the Saxon invaders, represents the ascending North Node, while the red dragon, for the Welsh, represents the descending South Node.

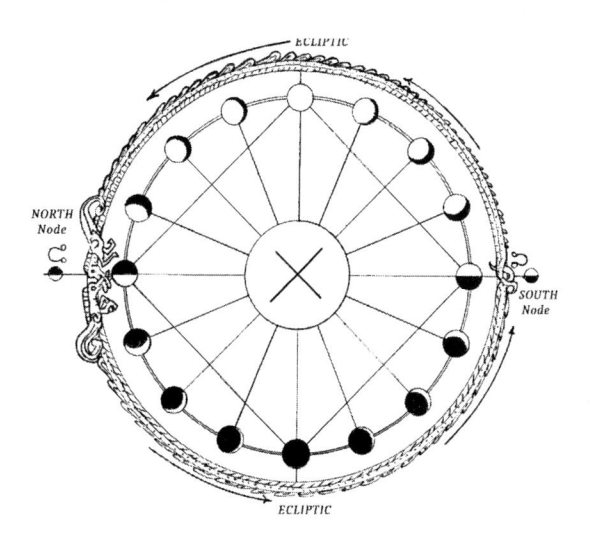

The white and red dragons along the moon's pathway. Caput Draconis: Pennos Ambeios/ Qendos Ambeios, the North Node (ascending); color white; Cauda Draconis: Lostos Ambeios, the South Node (descending); color red. Author's drawing.

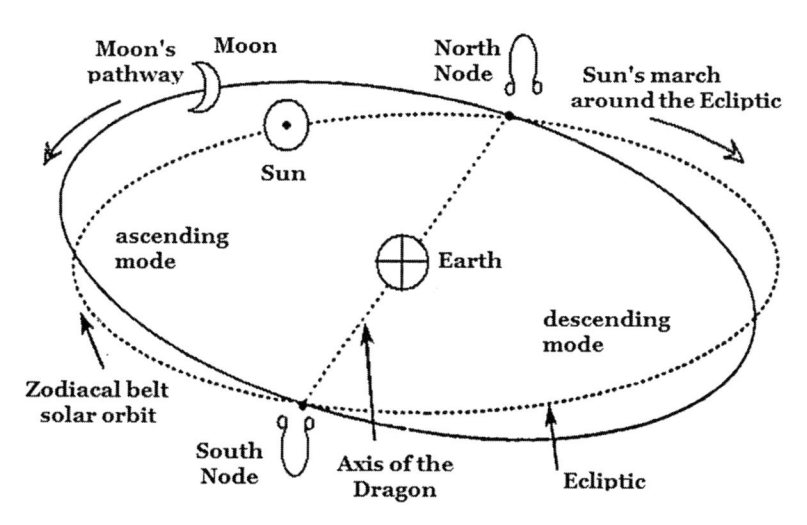

North and south positions on the intersections of the eliptic and zodiacal belt. Author's drawing.

The Moon Grid

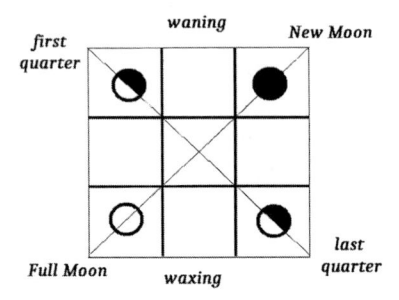

```
           waning       New Moon
first
quarter   ◐  |    | ●
         ----+----+----
             |    |
         ----+----+----
          ○  |    | ◑   last
                         quarter
Full Moon   waxing
```

The moon has often been seen as a large mirror or a large bowl. In antiquity, the moon shaped mirror was long used as a divining instrument for communicating with the Other World. Mirrors reflect indirect light and are therefore thought to be instruments of mind projection. The moon was once seen as the place from which emanated the mind of the Cosmos. Conversely, the radiant and bright sun represented the spirit of the cosmos.

In astrological graphic art, the moon grid is found at the center of the solar grid. The lunar grid consists of two hashed vertical and horizontal lines. This four stroke grid forms a magic square of nine spaces. This square is placed to the north/south position where the two lunar nodes are found. Number nine is for the nine holy days of the novena, the nine tables of fate and destiny, while eight represents the phases of the moon. Thus, the moon grid has four main squares for each of the major phases being: the full moon, the two crescents and the new moon.

This idea of four part place or mansion was called Bri Leith or Liath Bri[3] in Irish myth. The area in which was found the Liath Bri was referred to as mide mag. This lunar palace was governed by Medb (< Medua), the queen of the night sky, the moon goddess. Medb refers to the sweet intoxication of fermented beverages, especially mead. It is a known fact that the fermented beverages affect thinking and excite the tongue. Celestial waters, as it was believed, flowed from the moon, thus affecting thought. Did not its rays strike the minds of mortals? Therefore, Medb, from her lunar domain, had mastership over the watery element. The three sovereign fairies who assisted with Medb were her daughters: Aobh, Aoife and Arbha.[4] They are also called the three Étain, "Poetry." And they each embody one of the aspects of the Triple Goddess and mind the activities of the arts and healing. In short, each fairy is the allegory of the three stages of womanhood and the three phases of the Moon.

The Sun

> "Magnificent astronomy, when communicated, sees all that is high.
> When the mind is active, when the sea is pleasant, when the race is valiant,
> when the high one is supplicated, or the sun when it is given,
> when it covers the land.
> Covering land of what extent?"
> —Taliesin, *Book of Taliesin VII, Angar Kyfyndawt, The Hostile Confederacy*

IV: The Luminaries 75

Gallic coin depicting the sun with its eight acmes represented by circles and oak leaves. Drawing by the author.

As with all other questions concerning the cosmic mythological order, the conceptual scheme surrounding the heavenly bodies entertained by the Celts was essentially Indo-European. Thus, a basic conceptual model for the settings of the macrocosm was inherited by most of these cultures. First, the Cosmos was represented as a large covered dome prosaically called "the vault of heaven." Aether or Ether, the firmament, was called *nem* in Old Irish, *nef* in Welsh and Cornish and *neñv* in Breton, all from the Old Celtic root *nemos*. The whole universe, from top to bottom, was imagined as consisting of two large hollow spheres specked with holes from which shone the primordial light as stars. And at its center was a gigantic central sun around which other worlds and suns such as our own revolved. The world was made up of several domains or places that the Celts referred to as *Magoi* "plains" and that the Vedic seers called *Lokas*. These worlds, in constant motion around the axis of the center of the universe, were represented as a pole, a shaft or a tree. Its associated color was white, for daylight.

The Sun Grid

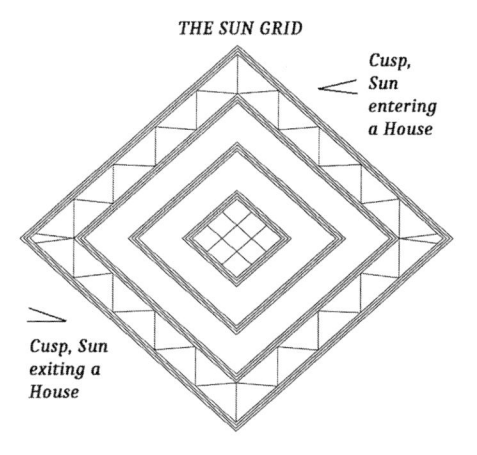

THE SUN GRID

Cusp, Sun entering a House

Cusp, Sun exiting a House

Drawing by the author.

The Sun grid consists of four horizontal lines and four vertical lines thus forming a magic square of twelve spaces, with at its center in the two tier, the moon square. It illustrates the four-part plan that the sun covers at each season. And for each of the seasons, correspond three zodiacal months of thirty days. At the summer solstice, the sun is at its paroxysm or peak, while at the winter solstice, the sun is at its lowest. The sun at the vernal equinox is peaking, or in exaltation, whereas at the autumnal equinox, it is at its downfall or in debilitation.

Much more than just a magic square, or sacred grid, the solar clock not only helps define the time and position of the sun in the annual sky, but also establish the powers, yokes and prognostics for astral themes. In Antiquity, and on to the Medieval Ages following Ptolemy's fashion, the grid, and not the circle, was the usual plan for setting up a zodiacal chart. It is in fact this same squared layout that appears in the forfedha (additional signs) of the Ogham under the designation of Aemhancoll.

These eight strokes must be understood as power lines or energy sources similar to the concept of the *Ashtakavarga*[5] in the Jyotish Vedic Astrological system. According to the Vedic astrologers, each of these lines represents a cosmic force emitted by the all-pervading sun lighting up ground space and there influencing the (known) seven planetary planes of the solar system. The astrologer's purpose is to determine whether these forces (positively or negatively charged) influence current or future events. Their influence is manifested when these cosmic rays penetrate given stars, celestial bodies and other objects.

Here, the eight rays act as transit lines channeling energy on to the seven main planetary courses. Graphic symbols found in Gallic coinage show that the Druids also entertained this notion of the eight acmes of the sun symbolized by orbs and oak leaves. The oak, traditionally linked to solar symbolism, was symbolic of the sun's ascent after the spring vernal equinox.

More than just a grid measuring the passages of the sun on its annual course, it was mainly used to chart planetary transits and positions in the various astral houses. We also must remember that the sun, as well as the other luminaries, was considered a planet by astrologers and was never treated independently from the other planets. Each planet had its allotted force or cosmic power along with its own course and hierophany (sacred manifestation or appearance). Or again, these epiphanies serve to predict its eclipses, returns and cyclical appearances. In turn, each of the planets enters an astral house kept by a given house master or lord. In Gaelic, the house master was probably called *tech-duin*.[6] And in Irish mythology, Tech Duin, "House of Donn," was a mystical island situated on the Ocean to the southwest. The Old Celtic name *attegioranda*, for "domain with land and mansion," or "lot with buildings," also neatly renders the notion.

Because of cosmic events described in mythology, it is possible to access the underlying astrological themes and motifs. For example, consider the story surrounding the bard-poet Fer Cherdne[7] who had eloped with Blathnáth[8] after Cuchulainn had killed his master, King Cú Roi.[9] In some versions, Cú Roi, seeing his fortress blazing, rushes into the sea and there drowns. And according to other versions, he was killed in his sleep.

Henceforth, Cú Roi, King of Munster and Lord of the Other World, kept Blathnáth, the beautiful fairy maiden, prisoner in his fortress. After Cú Roi's death, Cuchulainn took Blathnáth and carried her to the cliff-side coast of Beara peninsula. Seizing the opportunity, Fer Cherdne seizes her by the waist and jumps with her over the cliff.

In prosaic terms, this theme illustrates the moon and sun dipping under the horizon into the sea. Blathnáth represents the moon while Cuchulainn symbolizes the sun's path. The attributes of Cú Roi are described as dark and mysterious and his coat is described as grey and mottled. He has the ability to shape-shift taking on the appearance of a hero giant. Like Ogma, he has the power to bind others with magic. This characteristic likens him to Herakles who, in one of his twelve labors, must capture Kerberos, the hound keeper of the gates of Hades. Likewise, Cú does stands for "dog" in Gaelic. The name Cú Roi (also Cú Ruí, Cú Raoi) is probably from Cu-Redios means "dog of the plain." The Dog Star was of course Sirius. Sirius rises at the start of summer and declines in autumn.

Furthermore, the province of Munster was traditionally linked to death and the moon was once held to be the residence of the souls of drowned mariners. The opposition between the two Cú "dogs," most likely represents the passing of the sun and moon over the ecliptic. Cúchulainn's true name was Setanta[10] which means "one who takes the path or the path," the path being of course the ecliptic or the zodiacal band. Thus, each of the spaces on the sun grid represents a plain in which the sun, much like Herakles, accomplishes twelve celestial labors.

The Astrological Workings of the Solar Grid

The sun grid is comprised of four horizontal lines crossed by four vertical lines. The square serves as graphic table for predicting themes and zodiacal calculations. In each of the outer square spaces is consigned one of the 12 zodiacal signs along with its astral house, their planetary position and ruling master, including their strengths and yokes. Also taken into consideration, are the planetary conjunctions and the significators for each planet and constellation. The chart begins in Libra at the fall equinox and ends with the twelfth house in Virgo. Therefore, House One corresponds to Libra and not Aries, as is the case with the Classical and Vedic Zodiacs.

Assigned Colors

As manifestations of light, colors, hot or cold, were always traditionally associated with the sun, rarely the moon which is confined to the grey and blue specter. As earlier mentioned, white represents the east or rising, while red represents the west, the setting. Color separation of white light is demonstrated by the prismatic effects of the rainbow or of water vapor and crystals. Vedic literature maintains that "all the colors are in the eye," here connoting the eye of the radiant sun.

Other passages found in the various Indo-European texts mention the body of the primordial cosmic man which formed the primitive earthly landscape. And as the story goes, from his mind was fired spirit and the principle of light. Since the eye belongs to the sun, the eye sees the color that is in the heart because it is said that the understanding of color came from the heart. Or as is was believed, these colors perceived by the eye originated in the heart of the sun.

According to Hindu mythology, the sun-goddess Aditi, mother of the heavenly light, gave birth to the twelve zodiacal deities. The Celts also maintained a similar idea of the sun and the eye in relation to the phenomenon of color. The Celtic sun goddess, Suleuia was worshiped in Britain (Cirencester, Colchester and Bath), as attested by the semi–Latinized names Sulis Minerva[11] and Sulevia. The Celtic name Sulis means "eye" and is a clever word-play with Saualis, "the feminine Sun" and Suleuia which means "well colored." The Vedic goddess Aditi and Aditya Surya, her male companion, therefore had Celtic equivalents. To conclude, each of the three classes of Celtic society correspond associated colors: white—Druids; red—Warriors; black or dark—the artisan producers. As for the Ogham, there too, each zodiacal constellation had a color assigned to it, when not for each of the 24 cusps.

Colors of the Zodiacal Constellations from the Ogham

Libra:
First cusp or in-cusp (entering constellation): wild apple tree;
Color: Cron < qrun-os/-a/-on, Brythonic, prunos > brunos, "brown";
Second cusp or out-cusp (exiting constellation): elderberry bush;
Color: Ruadh < roud-os/-a/-on roudios or "red."

Scorpio:
In-cusp: pine tree or cultivated apple tree;
Color: Allad < alat-os/-a/-on, "spotted" or albant-os/-a/-on, "bright white";
Out-cusp: birch tree;
Color: Bàn < Ban-os/-a/-on < bonos, "white (cream colored)"; bodi-os/-a/-on, "golden, yellow ochre, bay."

Sagittarius:
In-cusp: hawthorn tree;
Color: Scath < scat-os/-a/-on > scotos, "dark colored";
Out-cusp: vine or larch tree;
Color: Mbracht < Mrect-os/-a/-on > brectos, "varied, variegated," for melin-os/-a/-on, "yellowish," melinus, "dark yellow."

Capricorn:
In-cusp: guilder-rose bush, snowball tree, high-bush cranberry;
Color: Perc-os/-a/-on > ercos, "colorful, iridescent, stripped, fawn-colored, tawny-colored, or dark and iridescent";
Out-cusp: beech or viburnum lanthanum;
Color: Phorc-os/-a/-on, "shiny, glossy."

Aquarius:
In-cusp: ash tree;
Color: Orcis, "dark, black";
Out-cusp: rowan tree;
Color: Liath < leit-os/-a/-on, "pale grey, livid, hoary, grey."

Pisces:
In-cusp: coppice or sessile oak tree;
Color: Cud-os/-a/-on, "grey-green, moss-green";
Out-cusp: oak tree;
Color: Dubh < dubis < dubi-os/-a/-on, "black."

Aries:
In-cusp: green oak tree;
Color: thexsimon, "clematis, blue";
Out-cusp: ivy;
Color: Gorm < gorm-os/-a/-on, "dark blue."

Taurus:
In-cusp: heather bush;
Color: Ur < ur-os/-a/-on, ugros, "green, unripe";
Out-cusp: alder tree;
Color: Urd-os/-a/-on < uiridos, "green."

Gemini:
In-cusp: holly bush;
Color: Tamos/tem-os/-a/-os < "dark" < temellos, temil-os/-a/-on, "darkish," temis, "dark";
Out-cusp: reed grass;
Color: Nglas < glast-os/-a/-on, "blue, blue-grey, blue green."

Cancer:
In-cusp: poplar tree;
Color: El-os/-a/-on, "grey, greyish";
Out-cusp: willow tree;
Color: Sodath < sudati-os/-a/-on, or suliui-os/-a/-on, "well colored."

Leo:
In-cusp: hazel tree;
Color: Cocc-os/-a/-on, "adventure, red," crocn-os/-a/-on, "blood-red";
Out-cusp: barberry bush;
Color: Ðarn-os/-a/-on, "dark, dull."

Virgo:
In-cusp: yew tree;
Color: Irfind < areuind-os/-a/-on, "ultra-white"; it-os/-a/on, "straw-colored";
Out-cusp: myrtle tree;
Color: Necht < nect-os/-a/-on, "pure, authentic"; nigt-os/-a/on, "washed clean."

Cryptic Symbolism of the Colors

The zodiacal color code for the constellations is not only in relation to light, heat and sun, but also to textiles and clothing. As we have seen, colors should not only be taken as light effects, but can also represent the social order. Color pigments for paint may be found in minerals and in plants for dyes.

So, thus for each zodiacal cusp there is a corresponding tree and associated color.

In Indo-European worldview, and this is also the case for the Celts, everything was codified to the minute detail. There was, among others, an astrological Ogham, a planetary Ogham, a medical Ogham, and a plaid or tartan Ogham. And as reported by the classical authors, the Celts, who excelled in the art of weaving, were widely known for their colorful textiles. Needless to say that Roman dress styles were much less flamboyant. Since the earliest times, the Gauls were important exporters of woolen, hemp and fine linen fabrics. The "garb of the Gauls" was not as primitive and rude as suggested by the Roman authors in their commentaries. During the cold and wet season, sophisticated Romans found great comfort in Gallic clothing, coats, scarves, capes, breeches and dresses. Judging on textile related jargon, the Roman language is replete with Celtic borrowings. Latin authors mention names of plants and trees for textile dyes having Gallic etymologies. The related textile techniques are corroborated by the surviving Celtic traditions.

Diodorus Siculus in *Library of History,* Book V, notes that "The clothing they wear is striking; shirts which have been dyed and embroidered in varied colors, and breeches, which they call in their tongue bracae; and they wear striped coats, fastened by a buckle on the shoulder, heavy for winter wear and light for summer, in which are set checks, close together and of varied hues."[12]

The *Book of Ballymote* contains the weaving code for the draft of the different weft patterns and ply thickness. The name for plaid pattern, called *breacan* in Gaelic, comes from the Celtic root briccanos for "long pieces or patches." Tartan is from the Norman French tartarin "Tartar cloth," or from tiretaine "strong, coarse fabric."

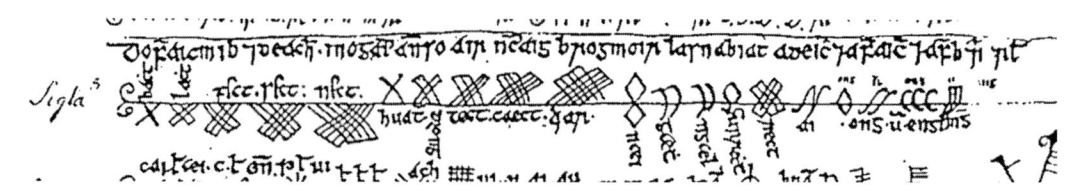

Sigla 5, *Book of Ballymote,* "Do foraicmib 7 deachaib in ogaim andso air na cumai(n)g brogmoir lasna biat a deich 7 a foraicme 7 a forbethi, 7 ri." Of extra groups and syllables of the Ogham here according to the excessive powers whereby there are syllables, extra groups, and extra letters of them, etc.—(the ogham line with syllables): bach, lact, fect, sect, nect, huath, drong, tect, caect, qar, nael (mael?), gaeth, ngael, strmrect, rect, ai, ong, ur, eng, ing.

Etymology and Meaning of the Acronyms

Bach., "breach, violent attack, surprise"; bach < bacos, "beech tree"; baccios "package; baccos, "small";

Lact. < lactos < mlactos, "milk";

Fect. < uecta, "turn"; uectos/uactos, "worse"; uectuon, "work";

Sect. < sect-os/-a/-os, "cut, sectioned";

Nect. < nect-os/-a/-on, "clean, pure, authentic, not mixed";

Huath. < uetes < scuetes < sqetes, "hawthon tree"; uatos, "long; uatos, "prophetic poetry"; uatis, "poet";

Drong. > droing, "people, race, tribe, folk"; drong, "chest, box"; drong-chlann, "soliers"; drong < drungos, "troop of cavalry"; drangos/druagos, "ghost, spectre";

Tect. < tectos, "messenger, the planet Jupiter"; tecto, "possession";

Caect. < cacta, cactos > caxtos, "captive"; cacto, "power"; cacteto, "grip, hold";

Qar. < qarios > coir, "cauldron"; qartis "part, lot, division"; qoriô verb, "to place";

Nael (mael?). < malos < malaios, "promontory, round hill, heap, mull";
Gaeth. < gata, "gust of wind"; gatos, "ray, beem of light"; gaito, "brush"; gaitanos "string, ribbon";
Ngael. < 'n-gel < in-gelu, "in cold torrential water";
Strmrect. < strì, "strife, contention" + -mrect-os/-a/-on, "variegated, spotted; strì, is from the Norse or Anglo-Saxon strið, a probable Celtic root: strta, "heap, hoard, bunch," from strtabrect-os/-a/-on.
Rect. < rectos, "right, rule of law";
Ai., "controversy, cause, region, territory, inheritance of land, possession"; ai sheep"; aiio, "affirmative";
Ong., "tribulation, chastisement, disease, restraint, sorrow; ong, healing"; ong, fire"; onco/oncu, "close, in proximity";
Ur. < uroica, "heath"; ur, "child, person"; ur, "tail, border"; ur, "fire"; ùr < ur-os/-a/-on, "fresh, cool";
Eng. > enig, aing > eiginn, "force violence, difficulty, distress, oppression, necessity"; engsis, "spear";
Ing. > ing, "force, compulsion, stir, neck of land, danger"; inguen, "ointment"; inguina, "finger nail."

What should we make of this group of 20 symbols for sigla 5? There are too many for a 12-sign chart and too few for a doubling of 12. The enigmatic caption preceding the signs informs us that they are in relation to excessive or extra powers: "Of extra groups and syllables of the Ogham here according to the excessive powers whereby there are syllables, extra groups, and extra letters of them, etc."[13] The most logical conclusion is that these sigla represent the decanates. Woven in the warp and weft, there are 10 significators and 10 rulers for each decan.

The Color Ogham from the Book of Ballymote

Virgo: Brown, Reddish Brown and Red (warrior class)
Red and reddish, these are the colors of dusk, dawn and twilight. This constellation, which buckles the ring of the zodiacal belt, marks the end of twilight that and heralds the dawn of the new solar year. The color brown is not only representative of the setting sun and the west, but also agricultural wealth symbolized by the dun bull. The annual sun retreats past the horizon on the Elysian Fields called Emain Ablach in the Irish myths. The apples of the crab apple-tree are eaten by the bay deer while in the elder-tree are perched many birds. The reddening of the setting sun and the dark reddish elder fruits are also associated with red, the color the warrior's class. Red also represents the three fate fairies.

Scorpio: White, spotted and speckled (priestly class)
Ophiuchus and Scorpio were the constellations that marked the beginning of the Celtic New Year. White was for the priestly class, the druid class which included filid poets and bards. It symbolizes brightness, purity, happiness, intelligence and beauty. In ancient times, it symbolized autumn flowers, winter snow and the birch-tree referred

to as the "old lady of the forest." Golden yellow represents wealth and abundance. The White Lady ghost and souls of the dead are on rendezvous for the autumnal celebrations of Samhain.

Sagittarius: Dark, obscure, yellowish and fair (class of artisans and producers)
The hues of dark, black, green or blue are symbolic of the third order guilds, laborers, farmers, artisans and merchants. Variegated, spotted, mottled tan and stripped color patterns express all that is wild, dark, obscure, magical, and occult, linked to Tantric sex and the martial arts. Blackish yellow recalls the shifting colors of dense smoke billowing from wet wood and leaves. Especially, those of the hawthorn or blackthorn trees which should never enter the house or be burning in the hearth. Vine twig is what burns more easily after the harvest. Larch is synonymous with devastation and destruction. The corresponding Gallic month of Sagittarius, Dumanios, was the time of ritual fumigation and thick fogs.

Capricorn: Dark, colorful and iridescent (crafts of the artisans and producers)
Capricorn, the goat-fish, is dark and mottled much like the salmon and trout or the colorful and iridescent as sturgeon. For the British people, this aspect of the dark times is found in the name given to the month in Cornwall as Kervardhu, "frankly dark," and in Brittany as Kerzu, "equally grim." The Gaelic calendar also hinted at this dark period with the "time of wolves." This sign is under influences of the lower world and its sub-aquatic psyche buried deep in dreams and in poetry. During this period, just before Capricorn on the winter solstice, the sun appears to stand still for twelve days on the horizon. The viburnum-tree, opulus, with its red berries is symbolic of the hues of the aurora or break of dawn and the symbol of the beech-tree reminds us that the sun is about to rebirth.

Aquarius: Dark and pale grey (crafts of the artisans and producers)
Aquarius pours its water into the mouth of the Southern Fish constellation. The Gaelic term *leith* (< leitos), which means grey, also connotes moisture. Ash and Rowan are symbolically associated with the moon and the element of water. This is probably due to their diuretic and laxative qualities.

Pisces: Green, Gray and black (crafts of the artisans and producers)
Green, grey and black, are the colors of the third order associated with magic and the occult arts. One of its tree names was the Sessile oak. In Latin, the name *robur* means strength and firmness while *sessile*, from the Latin sessilis, means "on which one can sit," that is to say, sit on the branches. The Old Celtic adjective *deru-os/-a/-on* "true, certain" and *derb-os/-a/-on* for, "hard to work," were the usual puns with deruos, "oak." In Gaulish iconography, the oak-tree represents the springtime rising sun.

Aries: Blue and dark blue (crafts of the artisans and producers)
The Celts did not clearly distinguished blue from green. These two colors were traditionally attributed to the third function and therefore signified fertility, prosperity and abundance. This time is marked by dark skies and heavy cloud cover with rain

showers over a lush and fresh green landscape. The holm oak grows with the undergrowth and scrubs of the woods. Much like oak, its symbolism is linked to the sun and sun light. The ivy-tree, present in winter, clings ever more tightly to cliffs and trees thus blocking off light with its green foliage.

Taurus: Green and verdigris or grey-green (crafts of the artisans and producers)
Giamonios, "germinating, Germinal," was the Gallic name given to this period and which was characterized by shoots and budding. It is obviously under the sign of greening and shoots, of the primeval period for, "prime vernal," that is, springtime. Green is the color representing country-folk, farmers and peasants, therefore, the third social function. Heath is known for its pretty pink or white (and sometimes greenish) flowers. Heather, unlike other types of grassland bushes, retains its nutritional quality all year round, thus making it an excellent fodder crop. From the shoots of the alder-tree, alnus-glutinosa, was extracted many hues of characteristic yellowish or cinnamon-colored dyes and from the bark mixed with iron sulphate a strong black dye.

Gemini: Dark blue and blue-green (crafts of the artisans and producers)
Gemini is the allegory of youth and duality and covers the period of midsummer. At this time of the year, foliage takes on a deep blue-green color while it thickens and darkens the undergrowth. Holly is the only non-coniferous evergreen flowering tree. That is, it is an aquifoliaceae, and the only living genus of that family. Only the female holly bush bears red berries. Phragmite reed or common and other perennial tall grasses are found in wetlands. Reed grows on the edges of rivers, lakes and ponds, in cool, wet soils. It is also used for the manufacture of pan flutes and reeds for musical instruments.

Cancer: Grey and well colored (crafts of the artisans and producers)
The term *sodath* (< sudatios), "good hue, or well tinted," expresses the subtle play of the reflections and shadows of the sun. Sodath is a shifting light color that can take on different amber hues of gold and silver. In the Gallic calendar, the parallel month to this zodiacal sign was Ecuos, under the sign of the horse. Poplar and willow, are rarely found in dense forests and you see them grow in damp places and on the waterfront.

Leo: Ruddy, rusty red and dull red (the warrior class)
The color red highlights this reddening season of plant life. The warrior aspect of this period is marked by battles and commemorations in honor of the king of gods Lugh. Hazel-tree, along with hornbeam, is traditionally associated with magic and innate knowledge. In the tale of Tristan and Isolde, love can only exist unless the hazel-tree can be entwined by honeysuckle. Barberry with its yellow and orange flowers and leaves of different shades is the sentinel of the fields. Its prickly thorns make it an impenetrable barrier appreciated for the formation of defensive hedges.

Virgo: Ultra-white, corn gold and clean colored (the priestly class)
The maiden of Virgo is dressed in pure white. Her lily white and golden appearance identifies her as a member of the class of priests. The golden yellow wheat ears are

signs of prosperity and promise of fertility. Yew, with its toxic and medicinal qualities, is in relation to medicine and war. It's hard and flexible wood was used for making bows and even arrow shafts. Yew, as the maiden was, "the best of creatures." Myrtle was used as pepper in ancient Gallic cuisine. For the Romans, myrtle was seen as one of the symbols of the goddess Venus. In Greece, a myrtle branch was worn by priestesses, candidates for initiation and mystics, in the mystery rites of Eleusis serving in the temple of the goddesses Demeter and Persephone.

Venus, the Morning and Evening Star

Gallic Armorican stater with the pentagram of Venus topped by a horse or mare (Ecuos July/Cancer?). The "horse" name is also found in the Irish Ogham labeled as *ech*. The ech mention is found in association with the sign of Virgo. Drawing by the author.

Venus, the third luminary, was the roving star that marked the passage between night and day, day and night, dusk and dawn, darkness and light. Therefore, given that Venus is the third planet in light intensity, the ancient astronomers sometimes added the planet to the list of the brightest heavenly bodies. The qualities of its vesperal (evening time) light added to the mystery of its dual passages. Venus (Freya in Germanic; Reiia in Celtic) was the queen of the in-between night and day and auroras associated with it. Greek astrologers saw Venus as a double planet: the morning star, Heôsphoros,[14] "the Bearer of Dawn," and the evening star Hesperos, "the Vesperal." The Romans called the morning star Lucifer and the evening star Vesper.

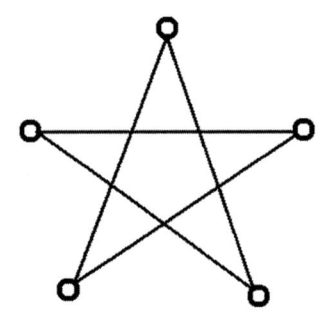

The Venusian pentagram.

The Venus Pentagram

In ancient times, the five-pointed star or pentagram was the symbol given to planet Venus. This number represents the five conjunctions needed for Venus to harmoniously rendezvous earth and the sun on the same day. In the past, there was a time where there was concordance between the five synodic revolutions of Venus and the eight tropical solar years. Henceforth, the symbolism of five for the synodic period of Venus. The cycle of Venus is of eight Earth years and more than thirteen Venusian orbit gives 21. Thus, following the sacred numbers 1, 3, 5, 8, 13, 21, is astrologically associated with Venus. Venus takes 8 years to accomplish a transit. Venus's orbital periods of 224.701 days cover an eight year period when it aligns Earth at the same position before the sun. That is, a Venus transit equals the time it takes Venus to meet Earth in conjunction with the sun. Its associated color was red, for dawn and dusk.

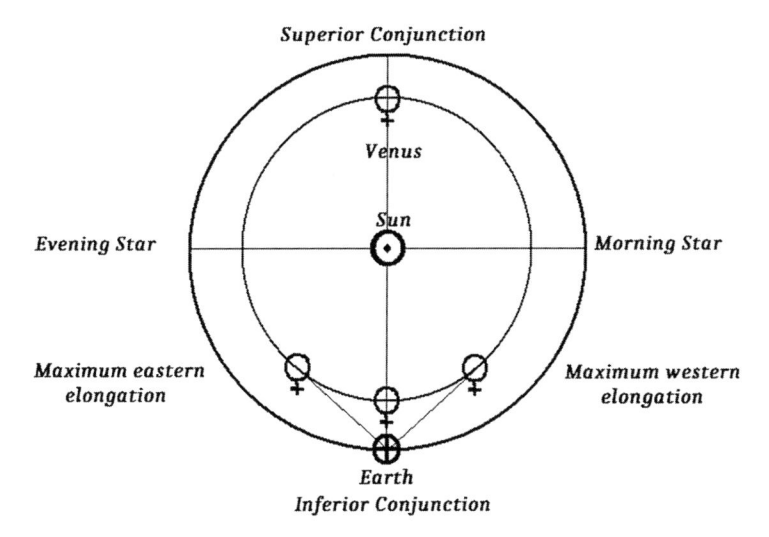

In short, the earth revolves around the sun eight times while Venus performs thirteen revolutions. Eight Earth years of 365 days equal 5 Venusian synodic episodes (365 × 8 years = 2920 and 29.5 days of the lunar cycle also equal 2920 × 99).

V

The Planets

"Seven airs there are, above the astronomer, and three parts the seas.
How they strike on all sides.
How great and wonderful, the world, not of one form, did God make above,
On the planets.
He made Sola, He made Luna, He made Marca and Marcarucia, He made Venus, He made Venerus, He made Severus, And the seventh Saturrnts."
—*Llyfr Taliesin LV, Kanu y Byt Mawr,* Book of Taliesin LV, Song of the Great World

Mars Cocidios figured on an embossed silver plate from Bewcastle, Cumbria, UK. Note the bear-headed warrior carrying a long-bow and holding a shield. Drawing by the author.

The Seven Known Planets of Antiquity

If we are to exclude the two luminaries, namely, the moon and the sun, only five planets were counted in ancient times. These were the observable planets and were then taken for wandering stars. At that time, astronomy was a naked eye science. For many centuries, the Mediterranean peoples, mainly the Greeks, saw Venus as two distinct wandering stars. But then again, some of the star gazing astrologers speculated on the hypothetical existence of additional non-visible outer planets. This was because of the missing count of planets which was in disharmony with the twelve zodiacal houses. Up until William Herschel's discovery in 1781, the existence of Uranus was almost completely ignored. It should be noted however that the ancient astronomers were not completely ignorant of its existence since it was sometimes visible in certain optimal conditions. As to regards of Neptune and Pluto, their discoveries were much more recent and were perfectly unknown to the ancients. Planet Neptune was discovered in 1846 by Le Verrier while Pluto (now regarded as a planetoid) was only sighted in 1930 by Tombaugh. More recently, on June, 2002, astronomers Michael Brown of the California Institute of Technology in Pasadena and Chadwick Trujillo identified a second planetoid orbiting the sun behind Pluto. These observations were confirmed by the powerful Hubble Space Telescope. This object is a small icy planet with a diameter of one-tenth of that of the Earth, about 1.280 km, according to NASA. In 2012, new NASA imagery has shown that Pluto formed with Charon a binary planetoid system with their four orbiting moons: Styx, Nix, Kerberos and Hydra. Subsequently, for the years to come, contemporary astrologers working on the planetoids in the outer solar system will have much more to speculate upon. Thus, in order to give each zodiacal sign a planet, astrologers, following Claudius Ptolemy's example, had to double some of the planets.

Following the Greco-Roman view, the old Welsh poets such as Taliesin maintained that there were seven visible planets.[1] In another of Taliesin's poems, the *Song of the Wind, Book of Taliesin XVII*, there are these verses concerning the seven planets:

> Llucufer the corrupter, like his destitute country
> seven stars there are, of the seven gifts of the Lord.
> The student of the stars knows their substance.
> *Marca mercedus, Ola olimus, Luna lafurus,*
> *Jubiter venerus,* from the sun freely flowing,
> the moon fetches light.

The Barddas adds eight invisible ones:

There are three kinds of stars: fixed stars, which keep their places, and are also called stationary stars; erratic stars, which are called planets, and are fifteen in number, seven being always visible, and eight invisible, except very seldom, because they revolve within and beyond the Galaxy; and the third are irregular stars, which are called comets, and nothing is known of their place, number, and time, nor are they themselves known, except on occasions of chance, and in the course of ages.[2]

From the *Prophecies of Merlin*, a chapter found in Montmouth's *Historia Regum Britaniae* or History of the Kings of Britain, there are more details of what the medieval Welsh understood as "visible," and "invisible," planets.

Visible	The shining sun, the planet Mercury from Arcadia, the helmet of Mars shall call to Venus, Jupiter shall emerge from his established bounds, and the star of Saturn, the chariot of the Moon shall disturb the Zodiac.
Invisible	Adriana[3] (Arianrhod, the Norther Crown) behind a closed door (the Postern) shall seek refuge in her causeways. At a stroke of the wand the winds shall rush forth and the dust of Uentu (Wind) shall blow on us again.

No matter how enigmatic and cryptic these lines may seem, an explanation to what they allude can likewise be found in Welsh mythology. For the great part, the mythological play for this cosmological motif can be found in the fourth portion of Lady Charlotte Guest's *Mabinogion* entitled *Math son of* Mathonwy.[4]

Math, Lord of Gwynedd,[5] loses the service of his foot holder due to the trickery of his nephews Gwydion and Gilfaetwy. Their intrigues lead to the death of Pryderi, lord of Dyfed. Then, Gwydion advises Math to take his sister Arianrod as his new foot holder. With his wand, Math changes Gwydion and Gilfaethwy into deer for one year and for another into wolves or wild dogs. The year after, they resume their original human form. Following this episode, Arianrod steppes over his magic wand after which she gives birth to twins. Then Math discovers that she is not a maiden. The twins were called Dylan Eil Ton[6] and Llew Gyffes.[7] Gwydion[8] manages to conceal Llew in a chest while golden haired Dylan runs off and leaps over a cliff into the sea.

Arianrod, daughter of Don, and sister of Math, resides in a circular castle by the sea. In one of the outer walls is found a door through which passed her servants. The Greek cognate, Ariadne (Arianna in Latin), goddess of Olympus and mistress of the Labyrith, possesses a spinning wheel on which she spindles the thread of fate. The Northern Crown, symbol of elevation, was given to Ariadne by Dionysos as a wedding gift. Arianrod also resided in this constellation. In Merlin's Prophecy, she hides behind a door hoping to take shelter from a powerful wind gust (uentu < uentos < auentos) generated by a magic wand.

Actually, there was a Gallic deity named Duoricos, the "Postern." According to the myths, the gods all have their place in the stars. The Postern was presumably the name of an invisible place, taken esoterically as a celestial "place." The Postern of the four towered fortress was substantially represented by a door in the area of the Northern Crown. This gate opened on Gwyfyd[9] (Celtic Uindobitu) when not, Annwn[10] (Celtic Andumnon), the Underworld. In hermetic Greek cosmology, Cancer was called "the Gate of Mortals." Through it passed the souls of the deceased descending to Earth from Heaven while Capricorn was "the Gate of the Gods," the portal of ascension through which the souls of the departed rose back to Heaven. Consequently, this gate opens to a higher spiritual plane. But then again, the Postern also hints at Astraios, the Greek Titan god of stars, winds, planets and of astrology. His daughter, Astraia, was the star maiden of Virgo. Her other aliases were Kore, "the corn maiden," and Demeter, "goddess of harvests." She is also linked to Taurus (an aspect of the god Jupiter) which the Greek astrologers referred to as Kore's Door, gate to the Underworld.

Astraios's four sons, Euros (east wind), Notos (south wind), Zephyros (west wind) and Boreas (north wind), commanded the winds from the four corners: Krios, the ram star, in Aries, Perses, the dog star (his daughter Hekatethe's dog-star), Sirius in Canis major, and Pallas the goat star, in Capricornus. Henceforth, the Postern probably refers to a dark circle of the sky in Taurus forming the galaxy's anti-center which is marked by the star Elnath, beta Tauri, the constellation's second brightest star. Western astrologers maintain a similar notion with the lunar nodes or black moon. This Welsh concept of Uentu[11] is similar in astrology to the mythic portico of winds of Greek and Roman Antiquity.

Dylan's twin, Llew, acts much like Balarama, Krishna's brother, who also escapes to the sea as a fish in the water. The Welsh Llew is the same as the Irish Lugh and the Gallic Lugus who was compared to the Roman Mercury. Dylan, an alias of the Manx Manawyddan, son of Lyr, is precisely the oceanic Apollo mentioned in Merlin's prophecy. On the Gundestrup Cauldron, we find him depicted as a boy riding on the back of a porpoise (or a sturgeon?). And Manawyddan, before being a solar deity of the sea, was primarily a weather god. Moreover, if Mercury is Lugus, Manawyddan is identifiable to Mars as a storm god. His Gallic name, Nabelcos, "the cloudy," was coincidentally worshipped in the mountains of Vaucluse on Mont Ventoux. Thus, we can safely say that this Celtic god was akin to the Indian Marut gods of winds. Let us add that Manannan is hardly present in the Irish cycles and does not show up at the famous battle of Mag Tured alongside the Tuatha Dé Danann. Not unlike planet Uranus, which comes and goes from sight, Manawydan or Manannan, with his cloak of invisibility, also has this ability.

To conclude, in addition to the generally accepted five or seven planets, ancient astrology included, two lunar nodes prosaically called the Dragon's Head and Dragon's Tail. Finally, if we should consider the Mountain of Winds and the Postern (Kore's Door ruled by Astraios, god of dusk and stars), the count is now of eleven planetary sojourns. And then, if we should include Uranus (Manannan/Manawyddan?), which is often invisible, this yields five invisible plus seven visible planets for a total count of twelve entries.

Planetary Names in the Book of Ballymote

I once asked Joseph Monard if he had a complete list of the Old Celtic names for the traditionally known planets and the answer was that apart from the two luminaries and planets Venus and Saturn, there were no certain denominations. Therefore, finding the other astronyms was shear speculation. Then I submitted him a list of acronyms found in the *Book of Ballymote* which I suspected were abbreviated captions for planetary symbols. At first he was skeptical, but upon closer examination he found that the captions did express planetary designations. Monard was very surprised to find the *tuct* name for Jupiter since it was a garbled rendering of the Old Irish *tect*, stemming from the root *tectos*, "messenger," and attested in earlier Gaulish. Now we were certain that we had found the Old Irish names for the planets.

Planetary names from the *Book of Ballymote*, Ireland

☽	Moon
Goac	Mars
|||	Sun
Tuct	Jupiter
Lct	Mercury
Rii	Venus
Milni/N. Uih	Saturn
Lth	Southern lunar Node (Dragon's tail)
Ean < (C)ean	Northern lunar Node (Dragon's head)

Celtic Etymology of the Gaelic Names from the *Book of Ballymote*

The **Moon** is not named and is represented by the crescent known in Old Irish as Éasca < Eidsciia, "in phases," and one of names for the moon.

Mars, Goac < Coccos, "the red."

Sun, represented by three rays for Greina, "radiant, bright, sunny," the deified Sun (in its feminine aspects). These are the three solar rays thrown by Jupiter to feed the fires of Mars, Mercury and Venus. All in all, there were seven bolts or cosmic rays in number.

Jupiter, Tuct/Tech < Tectos, "messenger, envoy," also for "planet," that is, a wandering star.

Mercury, Luct < Luctos/Luxtos "bright, assembly, gathering, troop, party, burden"; Luxstos "wanderer," for, "bright wandering (star)."

Venus, Rii < Riia/Reia/Reiia, the old common Celtic name for the planet, connoting, "free star, or lofty star," which is the same as for the Germanic Freya.

Saturn, Milni < Melnos, "slow, indolent (long-termed)," because of its long planetary revolution.

Also, N. < Nucturos, "nocturnal," and Uih < Uosiros, "laggard, straggler (extending)."

South Lunar Node, Lth < Losta/Losto, "tail," for Losto Ambeios, "dragon's tail," and Ean, hinting at the lunar north node, Cean < Qennos Ambeios, "dragon's head."

Or maybe connoting **Uranus** here called Ean < Eno/Ono, "liquid," or perhaps Ona/Ono, "Water," in wordplay with Etnos "bird?" Then again, Oinos from, "ean," corresponds very well to the changing element of the "Oceanic Mercury" who had the gift of ubiquity. In this case, ean-, from the Celtic root, ennodios, "temporary," could, along with other sets of possible connoting words, be ennos < uennos for, "cart vehicle," and endion for, "end, limit." All these speculative terms hint at Uranus since the planet occasionally appears shifting on and off. In light of this, Uranus is but a twin aspect of Mercury in that it recalls Venus's dual aspect. In short, the nodes have sinister Mercury-like and a Mars-like qualities reflected and mirrored by Uranus.

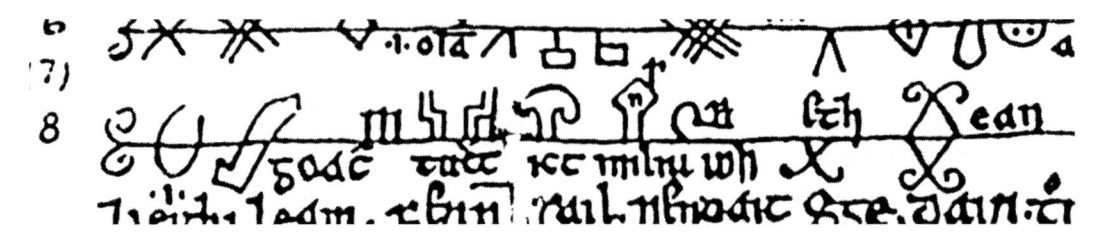

Symbols and acronyms for the Gaelic planet names, detail from the *Book of Ballymote*, an Irish manuscript dating from the 1300s.

Names of Planets in Old Celtic

The Welsh names *planed* and *blaned*, Breton planedenn and Gaelic *planaid* for "planet," are all from the Latin term *planeta* borrowed from the Greek *planetes*, "wanderer," and deriving from *asteres planetai*, "wandering stars" (from the verb *planasthai*, "to wander"). The question that comes to mind is what was the original Celtic name?

The Old Celtic name for "planet," in all likelihood, was also linked to the notion of "vagabond, wandering or roving star." Therefore, for the Indo-Europeans, the planets were stars that move. From the *Book of Ballymote*, we know that *tuct* or *tect* was the Old Irish name for Jupiter meaning, "traveler," and that luct connotes "wanderer," both these were analogous to the Greek name. Because of their apparent motion, it was normal that they were designated as such. Compared to bulky Jupiter advancing briskly, Mars is a lightweight runner and Saturn is a slow poke. Or as Joseph Monard wrote: "The apparent motion of the outer planets, such as Mars, Jupiter and Saturn, seemed all too confusing to the naked eye observer as they skipped to and fro, from east to west, periodically interrupted in their progress by episodic regressions. These backwards motions were enough to catch the attention of the observer. The Greeks tentatively explained this phenomenon by coining the term 'epicycloids.'"[12] The other attested Celtic name for planet was *seruons*, also meaning, "vagabond," yielding *seruonta retla*, or in one word *seruoretla* for, "wandering star."[13]

Comparison of Modern Celtic Names for the Planets Borrowed from Latin

English	Welsh	Breton	Gaelic	Latin
Moon	Lloer	Loar	Gealach	Luna
Sun	Haul	Heol	Grian	Sol
Mars	Maurth	Meurzh	Mhàirt	Mars
Jupiter	Iau	Yaou	Joib	Jupiter, Jovis
Mercury	Mercher	Merc'her	Mercuir	Mercurius
Venus	Gwener	Gwener	Uenir	Venus
Saturn	Sadwrn	Sadorn	Sartharn	Saturnus

The Welsh bard-poet Taliesin lists the seven anciently known planets accordingly: in addition to the luminaries, Sun and Moon, there is Mars, Mercury, Venus, Jupiter and Saturn. He also describes them as worlds: "seven worlds above the astrologer's head." And because of the observer's geocentric point of view, the Earth was never included in the list of planets and never treated as such.

THE OLD CELTIC NAMES FOR THE PLANETS

The Luminaries

Sun	Belinos, the Sun deified; Grannos (m), Greina (f), Sauelios (m), Sauelia (f), Sonnos (m), Sonna (f).
Moon	Deiouona/Diuona, the Moon as a goddess; Diuon (n), Luxna > Luana Gdl (=Goidelic), Eidscos (m), Esciion (n), Leucara (f), Gelacos (m).

The Wandering Stars or Planets

Mars	Cocidios, Mars deified; Coccos
Mercury	Lugus, Mercury deified; Luxtos, Boudios, Boduos
Venus	Riia
Jupiter	Taranis, Jupiter deified; Tectos
Saturn	Arualos, Saturn deified; Melnos, Nucturos Uosiros

Irish Medieval Order of the Planets from the *Book of Ballymote*:
Moon, Mars, Sun, Jupiter, Mercury, Venus, Saturn.

The Welsh Medieval Order of the Planets from Taliesin:
Sun, Moon, Mars, Mercury, Venus, Jupiter, Saturn.

The Gallic Godly Order after Julius Caesar in his *War Commentaries*:
Mercury, Sun, Mars, Jupiter, Venus (Moon or Saturn?).

The Order of Planets According to Vedic Literature:
Sun, Moon, Mars, Mercury, Jupiter, Venus, Saturn.

The planets were imagined by the ancient Indo-Europeans as heavenly bodies emitting light. Indeed, Deiuos, light and Deuos deified god, have the same common etymology as deiuo-, diuo-, "lightly, light emitting." The gods are therefore conscious and dynamic light manifestations.

The Ages of Life and the Revolutions of the Planets

The wandering stars visit their astral homes in varying time cycles. Since the microcosm reflects macrocosm, each planetary cycle corresponds to the seven ages of the world, the ages of the gods and those of the mortals. The seven ages of man thus correspond to the planets starting with the moon and ending with Saturn. Obviously, the periods allotted to the planets in astrology do not correspond to those of science. These periods or ages are essentially mythological and therefore should be taken as purely symbolic.

AIUITATE—the Ages of Life	Ruling Planet	In Number of Life Years
1. Brita (Brt [=Brythonic])/ Gnatutaxeto > nàidendacht (Gaelic) "birth"	Moon	0–1
2. Mapia (Brt)/ Maqotaxeto < macdacht (Gdl) "childhood"	Mars	1–7
3. Iouintica (Brt) "youth"/Geistlaxto < gillacht (Gaelic) "later childhood, adolescence"	Sun	7–21
4. Aesacos/hoclachus (Gdl) "adulthood"	Jupiter	21–49
5. Adbiutio "maturity"/ Senodageto < sendacht (Gaelic) "seniority"	Mercury	49–56
6. Anbiutio/diblidecht (Gaelic borrowing from Latin) "debility, decrepitude"	Venus	56–77
7. Duniobatus "time of death, mortality"	Saturn	—

The Planetary Revolutions

The planets do not all take the same time to complete a turn of the Zodiac from one house to another. As mentioned, it is obvious from the perspective of the observer, which is an essentially geocentric, these movements are only apparent.

- The sun tours the 12 zodiacal constellations in one year (365.2422 days).
- The moon swings around the earth in roughly 28 nights, 27 days and 43 minutes and a few seconds.
- Mars takes 320 days to appear again in the same Zodiac sign. A Martian revolution is of 1 year and 881 days.
- Jupiter takes 10 years and 315 days to go around the Zodiac and its revolution around the sun is of 11 years and 860 days.
- Mercury is always found in the company of the sun, moving from the side to the front, is never away from it more than an astral sign. Its revolution around the sun takes less than a year of 241 terrestrial days.
- Venus literally dances before the sun and never moves away from it more than two signs to each side. It accomplishes its revolution in 615 days.
- Saturn makes its round of the Zodiac in 28 years and 168 nights and its revolution is of 29 years and 460 days.

Iconic symbolism of Mercury's ram horns. Drawing by the author.

In Vedic astrology, a world *loka* generally refers more specifically to a region of the sky, of the cosmos, of the earth, of the sky, or the atmosphere or the lower regions. These sites are designated as follows: earth, sky, the firmament, the middle region, the place of rebirth, the abode of the blessed and the place of truth. The Lokas include seven worlds: Bhu-loka, the earth Bhuvar-loka, space between the earth and the sun inhabited by spirits or gods, the siddhas and the like; Svar-loka, the heaven of Indra above or between the sun, or the space between the sun and the North Star; Mahar-loka, the region above the North Star inhabited by Bhrigo and other wise men who survived the destruction of the last three lower worlds; Janar-loka, a place inhabited by the four Kumara, the sons of Brahma, including Sanat Kumara, and others; Tapar-loka, inhabited by the deified Vairagins and finally Satya-loka or Brahma-loka, the abode of Brahma.

The Gallic Venus Reiia as depicted on a coin minted for Tasciovanus, king of the British Catuvellauni. Drawing by the author.

VI

The Stars

"I have been a twinkling star. I have been a word among letters, I have been a book in the origin. I have been the light of lanterns, a year and a half."—Taliesin, *Taliesin Llyfr VIII Cad Goddeu*, "The Battle of Trees

Naiad nymphs with pouring pots. Above the arch are figured the three stars of Andromeda. The main star of Andromeda is located diagonally across the square of Pegasus which also groups: Alpheratz (alpha star of Pegasus), Mirach (Beta Andromeda) and Almach (gamma Andromeda). Author's drawing from a photograph taken under the joint auspices of the Museum of Antiquities, the Society of Antiquaries and the University of Newcastle upon Tyne.

The Constellations

An Irish manuscript of the Renaissance (circa 1500–1550) called *Ranna an Aeir*, "The Divisions of the Sky," describes the main constellations. It is a late manuscript, giving the names of the stars and describing the astral themes taught in classical astrology. Basically, it is an Irish interpretation of late Roman Ptolemaic astrology. Here is an excerpt of what is found in the *Ranna an Aeir*:

It is enquired here how many constellations are in the sky, in both southern and northern hemispheres. Easily told: thirteen constellations in the (northern), and eight in the (southern) hemisphere. And these are their names. Of the constellations of the southern hemisphere: Idurus, Canicula, Lepus, Eridanus, Cetus, Centaurus, Argo, Pisces, Ara. Of the constellations of the northern hemisphere: Septentriones, Draco, Arcturus which was called Bootes, Corona, Hercules which was called Nixus or Engonasin, Libra, Cygnus, Serpens, Cassiopeia, Perseus, Delaton, Eniochus, Andromeda, Pegasus, Ophiuchus, Delphinus, Aquila.[1]

Celtic Astronomy, Stellar Denominations

What we presently have on the astral knowledge of the ancient pre–Christian Celts is very limited. Most of it is fragmentary and partially evoked by the classical Greek and Roman commentators. Some of it was also leaked by Medieval Latin, Welsh and Irish authors and is principally found in the legendary and bardic corpuses. Some other bits of information were collected from the oral traditions. Star lore is maintained mostly by seafarers and farmers. To better chart the skies, astronomers divided the sky into four sectors arranged according to the seasons: North, South, East and West. Taliesin called these sections, "regions of the stars," that were, the realms of the stars of spring, the stars of summer, the stars of fall and the winter stars. Stars differ from the other heavenly bodies such as planets, comets and meteors, in that they are apparently stationary and do not move in the sky.... Not unlike crystals, they simply twinkle!

Ptolemy, in the *Almagest, Book 1, chapter 2, On the Order of Theorems*, thus describes the sky's geography in relation to the fixed stars:

> Those things having to do with the sphere of what are called the fixed stars would reasonably come first, and then those having to do with what are called the five planets. And we shall try and show each of these things using as beginnings and foundations for what we wish to find, the evident and certain appearances from the observations of the ancients and our own, and applying the consequences of these conceptions by means of geometrical demonstrations. And so, in general, we have to state that the heavens are spherical and move spherically; that the earth, in figure, is sensibly spherical also when taken as a whole; in position, lies right in the middle of the heavens, like a geometrical center; in magnitude and distance, has the ratio of a point with respect to the sphere of the fixed stars, having itself no local motion at all. And we shall go through each of these points briefly to bring them to mind.[2]

Not surprisingly, it is from the oral traditions of the various Celtic peoples that most of the star-lore is to be found. From early Welsh literature, the Hanes Taliesin, is a good source and in latter writing, comprehensive lists are found in the highly contested Barddas published by John Williams. Then, there are a few indications found in ancient Celtic epigraphy and numismatics such as the names: Nemoratta, "the celestial fortune, grace," Sirona or Dirona, "the stellar," Smertus, "the sword," (nowadays called Deneb, alpha star of Cygnus) Andarta/Andastra, "the super bear" (the Big Dipper), Artulla, "the Little Bear," and Artaios, "the Bear keeper or Bear-like," (Arcturus, alpha star of Bootes). These are corroborated by mythonyms found in medieval Irish literature: Starn and Nemanach.[3] Moreover, the remaining data has to be collected from the classical texts.

THE CONSTELLATIONS AND STARS FROM *THE BARDDAS*[4]

(1) Caer Arianrod, "the Circle of Arianrod";
(2) Yr Orsedd Wenn, "the White Throne";

VI: The Stars

(3) Telyn Arthur, "Arthur's Harp";
(4) Caer Gwydion, "the Circle of Gwydion";
(5) Yr Hotel Fawr, "the Great Plough-tail";
(6) Haeddel Fach yr, "the Small Plough-tail";
(7) Y Llong Fawr, "the Great Ship";
(8) Y Llong Foel, "the Bald Ship";
(9) Y Llatheidan, "the Yard";
(10) Y Twr Tewdws, "Theodosius's Group";
(11) Y Tryfelan, "the Triangle";
(12) Llys Don, "the Palace of Don";
(13) Llwyn Blodeuwedd, "the Grove of Blodeuwedd";
(14) Cadair Teyrnon, "the Chair of Teyrnon";
(15) Caer Eiddionydd, "the Circle of Eiddionydd";
(16) Caer Sidi, "the Circle of Sidi";
(17) Cwlwm Cancaer, "the Conjunction of the Hundred Circles";
(18) Lluest Elmur, "the Camp of Elmur";
(19) Bwa 'r Milwr, "the Soldier's Bow";
(20) Brynn Dinan, "the Hill of Dinan";
(21) Nyth yr Eryres, "the Hen-Eagle's Nest";
(22) Trosol Bleiddyd, "Bleiddyd's Lever";
(23) Gwynt y Asgell, "the Wind's Wings";
(24) Y Feillionen, "the Trefoil";
(25) Pair Caridwen, "the Cauldron of Ceridwen";
(26) Dolen Teifi, "Teivi's Bend";
(27) Yr Esgair Fawr, "the Great Limb";
(28) Yr Esgair Fechan "the Small Limb";
(29) Yr Ychen Bannog, "the Large-horned Oxen";
(30) Y Maes Mawr, "the Great Plain";
(31) Y Fforch Wenn, "the White Fork";
(32) Baedd Y Coed, "the Woodland Boar";
(33) Llywethan, "the Muscle";
(34) Yr Hebog, "the Hawk";
(35) March Llyr, "the Horse of Llyr";
(36) Cadair Elffin, "Elffin's chair";
(37) Neuadd Olwen, "Olwen's Hall."

Short Commentary on the Welsh Names:

(1) Caer Arianrod, the Circle of Arianrod (Northern Crown);
(2) Yr Orsedd Wenn, the White Throne or White Chair (Cassiopea);
(3) Telyn Arthur, the Harp of Arthur (Lyra);
(4) Caer Gwydion, Gwydion's Circle (Milky Way or Galaxy), Gwydion fab Dôn, and a nephew of Llew Llaw Gyffes and son of Don. He was one of three mystical astronomers of the island of Britain, whose name was given to this Galaxy.

(5) Yr Haeddel fawr, the Great Plow-tail (Big Dipper);
(6) Haeddel fach yr, the Small Plow-tail (Little Dipper);
(7) Y Llong fawr, the Great Ship (Navis);
(8) Y Llong foel, bald ship (Argo and Navis);
(9) Y Llatheidan, the Yard or Court (Orion);
(10) Y Twr Tewdws, the group of Theodosius (Pleiades); (Theodosius (347–395 CE) was the Roman emperor who destroyed ancient paganism in favor of Christianity. Therefore, this cannot be the old name for this constellation.
(11) Y Tryfelan, the Triangle (Triangulum);
(12) Llys Don, Don's palace (Cassiopeia);
(13) Llwyn Blodeuwedd, the Grove or Glade of Blodeuwedd (Coma Berenice); Blodeuwedd, the blossom maiden was Llew's wife.
(14) Cadair Teyrnon the chair of Teyrnon (Capella); From the Old Celtic Tigernonos "of the lord." Teyrnon Twryf Lliant was lord of Gwent and Pryderi's foster-father.
(15) Caer Eiddionydd, the Circle of Eiddionydd (?); Eiddionydd is a region of Caernarvonshire commonly called Eifionydd.
(16) Caer Sidi, the circle of Sidi (the Zodiac or Ecliptic);
(17) Cwlwm Cancaer, the Conjunction of the Hundred Circles (?); probably in reference a Welsh territorial unit composed of a hundred trefs. Tref, from Celtic trebon, "homestead, village."
(18) Lluest Elmur, Camp of Elmur (?); Elmur ap Cibddar with Cynhavel ap Argad and Avaon ap Taliesin is one of the three chief Bards of the Isle of Britain.
(19) Bwa'r Milwr, the soldier's bow (Sagitta);
(20) Brynn Dinan, Dinan Hill; Probably the present city of Dinan in Brittany, resulting from the contraction of two Celtic words Din-an(a), from Dunos, and Ana for "Ana's hill," in Old Celtic. Ana is one of Don's names as the protective mother-goddess and guardian of the gods and mortals of Brythonic mythology. The first written testimony to the existence of the city goes back to the eleventh century after the defeat of the lords of Dinan, the Dinantes, shown on the Bayeux Tapestry. Despite of this event, due to its strategic location above the valley of the Rance, its population prospered.
(21) Nyth yr Eryres, the Nest of the Hen-Eagle (Aquila);
(22) Trosol Bleiddyd, lever Bleiddyd (Lupus); Bleiddyd < Bediatis, "the wolf chaser." Bleiddyd son of Meirion or Bladud was the son of Lud Hudibras, mythical king of Great Britain (d. 269 BC to AD) and legendary founder of the city of Bath? Or the son of Bleiddyd, King Llyr of Shakespeare.
(23) Gwynt y Asgell, the Wings of the Wind (?);
(24) Y Feillionen, the Trefoil or Clover (a cluster of Aquarius);
(25) Pair Caridwen, the Cauldron of Ceridwen (Crater);
(26) Dolen Teifi, Teivi's Bend or Meander (Eridanus); Teifi or Teivi (< Tuerobios, "having the appearance of peat, turf-like") is the name of a river of Wales which takes its source in the Cambrian Mountains Other courses have similar names. Taff and Tawe.
(27) Yr Esgair Fawr, the Great Limb, a major or branch of the Milky Way (?);

(28) Yr Esgair Fechan, Small Limb, a branch or twig of the Milky Way (?);
(29) Yr Ychen Bannog, the Long-horned Oxen (Gemini);
(30) Y Maes Mawr, the Great Plain (Zodiac);
(31) Y fforch wenn, the White Fork (Taurus intersecting with the Milky Way);
(32) Baedd Y Coed, the Woodland Boar (Polaris, Ursa Minor);
(33) Llywethan, the muscle (Hydra), or Leviathan (?) Leviathan is from the Hebrew: livyathan (late Latin leviathan) meaning, "dragon, serpent, huge sea animal, sea monster or sea serpent," and regarded in Christian lore as a manifestation of Satan.
(34) Yr Hebog, the Hawk (Altair);
(35) March Llyr, the Horse of Llyr (Pegasus);
(36) Cadair Elffin, the chair of Elffin; a character mentioned in the Book of Taliesin. It was he who found the wonderous child poet.
(37) Neuadd Olwen, Olwen the Palace (Hare). Olwen, "the White Trace," was Yspaddaden Penkawr's daughter.

As evidenced by several of the names and expressions, the nomenclature in this list is not very old and dates no earlier than the late the Middle Age and Tudor period. Furthermore, if some of these are mythological, they do not seem to go back to earlier than the bardic era (ca. 600 to 700 CE) of the *Arthurian cycles*. That is, that these names are more or less in agreement with the older attested Gallic and Gaelic ones.

In former times, great importance was given to the stars and their names were often, if not always, in accord with their appearance, luster, fixity or apparent motions. In light of this, names changed along with beliefs. Henceforth, the old faith was outranked by the new one and the old names were dropped or replaced for others. Also, the occurrence and observation of new stars or wandering stars was interpreted as a good or bad omen. Most often the passing of a comet was seen a sign of bad luck therefore announcing disasters, pestilences, wars and famines.

The Attested and Hypothesized Celtic Astronomical Nomenclature for the Stars, Comets and Meteors

The Fixed Stars

The word star comes from the Old English steorra which is from the Proto-Germanic root sterron, or sternon. Likewise, the Latin word *stella* is at the root of words such as stellar and constellation. The Welsh seren and Breton sterenn are of the same Proto-Indo-European root reconstructed as aster- > ster-, which also gave other cognates such as Sanskrit star-, English star, and German stern. Thus, from ster- derive the Sanskrit *tara*, the Old Germanic *sternon* and the Old Celtic sdira > ðira/sira. In Goidelic there were two other names to distinguish stars: rendu (connoting *renda* "bunch, measure"), a star cluster, and retla (*reta* "wheel"), a disk-shaped star. These names were combined to designate the other celestial bodies such as comets and falling stars. These many terms show how sharply the Indo-European astronomers had observed the skies. From Vedic astrology, the Sanskrit term *dyotis* > jyotis is of the same etymology as the Celtic root diu-os/-a/-on and diuan-os/-a/-on for "light emitting, luminous." Hence, the Sanskrit name *jyotirjia* for "astronomer or star knower."

Shooting Stars

In classical Roman astronomy, the other category of wandering stars, known as comets or meteors, were called *stellae comans,* or "hairy stars." The Sanskrit term *Ketu* refers to any curious celestial object such as comets, meteorites and the southern lunar node. The term comet comes from the Greek *kômêtes* for "hairy." The Celts called comets "star tails." There were many variations of the name from one Celtic region to another: combondna ðira, lostoca ðira, ersaballaca retla and retla con ersaballu. There were also other designations such as: loscontia ðira, "smoldering star," scarbaca retla, "ragged star," seqorétana retla, "wandering star," mongaca retla, "star mane," and dregia "trace." In Old Celtic, a hairy star was called Cnabetica ðira or Cnabetioðira. The terms meteor and meteorite come from the Greek Meteora, meaning, "something high up in the air." The Celts also had many names for these: biua ðira, "live star," ðira redona or redona retla, "running star," and coris tenni, "circle of fire." In Antiquity, the first scientific speculation on the nature of comets was given by Aristotle in his *Meteorologica*:

> Let us go on to explain the nature of comets and the "milky way," after a preliminary discussion of the views of others. Anaxagoras and Democritus declare that comets are a conjunction of the planets approaching one another and so appearing to touch one another.
>
> Some of the Italians called Pythagoreans say that the comet is one of the planets, but that it appears at great intervals of time and only rises a little above the horizon. This is the case with Mercury too; because it only rises a little above the horizon it often fails to be seen and consequently appears at great intervals of time. A view like theirs was also expressed by Hippocrates of Chios and his pupil Aeschylus. Only they say that the tail does not belong to the comet itself, but is occasionally assumed by it on its course in certain situations, when our sight is reflected to the sun from the moisture attracted by the comet. [...]
>
> This is the case, first, with those who say that the comet is one of the planets. For all the planets appear in the circle of the Zodiac, whereas many comets have been seen outside that circle. Again more comets than one have often appeared simultaneously. Besides, if their tail is due to reflection, as Aeschylus and Hippocrates say, this planet ought sometimes to be visible without a tail since, as they it does not possess a tail in every place in which it appears. But, as a matter of fact, no planet has been observed besides the five. [...]
>
> An objection that tells equally against those who hold this theory and those who say that comets are a coalescence of the planets is, first, the fact that some of the fixed stars too get a tail. For this we must not only accept the authority of the Egyptians who assert it, but we have ourselves observed the fact.[5]

According to another of Aristotle's speculations, Seneca linking comets with wandering stars or planets, also speculated on the nature and frequency of their trajectories:

> Apollonius of Myndus differs in his view from Epigenes. He asserts that a comet is not one star made up of many planets, but that many comets are planetary. A comet, he goes on, is not an illusion nor a trail of fire produced on the borders of two stars, but is a distinctive heavenly body, just as the sun or the moon is. Its shape is not limited to the round, but is somewhat extended and produced lengthwise. On the other hand its orbit is not visible. It cuts the upper part of the universe, but only emerges when at length it reaches the lowest portion of its course. There is no reason to suppose that the same comet reappears; for instance that the one seen in the reign of Claudius was the same as the one we saw in the reign of Augustus; or that the recent one which appeared during the reign of Nero Caesar which has redeemed comets from their bad character was similar to the one which burst out after the death of the late Emperor Julius Caesar, about sunset on the day of the games to Venus Genetrix. Comets are as varied as they are numerous. They are unequal in size, unlike in color. Some are ruddy without any light; others are bright with a pure clear light; others are flame-colored, but the flame is not a pure thin flame, but is

VI: The Stars

enveloped in a mass of smoky fire. Some are blood-stained and threatening, bringing prognostication of bloodshed to follow in their train. They wax and wane like other planets. They are brighter when they come down toward us, and show larger from a nearer point, smaller when they depart from us, and dimmer when they retire to a greater distance.[6]

Concerning the trajectories of comets, for example, Halley's Comet visits us every 75 years as it once did in ancient times. In July 44 BCE, it was visible for seven days during the month dedicated to the great Julius. Normally, the appearance of such a comet is taken for a bad omen. For this event, it was decided that it announced the end of the tenth legendary age of Rome. The comet's passing was seen as a sign for the divinity of the Caesars that was subsequently claimed for Augustus, Caesar's step-son, in order to sanction his power over Rome.

"The Cauldron of Plenty" in which flows from the source of the heavenly waters. La Tène Art, of the third or second century BCE. Detail from an engraved weight scale. Author's drawing from a photograph by Lessing-Contrasto.

The Milky Way

Since the earliest times, the Milky Way was seen as a patch of white light, a bright trail, or path taken by celestial beings, elevated sages, dead heroes and gods. This cosmic view was well attested in Greek and Sanskrit vocabulary. However, the Celtic terminology is less known. Our word for the galaxy is from the Latin *galaxias* which was borrowed from the Greek, γαλαξίας, literally for: "Milky One." Sanskrit is quite evocative with its rich vocabulary: *Devapatha*, "the path of the gods," *Svargapatha*, "the way of heaven," *Somadhara*, "support of Soma," and *Nabhahsarit*, "the river of heaven." But then again, the Celtic expressions were no less suggestive than these.

Gaelic terminology abounds in similar imagery: Bealach na bó finne,[7] "crossing the white cow," Slighe bhainneach,[8] "the Milky Way," and sleigh clan Uisnech, "the way of the son of Uisnech."[9] And on the Brythonic side, we have: Hynt or Caer Gwydion,[10] "Gwydion's pathway," Llwybr Llaethog, "milky track," Hent an neñvou and Hent ar stered, "pathway to heaven" and "path of the stars," respectively.[11] Gwydion and Uisnech are interesting names in that they bring us back to the oldest Indo-European roots.

The mythic theme for the Milky Way went as follows: According to ancient belief, this divine path in the night sky was taken by the gods and the great sages on their way to the northern stars above. For example, the Welsh term Gwydion comes from the Celtic root-word uid-on/-ona/-ons for, "knowing, and understanding." It is also the name of the god Welsh god Gwydion, son of Beli and Dôn, the heavenly pair. He is the brother of Gilvaethwy,[12] the embodiment of the light principle. As for the Gaelic name Uisnech, the idea of elevation is here expressed. The Hill Uisnech or Uisneach[13] was formerly Balor's Hill and was considered as the Omphalos, the navel or center of Ireland. In this place was found the stone of Aill na Mirenn which marked the limits of the four provinces. Usnach, Usnagh or Uisliu[14] is etymologically linked to Uxouinos, the Gallic god of high places. The god-hero Usnach had a wife called Ebhla,[15] a daughter of the Druid Cathbad.[16] The sons of Usnach and Ebhla were three in number and were exiled warrior-heroes. If we go even further back in time, the Uxonacoi were the souls of the heroes on their way to the northern stars.

Another interesting mythological theme is that of the white cow and the Milky Way. The River Boyne in Ireland, like the mythical and mystical Saraswati River of India, was the embodiment of the great goddess. The name Boyne or Boand is reminiscent of the Indian cow-herder god Govinda but does not exactly share in the same meaning. The Celtic Boand is from bou-inda meaning, "ultimate cow," connoting bou-uinda, "the white cow," while Govinda is from go-, "cow," and vinda, "find." Although these root stems are paronymous, the suffixes are of different etymologies. This myth explains that Boand, while bathing in the pool of Segais, causes it to overflow, henceforth flooding the entire valley. The great or white cow was one the archaic Indo-European symbols of light and day. The Milky Way was said to be crossed by the "herds of Dawn" at the fords intersected by the ecliptic. Celtic cosmology maintained this arcane representation with great detail. The Athoi, or "fords," are bright spots intersecting the Milky Way at certain points on the ecliptic. Irish mythology often refers to them. Here are the best known:

> **The Ford of Sagittarius:** Ath Mor < Maros Athos, the "big ford";
> **The North Ford of the Ecliptic:** At Mhadra Alta < Athos Allti Madri, the "ford of the wild dog or wolf";
> **The Ford South of the Ecliptic:** Ath Brassail < Brassellos Athos, the "very broad ford";
> **The Ford of Taurus:** Ath Gabla < Athos Gabulas, the "ford of the fork"; Ath Grenca < Athos Granacos, the "gravel ford";
> **The Ford of Cassiopeia:** At Mhedbha < Athos Meduas, the "ford of Medb."

The North Star

Alpha Ursa Minoris is the present star of first magnitude in the Little Dipper constellation. In the early period of star reckoning, the Pole star was in Cepheus. This Cepheus pole star, Alderamin (Alpha Cephei), will again return to the north position in the year 7500. But from 2830 to 2700 BCE, the Pole star was Thuban, the alpha star of the Dragon. Then, around 1793 BCE, Thuban moved to the north of theta Boötis, "the clamorous, or ox driver." Arcturus, alpha Boötis, was then called Artaios, "the Bear-keeper or watcher," in Gaul. Artaios was an alias of the god Lugus assimilated to Mercury by the Romans.

Therefore, Polaris was not the Pole star in Antiquity more than two thousand years ago. In 2000 BCE, the North Pole was marked by the alpha star of the Dragon. It was called *Dhruva tāra*, the "Firm Star," in Sanskrit. The Old Celtic form could have been *Drua ðira*, but from what can be surmised from the Gundestrup Cauldron, it was probably called Druuios, "the Wren." The Greeks called the Little Dipper *Arcas* or *Cynosūra*, "the dog's tail." Jupiter placed Arcas there and dislodged the old Polar Star Hera. The Old Norse name for it was *leiðarstjarna*, for "guiding star." The top of the sky was perceived by the Celts as the pinnacle of the world tree called Bile Medba[17] where the Wren perched.

Polaris (Little Plough-tail or Little Dipper) was called Eburos, the Boar, in Old Celtic. The following image is a representation of the bear watcher (seen as a boar) on a coin from the third century BCE.

Gallic coin. Author's drawing from a photograph by Erich Lessing, National Museum of Budapest.

Stars and Asterisms of the Zodiacal Band

Libra

Alpha Librae, Zuben Elgenubi, "South claw of the scorpion," and beta Librae Zuben Eschamali, the "northern claw of the scorpion."

Old Celtic, Sidos or Caruos, for "deer," and Gallic Cantlos, meaning "looping, buckling" and by connotation, Cantalon, "memorial pillar."

The ancient Deer constellation comprised of the constellations of Libra, Ophiuchus and Scorpio. The other modern Celtic names for these constellations and their asterisms were all modelled on Latin nomenclature.

Scorpio

Alpha Scorpii, Antares.
Celtic, Sidos/Caruos, "deer," as a region of the sky; Gallic Samonios, "the Sower."
Antares, a red giant, is the brightest star in Scorpio.
Its modern name comes from the Greek anti–Ares, that is, anti–Mars. In May, it

is very visible on the horizon when it dips under it in conjunction with the passage of the moon in the east.

Sagittarius

Alpha Sagittarii, Rucba; Gamma Sagittarii, Alnasl.

Gallic, Dumannios, "the Darkening" or Dumannos, the "dark horse"; Breton Gwareger < Uarcustos, "archer"; Boghadair in Gaelic and in Manx Gaelic, Boogheyder < Bogdarios, the "archer."

Sagitta, the Arrow Asterism

Alpha Sagittae, Sham.
An asterism of the constellation Sagittarius.
Breton Birrêc < Beruacos, the "arrow"; Welsh Bwa'r Milwr, the "soldier's bow."

Capricorn

Alpha Capricorni, Algedi; Capricorni beta Dabikh.

Gallic, Riuros, "frozen," in wordplay with Riuoros, "radiant," and connoting Ariurocon, "before the bucket, or pot"; Breton Bouc'h < Boccos "goat"; Welsh Bwch Gafr < Boccos Gabros, "goat, billy-goat"; Gaelic, an Gabhar < Gabros, the "goat," and/or Bocan < Boccos, the "goat."

Aquarius

Alpha Aquarii, El Melik.

Gallic, Anagatios, "calamitous," Anaxs, the "cup, pot"; Breton, Hoch < Succos, "pig"; Gaelic, Uiscioch < Udesciocos, "aqueous, watery."

Pisces

Alpha Piscium, El Rischa, beta Piscium, Fum al Samakah.

Gallic, Ogronoi, "cold-blooded"; Breton Eoged < Esoxs, "salmon"; Welsh, Eogiaid < Esogate (collective case of esoxs); Gaelic, na hÉisc < eiscos, eisconos "fish, of fish."

Aries

Alpha Arietis, Gamal, beta Arietis, Sharatan.

Gallic, Qutios, "ram"; Breton, Tourz < To-riiotios, "ram" (?); Gaelic, Reithe < Riiotios, "ram."

Taurus

Alpha Gamma Tauri Tauri Tauri beta, delta Hyadum I Hyadum Tauri II.

Gallic, Giamonos, the "germinator," and connoting, Gammos, "ox or deer buck," and Taruos, "bull."

In Celtic mythology, it is called the bull with three horns, the bull with the three cranes, the seven cows or the hazel brown bull of the plain. The old Celtic name was without doubt Taruos Donnotaruos, the "brown bull," in wordplay with "lord bull."

VI: The Stars

Maia, the Alpha star of the Pleiadean Asterism

The Pleiades asterism was called Treis Garannai, "three cranes." The Greeks believed that the seven daughters of Atlas resided there.

An old belief was that the souls of the Celts came from this group of stars. This constellation is mainly composed of a remarkable set of six stars. The symbolism of the six stars is linked with the triple goddess Brigantia/Brigindu or Bouinda. Regardless of the name, it is in relation to the sovereign sky goddess and represents the creative forces of the universe. One of the attributes of the Pleiades is given in the Irish myths surrounding the legendary crane skin bag of the stormy Manannan mac Lir. In Celtic mysteries, the Pleiades are associated with destiny, fate and fatality. Cranes, of course are not just birds but also fate fairies. Manannan's bag contained magical items such as a knife, a shirt, a leather harness, a whale hook, blacksmith's tongs, a helmet and pig bones. These tools and objects are in the bag at high tide but then disappear at low tide. The bag was made from the skin of the fairy Aoife after she was killed in the guise of a crane. In the Hanes Taliesin, the Pleiades are called Group of Theodosius (Twr Tewdws). Theodosius was the name of a Roman Christian emperor. This Latin name is a later rendering of the older Celtic name, most likely a Christian gloss of Teutatis, "tribal agent." The other names of this divine trinity were also identified as Gallic star names: Taranis and Esus. This godhead was linked to the symbolism of the three-horned bull as an aspect of the god of the Gallo-Roman god death Dis Ater. His alias was Belos (Bile or Beli in Ireland and Wales). Caesar reported that the Gauls believed that Dis Pater (Dis Ater in Gaulish) fathered the Celtic race.

The stars of Taurus, the Pleiades (crane) and Hyades (cat).

Aldebaran, Alpha Tauri, the Brightest Star of Taurus

Alpha Tauri, or Aldebaran Palilicium; Beta Tauri, Alnath; gamma Tauri, Eta Tauri, Alcyone, Epsilon Tauri, Oculus Boreus.

Gallic, Donnotaruos, the "brown bull"; Breton Ruzan < Rudianos, "the red one"; Gaelic Donn Cuailnge < Donnos Caulinigos, the "brown of Cuailnge." The Aldebaran star was called the Bull. In Irish stories, it is referred to as the Dun Bull of Cooley or Don Cooley. Aldebaran, a big bright red star, is the brightest of the asterism of the Hyades. The Greeks called it Omma Boos, the Romans, Oculus Tauri, the "Eye of the Bull," which in Old Celtic would yield: Sulis Tarui. In the Vedic texts it was called Rohini, the "red deer." In the Irish tale of the *Tain Bo Cualgne*, "The raid of Cooley cows," it is mentioned that it was so big that fifty young people could jump on his back. The ancient Indo-Europeans saw the ox as the allegory for the heat of day, the bright time of day, as well as springtime and summer. In the various Indo-European myths, it is described as being attacked and eaten by a monstrous oversized cat when not a great lion.

Bottom of the Gundestrup Cauldron, a big cat attacking a bull. In former times, the cat was identified to Hyades. Drawing by the author.

The Hyades, the Cat star

Gamma Tauri, Hyadum I; Hyadum delta Tauri II.

Gallic, Cattos Pilaxs, "the mouser cat"; Welsh, Cat Palug < Cattos Pallucos, "the defective or customary cat (Hyades)."

Cat Palug was a big sized wild cat, possibly a lynx because it was described as a spotted cat. The Welsh tales relate on how it suddenly leaps out from the water on the island of Ynys Mon and then devours 180 warriors. The cat was eventually killed by the warrior Cei[18] there putting an end to its terror. Planet Venus can also be compared to a feline. In Greek myths, Atalanta and Hippomenes were turned into lions after having failed to show gratitude to Aphrodite. The Hyades asterism is crossed from above the ecliptic in Taurus by approximately 24 degrees. And as the Roman astronomer Manilus wrote these words on their rising: "Those born at this time take no pleasure in tranquility and set no store by a life of inaction; rather they yearn for crowds and mobs and civil disorders. Sedition and uproar delight them ... they welcome fights which break the peace and provide sustenance for fears."[19]

The god of the Dioscuri. Detail of Gundestrup Cauldron. Drawing by the author.

Gemini

Alpha Geminorum (Apollo), beta Geminorum (Hercules); gamma Geminorum Alhena.

Gallic, Semiuisonios/Simiuisonios, "capricious breeze," Simiuisunoi, "the spirited, vivacious, dashing one," connoting Semiuesses, "small light, dashing pigs." The Dioscuri, "twins," were called Emnoi in Old Celtic, in Gallic: Diuanno, "daylight, illuminating" and Dinomogetimaros, the "protector or colossus of dawn" and/or Momoros, the "graceful," and Atepomaros, the "great sponsor or Cavalier." These characters were very popular in the whole of Gaul. One of these Dioscuri was also called Uintios and was compared to the Greek Poludeukès (Pultuke and Pollux in Latin and Etruscan), the twin brother of Castor (Kasutru in Etruscan). They guide travelers and navigators and provide protection for riders. They also play a role as guides for lost souls. The area intersecting the Milky Way with Gemini was called the Well of Sionan (genitive Siannas, Sianna "the binding"), a fabled fountain on the River Shannon in Ireland. Legend had it that the water nymph Sionan caused a great flood after having taken a dip into this forbidden pool. Sionan was a naiad identical to Boann.

The Fiery Eye (Gemini)

This sub-constellation Gemini, the twins bathing in the Milky Way, is composed of the stars Tejat and the star cluster of M 35. It was called Aedh (Aedus, "fire") in Gaelic. Aedus was the deified morning sun. According to Irish myth, Aedh was the father of Fand (Uednalo) and foster father of Mananann (Manauionos). His name, Aedh Abrat (Aedus Abruentios), meaning, "fire eyebrows," is a description to this asterism which is shaped like an eye.

Cancer

Alpha Cancri, Sartan, beta Cancri, Tarf, gamma Cancri Asellus Borealis. Gallic Equos > Ecuos/Epos, "horse"; Breton, Gwiz < Uestis, "sow."

Leo

Alpha Leonis Al Kalb al Asad, beta Leonis, Deneb Aleet; gamma Algeiba. Gallic, Elembos, "fawn."

Asterism of the Front Part of the Lion

Gaelic year Corran < Corranos, "the sharp sickle."

Virgin

Alpha Virginis, Corn, Beta Virginis, Minelauva; gamma Arish, Celtic Edrinos, "judge-arbitrator."

For the druids, the constellation of Ophiuchus (Ophiuchus) once served as a marker for the start of the zodiacal cycle. That is, at just about the time the sun enters Scorpio. Author's drawing after a detail from the Gundestrup Cauldron.

Celtic Names of the Non-Zodiacal Constellations

The Northern Circumpolar Stars (including Ophiuchus)

The circumpolar stars reckoned in the past consisted mainly of the constellations surrounding the North Pole, These included: Draco, the Bees (the many small stars between Cepheus and Ursa Major, now called Camelopardus), Ursa Minor, Cepheus, Cassiopeia, Cygnus, Lyra, Hercules and Ursa Major, the Big Dipper. Further down to the ecliptic, there are eleven other constellations: Pegasus and Andromeda, the Triangle, Perseus, Auriga, Boötes, the Northern Crown, the Serpent, the Eagle, the Dolphin and the Small Horse.

Draco, the Dragon

Welsh, Afang Ddu < Dubis Abancos, "the black beaver."

Camelopardalis, the Giraffe

Welsh, Gwenyn < Beccena, "the bees," Modrydaf < Matridamon, "the honeycomb"; Breton, Ninian < Ninauos < Neinauos, "of the zenith."

Ursa Minor, the Little Bear

Gallic, Artulla, "little bear," Medwed, "honey bear," or "sweet knower," from meldos, "sweet," + uidions, "knower, scientist)."

Ursa Major, the Great Bear

Gallic, Artaio/Artaiona/Artio, "bear"; Welsh, Arth Vawr < Maros Artos, "the big bear"; Breton, Karr Arzhur < Carros Aretorii and Welsh, Cerbyd Arthur < Carbantos Aretorii or Artouiri, "Arthur's chariot"; Gaelic, Camchéachta < Cambon cexton, the "crooked plough."

Although the agrarian theme of the plough is of Indo-European origin, the Bear harks back to the Stone Age. Not only do we find the stellar bear theme with the Basques, Pelagian Greeks and Caucasians of Europe, but also with the Algonquians of North America. It would therefore be sage to conclude that this astral motif originated within the prehistoric shamanic culture of northern Eurasia. We can also assume that it was maintained as an archaic motif by the Indo-Europeans. The Celts knew it as Andarta while the Greeks knew it as Callisto or Artemis. In this case bear symbology is linked to the birthing process, pregnancy and wedding of young women. The Greeks maintained that the she-bear and her son Arcas resided in the constellations of Ursa Major and Ursa Minor. And Matus or Artos were the two common names for bear in Old Celtic. There is no doubt that Artio was some sort of Celtic Artemis.

Arta was the she-bear, and Artulla was the bear-cub. All of these names reminisce of King Arthur, a medieval version of the older prototype Artaios. Artaios was an alias of the god Lugus, and his female counterpart was Artaio, the Gaulish Bear goddess. The many other forms of the name were: Arduina, Andarta, Andrasta, and all attest to the popularity of the goddess. She was mostly celebrated as a war goddess from whom heroes and warriors sought protection. This Andarta was seen as the star mother known as the Great Bear or Big Dipper. Her cub, the Little Bear or Little Dipper was called Artulla. Then again, the stars bellow the Big Dipper were called Eburos, meaning, "boar," or the "yew." The M 97 nebula was called the "Owl" by the Anglo-Irish astronomer Lord Rosse in 1848. Was not the fairy Blodeuwedd of the Welsh myths changed into an Owl? Interestingly, Gwyddyon, son of the goddess Dôn (Cassiopea) and the nephew of Math (Bear), was said to have changed Blodeuwedd (knower of blossoms) into a Night Owl (Minerva). Lord Rosse (William Parsons 1800–1867) probably knew more than expected!

The Bear cult is well attested since the early Magdalenian pre–Basque culture in the Pyrenean Mountains of Spain and France. We may also presume that the pre–Celtic highlanders of many areas of Gaul continued to practice the bear cult long after. The Breton saint, Saint-Ursula (from ursua, "bear" in Latin) was the Christianised form of Artio. According to legend, she was kept secluded underground. This of course in reference to the bear's den. It is a known fact that when the bears emerge from their retreats, that they crave for honey and berries. Berry pickers would often encounter hungry bears and often have to pray to the goddess for their safe return. Also, wine urns, kegs and barrels of mead and berry-wine were kept in underground cellars for the maturing process. This special wine was most likely used during sacred rituals commemorating Artaios/Lugus at the Lugi Naissatis celebrations or during victory celebrations to the goddess Artio. It seems that Artaios was another star altogether, possibly Arcturus in Boots since it was known by the ancients as "the Bear Watcher" (Arktouros), a giant fixed star of the first magnitude.

In the Pyrenean mountains a stele bearing the inscription; LEXIIA ODANNII ARTEHE VSLM, for Lexiia (daughter) of Odan to Artaha (Artaio) accomplishing willingly a vow, was discovered in the small town of Saint-Pé, not far to the west of Lourdes in France.[20] Few scholars will maintain as Jean Markale, that the etymology of the goddess Arduina or the Hills of Ardennes stem from Arta (she-bear). A better etymology for Arduinna or Arduinna, as Mr. Monard claims, could be, "steeped, sloped," for a mountain goddess.

Left: the head of Apollo (incarnated as Alexander the Great) with curls and torque bearing. Right: winged figure (Mercury or Cepheus, the bumble-bee?) holding a torque. Silver coin of the of the Vangiones Celtic nation found in Germany. Author's drawings from a photograph at the Money Museum, Zurich, Switzerland.

Cepheus, the Head, the Chief

Breton, Marzhin < Myrddyn < Moridunios, "man of sea, seafarer," that is, Merlin.

Cassiopeia, Cassiopeia

Welsh: Llys Dôn,[21] "the "court of Don."

The "present," or the "gift," was the Brythonic name for the Irish goddess Danu. She was the mother goddess of the Celts, the Tuatha Dé Danann. She was also called Matrona in Gallic, Modron in Welsh and Ana or Anu in Ireland Modron. The mountains Da Chich Anand *Dá Chích Anann,* or Paps of Anu[22] were named after her. The name Paps of Anu in County Kerry, literally means, "The nipples of Anu," and could have been an earthly representation of this m-shaped constellation. The Celtic myths describe her as the wife of the god Bilé or Beli,[23] "the bright," as owner of the sacred tree. According to Greek literature, for her beauty, Cassiopeia, wife of Southern King Cepheus, was to be sacrificed to a sea monster by Poseidon. She will then be delivered by Perseus, who marries her and takes her to the northern constellation named after her. Cassiopeia was also called the "chair" or "throne." In short, this constellation is traditionally seen as the heavenly abode of the mother-goddess Ana, Anu and/or Danu, Dôn.

Cygnus, the Swan

Breton, Alarc'h < Alarcos, "the swan."

Lyra, the Lyre

Gallic, Esus; Breton, Telenn and Welsh, Telyn, the "little harp," or Telyn arthur,[24] "Arthur's little harp"; Gaelic, Uaithne,[25] the name of Dagda's magic harp.

Vega, alpha Lyrae, is a star of the first magnitude. The genitive case lyrae meant "of the harp," in reference to the harp's string. The Cad Godeu, the "battle of the trees," states that Taliesin is "the magic harp string of nine years." Its current name comes from the Arabic Vega, Al-Waki, and meaning "falling vulture." It therefore has nothing to do with either Greek or Latin star names. The Etruscans called Mus, the "field mouse," or "little rat." The lyre star was called Uaithne in Gaelic, which was the name of Dagda's harpist. Indeed, if we are to compare, the Lyra was in the hands of Hercules as it seemed to float above this constellation. Was it not said that Dagda's enchanted harp flew to his hand when he called it? According to legend, Uaithne harper of Dagda had a love affair with the nymph Boann with whom he had three sons: Goltrade, Gentrade and Suantrade. Henceforth, Lyra the harp crosses the Milky Way (the path to cows Boann) by Cygnus on to Dagda's arm. Nymphs or fairies also had the power to transform themselves into a swan. Regarding the Dagda, he is in the same area as Hercules. His three sons were not far between these three constellations and found in the location of the two small asterisms between the Swan and the Arrow now called Vulpecula (Little Fox) and Anser (Goose) in Latin.

Vulpecula cum Anser (The Little Fox and the Goose)

This small double constellation Vulpecula and Anser was named by Hevelius in 1660 to bridge the gap between the Lyre and the Arrow. The three major stars that form the asterism or Anser, the cluster of Brocchi and the Dumbbell Nebula, correspond to three sons of Boann and Uaithne: Goltrade, Gentrade and Suantrade.[26]

Hercules

Gaelic, Ogme < Ogmios, the "champion," or Dagda < Dagodeuos, the "good god."

Gallic gold stater of the Aulerci and Cenomani tribes (80 to 50 BC). Drawing by the author.

Pegasus (Pegasus)

Welsh, Llyr Marc'h < Marcos Leronos, "the horse of Llyr," or Baedd Coed < Baedos Caiti, "the boar of the woods," or the "old boar."

The square of Pegasus stays firm in the autumn sky since it is not obscured by the Milky Way. Pegasus therefore serves as the starting point in order to find the other northern constellations.

The Square of Pegasus: Pegasus and Andromeda

The Greeks regarded Pegasus square as a winged horse while the Welsh imagined it as a boar. This constellation, which forms an almost perfect square, incorporates Sirrah, the alpha star of Andromeda. According to Greek mythology, Pegasos, by the blows of his hooves, provoked a strong flow pouring from Mount Helicon. It was at the source of poetic inspiration. The horse was cared for by the naiad water nymphs and at maturity was mounted by Perseus and Bellerophon. Irish mythology also associated this constellation with poetry, each star being the residence of one of the four master poets of Ireland (*Cath Maige Turedh*, translated from C. Guyonvarc'h and F. Leroux, Ogham celticum).

"There were four cities in which they learned science, knowledge and the diabolical arts, namely Fallias and Gorias Murias and Findias. (…) There were four Druids in these four cities. Morfesae was in Falias. Esras was in Gorias. Uiscias was in Findias. Semias was in Murias. These are the four poets from whom the Tuatha Dé learned science and knowledge."

In Irish cosmology, each of the four stars forming the square is one of the four mythical northern cities of the world ruled by a poet-seer.

Uiscias (< Uesciatis or Uindiassos)	From the city of Findias (Uindia)	The star Sirrah
Semias (< Semiuis, Semiatis or Moriassos)	From the city of Morias (Moria)	The star Scheat
Morfessa (< Marouesos or Ualiassos)	From the city of Fallias (Ualia)	The star Markabet
Esras (< Uros Esdratis or Goriassos)	From the city of Gorias (Goria/Gortia)	The star Algenib

On the advent of the equinoxes and solstices during the seasonal cycles, these druid-poets were posted at each of the four corners overlooking world affairs. They were later displaced by the four Evangelists.

Andromeda

Welsh, Essylt and Breton, Eselt: Yseult < Esuueleda, the "noble lady-seer," and/or Adsilta, "looked upon."

Triangulum, the Triangle

Gallic, Trigenacos; Gaelic, Triantàn, the "triangle."

Perseus

Drestan Breton; Welsh Drostan < Drustannos/Drustennos, "vigorous fire"; Gaelic Nead < Nedos/Neððos, "close, close by, in proximity."

Auriga, the Charioteer or Driver

Breton, Saezh, from the Latin Sagitta, "arrow"; its true Celtic names were: Welsh, Cerbidwr < Carbantouiros, "charioteer"; Breton, Karr an Ankou < carros ancouos, "the carriage of death."

Alpha Aurigae, Capella

Latin, Capella, "goat," is a star of the first magnitude in the constellation of Auriga. It is located at approximately 46° north in the vernal sky between Perseus and Gemini. Its location makes it a useful marker for lunar adjustment for the winter solstice. It appears during the period set between the Irish holidays of Imbolc and Beltaine. In Celtic cosmology, the goat (in association with Capricorn) seems to be a borrowing of the Greek or Roman Zodiac. The ancient city of Rome was under the patronage of the god Silvanus. According to the Roman interpretation of the Gallic pantheon, Silvanus or Pan was identifiable to the god Uiducos.

Coma Berenices, Berenice's Hair

Breton, Heulwenn < Ollouindas, Welsh, Olwen, the "all-white"; Llwyn Blodeuwedd < Luianos Blotiaueidonos, "the thicket of Blodeuwedd"; Gaelic, Eithne < Etiana, the "country," punning with Etnia, the "acme" and Eithne Aitenchaitrech < Etiana Acstinocaitorixtio, the "country that looks like a gorse thicket."

Bootes, the Herdsman

Gallic, Otis, the "bear catcher"; Welsh, Math < Matus, the "bear."

Arcturus Alpha Boötis

Gallic, Artaios, "bear-like"; Welsh, Arthur < Aretorios, the "charioteer."

The Greek meaning of the name Arcturos is from the compound Arktos, "bear," and ouros, "tail," that is, "tail of the Bear." Thus, Arktophulax, the "guardian or keeper of the bear." Arcturus is the star closest to the Bears (Ursa Major and Minor) in Boötes and was imagined as the chariot driver of the Big Dipper. In remote times, it was the closest star to the North Pole. The Ancients believed that Arcturus was the world's highest abode of the wise souls. Because of its high visibility in the May sky, the star Arcturus was also associated with the cattle of the Milky Way's high path. Its position north of the zodiacal band is a significant landmark for the year's seasonal changes. Moreover, according to Hesiod, the star marks the beginning of spring and sunrise upon late February evenings and fall in the morning at mid–September. Its presence corresponded to early spring and fall in Greece. Sirius brought the first warmth of spring and Arcturus prosaically carried the grain harvest in its chariot. In Gaul, Artaios, which the Romans identified to Mercury, represented the pastoral aspects of the god Lugus.

Corona Borealis, the Northern Crown

Breton, Arc'hanrod < Argantoreta, the "silver wheel"; Welsh, Caer Arianrhod < Qataira Argantoretas, the "citadel of Arianrhod," Llys Arianrhod < Lettos Argantoretas, "Arianrhod's court." The gate of the citadel was also guarded by two of Arianrhod's porters.

Ophiuchus, the Serpent

Breton, Naertaer < Natronouiros, the "snake"; Welsh, Peredur < Priteros, the "hesitant"; Gaelic, Diancecht < Deinacacteto, "of the hard grip," the Goidelic equivalent of the Greek Aesculapius.

Coinage of the Meldi kingdom, depicting a spreading eagle. Museum of Troyes. Author's drawing after a photograph from *Publication Art Gaulois, magazine d'art, Zodiaque.*

Aquila, the Eagle

Welsh, Eryr and Breton, Erer, Erur <Eruros, the "eagle"; Gaelic, Ochill < Uxellos, the "lofty," the eagle or the hawk.

Aquila, Altair

Welsh, Yr Hebog, "the hawk."

Delphinus, the Dolphin

Breton, Morhoc'h and Welsh, Morhwch < Morisuccos, the "porpoise."

Stater of the Trevere tribe, Museum of Troyes. Author's drawing after a photograph by Blanchet.

Equuleus, the Colt

Breton, Ebeul and Welsh, Ebol < Epalos, the "colt."

The Stars Around and Below the Ecliptic

Eridanus

Welsh, Stêr < Stura, "the impetuous" or Dolen Teifi < Dola Tuerobios, "the meander of Teifi or Teifi's bend"; Afon Teifi, the Teifi River in south-west Wales; Gaelic, Fual Mhedba < Uoglon Medba, the "veil of Medb (cf. Latin velum)"; or uoglon, there punning with "urine."

Eridanus, Achernar

According to the Greek myths, the Eridanus River, is located in the Other World and cannot be seen by any mortal being. It is therefore a hidden mystical place.

Pisces Austrini, the Southern Fish

Breton, Pellez and Welsh, Pwyll < Peislos, "Psyche"; Ireland Fintan < Uindosenos, the "splendid/white (headed) elder."

The name Fomalhaut, alpha star of the Southern Fish, is from the Arabic *Fom al-Hat* or *Fam al-Hut,* meaning "mouth of the fish."

Some zodiacal charts show Aquarius pouring her pitcher into the mouth of a large fish. The Crane cluster was part of the Southern Fish until the astronomer Johann Bayer created Grus in the 17th century as a distinct constellation. From an astral theme found in Greek mythology, Aphrodite and Eros were pursued by a monster on the bank of a river and were rescued by two fish. In Irish mythology, the Southern Fish was identified to Fintan seen as the "Salmon of Knowledge," bathing in the pool of Segais.

Cetus, the Whale

Breton, Morvil and Welsh, Môrvyl < Morimilo, the "whale, a large marine mammal"; Gaelic, Miol Mór < Milo Morias, the "whale."

Orion

Breton Ri or Roue < Rixs (cf. Latin Rex), "king"; Welsh, Cadlas Arthur < Catuletos Aretorii, "the Wall of Arthur"; Gaelic, Meadhan < Meduanos, the "soft middle"; and Nighean Ri < Neqtis Rigos, "the niece of the King," and Fionn < Uindos, the "white, splendid (or perhaps Goibniu/Guibne < Gobanio/Gobannos (?) "the blacksmith")."

The Greek mythological theme surrounding Orion resembles that of the Fianna of Ireland. After his heroic earthly existence, the god hunter Orion was removed in the summer night sky. As with many other similar cases, it would be too simple to coin a Celtic equivalent for this Greek mythonym. With all caution, Monard offers Selgarios, "the hunter," as a Celtic translation for Orion. This description also fits Fionn Mac Cumhail, who is also involved in a hunting spree accompanied with his two dogs, Bran (< Brannos for Canis Major) and Sceolan (< Scelonos for Canis Minor). They were in fact his two cursed nephews changed into dogs.

Bas-relief from the Musée St-Rémi of de Reims representing Cernunnos flanked by Belenos (left) and Lugus. Author's drawing.

The Mythic Cosmological Theme for Fionn's son Oisin

The constellation of the Fawn (Elembiui Prinnios) is the same as the constellation of Leo. In Gaelic myths, the fawn was embodied by Oisin,[27] son of Fionn. Legend has it that Fionn, after having retired to a cave, slumbered there for a day before his return in order to save Ireland. Like the salmon, Fionn embodies the warrior magician infused with innate knowledge. He possesses the same attributes and instruments as those given to Orion. His were given by the blacksmith-god Goibniu, and one of those attributes was the belt. As we will see, many other instruments were given to Fionn. Fionn can be seen as an avatar of Cernunnos, the horned lord of animals. Cernunnos was depicted as a serpent-bearer and as lord of beasts on the Gundestrup Cauldron. Goibniu, the blacksmith has a girdle which ends up with a series of other magical objects contained in Mananann's crane-skin bag. This being said, Goibniu was one of the triplets along with Cian and Samhan (or Samhain). Judging from certain mythological themes, Fionn compares with Arthur. The expression "Arthur's wall, enclosure or pen," also hints at husbandry and animal keeping. The Welsh tradition clearly describes this constellation as being King Arthur's castle. The ancient Celtic theme of the walled domain or circular fortress is here felt.

The Asterisms of Orion

The Girdle or Belt, Also Called the Three Kings or Three Marys in Christian Lore (the three bright stars of Alnitak, Alnilam and Mintaka)

Orion's Belt

Gaelic, Crios Goibne < Cerdsua Gobanni, the "belt or body harness Goibnu," or Crios Fraoich < Cerdsua Ureccis, "the belt of Goibnu or Fraoch."

Lepus, the Hare

Breton, Kammed Heulwenn < Cambita Ollouindas, "Olwen's girdle"; Neuadd Olwen < Gnauosedon Ollouindas, "Olwen's palace." In the Constellation of the Hare, the alpha star is on the meridian at the end of January. Its Celtic name was Corbmacos > Corbmac > Cormac, the "light chariot driver," named after one of the three son of Conchobar Mac Nessa. It is among the brightest stars of the constellation, the others being: Leporis gamma (Corbmac Cond Longes), Alpha Leporis (Cairbre Caitchean) and Leporis beta (Cuscraid Mend Machae).

Canis Major, the Great Dog

Breton, Ki Bras < Bratuos Cu, the "large dog"; Welsh, Ci Mawr < Maros Cu, the "great dog"; Gaelic, Madra Mór < Madros Maros, the "big dog."

Sirius, the star "dog," is so called because of its strategic position in the constellation of the same name (Canis Major). The ancient Celts most certainly called this star Cu, for "dog." The Bretons still call it Steredenn ar C'hi.[28] The Irish call it Reul na Madra,[29] "star of the dog." The Old Celtic names Ðira and Retla were synonymous of "star" and maddos < masdos for "mastiff, bull-mastiff," was another name for "dog." There is also another Gaelic name for this star which is Reul an Iuchair,[30] "the star of Iuchar," or "star of the key." Iuchar was a son of the Dé Danann, Tuireann (< Toranis/Taranis, "the thunderer"). Also note that there may be a confusion between the genitive of cu, "dog," connos cunos, and the nominative cunos "puppy," with the adjective cun-/os/a/on, meaning, "high and noble." This cuno- prefix is found in ancient Celtic names such as Cunomaglos, "noble prince," Cunomaros, "the great noble," Cunocobarios, "the highly helpful," are all related to Cunobelinus (Cunobeleinos, the "high glowing"). He appears in one of Shakespeare's plays as Cymbeline, the legendary British medieval king. The Latin term Sirius comes from the Greek Seirios and meant the "flamboyant." This principally because it is the brightest star in the sky and most visible in the winter in the northern hemisphere. In summer, it is virtually invisible since it is high up in the sky in broad daylight thus coinciding with the coming of dog days, the hottest time of year. No wonder if Sirius was identified to the flamboyant sun of summer. The Celts described it as the Great White dog with burnt red ears. The Hindus, who also shared this motif, called it Cvan, "dog," or more prosaically, Maha Kamuka, the "great lover." Also found in Vedic literature, was the bitch Sarama who kept the flock of Indra of seven bulls and fifty cows.

Canis Minor, the Small Dog

Breton, Ki bihan; Welsh, Ci Fychan < Beccos Cu, the "little dog"; Gaelic, Madra Beag < Beccos Madros, the "little dog."

Canis Minor or Canicula, the "little dog," shows up on the meridian just a few weeks after Canis Major. In Celtic culture, dog and wolf are inseparable, in that wolves are wild dogs. The time of Wolf winds marks the start of springtime and heralds the rise of the dog stars. In Rome, Lupercus was the name of an ancient priest caste called the twelve Luperci. The creation of this institution was believed to be prior to the days of Romulus. The Luperci were recruited from two great patrician families: the Quinctilii and the Fabii. Every year in February, the priests performed ceremonies in sheepfolds in hope of protection against the attack wolves. Afterwards, during the Lupercalia, they would roam the streets of Rome, half-naked, and with goat leather straps, strike all those who wanted children, livestock and good harvests. The Lupercalia rites were therefore fertility festivals celebrating the glory of Lupercus, the wolf god. Lupercus was also associated with the lynx and was an alias of Faunus who was later equated with the Greek god Pan.

Hydra, the Water Snake

Gallic, Adrouantos and Breton, Aerouant < Aterouantos, "aggressor, recurring monster, dragon"; Gaelic, Abhainn Eascainne < Abon Eiscanguion, "river eels."

Hydra was presumably called Eiscanguis, Abon Eiscanguios or Segeandera in Old Celtic. Irish legends speak of a monster from the River Shannon called the Cata (< Catta, "pugnacious"). It is described as having a horse-like head with a mane, gleaming eyes, thick claws with nails of iron and a whale's tail. This description reminds us of Hydra.

Crater, the Mixing Bowl

Welsh, Pair Caridwen < Parios Gerradunias, the "cauldron of Ceridwen."

Corvus, the Raven

Breton and Welsh, Bran < Brannos, "crow"; Gaelic, Bodbh < Bodua, "crow." In all likelihood, the small constellation of Corvus, the "raven," was called Bodua, "the crow," when not, Brannos, the "raven."

The small constellation of the Raven was known as Bodua, the female crow. It was imagined perched just above the waters where swam a water monster.

Lupus, the Wolf

Breton, Bleiz < Bleðios, the "wolf"; Welsh, Trosol Bleiddyd < Troudslios Bleðiation, the "lever of wolves." The constellation of the Wolf culminates in late June just before the summer solstice. The wolf, like the bitch, symbolizes the hot flux and heat of summer. Not unlike the Indo-European astronomers, the Chinese maintained that wolf was a Cerberus identified to the star Sirius.

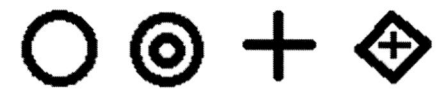

Star representation in Celtic coinage.

VII

The Astral Cusps

"The wise man of the primary science, the astrologer reasoned, about wrath, about the resolvent, about the man describing windings. About men well versed in praise. Let us proceed, God it is, through the language of Talhaearn, Baptism was the day of judgement that judged the characteristics of the force of poetry. He and his virtue gave inspiration without mediocrity, seven score Ogyrven are in the Awen."—Taliesin, *Book of Taliesin VII, The Hostile Confederacy*

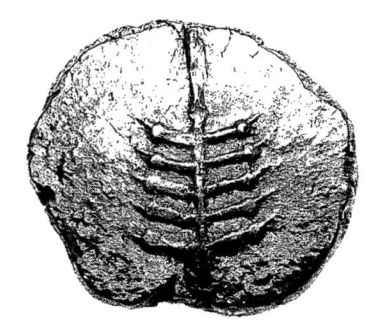

The Cosmic tree depicted on a hammered British Gold Stater of the Dobunni, minted circa 10 BCE. Drawing by the author.

The Cosmic Origins of Sacred Key or Seed Sounds and Letters in Early Indo-European Cultures

The link between syllables and writing is clear. However, for the non-initiated, more ambiguous is the relation between writing and cosmology. From Taliesin we have this passage explicitly stating that the astrologer intently and magically binds meaning and science: "The wise man of the primary science, the astrologer reasoned, about wrath, about the resolvent, about the man describing windings." This magical binding described in the *Book of Taliesin VII, The Hostile Confederacy*, is directly linked to letters and writing: "He and his virtue gave inspiration without mediocrity, seven score Ogyrven are in the Awen." Here, the poet mentions that there are "seven score" (140) Ogyrven (letters).[1] The Awen is the inspiration or the muse.[2] Seven score is for 140 days which represent the fleeing of Saturn deserting the others planets; meaning that Saturn is in retrograde motion for 140 days and is stationary for approximately another 10 days. Not surprisingly, the poet here insists on the wrathful qualities of these windings.

According to a hymn from Vedic literature, Shatpatha Brahmana and *Rig Veda*:

> When the four-headed Brahmâ projected the universe from his mind, the seed ingredient was Shabda, the sound. The prime sound was the original Ôm or Aum. And from that Ôm, the mantras were born. In the midst of this sound, the fourteen planetary worlds spew forth as expressions of pure sound. Therefore, the constellations and planets are also expressions of sound and each is an utterance of the Brahmâ.

And according to the traditions of the *Lebor Gabala Erren* (Book of the Taking of Ireland) and the *Auraicept na N-Éces* (The Scholars' Primer), the Irish peoples originated in Scythia and were the descendants of King Feinius Farsaid, a King of Scythia. This Feinius Farsaid and his son, Nel, went into Asia to work on the Tower of Nimrod (the fabled Tower of Babel in biblical texts) and were present at the subsequent dispersal of the races after the destruction of the tower. Feinius and his son, both learned of these new languages and after their dispersal, they returned to Scythia where Feinius opened a great school of languages on the Scythian plain. From The Scholars' Primer, Chapter I:

> Query, well, then, from whence were the Ogham vowels and consonants named? Not hard, Secundum alios quidem, it is from the school of Fenius Farsaidh, to wit, the school of poetry which Fenius sent throughout the world to learn the languages. There were five and twenty that were the noblest of them so that it is their names that were put for the Bethe Luis Nin of the Ogham, both vowels and consonants; and there were four who were the noblest of these again, so that it is their names that were given to the seven principal vowels: 15.
>
> It is Gaedel Glas who fashioned the Gaelic language out of the seventy-two languages: there are their names, Bithynian, Scythian, etc. Under—poeta cecinit- who of the school went to it thither? Not hard. Gaedel, son of Ether, son of Toe, son of Baracham, a Scythian Greek.
>
> To what is this beginning? Not hard. To the selection that was selected in Gaelic since this is the beginning which was invented by Fenius after the coming of the school with the languages from abroad, every obscure sound that existed in every speech and in every language was put into Gaelic so that for this reason it is more comprehensive than any language. "Er" then is every beginning, for this was the beginning with the poets that every obscure sound should come in the beginning, to wit, the Beithe Luis of the Oghan on account of obscurity.
>
> Query, what is the reason why select language should be said of Gaelic?
>
> Not hard. Because it was selected from any language; and for every obscure sound of every language a place was found in Gaelic owing to its comprehensiveness beyond every speech.
>
> Query, how much did he bring of it? Not hard. The whole of it except what the poets added by way of obscuration after it had reached Fenius.
>
> Query, what language of the seventy-two was published by Fenius first?
>
> Not hard. The Irish language ... for it is he whom he preferred of his school, and whom he had reared from his youth, and it is he that was the youngest of the school, and on account of its comprehensiveness beyond every speech, and it was the first language that was brought from the Tower. Fenius had Hebrew, Greek, and Latin before he came from Scythia, and he had no need to establish them at the Tower, wherefore on that account it was published first.[3]

The seed sounds are the three first utterances of the god of eloquence, Ogma. Each of the strokes simultaneously represents a vowel and a consonant. For example: -|- = "A" and "M," -||- = "O" and "G" and -|||- = "U" and "Nc > Ng." In this respect, the three strokes combined -||-: O/G,-|-: M/A not only spell out the name of the god Ogma < Ogmios, the name of the signs of the Ogham < Ogmon, plural Ogma, but also

VII: The Astral Cusps

O.G.A.M., the most sacred prime or seed sound expressly found in Vedic mysticism. That is, Og-aM, acts as a mystic syllable comparable to the Vedic ÔM or AUM.

OGAMos/-a/-on = "greatly, intact, mystic groove";
O:-||- Og- : Og-os/-a/-on, "pure, virginal, intact"; Ogios, the youth of sound;
A: -|- Am- : Am-os/-a/-on, "great, super, empowered"; Ama, the mother of sound;
M: -/- Ma- : Ma-/ios/-ia/-ion, "greater, much greater"; Maiia, the home of sound.
Nc: -///- U: -|||- : Ncu/'Ncu < Ancu < Ancouo, "fatality, fatal outcome, death."

The Auraicept maintains that Soim was the first thing to be written in Ogham and that "R" is for Graif. What is the meaning of this? First, Soim, from soimos < soibos meaning "magic, illusion," and Graif < grauon, "writing." It couldn't be clearer, Ogham is magic writing! Og-uaim < actusama, "perfect alliteration," the Ogham, in accord with sound, comes from Ogma, if not Fenius, its prime inventor. And the learned are the prime agents who apply it to poetry. In the order of intellectual values, thought is superior to the spoken word, most often its imperfect expression. The spoken word is superior to writing, which kills it by fixing it forever. This fixing of word is nevertheless bonded by magic. Graif (grauon), writing, is superior to Delb (Old Celtic, delua, "image"), in that writing is the property of the learned, the initiated to the mysteries, while imagery is understood by the ignorant and unlearned, therefore the initiated.

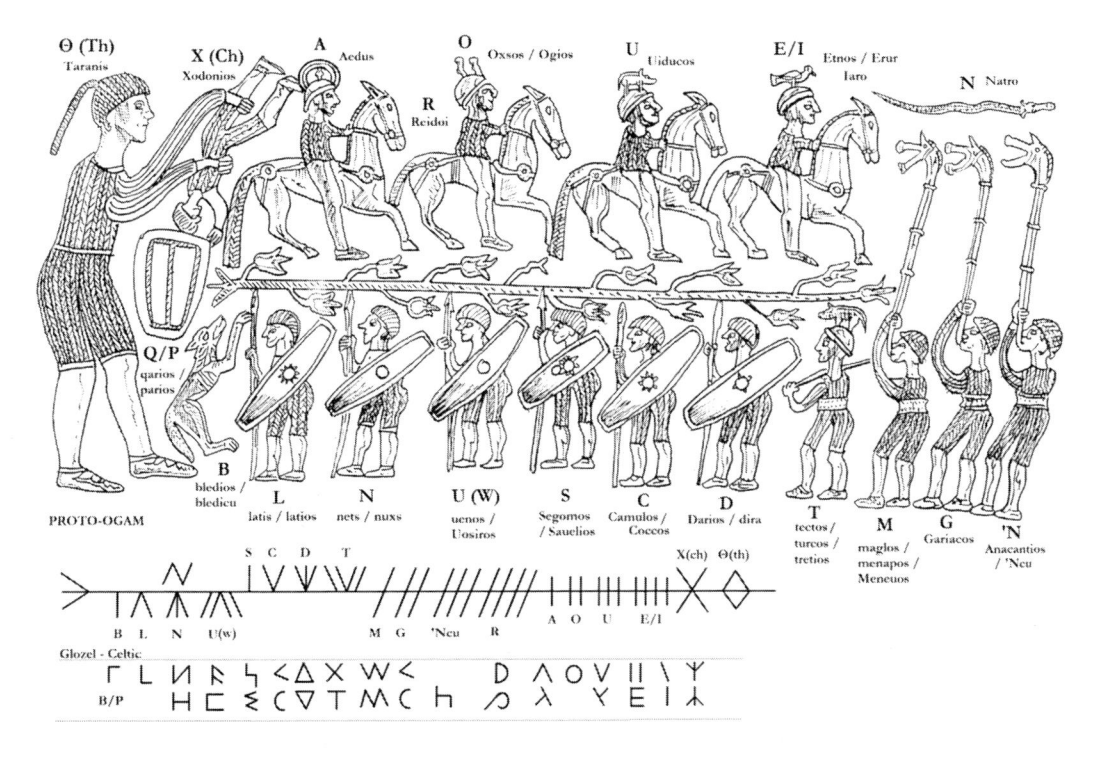

The World Tree, Cauldron of Transformation with the Lord of the Cosmos and warrior heroes. Each one represents a letter of the Celtic he alphabet. Author's drawing of a detail from the Gundestrup Cauldron.

On the Antiquity of the Ogham

In strict archaeological terms, the Oghams are dated at best at the time of Ireland's Christianizing by St. Patrick and followers around the 4th and 5th centuries CE.... This argument is solely based on epigraphical evidence provided from scattered bilingual inscriptions in Goidelic Oghams and Latin letters from the Isle of Man, Southern Wales and Devon. In this light, the Oghams are viewed strictly as an Irish invention and its diffusion restricted to parts of Man, Scotland and Wales. Its origin is explained as the alphabetization effort in the hope to recruit illiterate members of the druidical class. The problem with this theory is that the Druids were far from being illiterate, mastering Oghams, (apart from their Glozelian script from which the Coelbrenni, Celtiberian scripts derive) at least three of the four or five different alphabets known to the Celts: Greek, Etruscan and Roman.

Julius Caesar in *The Gallic Wars,* Book VI, stated that:

> It is said that these young men have to memorize endless verses, and that some of them spend as long as twenty years at their books; for although the Druids employ Greek characters for most of their secular business, such as public and private accounts, they consider it irreverent to commit their lore to writing. I suspect, however, that a double motive underlies this practice; unwillingness to publicize their teaching and a desire to prevent students relying upon the written word at the expense of memory training; for recourse to text-books almost invariably discourage learning by heart and to dull the powers of memory.

In most cultures of Antiquity, literacy was a guarded secret in that it was an instrument, the key of power. It was not only irreverent to commit teachings to writing but politically dangerous to disseminate the secret code of written language. The alphabetization effort of masses is a recent event in history. The more informed sources (C. Sterckx, J. Monard) see the Oghams as a transitional sign system constructed from tally marks (Azilian Art) notched on wooden rods prior to the generalized use of the Latin script adapted to the Irish usage.

The most ancient Irish artifacts show that the Oghams were used in very short dedications of one or two words, most often the name of the deceased on the edge of commemorative gravestones. This practice leads to necessary upkeep of glossaries such as the "Auraicept Na n'Eces" and the *Leabhar Bhaile Mhota* or *Book of Ballymote* given in latter horizontal form. However, these myopic views are broadened by other experts such as Prof. Claude Sterckx of the Université Libre de Bruxelles and linguist Joseph Monard. Sterckx has demonstrated how the Ogham inscriptions were written in a standardized archaic Proto-Irish very close to Gaulish and Latin. For example, the inscription "Degos maqi Mocoi Toicaci" (singular genitive) reading (Grave) of Degos, "the studded," son (of) the descendant of Toicacos (or Togicocos), "the Charming Red," (Maqi and Toicaci being singular genitives and Mocoi, a plural genitive).[4]

According to J. Monard, the Oghams are (our translation) "writing solely of Celtic or of Goidelic origin most probably elaborated by the Druids from an analysis of sound, sorting out vowels from consonants: truly a systematic and original alphabet."[5]

VII: The Astral Cusps

Gallic gold stater attributed to Tasciovanos, first century BCE, showing the two crescent moons set by the solar orb along with ears of corn representing the ecliptic band.

Table for the Esoteric Meanings of the Forfedhas

Forfedha	Cosmology	Element
X/EA	The Four Directions	Xdonion, "chthonic, earth (ground)"
Th/OI	The Dragon's Head	Tepnia > tennia, "fire"
P/UI	The Dragon's Tail	(P)idsca/udesca, "water"
PH/IA	The Moon Grid	Auela, "air breaks, blasts"; auentos > uentos, "wind," auentia, "inspiration breath"
XS/AE	The Sun Grid	Uxon "high," uxdulon, "high element" (aether/ether)

Therefore, the Forfedhas have nothing artificial, awkward, or added on if we are to compare these with the other fews which were assumed to be much older.

Esoteric Meaning of the Astral Cusps for the Directional Sun Wheel

Etymological rundown of the "fedha" (along with their hidden meanings):

A, ailm < alamios, "arolla pine"; alamos, "livestock, cattle, wealth, possessions";
B, beth < betua, "birch"; betis, "road"; bitu, "world (of the living)"; bitus, "life."
H < sq/sp < sc, huath > uath < squiats, "hawthorn"; squertos, "thicket"; scetlon/squetlon, "narrative, narrative history";
M, muin, min < muinia, "bramble or vine"; muinos/moinos, "treasure"; muinon, "the blessing."
P/Ui, peith, pethbol < petios/quetios, "opulus"; || uillean < uillo, "honeysuckle"; uillos, "horse"; uilia, "willingness, honesty."

Ph <B || sp/ia < fea < phogos < bagos, "beech"; bagios, "boar"; bagacos, "fighter, warlike"; || iphin < spiðna, "gooseberry (mackerel)"; spina/sparna, "thorn."

O, I, ohn < ocstino/acstino, "gorse"; acunos, "spice";

L, luis < lusis, "rowan"; lugos, "shine, splendor"; louxsnos, "light";

C > K < Ch < X/ Ea, choad < coiton/caiton, "thicket"; caitos, "woody, bush"; coitos, "common"; || eashadh < esados/elto, eltos, "(white) poplar"; esa, "cascade";

D, daur < daruos/deruos, "oak"; deruos/derbos, "safe, certain, proven."

Th < T/Oi(r), tharan < taranos, "green oak"; tarannos, "thunder"; tarandos, "reindeer"; thesmerion, "hibiscus"; || oir < feorusoir < uorosorios, "charcoal"; uorricé, "goat willow"; uoros,"wise"; Uornoctos, "bare, naked";

G, gort, gart < gortia, "ivy, "thorny bush"; gorton, "garden"; gorta, "famine."

U, ur < uroica/broica, "heather"; ur/uron, "fire";

F < V < U, fearn < uernos, "alder"; uernos, "good"; uiriona, "sincerity"; uira, "truth."

T, tinne < tennos, "holly"; tepnia > tennia, "fire (wood)";

Ng < Nc, ngetal < ingaitalis < caitalis, "reed"; ancouo > ancu, "death (personified)"; anacantios, "disastrous."

E, eadha/eodha < idato, "aspen"; edemnos, "need"; iduna, "wisdom";

S, saille < salicos/salixs, "willow"; suligu, "harmony"; sauelios, saulios, "sun"; sulis, "eye"; sulisma, "the look."

C, coll < coslos, "hazel"; cailos, "pomp, favorable, auspicious";

St (Sd), straif < sdragenos < ðragenos > dragenos, "barberry"; draco, "head, chief, chieftain"; drangos, "ghost."

I, ioho, idho < iuos, "yew" || iubhar < iburos/eburos, "yew"; iuos, "good, suitable, safe, valid"; eburos, "(old) boar, solitary boar";

N, nuin, nion < onna, "ash"; ninatis, ninnatis > nenadis, "nettle"; nentios < nantios, "(war) injury."

Q, quert < qerta, "apple"; qarios, "cauldron"; qartis, "(war) party, troop";

R, ruis < ruscia, "elder"; roudios, "red, ruddy, rusty (ruined)."

Setanta the Sun's Path and the Zodiacal Cusps

While studying the Gallic nomenclature found on the Coligny Calendar, Monard pondered on the abbreviated term Prinn and longer Prinni, which he read for "arborescence," following the names of the month. He concluded that this had to be the name of the constellations. It then became clear that these out branching constellations formed the zodiacal belt. Could these terms be further explained in the older myths? It just happens that this is the case. After all, cosmology is expressed through mythological motifs. In 1902, Lady Augusta Gregory translated the Irish tale *Cuchulainn Muithemne* relating of Cuhulainn's Death into English as which explains the sun's path and solar stations in highly prosaic language. Let's not forget that Cuchulainn's real name is Setanta, "the Path."

The story is set at the start of winter and snow just fell on the ground. The hero Cuchulain, son of Lugh, the god of Light, goes to his mother's house to bid her farewell.

Her name, Dechtire, literally means "the right-handed, dextrous." For her son, she fills a vessel which reddens with blood three times. In Celtic cosmology, the vessel, or mixing bowl, represents the constellation of Crater. Upon leaving his mother's house, he meets the Druid Cathbad, "the Death battle," who follows him. The come to a ford where they encounter fair maiden washing blood-stained linen. Now, the area of the sky where the Zodiac crosses the Milky Was is referred to in Gaelic terms as an ath, a "ford." There are two fords crossing the Galaxy: the summer ford crosses Taurus and Gemini and the winter ford passes through Scorpio and Sagittarius. This winter intersection was also referred to as the ford of the wolf since the constellation of Lupus lies just below. Bear in mind that in Gaelic, faol, "wolf," was also called cù allaidh, "wild dog." All types of dogs were meant as curses toward Cuchulainn.

Then Cuchulainn leaves Cathbad. And on his way, he encounters three hags blind of the left eye who were cooking hound on rods of rowan tree. As we proposed, rowan is the posited exit cusp marker for Aquarius. They offer him dog meat but he vehemently refuses to be tricked by them. Cuchulainn goes his way mounted in a chariot performing thunderous feats with his spear and sword. The solar Apollonian imagery is here self-evident. The storyteller goes on to say that the battlefield was scattered with the limbs and the severed head of fallen warriors, like stars in the sky, like leaves on a tree and like buttercups in a meadow.

Then Lugaid, "the luminous," spears Cuchulainn. The spear here symbolizes the westerly direction of the sun's rays. Cuchulainn then ties himself to a stone-pillar so as to meet death standing up where he is flanked by his steed, the gray of Macha and where a bird is perched. Aquila, "the Eagle," is found just on the north side of the Milky Way above Sagittarius. As for the pillar, it represents the buckling of the annual cycle in Libra.

Then Cuchlainn's head is severed by Lugaid and taken south to the Lifé River. At each cardinal point, the head of a fallen king is placed on a pillar top:

> To the south, the black head of the king of Meath, Erc, son of Cairbre of Swift Horses;
> The head of the son of Maeve; a destroyer of harbors, yellow-haired Maine, man of horses;
> The head of the son of Fergus of the Horses, a destroyer in every battle-field.
> To the west, the head of Lugaid, son of Curoi of the Rhymes;
> The heads of Laigaire and Clar Cuilt;
> To the east, the heads of brave Cullain and hardy Cunlaid.
> To the north, the three evil black, blue faced heads of the sorceress daughters of Calatin;
> The golden head of the son of Red-Haired Ross, son of Necht Min, the high king of Leinster of Speckled Swords.

Please note that there are twelve heads in all on this list. It can't be a coincidence. The story ends magnificently with Cuchulainn riding in his blazing chariot in the great plain of Emain Macha before a hundred and fifty maidens singing to the music of the Sidhe.

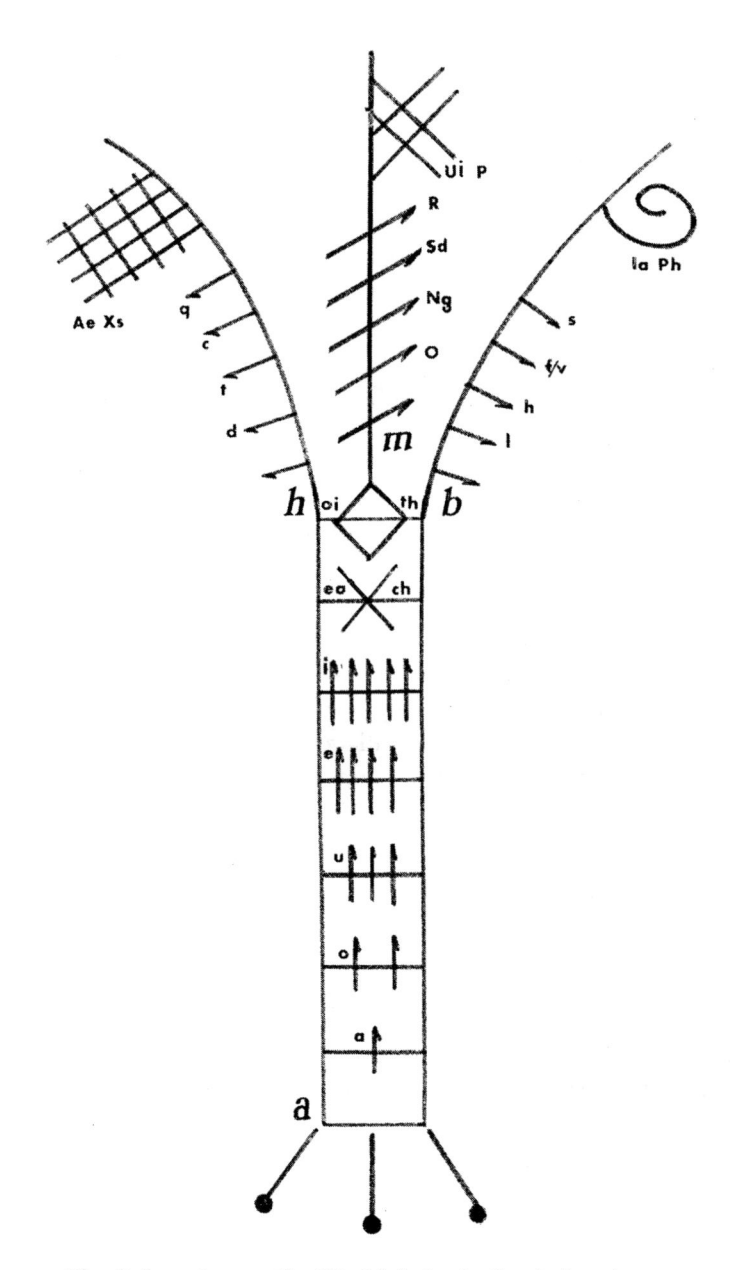

The Ogham tree as the World Axis. Author's drawing.

The Cusps, in the Irish Ogham Scheme

Star Chart

Please note that the words within brackets [...] indicate the meaning traditionally given to the houses in Vedic astrology.

Libra: Indouelicon, "ring or circle ultimate"; cantos, "ring"; Cantli Prinnios, "constellation of the ring, buckle"; Indamia, "servant";

In cusp (entering constellation): querta, "apple";
Bird sign: qarca < carca, "hen";
Animal sign: qrumis "worm, maggot";
Out cusp (constellation exit): rudioscaua/ruscia, "elder";
Bird sign: rucinatis, "rook";
Animal sign: ructu, "pig";
House XII: Indon, "end, result"; [losses, costs, waste];
Ruling planets: Venus and the South Node, as an aspect of Mars.

Scorpio: Lingonis, "jumper, dancer or fetcher"; Siltarios/Samonios, "the sower"; Samoni Prinnios, "constellation of the gathering, of the sower";
In cusp: alamios, "arolla pine";
Bird: alauda, "lark";
Animal: alcis, "big deer, and elk";
Out cusp: betua, "birch";
Bird: boduos, "crow";
Animal: baedos/bagios, "boar";
House I: Lingmen, "arriving on scene, coming to place"; [birth, origin, commencement];
Ruling planets: Mars and the North Node, as an aspect of Saturn.

Sagittarius: Bogdariios, "the archer"; Dumanni Prinnios, "constellation of darkness, of the horseman";
In cusp: squiats, "hawthorn";
Bird: sciatos, "duck," or scrauo, "black-headed gull"; or screua/scriua, "skua gull";
Animal: scobarnocos, "hare";
Out cusp: mUinia, "bramble or vine";
Bird: mesalcos, "blackbird";
Animal: morimoccos, "porpoise";
House II: Artigatiom, "plowing"; [life, livelihood, work];
Ruling planet: Jupiter.

Capricorn: Lucius, "pike"; or Attiluis, "sturgeon"; Riuri Prinnios, "constellation of frost";
In cusp: petios/qetios, "opulus";
Bird: pincio/pinciu, "finch";
Animal: peigno < pencinio, "salmon";
Out cusp: phagos > phogos/bagos, "beech tree"; or spidna, "mackerel currant";
Bird: sparuo, "sparrow";
Animal: phrucnios < sprocnios, "horse";
House III: Eluetia, "abundance (of goods)"; [fraternal relations, friendly and social];
Ruling planet: Saturn.

Aquarius: Udesciocos, "aqueous, watery"; or Uisucios/Uiseceos, "beautiful"; Anaganti Prinnios, "constellation of the calamitous";
In cusp: onna, "ash"; acstino/ocstino, "gorse";
Bird: olerca/olerica/alarca, "swan";
Animal: ouios, "sheep," ouica, "sheep," ognos, "lamb";
Out cusp: lusis, "rowan";
Bird: lugos/luogos, "crow";
Animal: lucius/lugius "pike";
House IV: Uindobios, "happiness, bliss"; [maternal relationships, happiness];
Ruling planet: Saturn.

Fish: Escoi, "fishes"; Ogroni Prinnios, "constellation of coldness";
In cusp: xoiton, "thicket";
Bird: cauacos/cauocos, "jackdaw"; or couixs, "cuckoo";
Out cusp: daruos, "oak";
Bird: druuos, driuolos, "wren";
Animal: damatos, "sheep";
House V: extincón, "abundance, with the meaning of waxing"; [offspring, brood, children];
Ruling planet: Jupiter.

Aries: Aros, "Ares/Mars"; Qutios, "ram"; Cutii Prinnios, "constellation of the fiery, the blazing, the ardent, connoting of the ram";
In cusp: taranos, "green oak";
Bird: tarascala, "thrush, song thrush";
Animal: tarandos, "reindeer";
Out cusp: gortia, "ivy";
Bird: gansa, "wild goose"; garannos, garanna, "crane";
Animal: gabro, gabros, "goat";
House VI: Aruos, "striker"; [opposition, diseases, obstacles];
Ruling planet: Mars.

Taurus: Insciatos/'nSciatos Ander, or Ander Sciatos, or "winged ox"; Taruos, "bull"; Giamoni Prinnios, "constellation of shoots";
In cusp: uroica, "heather";
Bird: udarocrago, "corncrake";
Animal: uros > urus, "bison, ure, aurochs"; and/or urleo, "wild cat";
Out cusp: uernos, "alder";
Bird: uailennos > uoilennos, "seagull";
Animal: uerbis < uerba/uerua, "cow"; uetsis > uisis, "young sow, sow"; and/or ualos/uolcos, "wolf";
House VII: Insqiiate/Eniscuiate, "speeches, colloquy, discourse"; [partnerships, marital relations];
Ruling planet: Venus.

Gemini: Roudiosuccoi, "the red pigs"; Simiuisoni Prinnios, "constellation of the frisky breezes";
In cusp: tennos, "holly";
Bird: trosdis > trodis, "starling";
Animal: trucos/tretios, "boar";
Out cusp: 'nGaitalis < incaitalis, "reed";
Bird: engnaca, "hooded crow";
Animal: ancoracos > ancoragos, "male salmon, old salmon";
House VIII: Roudios, "ruin, fall (from prestige or eminence)"; [death, destruction, annihilation];
Ruling planet: Mercury and Counter-Earth.

Cancer: Uillos, "horse"; equos, "horse"; Equi Prinnios, "constellation of equity, of the horse";
In cusp: elto/eltos, "poplar";
Bird: eruros/eror, "eagle";
Animal: epos/eqos, "horse";
Out cusp: salicos, "willow";
Bird: sebacos, "hawk";
Animal: sidos, "deer";
House IX: Uilia, "honesty, will"; [the Dharma, the law of good order of the world and of his own nature];
Ruling planet: Moon.

Leo: Aga, "doe"; Elembos, "fawn"; Elembiui Prinnios, "constellation of fawns";
In cusp: coslos, "hazel";
Bird: caliacos/calliacos, "cock, rooster";
Animal: cattos, "cat";
Out cusp: sdragenos < ðragenos < dragenos, "barberry";
Bird: ðragena < draena/drasina/drascina, "thrush";
Animal: ðragenocos, "hedgehog";
House X: Agtate/Actate, "acts, facts, actions, decisions to act"; [actions, rewards, karma];
Ruling planet: Sun.

Virgo: Ecco, the "country priest"; edrinos, "umpire, judge, and arbitrator"; Edrini Prinnios, "constellation of the judge";
In cusp: iuos/iburos, "yew";
Bird: iaro/iar < giar, "cock-bird, gallinaceous";
Animal: iorcellos < iorcos, "deer"; and/or, isoxs/esoxs, "pike";
Out cusp: nertos, "myrtle";
Bird: naudauica/nauscua, "snipe";
Animal: natris/naðris, "snake";
House XI: Ecuodecs, "perfectly fair"; [gains, profits, and possessions];
Ruling planet: Mercury

Table for the Degrees of the 24 cusps

Ogham (astrological symbols of the cusps) with respective degrees		Cusps
Q	330°–345°	**Libra/Scales—House XII** Indon end, "issue" In cusp: querta,"apple tree"
R	345°–360°	Out cusp: rudioscaua/ruscia,"elder berry"
XS	360°–0°	Xs < exs- Extimu, "exit" Sonnocinxs,"the sun's course, the annual solar cycle"
A	0°–15°	**Scorpio—House I** Lingmen, "entry, on scene" In cusp: alamios, "arolla pine"
B	15°–30°	Out cusp: betua,"willow"
Sc (H)	30°–45°	**Sagittarius—House II** Artigatiom,"ploughing" In cusp: squiats,"hawthorn"
M	45°–60°	Out cusp: mUinia < uiniia, "vine"
P	60°–75°	**Capricorn—House IV** Eluetia, "riches, abundance (of goods)" In cusp: petios/qetios,"snowball tree, elder rose"
PH	75°–90°	Out cusp: phagos > phogos/bagos, "beech tree" or spidna "gooseberry"
O	90°–105°	**Aquarius—House IV** Uindobios,"happiness, bliss" In cusp: onna,"ash tree"; acstino/ocstino, "gorse, furze"
L	105°–120°	Out cusp: lusis,"rowan, sorb tree"
X	120°–135°	**Fish—House V** Extincon,"abundance, waxing" In cusp: xoiton,"copse, coppice"
D	135°–150°	Out cusp: daruos,"oak"
TH	150°–165°	**Ares—House VI** Aruos, "attacker, striker" In cusp: taranos, "green oak"
G	165°–180°	Out cusp: gortia,"ivy"
U	180°–195°	**Taurus—House VII** Insqiiate/Eniscuiate, "discourses, speeches, talks" In cusp: "uroica heather"

Ogham (astrological symbols of the cusps) with respective degrees	Cusps
U (V F) 195°–210°	Out cusp: "uernos, alder"
T 210°–225°	**Gemini, Twins—House VIII** Roudios, "ruin, fall (fall from prestige or eminence)" In cusp: tennos, "holly"
'N/ NC (NG) 225°–240°	Out cusp: 'nGaitalis < incaitalis, "reed"
E 240°–255°	**Cancer—House IX** Uilia, "honesty, will" In cusp: elto/eltos, "aspen, poplar"
S 255°–270°	Out cusp: salicos, "willow"
C 270°–285°	**Leo—House X:** Agtate/Actate, "deeds, facts, actions, decision for action" In cusp: coslos, "hazel"
Ð 285°–300°	Out cusp: sdragenos < ðragenos < dragenos barberry"
I 300°–315°	**Virgo—House XI** Ecuodecs, "well balanced, perfectly fair" In cusp: iuos/iburos, "yew"
N 315°–330°	Out cusp: nertos, "myrtle"

The Cusps in the Welsh Bardic Tradition

List of trees in Taliesin's the Cad Goddeu

The Welsh list of 27 (or 28) trees allows for a lunar mansions chart.

1, alder; 2, willow; 3, mountain ash; 4, gooseberry; 5, medlar tree; (It was decided that raspberries would be withdrawn from the conflict); 6, wild-rose; 7, privet; 8, honeysuckle; 9, ivy; 10, poplar; 11, cherry tree; 12, birch; 13, laburnum; 14, yew; 15, ash; 16, elm; 17, hazel; 18, beech; 19, holly; 20, hawthorn; 21, vine; 22, fern; 23, broom; 24, gorse; 25, heather; 26, oak; 27, pear tree.

Chief tree: Aballos, "apple tree"; Abelio, "the Sun God"; abelio, "departure";
1) Uernos, "alder tree"; uern-os/-a/-on, "good";
2) Salixs, "willow tree"; selua, "property"; selos, "origin, source, descendance, offspring";
3) Lusis, mountain ash; luca, "light"; luci-os/-a/-on, "stunning, remarkable"; Luxna, "moon";

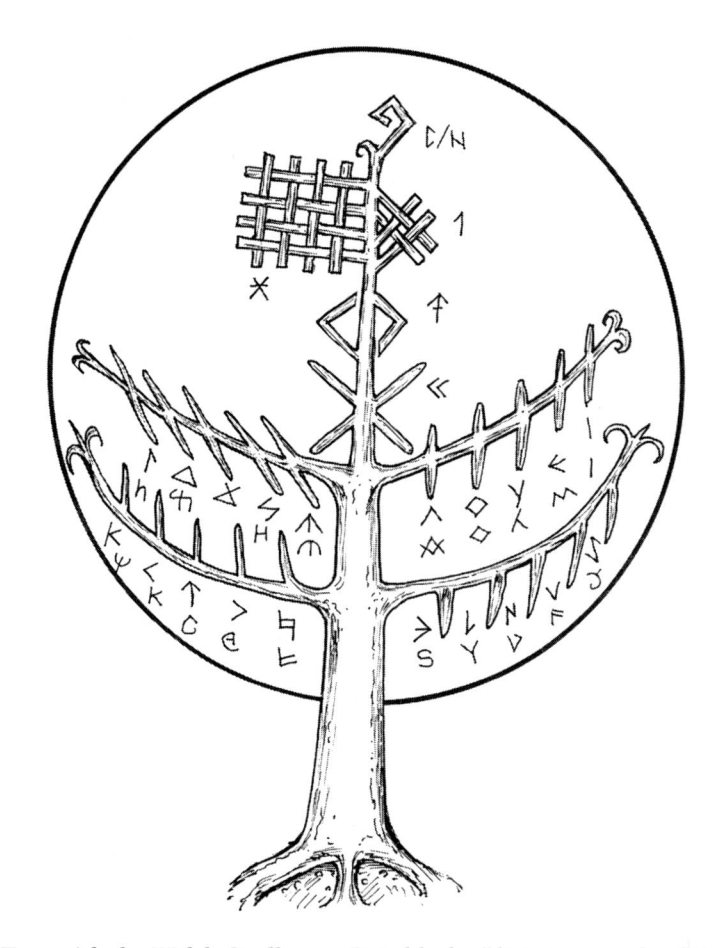

The World Tree with the Welsh Coelbren y Beirdd, the "divining woods of the Bards."

4) Spiiats, "gooseberry"; spidna/spina, "gooseberry"; spidsca, "speed, diligence"; Spidna/spina/spiiats, "thorn, gooseberry bush"; spidscu/spidsca, "speed"; spidscu-os/-a/-on, "hasty, speedy";

5) Mespilos > Nespila, medlar tree; mescis, "confusion"; messos/mestos, "fruits";

6) Acuilentos > apilentos, from Latin, aculentum, wildrose; also Broica/Uroica, briar; Ur, "fire"; ur-os/-a/-on, "pure, fresh";

7) Gabromelxos, "privet"; melso, "softly, slow";

8) Gabrostos, "honeysuckle"; garmen, "invocation, calling";

9) Edennos, ivy; edan-os/-a/-on, "nourishing, sustaining";

10) Elto/Eltos, "poplar, aspen tree"; elata, "ability, knowledge";

11) Carasos, cherry tree; caros/cara, "friend"; carantia, "friendship";

12) Betua, "birch tree"; betis, "road; bitu/bitus, "world";

13) Cista (c.f. Greek, khistos), labdanum; cesta, "projectile, spear, arrow, ray";

14) Iuos, "yew"; iuos, "clear, distinct";

15) Osnos, "ash tree"; onnos, "solid";

16) Lemos, "elm tree"; lemos, "soft"; cedtis, "back and forth";

VII: The Astral Cusps

17) Coslos, "hazel tree"; colia, "group, company";
18) Bagos, "beech tree"; bogos, "fight, brawl";
19) Colenos, "holly"; coleinos, "child, kid";
20) Acinarios, spetes, "hawthorn"; acenis < adcenis, "opening";
21) Uiniia, "vine"; uindsiu, "perception";
22) Ratis, "fern"; raton, "favor, love";
23) Banatlos/genista, broom; genio/gena, "birth, progeny";
24) Actina, gorse, furse;
25) Broica/Uroica, heather;
26) Deruos, "oak tree"; deruuidia, "truth, certainty"; actos, "decision to act, action";
27) Periarios/pesiarios, "pear tree"; pados, "pine"; pennantos, "set, determined."

Plus the other trees which were removed from the list:

28) Subitocrobio, raspberry; subios, "good humor."

And maybe larch in place of medlar for "M": Melixs/mletto/bletto, "larch"; mileto, "devastation, destruction, devastating attack"

For the above ascriptions, the names for the Welsh letters do not exactly match those from the later names given in *The Barddas*. The Celtic names are from etymologies given by Joseph Monard.[6]

VIII

The Astral Houses

"The twice six houses of the stars shall mourn over the wayward wandering of their guests (the seven planets)."—Geoffrey of Monmouth, *Histories of the Kings of Britain, The Prophecies of Merlin, Book VII, Chapter IV*

The Gallic goddess Nantosuelta, holding a caduceus mounted by the representation of a house, along with her companion Succelos holding the regulating mallet of time. Author's drawing of a bas-relief from Sarrebourg, Metz, France.

The Twelve Houses, Astral or Solar

Queen Medb and King Ailill had a wonderful palace called Rath Cruachan. The *Fled Bricrend:The Feast of Bricriu* provides an amazing description of this unusual palace:

> On the arrival of the Ultonians, Ailill and Méve with their whole household went and bade them welcome. "We are pleased" quoth Sencha, son of Ailill, responding. Thereupon the Ultonians come into the fort and the palace is left to them as recounted, viz., seven "circles" and seven compartments from fire to partition, with bronze frontings and carvings of red yew. Three stripes of bronze in the arching of the house, which was of oak, with a covering of shingles. It had twelve windows with glass in the openings. The dais of Ailill and of Méve in the center of the house, with silver frontings and stripes of bronze round it, with a silver wand by the fronting facing Ailill, that would reach the mid "hips" of the house so as to check the inmates unceasingly. The Ulster heroes went round from one door of the palace to the other, and the musicians played while the guests were being prepared for. Such was the spaciousness of the house that it had room for the hosts of valiant heroes of the whole province in the suite of Conchobar. Moreover, Conchobar and Fergus mac Roich were in Ailill's compartment with nine valiant Ulster heroes besides. Great feasts were then prepared for them and they were there until the end of three days and of three nights.[1]

According to Peter Berresford Ellis, this astral palace of Ailill and Medb represents the lunar mansions, which were the Irish equivalent of the 27 Nakshatras of Hindu or Vedic astrology.

In *Mythe et épopée II*, Dumézil clearly identifies the Irish king Eochaid to the Indian king Yayati of the Puranas. Yayati, son of Nahusha, was the king of the of the lunar sky gods' dynasty. Nahusha was one of those god-kings, a protector of the world, of water, of death and of wealth. According to the myths, he was transformed into a serpent by the sage Agastya for having usurped the throne of Indra in the heavenly kingdom. As with Yayâti,[2] who was the father of Mâdhavî,[3] Eochaid was the father of Medb. And not coincidentally, as we have seen, the names of Madhavi and of Meadb,[4] both stand for "drunkenness," or "intoxication," through mead! That is, in Sanskrit, the name Madhavi is relative to madhu, for "mead" and is of the same etymology and meaning as the Old Celtic medu or medus. The Irish Medb, from Old Irish Medba, is also of the same root. The Sanskrit name Soma, however, does not define the same drink. It is rather similar to the holy ambrosia of the Greek gods through which immortality is gained. In the Indo-European myths, intoxicating drinks were allegorically linked to moon. Chandra was one of the important Sanskrit names for the moon and its moon god. It was also on the moon that this elixir was kept and guarded by the lunar deities.

As Dumézil remarked, the Indian Madhavi, daughter of the universal king Yayati, was also wife and mother of the many Aryan mortal kings. When we learn the story of her quadruple performances as she is imbued with pious thoughts and growing accordingly to law, canon and civil law, we understand that she embodies the most respectable aspects of Brahmanic society. The stories surrounding the Irish moon goddess Medb make it clear that we have access to extremely old and well preserved mythological themes which through her guise, better explain the other two episodes from the life of Yayati found in the Bhagavata Purana.[5]

In light of these compared myths surrounding the Indian Yayati and Madhavi, we can now better understand the godly attributes of the Irish Ailill and Medb royal couple.

The Attributes of Medb	Attributes of Ailill
Fual Medba, "the veil of Medb or the outpouring of Medb," (Eridanus)	The brown bull Cualgne and 50 heifers (Taurus/Pleiades)
Ath Medba, "the ford of Medb," (area of intersection of the Milky Way with Cassiopeia) Dindgna Medba, "the hill of Medb," (the top of the world) Pupall Medba, "the tent of Medb"; (the canopy or sky vault) Bili Medba, "the tree of Medb," (the world tree or axis).	The gold Imscin or Imscing < imb-scena "skene belt."

However, Ailill and Medb are not the only ones in possession of such a palace in Ireland. Think of those belonging to Bricriu and Mac Datho. In the *Fled Bricrend* there is a similar account concerning Bricriu's mead hall:

> Bricriu, of the Evil Tongue, held a great feast at Bricriu's hall for Conchobar mac Nessa and for all the Ultonians. The preparation of the feast took a whole year. For the entertainment of the guests a spacious house was built by him. He erected it in Dun Rudraige after the likeness [of the palace] of the Red Branch in Emain. Yet it surpassed the buildings of that period entirely for material and for artistic design, for beauty of architecture—its pillars and frontings splendid and costly, its carving and lintel-work famed for magnificence. The House was made on this wise: on the plan of Tara's Mead-Hall, having nine compartments from fire to wall, each fronting of bronze thirty feet high, overlaid with gold. In the fore part of the palace a royal couch was erected for Conchobar high above those of the whole house. It was set with carbuncles and other precious stones which shone with a luster of gold and of silver, radiant with every hue, making night like unto day. Around it were placed the twelve couches of the twelve heroes of Ulster. The nature of the workmanship was on a par with the material of the edifice. It took a wagon team to carry each beam, and the strength of seven Ulster men to fix each pole, while thirty of the chief artificers of Erin were employed on its erection and arrangement. Then a balcony was made by Bricriu on a level with the couch of Conchobar [and as high as those] of the heroes of valor. The decorations of its fittings were magnificent. Windows of glass were placed on each side of it, and one of these was above Bricriu's couch, so that he could view the hall from his seat, as he knew the Ulster men would not suffer him within. When Bricriu had finished building the hall and balcony, supplying it both with quilts and blankets, beds and pillows, providing meat and drink, so that nothing was lacking, neither furnishings nor food, he straightway went to Emain to meet Conchobar and the nobles of Ulster.[6]

Then in the *Scéla Mucce Meic Dathó*, "The Story of Mac Datho's pig," Rudolf Thurneysen's translation from the Angela Grant edition, there is another description of such an edifice:

> There was a famous king over the men of Leinster, Mac Dathó was his name. He had a dog. The dog used to protect all the Leinstermen. Ailbe was the name of the dog, and Ireland was full of the dog's fame. Messengers came from Ailill and from Medb to ask for the dog. At the same time there came messengers from the Ulstermen and from Conchobar to ask for the same dog. Welcome was made to them all, and they were taken to Mac Dathó in the hostel. That is one of the five hostels that were in Ireland at that time, this and the hostel of Da Derga in the district of Cualu, and the hostel of Forgall Manach, and the hostel of Mac Da-Reo in Brefne, and the hostel of Da Choca in the western part of Meath. Seven doors were in the hostel and seven roads through it and seven hearths in it and seven cauldrons. There was an ox and a salt-pig in each cauldron. The man who came along the road thrust the flesh fork in the cauldron, and whatever he got from the first taking, it is that he ate. If, however, he got nothing from the first attempt, he got no other.

[...]
On the same day, indeed, they had arranged to meet, both (the Connachta) from the west and (the Ulstermen) from the east. Nor did they neglect to appear. Two provinces of Ireland came on the same day until they were at the doors of the hostel of Mac Dathó. He himself came to meet them and welcomed them. "Warriors, we were not expecting you," said he, "nevertheless you are welcome. Come into the courtyard!" Afterwards they all went into the hostel, half the building then by the Connachta and the other half by the Ulstermen. The house was indeed not small, seven doors were in it and fifty couches between each two doors. They were not the faces of friends at a banquet, however, that were in the house. A large number of them had feuded against others. The war between them was three hundred years before the birth of Christ.[7]

The Seven Messengers or Seers of the North

> "Messengers went from Medb to the Maines to bid them come to Crúachu, the seven Maines with their seven divisions of three thousand, namely, Maine Máithremail, Maine Aithremail, Maine Condagaib Uile, Maine Mingor, Maine Mórgor and Maine Conda Mó Epert."—*Táin Bó Cúalnge*, Book of Leinster, translated by Cecile O'Rahilly

The seven seers of the North (Septentriones in Latin, and Sanskrit Saptarishaya[8] or Sextanðirionesin Old Celtic) were the seven prime seer princes who lived in the stars of the northern region which comprised of the stars of the constellation of Ursa Minor. Vedic literature describes them as the emanations of the first Manu, the first "man." Each Manu was in charge of a celestial house called and Mandira in Sanskrit (cf. mantera or mandera Celtic).[9] The Teutonic Mannus, Welsh Mynogeni[10] and the Irish Maines were the European equivalents of the Vedic Mânavas. When the sun was positioned in Capricorn, there emanated the seven cosmic rays that fed the worldly vital energy. On the Old Celtic side, the sextanriuones, "the seven rays," originated from Riuros Prinnios, the constellation of Capricorn. Here, riuros, "frost," puns with riuoros "the ray, beamer"; from riuo "ray," pl. riuones. In turn, each of these Riuones supplies solar energy to one of the seven worlds or planets. According to the Vedic texts, with each of these cosmic rays comes vital energy (Tantra), empowered through the supervision of the seven seers embodying the seven sciences of the universe. These seven stars of the north sky take a slow revolution around the pole much like the ox ploughing around an obstacle, a tree or a rock. This is the reason why Arcturus (Celtic, Artaios), the alpha star of Boötes was called the "bear keeper or bear watcher."

Comparative Table of the Seven Seers, Vedic and Celtic Myths

Vedic	Celtic
1-Gautama or Marìci	1-Fios/Fis
2-Bharadvàja or Angiras	2-Fochmarc
3-Visvâmitra or Pulaha	3-Eolas
4-Jamadagni or Kratu	4-Ferann
5-Vasistha or Pulastya	5-Fors
6-Kasyapa or Bhrgu	6-Anind
7-Atri or Daksa	7-Finn/Find/Fionn

Etymologies for the Irish Gaelic Names:

1. Fios/Fis < Uesos, "the knowing, learned";
2. Fochmarc < Uocomarcos, "the research";
3. Eolas < Eulaxsos/Sulaxsos, "the expert";
4. Ferann < Uirionos, "the truthful, the fair";
5. Fors < Uoros, "the wise";
6. Anind < Andiendos, "the super great, the famous";
7. Fionn/Finn/Find < Uindonos "the splendid, the white"/Uindosenos, "the splendid or white-elder."

The Seven Maines (from the Cath Boyne)

Maine Athramail (like his mother Medb), also called Fedlimid;
Maine Màthramail (like his father Ailill), also called Coirpre;
Maine Andoe (the quick, the speedy), also called Eochaid;
Maine Tai (the quiet), also called Fergus;
Maine Mógor (of great duty, duty-full), also called Ceat;
Maine Milscothach (the sweet tongued), also called Sin;
Maine Móepirt (above all description), also called Dàire.

And according to another list:

The Children of Ailill and Medb

The Seven Maines:
1. Maine Mathramail, "the boy like his mother";
2. Maine Athramail, "the boy like his father";
3. Maine Mórgor, "the boy of great duty";
4. Maine Míngor, "the boy of lesser duty";
5. Maine Mo Epirt, "the boy above description; also called Mílscothach, the sweet tongued";
6. Maine Andoe, "the speedy boy";
7. Maine Gaib Uile, "the boy of all qualities";

The three sisters:
8. Findabair, "the white ghost (the white lady)";
9. Cainder, "the songstress";
10. Faife, "the breeze (?)."

The Many Pleiades Fairies, in Groups of Three, Six or Seven

The three druidesses, Badba, Macha and Morrigan claimed they could prevail over their enemy after having sent clouds of hail and poisonous gases and made them weak and confused so that they would be denied of intelligence and common battle sense. And as we find in the following passage, on some occasions, these fate fairies not only come in sets of three but also pairs: "'And you, Bé Chuille and Díanann,' said Lug to his two witches, 'what can you do in the battle?' 'Not hard to say,' they said. 'We will enchant the trees and the stones and the sods of the earth so that they will be a host under arms against them; and they will scatter in flight terrified and trembling.'"[11] Here, the translator gives the Irish name Bandrui as meaning "witch," instead of "lady druid," which was the pejorative Christian understanding of the name. In late Antiquity, Druidesses, much like their masculine counterparts, were of the first holy function acting on behalf the sky gods for their communities.

The fairies or nymphs of the Pleiades, were generally seven in number, that is, six including Maia. They were the consorts of the seven sages and the nurses of Arcturus, the young cow-herder. In ancient Greece, these fate goddesses, the daughters of Hesperus (the Evening star) looked over the fate of men in their garden of the Hesperides, an otherworldly realm where grew a marvelous apple orchard. This theme is also found in the Celtic myths with the Irish Emain Ablach and Welsh Avalon. In Welsh myths, they were thus called: Moronoe, Gliten, Glitona, Gliton, Tyronoe, Thiton and Thiten.[12] The Irish texts refer to them as the Cailleach. They had seven periods of youth, and they, too, were six in number. Here were their Irish names: Cailleach, Cailleach Bolus, Cailleach Corca Duibhne, Caileach Bui, Cailleach Beara and Cailleach Beinne Bhric.[13]

According to the book of Lecan, Cailleach Bui, the companion of the seven Lughs, had seven periods of youth and had custody over his fifty foster children, who the ancestors of the Irish nations. The Book of the Takings of Ireland gives another list: Tea, Fás, Fial, Liben, Odba, and Scota.[14] These seven sisters, referred to as cows in Indo-European myths, express the feminine aspects of incarnation, while the seven bulls, the masculine aspects. Thus, the six or seven stars of the Pleiades were embodied by the fate fairies led by Maia, the goddess of Sovereignty and Destiny.

According to the ancient Greeks, these included the six main stars of the Pleiades including the smaller, Pleione. The Pleiades were generally named as follows: Alcyone, Asterope, Electra, Atlas, Maia, Merope, and Taygetos. In Vedic astrology, the Krittikas, the Pleiades, represented by a flame, were named as follows: Amba Doula, Nitaoui, Abrayanti, Maghayanti, Varshayanti and Choupunka. The triune river goddess Sarasvati also had seven sisters. Her two main sisters, Ida and Bhatrati, were the goddesses of ritual sacrifice and sacred speech.

The Astral or Solar Houses

The twelve equally divided sectors of the zodiacal belt are referred to as "astral Houses." This way of dividing the astral sky is a very old concept that has no connection with our modern scientific conceptions of stellar mapping. It is therefore preferable to always treat ancient astral science as a totally different mind view from our modern science.

It was a traditional practice to divide the sky into four pie shares. These corresponded to the four cardinal points to which three equal houses were allotted. Each quarter was called a magh (< magos, for "plain, area, field"). This term was somewhat comparable to the Sanskrit term bhava, which roughly has the same meaning. Although the area of the houses varies greatly in the northern skies, the Druids gave equal value to each of the houses. Following this pan, for each of the 12 constellations there were two cusps:

Belenos and Rosmerta in their home, Romano-British bas-relief from Gloucester, England. Note the coq-rooster, the double snake caduceus of Hermes, the pots and the water bucket along with Rosmerta's double ram-horned staff. Author's drawing from a photograph by Betty Naggar.

an in-cusp and an out-cusp. Cusps served to mark the sun's passage through the house and were placed at equal distances from the center of the house. The first cusp was in Libra, taken as the initial sign, and was set between five and ten degrees while the second between the twentieth and twenty-fifth degree points. This progression was carried so on and so forth from one sign to another finally back to Libra again. The cusps were most certainly called *prenn* (< prennoi) in Brythonic and *fidh* (< uidoues) in Goidelic. In classical astrology, a cusp was defined as the first point of a house at its first degree. For this old Celtic scheme, each cusp was designated by a tree name. Constellations in this great celestial forest of *Litana Uidua* (the old Gallic designation) were thus viewed as trees. As previously mentioned, each tree of this forest marks the point of passage of the sun in the constellar home. Here, the trees were seen as roadside sentinels guarding the passage of the Sun. Alternately, cusps were represented as doors or gates to the astral houses. When the bardic poets Taliesin and Amorgen declared that the sun passed through a door, they really meant that the sun was entering a constellation.[15]

For example, the *Song of Amorgen* (from the Books of *Leccan* and *Ballymote*, John MacNeill's translation) is replete with cosmic symbolism:

VIII: The Astral Houses

(...) thus Amorgen sang this lay:
I am the wind on the sea [for depth];
I am a wave of the deep [for weight];
I am the sound of the sea [for horror];
I am a stag of seven points [? for strength];
I am a hawk on a diif [for deftness];
I am a tear of the sun [for clearness];
I am the fairest of herbs;
I am a boar for valor;
I am a salmon in a pool [i.e., the pools of knowledge];
I am a lake on a plain [for extent];
I am a hill of Poetry [and knowledge];
I am a battle-waging spear with trophies [for spoiling or hewing];
I am a god, who fashions smoke from magic fire for a head
    [to slay therewith];
[Who, but I, will make clear every question?]
Who, but myself, knows the assemblies of the stone-house on
   the mountain of Slieve Mis?
Who [but the Poet] knows in what place the sun goes down?
Who seven times sought the fairy-mounds [sidhs] without fear?
Who declares them, the ages of the moon?
Who brings his kine from Tethra's house?
Who segregated Tethra's kine?
[For whom will the fish of the laughing sea be making welcome,
   but for me?]
Who shapeth weapons from hill to hill [wave to wave, letter to letter,
   and point to point]?
Invoke, O people of the waves, invoke the satirist, that he may make
   an incantation for thee!
I, the druid, who set out letters in Ogham;
I, who part combatants;
I, who approach the fairy-mounds to seek a cunning satirist, that he
   may compose chants with me.

In Amairgen's poem, the planets are prosaically called fairy-mounds: "Who seven times sought the fairy-mounds (the places of peace, the Sidhs)?" The house of Tethra[16] here mentioned, is found on the ecliptic at sunset while Tethra's herd is obviously the Zodiac populated by its constellar beasts and characters. This cosmic order was organized according to the druidical plot where darkness precedes light. Medium Coeli, "middle of the sky," roughly corresponds to the vernal sky marked by the stars of Aries and Taurus. The sun's acme at noon is but a small-scale reminder of the yearly macro-event of "mid-summer (Mediosamonios in Old Celtic)." As we all know, this major solar event occurs in late June just in time for July; months which are overlapped by Gemini and Cancer. The poets called these, the stars of the summer sky. And these cosmic events had to be regulated by some power of intelligence.

According to the underlying scheme, the astral houses were believed to be governed by its resident planetary lords. That is, planets entering a house fell under the influence of a given planet. But then again, planets wander. In light of this, the power of their influence was greater whether they were at "home" or just "visiting." In astrological terms, when planets met, they came into conjunction. And since every House had its resident ruler, heavenly bodies that passed through were subjected to it.

In short, a non-resident visiting planet is inevitably influenced by its host. Either it falls under its control, is subjected to its regency or benefits from its hospitality.

Therefore, according to the logic, wandering planets suffer of benefit when transiting from one House to another. In Old Celtic, these influences were either termed *mata*, "beneficial," or *anmata*, "non-beneficial." In itself, no House, planetary ruler, or sign, is neither completely good nor bad. Planets also have their own forces or powers which are exerted by the strengths of their yokes during each passage, meeting or conjunction. The grip of a yoke is determined by the angle and speed of the planet's passage while entering of exiting a given House. In other words, if its entry or departure is taken directly in prograde or retrograde motion.[17] Also, each planet has its own quality and strength, be it borrowed from a House ruler or granted on its own according to the characteristics of its zodiacal sign or House significator. In astrological terms, the significator is either aspected by the faster moving planet or is aspected by the slower one.

The solar or astral houses were roughly defined as follows: The ascendant is marked by the closest star at the front of a constellation and there marks the entry point given by the first cusp. The zodiacal cycle starts at the first cusp in the sign of Libra and ends with the second cusp past Virgo. That is, at the moment when the sun leaves the constellation past the second cusp, there it falls out of influence and enters another sign. The astral houses are opposed in pairs and are complemented by their oppositions. Each house is governed by a lord or ruler, each having his own characteristics exerting in a given area or field of activity. In turn, each of these individual rulers is conditioned by a specific element:

- The earth houses are considered physical, laborious and sluggish (IIII, VIII, XII);
- The fire houses are seen as passionate, ardent, fervent and creative (III, VII, XI);
- The water houses are seen as deterministic or fatalistic, wavering and emotional (II , VI, X);
- The air houses are seen as fresh, communicative, honest, and intellectual (I, V, IX).

In short, the House system gives each planet a seat in its appropriate sign and there precisely where its greatest strength of influence is presumed.

The equal house division is therefore consistent with the allocated time and location for the planets in the corresponding astrological signs. But then again, this equal space distribution is not made without causing some structural problems since these houses can only be twelve in number regardless of their very different sizes. Let us note, however, that although Western and Celtic astrologies focus primarily on the sun's passage through the constellations of the zodiacal belt, the other five planets also play a major part as house significators. The officially recognized seven planets of Antiquity, including the two luminaries, were roughly ranked in importance as: Moon and Sun; Mars, Mercury and Jupiter; Venus and Saturn.

The moon, with its two nodes, North and South, was counted as triple. Although the Earth is not counted as a planet, the ancient druid-astronomers saw it as a sphere called Crundion, "sphere." In addition, these ancient astronomers placed a second invisible earth in orbit behind the sun always hidden behind its orb. This planet was called "anti–Earth" or "counter–Earth" by the Romans and Greeks, and was in complete opposition with ours. Ancient astronomers sometimes included Uranus which was periodically visible under certain optimal conditions. This new count permitted for eleven bodies which could be counted as House ruling planets. Since there was one missing, some rather mystical astrologers, counted Arcturus, alpha star of Boötes as a twelfth planet. Arcturus, the alpha star of the Boötes system, was the one who led the heavenly flock.

Hence Amorgen sang tis lay: "Who brings his kine from Tethra's house? Who segregated Tethra's kine?" Tethra's kine refers to those of the sea or ocean. Most likely those planets which fall below the horizon into the sea. We should also consider that the long orbiting distant giant planets, including Jupiter and Saturn, after a long visual absence, linger longer in each zodiacal house. And unlike these, the smaller inner planets orbiting near the sun quickly run through all the houses several times a year. For example, Mars, the most distant of small planets, in its raids, takes over a year to go around the zodiacal belt, while Mercury travels to and fro four times a year.

Astronomical Planetary Revolutions

Moon	27.32166 days per revolution around Earth
Moon	29.53058 days for the duration of one lunation
Sun	365.24221 days for one tropical solar year (that is, one turn of the Zodiac)
Mercury	87.96858 days for its revolution around the Sun
Venus	224.70068 days for its revolution around the Sun
Mars	686.98044 days for its revolution around the Sun
Jupiter	11.86222 years for one complete turnaround the Zodiac
Saturn	29.45776 years for one complete turnaround the Zodiac
Uranus	84.01312 years for one complete turnaround the Zodiac
Neptune	164.79334 years for one complete turnaround the Zodiac
Pluto	248.40299 years for one complete turnaround the Zodiac

The revolutions of the stars are good indicators for interpreting the characteristics or personalities of the planetary lords. This interpretation is facilitated by the fact that Celtic myths are rich in detail concerning the astral Houses. This data is not only found in the myths of Ireland and Britain, but is also noticeable in Gallic numismatics and, to a lesser degree, in Gallo-Roman art and epigraphy. The following list was constructed using data from Irish mythology.

Ráth Crúachan < Ratis Cruccon—"The Fortress slopes"

Reagarding the Celtic astronyms:
- Gaelic astral house names are attested in Old Irish literature. There were probably other collective names in the other ancient insular and continental Celtic traditions. The oral traditions of these cultures need further analysis.

- Some of the Old Celtic astral names were obtained through compared etymological study.
- Also note that for the Old Celtic Zodiac, houses began in Libra, not in Aries, as was the case for the ancient Classical Zodiac, and now the case for modern Western astrology.
- Henceforth, House I, for "birth," is in Libra and not in Aries. For Aries, we have House VII, for "marriage." And as previously noted, the Celtic annual and cosmic cycle starts on Samhain (< Samonios, roughly November), is midway through on Beltaine (< Belotennia, May celebrations), and ends on the eve of the following Samhain feast in late October.

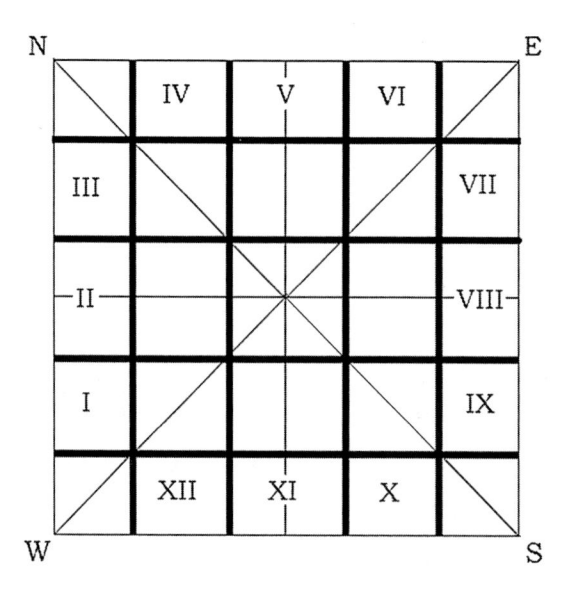

Solar grid chart for the astrological houses. Author's drawing.

Na Muintireacha < Manuterai, the Houses (households)

HOUSE I

Significator: Indon, "end, limit";

Meaning: losses, the buckling of the sign;

House ruler: Atramalis Manios > Maine Athramail, "like the father"; paternal relations, grandparents, uncles, aunts, cousins, in-laws and other relatives on the father's side; Atir, "father"; Ailill < Alpillis, "the elf," along with Medb Leithderg < Medua Letos Dercos, "Medb of the grey eye," a pun on "eye with red"; along with Indamia, "the servant, the household member, of the suite";

Planet: Venus, Riia, "the free," along with Ersa Ambieios (Cauda Draconis, the south node), with qualities of mercury;

Associated planets: Venus, Mercury;

Corresponding astrological sign: Libra, Indouelicon, "the ring," or "the ultimate circle."

HOUSE II

Significator: Lingmen, "on the scene, in action";

Meaning: birth, the foundation, life, source of death, the beginning, the arrival, the birth, the advent of the self, the physical body and its aspects, family, shape, appearance;

House ruler: Matramalis Manios > Maine Mathramail, "like the mother"; maternal relations, grandparents, uncles, aunts, cousins, in-laws and other relatives on the mother's side; Matra (mother); Medb Derg < Medua Derga "Medb the red," punning with, dercos, "eye";

Planet: Mars, Cocos > Goac, "the red," along with Qennos Ambieios (Caput Draconis, the north node), with martial qualities, the red riders or Eqoredioi/Eporedioi, "the fast riders";

Associated planets: Jupiter, Moon and Sun;

Corresponding astrological sign: Scorpio, Siltarios "the sower."

HOUSE III

Significator: Artigatiom, "plowing";

Meaning: acquisition, property, finance, and the brood, children;

House ruler: Manios Ollogabion > Maine Gaib uilé, "of all the qualities," for precision and finesse of voice or speech;

Planet: Jupiter, Tectos > Teach, "the traveler, the planet";

Associated planets: Sun, Moon and Mars;

Corresponding astrological sign: Sagittarius, Bogdariios, "the archer."

HOUSE IV

Significator: Eluetia, "abundance, riches, and property";

Meaning: profit growth, gain, wealth, home, longevity and age;

House ruler: Manios Minocuros > Maine Mingor, "the finely helpful," for longevity, brood, offspring, children, descendants;

Planet: Saturn, Melnos > Miln, "the slow";

Associated planets: Venus and Mercury;

Corresponding astrological sign: Capricorn, Attiluis, "the sturgeon."

HOUSE V

Significator: Uindobios, "happiness, bliss";

Meaning: longevity and age;

House ruler: Uindasoibra > Findabair, "the white lady, the ghost," or Aiba > Aobh, "the pretty face," or again, Etana > Etain, "poetry";

Planet: Saturn, Melnos, along with Artaios, Arcturus, "the bear watcher," maybe;

Associated planets: Venus and Mercury;

Corresponding astrological sign: Aquarius: Udesciocos, "aqueous," and Uisucios/Uiseceos, "raven."

HOUSE VI

Significator: extincón, "abundance within the meaning of brilliance,"
Meaning: the brood, children;
House ruler: Aiunia > Aoife, "of age";
Planet: Jupiter, Tectos, along with Uranus, maybe;
Planetary associations: Sun, Moon and Mars;
Corresponding astrological sign: Pisces, Escoi, "the fish."

HOUSE VII

Significator: Aruos, "the striker";
Meaning: marriage, partnership, partners;
House ruler: Mogocuros Manios > Maine Mogor, "well over";
Planet: Mars, Cocos;
Associations planets: Jupiter, Mercury, Moon and Sun;
Corresponding astrological sign: Aries, Qutios "ram"; Aros, "Ares/Mars."

HOUSE VIII

Significator: Insqiiate/Eniscuiate, "of speeches, of talks";
Meaning: wealth, heritage, sacrifice;
House ruler: Mou Epirtos Manios > Maine Mo Epirt, "highly attractive"; also called: Melissogutacos Manios > Maine Milscothach, "the honey tongued";
Planet: Venus, Riia;
Planetary Associations: Mercury and Saturn;
Corresponding astrological sign: Taurus, Sciatos Ander, "the winged ox."

HOUSE IX

Significator: Redsicos, "zippy, swift," and/or Roudios, "ruddy, reddish";
House ruler: Andouios Manios > Maine Andoe, literally "not slow, nimble";
Planet: Mercury, Louctos > Luct, "flashing";
Associated planets: Sun, Mars, Venus;
Corresponding astrological sign: Gemini, Roudiosuccoi, "the red pigs."

HOUSE X

Significator: Uilia, "honesty, will"; Uelia, "visualizing, seeing, observation," Ueilis, "festivity, joy";
Meaning: mother and maternal relations;
House ruler: Medua > Medb, "drunkenness";
Planet: Moon, Eidscos, "Moon";
Planetary associations: Sun, Mercury;
Corresponding astrological sign: Cancer, Uillos/Equos, "horse."

HOUSE XI

Significator: Agtate/Actate, "acts, facts, actions, decision to act";
Meaning: father, king, right, law, fairness, moral law;

House ruler: Alpillis > Ailill, "elf";
Planet: Sun, Greina > Grian, "beaming";
Associated planets: Moon, Mars, Jupiter;
Corresponding astrological sign: Leo, Aga, "doe," Elembos, "fawn."

HOUSE XII

Significator: Ecuodecs, "perfectly fair"; Exagon, "purge";
Meaning: work, health, illness, and hygiene;
House ruler: Arba > Arbh, "heir";
Planet: Mercury, Louctos, and maybe Andecrundion, Counter-Earth;
Planetary associations: Sun, Mars and Venus;
Corresponding astrological sign: Virgo, Ecco, "the country priest"; Edrinos, "the judge, umpire, arbitrator"; and/or Esoxs, "salmon, pike."

Compared Vedic and Celtic Planetary Attributions

Luminaries	
Sanskrit	*Celtic*
SUN	
Surya/Ravi/Âditya/Vivasvat Atman, "the Soul Master: Pitrukaraka, "paternal master"	Sauelios/Sonnos/Greina, "the sun"; Gods: Belinos, "beaming," Abellio, "the striker; punning with: departure." Sulis, "the eye"; Suleuios, "appointed, protector"; Suleuia, "well colored"; Suligu, "harmony"; Grannos, "beaming, bearded." Anatmon, "the Soul, vital breath"; Master: Ailill < Alpillis, "elf."
MOON	
Candra/Soma Mana,"the mind" Master: Matrukaraka, "Maternal master.	Luxsna /Eidsciia,"the moon"; Gods: Iuocatus,"good fighter" Medua, "drunkenness"; Mana, "mind, intelligence"; Mênmen, "spirit, psyche"; Master: Medb < Medua.
Planets	
Sanskrit	*Celtic*
MARS:	
Kuja/Mangala/Angaraka, courage, actions, ego Master: Bhratukaraka, "brotherly master.	Coccos, "the red/ Coxsinacios, "spry, nimble"; Gods: Aros, "Ares/Mars"; Toutatis Cocidios, "tribal red agent"; Aedon, "fervent, zealous"; Camulos, "dynamic"; Master: Ceat < Cetus, "ardor, rage," for, Maine Mógor < Mogocuros Manios, "the responsible lad";

MERCURY:	
Budha, commerce, trade, communications, diplomacy Master: Gnathikaraka, "master of relations."	Luctos, "troop, party, group, light"/Boudios, "free"; Gods: Artaios,"bear keeper"; Uisucios, "perceptive, voracious, respectable"; Master: Eochaid < Iuocatus, for Maine Andoe < Andouios Manios,"the quick lad";
JUPITER:	
Brihaspati/Guru, teaching, learning, law Master: Putrakaraka, "master of children and youth.	Tectos,"traveler, messenger"; God: Taranis, "thunderer"; Tectomaros,"possessor, owner"; Dagia,"goodness"; Milscothach < Melissogutacos Manios, "the sweet-mouthed lad"; or Maine Gaib Uile < Manios Ollogabion,"the lad of all gifts";
VENUS:	
Sukra, beauty, health, riches and pleasure Master: Darakaraka, "master of spouses."	Riia, "the free/ Uosris, Uâsria,"aurora"; Goddesses: Belisama, "the bright"; Briantia,"noble, lofty"/Brigantiia,"morally high"; Master: Dàire < Darios, "tumult," for Maine Móepirt < Manios Mou Epirtos, "the indescribable lad."
SATURN:	
Sani ou Ani/Sanaiscarya, trials and gains, work and experience; Master: Sani, "master of longevity and death.	Melnos, "indolent/ Nucturos Uosiros, "the nocturnal slowpoke"; Gods: Arualos, "the god Saturn"; Brestos, "the split, broken, bent"; or Bretos, "judge, umpire"; Master: Fergus < Uirogustus, "the true choice"; for Maine Tai < Manios Tausios, "the silent lad"; or Minocuros Manios, "the responsible or smart lad."

Lunar Nodes

Rahu, the dragon's head, northern lunar node, Chaos, anarchy, disorder. Saturnine aspect. Master: Matrukaraka, "maternal master."	Quendos Ambeios, "the dragon's head," Caput Draconis, northern lunar node (ascending); God: Balaros, "the luminescent"; Anacantios, "the calamitous"; Master: Coirpre/Cairbre < Caburtarios, "the night, rider," for Maine Màthramail < Maine Matramalios, "the lad like his mother."
Ketu, dragon's tail, southern lunar node. Occult influences, esoterica. Aspect martial. Master: Pitrukaraka, "paternal master."	Losta Ambeios, "the dragon's tail, Cauda Draconis, "the southern lunar node (descending)"; Gods: Tepthra,"the runaway"/ Spadonios, "the castrated"; Master: Fedlimid < Uedlimatis, "constant, ever good, to the point"; for Maine Athramail Manios Atramalios, "lad like his father."

Hidden Planets	
Mandi, a twin planet of Saturn **Makara,** a death inflicting planet.	Dubitus, "the evil world, the Bad-Earth," the dark invisible world, that is, Andecrundion, "the Counter-Earth, the Fore-Earth."

Masters (Rulers or Lords) of the Astral Houses (Mansions of the Sun)

MOON

MATRA (mother)/Matrona (matron): Queen Medb (Medua), the Celtic Soma, holding the throne of the gods of the lunar dynasty. True queen bee, she is strong, willful, ambitious, bellicose and desperately competitive. It is she who gives sacred intoxication to the men of Ulster of the warlords' class. She is King Ailill's (Alpillis) wife whom she dominates authoritatively. Her sole glance is enough to remove two-thirds of man's virility. It is said that she is never seen without a man in her shadow. As Goddess of Sovereignty, she was in possession of the World Tree called Bile Medba (< Bilion Meduas). Her name is associated with several stars, Alpha Centauri, among others. Another of her names was Awen (< Auentia), the Muse. She is the equivalent of the Vedic Madhavi, daughter of Yayati, father of the lunar dynasty.

Vedic Astrology: Matru (mother), Chandra (Moon), Matrukaraka, the mother mistress.

SUN

ATER (father)/Attios (foster father, stepfather, and educator): the solar king Ailill (Alpillis) is the good father of the sidereal world. In promise for his daughter Etain (Etana), the most beautiful girl in the world, Aongus (Oinogustios) clears twelve plains. Oinogustios was the Goidelic name for the Gallic Maponos Belenos. As rialtóir (Rextuarios, "regulator") he shares sovereignty with the queen Medb. In appearance, a sweet, naive shorty, Ailill proves to be very smart and crafty. Ailill is rich in cattle and prosperous in livelihood as owner of the prized dun bull of Cooley (< Donnotaruos). This brown bull attracts the envy of Queen Medb who raids the twelve newly cleared plains. In addition to Etana, he is the father of three fate fairies, Aoib, Ain and Arba, and the seven sons of Medb, the Maines. His Vedic counterpart was none other than Vishnu, father of the Avatars.

Vedic Astrology: Pitru (father): Ravi, sun, Pitrukaraka, the father master.

MARS

BRATIRES (brothers)/ Bratonos (fraternal): the older brother is the one who takes things in hand. The big brother is Mogocuros Manios. His other names were: Ogmios Grannos Aneponos, "the radiating/bearded face," Labratonos, "the eloquent," Elcomaros, "the envious, the big bad one," Celtocaros, "the noble friend," and Curmitos, "the brewer." This demiurge, in his Uranian aspects, epitomizes everything that is cloudy, dark, mysterious, mystical, magical and sinister. He is the binding god, the Tantric magician, the yogi, the eloquent teacher and the inventor of scriptures. His companion is Etain (Etana), the muse of Poetry. He is the twin brother of the Dagda (Dagodeuos), the good god.

When there is no war, which he embodies, as chief hero, the tribal father and oversees the warrior's society. In Greek myths, Heracles is the father of Nemia, the sky goddess of the starry vault. His counterparts were therefore the Greek Ouranos and the Indian Varuna.

Vedic Astrology: Bratru (brother): Kuja, Mars, Bhratukaraka, and master of brothers.

JUPITER

DANNOS (judge), Olloudios (the absolute master): That was Manios Ollogabion, "lad of all gifts," Jupiter, lord of creatures and of gods. His Vedic counterpart was Purusha. Following the example of Mithra, he embodies all that is good, fair and clear in quality. It has a good childish side, playful but rough and rustic. His many Irish names were: Eochaid Ollathair, Aedh[18] and Ruad Rofessa.[19] He shares the holy site of the astral houses of Bruigh na Boinne along with the young Aonghus Óg, and gave his divine kingship to his son Bodb Dearg.[20] It was from this princely son's red eye that emanated planet Jupiter's cosmic ray.

Vedic Astrology: Guru, Jupiter, Putrakaraka, lord of small (children).

MERCURY

PLANTA/QLANNA||GENETLA (brood, clan, extended family): Whose Lord was Andouios Manios, "the nimble." He had long legs and long arms with which he moved so overwhelmingly. His heavenly abode was called Rodrubán.[21] He replaces Nuada[22] for a time as king of the gods. With his wife, the mortal Dechtiré,[23] he has a son, the famous Achilles-like hero Cuchulainn.[24] The Gallic Mercury is often depicted with a triple face and accompanied by a pet spaniel. The spaniel, along with the cock-rooster who announces the new day, rises early and is active all day. His spouse was Rosmerta, goddess of "Providence." He had two brothers called the Lugoues or Lugones.

Vedic Astrology: Budha, Mercury, Gnathikaraka, lord of relatives and friends.

Tigernoi, the Gallic Planetary Lords and Rulers

Matrona Nantosuelta, "the Matron who flits around the valley"; Planet: Diuon, moon;

Sucellos Ipadcos, "the good striker horseman, the well-hitting rider"; Planet: Saulios, sun;

Toutatis Albiorix, "king of the cosmos," Toutatis Olloudios, "the totalitarian or absolute master," Toutatis Rigisamus, "the very royal or majestic," Toutatis Rigonemetos, "the royally crowned," Toutatis Nodens, "the angler tribal lord"; Planet: Tectos, Jupiter;

Toutatis Camulos,[25] "the dynamic tribal lord, the lord who strives to be active," Toutatis Medros, "the clever tribal lord," Toutatis Segomo, "the ace tribal lord"; Planet: Boudios, mercury;

Toutatis Cocidios, "the red glowing tribal lord," Toutatis Caturixs, "the tribal lord king of the battle," Toutatis Lenos, "the wealth or flow tribal lord," Toutatis Roudianos, "the reddening tribal lord"; Planet: Roudios, Mars;

Toutatis Mullo, "the heap tribal lord," Toutatis Nabelcos, "the nebulous tribal lord," Toutatis Sinatis, "the tribal lord of the weather"; Planet: Nucturos, Saturn;

Toutatis Loucetios, "the light emitting tribal lord," Toutatis Tincsos, "the slick or glossy tribal lord"; Planet: Reiia, Venus;

Toutatis Uorocios, "the advanced tribal lord"; Planet: head of the dragon, northern lunar node;

Toutatis Condatis, "the tribal lord of the union or the confluence"; Planet: tail of the dragon, southern lunar node;

The three Matres, the Suleuiai, the Sylphids or young Sylphs, "thin and graceful women or girls"; Suleuia, "the well colored, or watching over (someone), a guardian or protector."

Planets: any of the three invisible planets, Uranus, Counter-Earth and the Postern (Kere's Door, a gate of Taurus leading to the Underworld, a dark circle marked by Elnath, beta Tauri, near the galactic anti-center). In Irish lore, this gate to the Underworld was kept by the two door-keepers of Tara, Camal and Gamal.[26]

Proposal for a Gallic or Old Celtic Table of the Zodiacal Houses— Manuterai Đironai, "Astral Households"

House I

Libra, Cantli Prinnios, "looping, buckling";
House Ruler: Marta Suleuia;
Significator: losses, the cycle's end;
Planet: Venus (spouses, master and mistress of the house);
Cusp: R. Ratis, "fern"; connoting: "rat, favor, love, grace."

House II

Scorpio, Samoni Prinnios, "the sower, the meeting, the assembly";
House Lord: Toutatis Roudianos;
Significator: the coming to life, renewal, birth;
Planet: Mars (brothers, fraternal relations and siblings);
Cusp: D. Deruos, "oak"; deruuidia, "certainty."

House III

Sagittarius, Dumanni Prinnios, "depth, vastness";
House Lord: Toutatis Olloudios;
Significator: acquisition, property, finance;
Planet: Jupiter (the brood, children).
Cusp: T. Tanno, "holly (and uidion/amistros "mistletoe"); tana, "time"; tepneton, "fire."

House IV

Capricorn, Riuri Prinnios, "the cold, radius";
House Lord: Toutatis Mullo;
Significator: prosperity and property;
Planet: Saturn (longevity and age).
Cusp: P. Pados, "pine"; pennantos, "set, minded, determined."

House V

Aquarius, Anaganti Prinnios, "without activity, calamity";
House Lord: Toutatis Mullo;
Significator: unhappiness and happiness;
Planet: Saturn (longevity and age).
Cusp: S. Salixs, "willow"; selua, "property"; selos, "origin, strain, source, descendant, offspring."

House VI

Sign: Pisces, Ogroni Prinnios, "cooling, cold blooded (reptile, snake, fish)";
House Lord: Toutatis Olloudios;
Significator: difficulties, illness, opposition;
Planet: Jupiter (the brood, children).
Cusp: M. Mleto/Bleto, "larch"; mileto, "devastation, destruction, devastating attack."

House VII

Aries, Cutii Prinnios (fiery, dangerous);
House Lord: Toutatis Roudianos;
Significator: the self, the ego;
Planet: Mars (brothers, fraternal relations and siblings).
Cusp: N. Nertos, "myrtle"; nertos, "force, strength."

House VIII

Taurus, Giamoni Prinnios (Germination);
House Lord: Toutatis Loucetios;
Significator: growth and progress, intervention;
Planet: Venus (spouses, master and mistress of the house);
Cusp: G. Gabromelxos, "privet"; garmen, "invocation call."

House IX

Gemini, Semiuisoni Prinnios, "capricious breezes";
House Lord: Toutatis Segomo;
Significator: ambition, ruin;
Planet: Mercury (work, occupations, professional activities).
Cusp: C. Coslos, "hazel"; colia, "group company."

House X

Sign: Cancer, Equi Prinnios, "equalized, balanced, and set";
House Ruler: Matrona Nantosuelta;
Significator: the willingness and improvement;
Planet: Moon (mother, maternal relations).
Cusp: B. Betua, "birch"; betis, "road."

House XI

Leo, Elembiui Prinnios, "of complaints, of fawns";
House Lord: Sucellos Ipadcos;
Significator: actions and decisions;
Planet: Sun (father, paternal relations).
Cusp: X (Ch) Xista < cista (cf. Greek khistos), "laburnum," or Ximalos, "hops"; Xdonios, "chthonian, earth."

House XII

Virgo, Edrini Prinnios, "arbitration, heat stroke";
House Lord: Toutatis Segomo;
Significator: loss, decay and debility;
Planet: Mercury (work, occupations, professional activities).
Cusp: L. Lemos, "elm"; lemos, "soft."

IX

The Lunar Mansions

"Nine little white hands on the table in the area near the tower of Lezarmeur with nine mothers who moan a lot. Nine Korrigans (goblins) dancing with flowers in their hair and in robes of white wool around the fountain in the full moon light. The sow and her nine piglets at the door of their lair, groaning and burrowing, burrowing and growling; little ones! Little ones! Little one! Hasten to the apple tree! The old boar will give you a lesson."—*Barzaz Breiz*; *The Series; or, The Druid and the Child* [author's translation]

The Belgian goddess Nehalennia from a Celtic sanctuary in Holland. Author's drawing after a photograph from the Rijksmuseum van Oudheden, Holland.

The 27 Moon Mansions

The method of star divining using the zodiacal lunar mansions was once by far the most popular since it permitted accurate predictions for lesser time. Many seasoned astrologers preferred it before the other traditional methods using the astral houses system. The Greeks divided the lunar mansions into 27 or 28 shares of the ecliptic covering roughly the period of one month. In India, the lunar mansions or Nakshatras[1] were divided into 27 shares. Not unlike the Greeks, Druid-astronomers also counted 27 lunar houses and occasionally adding a twenty-eighth sign for adjustments. Moreover, it is understood that these sidereal periods should not be confused with the days of calendar months which are synodic.

In the *Red Branch* of the Ulster cycle, is found the mention of a series of heroes called Lá. Here again is an occasion for traditional bardic wordplay using lá, "hero" and la "calendar day": lá < lato, latios, "hero"; lata, latis, "heroin"; and la < latis, "calendar day," or "nycthemeron." Other puns included: latis, "liquor, beer," and lettos, "castle." It goes without saying that the moon and its houses were under the auspices of Queen Medb, the Soma queen of the Gaels.

In short, these *la* words represent the sidereal lunar mansions of the stellar month which is shorter than the synodic month. Therefore, there is a lag between the two months. This being that the synodic month is marked by an interval of two moons having a period of 29.53 days or 29 days and 12 hours. As for the sidereal month, its period is of 27.32 days, 27 days, 7 hours, 43 minutes and 11 seconds, to be exact. To compensate, Greek astrologers tended to add a 28th house every three years.

Detail from a panel from the Gundestrup Cauldron. Author's drawing from a photograph by Werner Forman, National Museum of Denmark, in Copenhagen.

The Two Medbs

According to the *Dinnsenchas Achall,* there were two separate Medbs: Medb Leithderg and Medb Derg. If Medb is the Moon deified, each one corresponded to one of its major phases: (1) Medb Leithderg < Medua Letos Dercos, "Medb of the grey eye (derg, a pun on 'eye and red')"; for the waning moon, that is, the last quarter seen as an eye of Medb. (2) Medb Derg < Medua Derga, "Medb the red"; for the waxing moon that is, the first quarter seen as the other of Medb's eyes. This double identity could also imply that Medb, "of the grey eyes," was the mother and that Medb, "the Red," was her daughter. This lunar period was initiated at the end of the last quarter.

Taken as a representation of the lunar phases in line with the Moon Goddess, it roughly corresponds to what the other Indo-European traditions related on the subject. "They (the Shaktis) indeed honored the Goddess (Kali) on some moonless nights."[2] Symbolically speaking, this new moon phase seems to mark certain intimate moments, a mysterious and disturbing event, here dedicated to the Goddess. The waning phase is associated to the novena since this period could not be initiated at the full moon, that is, the bright and clear period.

In one of the three Irish destiny tales, the name of the goddess Nemain, "the venomous," evokes the novena period of nine days. As the triune goddess, her other aliases were Fea (Hate), Badb (Fury), Macha (Battlefield) and Morrigan (the great Queen/born of the Sea). Morrigan was the main fate goddess as the allegory of death (mainly death suffered on the battlefield). This disturbing side of the Celtic triune goddess recalls the Indian Kali and her sisters. In light of this, the eye symbolism cannot be applied here in that the new moon is in fact blind and occulted. The novena period had to precede this moonless moment. But there again, one can imagine the goddess winking an eye.

The two quarters or halves, were symbolized by the horn, mainly that of cattle. The sons of Ailill and Medb were all called Maine which meant "lad," or "boy." According to legend, they were all lawless and sent in exile to Britain to the court of Ingcel Càech, son (or grandson) of the blind king of Britons. From there, they led raids in Ireland on Da Derga's hostel. The High King of Ireland, Conaire Mór, was killed in these attacks. Afterwards, they all answered their mother Medb's war call in the war of the Tain Bo Cuailgne, the raid of the Ulster cows.

Medb's 27 Handmaids

The antiquity of the Nakshatras, or 27 lunar houses system, also found in other Indo-European myths, is reflected by the records of the 4,000-year-old *Rig Veda.* The Nakshatras moon signs all put together work in conjunction with each of the zodiacal signs, there sublimating in a monthly period of the solar cycle of 360 days. Their allegorical significations roughly reproduce the moon's movement through the constellations it visits during one month. This apparent movement inevitably comes in conjunction with certain stars and therefore does not actually match the displacement of the sun through the same stars, clusters and constellations, it crosses.

The constellations visited by the moon in these 27 days, and so, are measured for a full day, that is, a period alternating day and night (marked by one night and one day).

The Greeks called this 24-hour period a nycthemeron, the Indians called it a tithi,[3] while the Celts a latis (pl. lates). Unfortunately, the Irish texts do not give us a complete list for the names of the different lunar mansions identified as maidens. Nevertheless, it is possible to identify some of the maids surrounding Medb and Ailill and complete this list following the instructions found in the *Auraicept na Do Eces* or "Scholars' Primer": "Tosach fregra, beginning of an answer, to wit, that is ailm, A; for the first expression of every human being after his birth is A."[4]

The following is taken from the book in the ogham word list of Morann Mac Main:

> Word Ogham of Morann Mac Main here. Feocus foltchain, faded trunk and fair hair, that is for birch, B, in the Word Ogham, because names which Morann gave of himself to the Ogham letters, these are they which take the effect of letters in the Word Ogham. Feocus foltchain for B, for these are two aspects of the birch, and it was hence put for the Ogham letter which has taken a name from it.[5]

In short, an Ogham ranking for women's names, as Calder explains, follows the same method:

> Woman Ogham: heroines for group B after the same procedure (or method), to wit, one for B, two for L, thus all down.
> Nuns for group H similiter.
> Maidens for group M similiter.
> Girls for group A similiter, to wit, one for a, two for u.[6]

Please note that *similiter* is a Latin word meaning "in like manner."

The Possible Irish Star Maidens

> The driver turned the chariot and Medb came back. She saw something that she deemed wonderful, namely, a women coming towards her by the shaft of the chariot. The girl was weaving a fringe, holding a weaver's beam of white bronze in her right hand with seven strips of red gold on its points (?). She wore a spotted, green-speckled cloak, with a round, heavy-headed brooch in the cloak above her breast. She had a crimson, rich-blooded fair-faced, countenance, a bright, laughing eye, thin, red lips. She had shining pearly teeth; you would have thought they were showers of fair pearls which were displayed in her head. Like new pertaining were her lips. The sweet sound of her voice and speech was as melodious as the strings of harps plucked by the hands of masters. As white as snow falling in one night was the luster of her skin and body *shining* through her garments. She had long and very white feet with pink, even, round and sharp nails. She had long, fair-yellow, golden hair; three tresses of her hair wound round her head, another tress falling behind which touched the calves of her legs.[7]

The mythological motif of the Druidess Feidelm holding a weaver's beam clearly identifies her as a fate fairy. Additional names can be gleaned, here and there, in other passages of the same tale surrounding Medb: "Medb told a handmaid of her household to go to the river and fetch her water for drinking and washing. Loche was the maid's name. Then Loche came, wearing the golden diadem of the queen on her head and accompanied by fifty women."[8] It is difficult to accurately guess the names of the 27 girls or 50 women who were in Medb's entourage, but nevertheless, the following list gives an overview of various possible mythonyms:

> (1) Áine < Ainu, "ship," or Annia, "ring," goddess of love and fertility, Eogabail's daughter, himself a foster son of Manannán; her mound: Cnoc Áine, Knockainy, County Kerry.

(2) Almha < Alma, "farming," a goddess of the Tuatha Dé Danann, and name of a mound of southern Ireland;
(3) Aobh < Aibo/Aiba, "physiognomy, mien, air, demeanor, fair faced."
(4) Aoife < Aisuia > Esuia, "the (divine) breath," Esuuia, "the terrible," a sister of Scathach.
(5) Arbha < Arbhar < Arbara, "herb, grass, cereal," or punning with Arua, "Furrow," another of Aoife's sisters.
(6) Badb < Bodua, "crow," one of the triple battle furies or Valkyries, wife and sister of Net Morigann and Macha.
(7) Becuma/Becuna Cneisgel < Bnacuma Gela Cnidta, "grief woman with light skin."
(8) Caer Ibormeith < Cadra Iburomatia, "beautiful yew lover," Aonghus Mac Óg's lover, the swan-maiden. She stayed at Bruigh na Boinne to the north of Tara.
(9) Collach < Cailiaca/Coiliaca, "prophetess, seer woman, vaticinator, augury, witch."
(10) Clothra < Clotara, "fame," a daughter of Eochaid Feidleach, sister of Medb, and another of Conchobar's wives, She was the mother of Cormac Conloinges, while others say that it was Ness, daughter of Eochaid, "of the yellow heels," who was Cormac's mother.
(11) Dechtire < Dexsiutera, "the rightful."
(12) Eadon < Aedonia, "fervent, fiery."
(13) Eibhir < Ebara, "forgetful," a foreign blonde star-maiden from the sunny countries courted by Oisin.
(14) Eile < Aella < Aetla, "gale," a daughter of Eochaid and another of Medb's sisters. She was Fergal mac Magach's wife. Her name was given to Bri Eili in Leinster. After being with Fergal, she became the wife of Sraibgend mac Niuil from the tribe of Erna, with him, she had a son called Mata, the father of Sraibgend Ailill mac Mata.
(15) Eithne/Ethne < Etana, "poetry," the daughter of Eochaidh Féidhleach and wife of Conchobar.
(16) Fedelm/Feidelm/Fedelma < Uidlma, "seer, witch." One of the druid-fairies of Sidh Cruachan prophesying Medb's defeat. She is described as a blonde with long braids and wearing a green coat.
(17) Fethan < Uetona, "veil," also called Fea < Uico, "fury."
(18) Findabair < Uindasoibra, "the white ghost, or specter," the name matches that of the Welsh Gwenhyfar (Guinevere in French and Jennifer in English, wife of King Arthur) and later on, the White Lady of folk tales.
(19) Fleidlimid Noichruthach < Uoltiatama, "great fleece," is a daughter of Conchobar, king of Ulster. She was also called Fedlem Noichruthach < Uoltitamos Netscrutacos, "heroine of the abundant fleece."
(20) Garmuin or Carman/Carmun < Carmantio, "the distaffer," a seasonal goddess sponsoring the Assembly of Tara.
(21) Inda < Enda/Inda, "the end, the ultimate," a daughter of Eocho Salbuide and wife of Cethern.
(22) Lebarcham < Labarocama, "bed talking," the daughter of Aue and Adarc. In the *Raid of the cows of Cualnge*, she is described as a beauty of noble face having large eyes and round cheeks.

(23) Loche/Lochu < Loca/Locua, "pond, lake."
(24) Mugain Attenchaithrech or Mumain Etanchaithrech, also spelled as Mór Muman and Ethne Aitenchaitrech. She was one of Medb's sisters. When Cuchulainn returned to Emain Macha taken with battle frenzy, she and her damsels stripped naked in order to calm his rage. Mugain < Mogontia, "adolescence" and Mumain < Momonia, "of Mumha," Munster. The name also puns with Mudsmia, "nurse," and Mór Mumain < Mara Momonia, for "Great Munster." Etanchaithrech is a compound of Etana "poetry," caitra "round shield" and suffixed by the feminine qualifier –aca, for "the shield of poetry." She was one of the representatives of the solar goddess and the shield was one of her attributes.
(25) Nemain < Nemetona, "sanctuary," or Nimneto, "intoxication, poisoning," one of the three Badbs (battle-furies), a sister of Badb and Morrigan.
(26) Odras < Adrastia, "invincibility," the daughter of Odarnatan Udarnatanos, "of the river of otters."
(27) Oonagh < Oinaca, "the meeting, the assembly," a goddess of the Tuatha Dé Danann and wife of Fionnbharr. They resided at Sidhe Medb near Tuam. Site of the Giant's Causeway, a visible volcanic formation on the Ulster coast, 3 km north of the town of Bushmills in County Antrim. Her name was in reference to the magic of her coat.
(28) Reid> Redia, "plain or field passable by cart."
(29) Scandlach > Scandlaca, "the tease, teaser," the princess of ladies.
(30) Scathach Buanand < Scataca Bouenda, "the suspicious and ultimate cow."
(31) Sgeimh Solais, traditionally given to mean "beautiful light," but most likely meaning "the great cutting light." She was a daughter of King Cairbre. Her marriage with the son of Desi created a conflict with the Fianna. Sgeimh probably derives from scei-, sceiô v. "to cut, break, chisel," a feminine superlative suffix –ama, for "greatly cutting one"; and Solais, probably from suelnestio "luminosity, light."
(32) Slaine ní Seren < Slania Sdironia, "health of stars"; from sdira > ðira/sira "star." She was a Milesian goddess, daughter of Scethern, wife of Craiphtine and sister of Forgall Manach. She had an affair with Cormac Cond Lanyards. Furious, Craiphtine killed Cormac and turned his army of 150 youths into birds. In the *Leabhar Gabala Eireann* or "Book of the Takings of Ireland," she is, along with Tea (Tea- Mhair), Fás (Feart Do/Do Gleand), Fial Liben, Odba and Scota, one of the seven Milesian fairies. A site is dedicated to her at Inber Slaine.
(33) Sionnan < Sianna/Sionna, "binding," she was the daughter of Mac Lir Lodan and her name is eponymous with the River Shannon which flows to southwest of Ireland.
(34) Tea < Tega, "support, cover," a goddess of the Tuatha Dé Danannn and wife of Eremon associated with Teamhair or Tara. Tea > Tee puns with the Middle Irish Tee, for "woman, girl, female."
(35) Tlachtga < Tlagtetica, "woolen dressed," a goddess associated with the Samhain ritual sacrifice performed on a hill of Meade.

(36) Uathach Buanand or nUanaind < Uataca Bouenda, "Boand, the sorceress, or witch."

The Top Six Women of Ireland Drawn from the *Dinnsenchas of Achall*: Medb, Sadb, Sarait (who embellishes verses), Er, Emer and Achall

(1) Medb II, that is, Medb Derg as daughter of Medb.
(2) Sadb < Sadua/Sedia, "the doe."
(3) Sarait < Sagreta, "the insistent."
(4) Er < Eria, "the West."
(5) Emer < Amaro, "sorrow, sadness."
(6) Achall < Uxella, "the highest."

The Bean Sidhe (anglicized as banshee), "the ladies of the mounds," which numbered three to seven, were comparable to the Roman Parcae and Greek Moîrai or Moires. They were sinister figures who presided over the destiny of mortal men and who decided on the span of life, work, marriage and time of death. According to Hesiodus, there were three Moires, Klôthô, "the spinner," who spins the thread of life, Lachesis, "the distaffer," who rolls the thread, and Atropos, "the inflexible," who cuts the thread. In Irish folklore, the banshees are said to be attached to some families as they are heard like sirens singing at the time of death or of birth. They are found in all of the Indo-European traditions and were named as follows: the Parcae, Fates, or Tri Fata, among the Romans, the Norns among the Germanic peoples, the Rozenicy among the Slavs, and the Niyati among the Indians.

The Sidh is a mound or hill whose underground entrance is a door to the Other World. The Irish countryside, as it is believed, is dotted with hundreds of Sidhs. The Sidh of Cruachan was such a magical place that it had its parallel in both worlds, that is, in the world of the mortals and in the realm of the spirits.

The 27 Irish Lunar Houses Compared to the Indian Nakshatras

(According to the Gaelic astrological scheme, along with the Vedic lunar mansions and constellations crossed by the moon.)

Names of the Gaelic constellations and Gallic (initial equinox in autumn) and their houses:	In-cusps and out-cusps with their constellations:	Medb's 27 handmaids and maidens (after the Irish tales):	Star chart (according to Vedic astrology) with astral houses, degrees and planets:	Vedic Lunar Mansions with the 27 daughters of Daksha and companions of Soma (the Moon God):
Scorpion: Siltarios || Samonios, "The Sower" / Samoni Prinnios **House I** Lates I	.ln./.lii. A, Ailm	01. Almha	From 20.00 Libra to 3.20 Scorpio, Jupiter	16. Vishakha, "The Forked"

IX: The Lunar Mansions

Names of the Gaelic constellations and Gallic (initial equinox in autumn) and their houses:	In-cusps and out-cusps with their constellations:	Medb's 27 handmaids and maidens (after the Irish tales):	Star chart (according to Vedic astrology) with astral houses, degrees and planets:	Vedic Lunar Mansions with the 27 daughters of Daksha and companions of Soma (the Moon God):
Lates II Scorpio	.ln./.lii. A	02. Achall	**House VIII** 3.20 to 16.40 / Scorpio Saturn	17. Anuradha, "Student of the divine spark"
Lates III Scorpio	B, Beth	03. Badb	16.40 to 30.00 Scorpio, Mercury	18. Jyeshta, "The Oldest"
House II Sagittarius: Bogdariios "the Archer" / Dumanni Prinnios **House II** Lates IV	.rii. H, Huath, Uath	04. Uathach Buanand, and Scathach	**House IX** From 0.0 to 13.20 / Sagittarius, Southern lunar node	19. Mula, "The Root"
Lates V Sagittairius	.rii. M, Muin, Min	05. Mugain Attenchaithrech or Mumain Etanchaithrech or Mór Muman or Ethne Aitenchaitrech	13.20 to 26.40 Sagittairius, Venus	20. Purva Ashadha, "The early victory or the undefeated"
Capricorn: Attiluis, "the Sturgeon" / Riuri Prinnios **House III** Lates VI	.lu. P/Ui, Peith, Pethbol/Uilléan	06. Fethan	27.40 Sagittarius to 10.00 Capricorn, Sun	21. Uttara Ashadha, "Late or not yet conquered victory"
Lates VII Capricorn	.lu. Th/Oi(r), Tharan / Oir, Feorusoir	07. Odras	**House X** 10.00 to 23.20 / Capricorn, Moon	22. Shravana, "The Hearing"
Aquarius: Udesciocos / Anaganti Prinnios **House IV** Lates VIII	fii. O, On, Ohn	08. Oonagh	**House XI** 6.40 to 20.00 /Aquarius Northern lunar node, 23.20 Capricorn to 6.40 Aquarius, Mars	23. Dhanistha, "The Richest"

Names of the Gaelic constellations and Gallic (initial equinox in autumn) and their houses:	In-cusps and out-cusps with their constellations:	Medb's 27 handmaids and maidens (after the Irish tales):	Star chart (according to Vedic astrology) with astral houses, degrees and planets:	Vedic Lunar Mansions with the 27 daughters of Daksha and companions of Soma (the Moon God):
Lates IX Aquarius	fii. Ph/Ia, Phogos/Iphin	09. Eibhir	Aquarius 6.40 to 20.00	24. Shata-bhishak, "The Hundred healers"
Pisces: Escoi / Ogroni Prinnios **House V** Lates X	ict. L, Luis	10. Lochu	20.00 Arius to 3.20 Pisces, Jupiter	25. Shata-bhishak "The Hundred healers"
Lates XI Pisces	ict. L	11. Lebarcham, daughter of Aue	**House XII** 3.20 to 16.40 Pisces Saturn 16.40–30 Pisces, Mercury	26. Uttara Bhadrapada, "Happy feet of the Future"
Lates XII Pisces	ict. D, Daur	12. Daireann, Dairine	16.40 to 30.00 Pisces	27. Ravati ou Revati, "The Rich"
Aries: Aros,"the god Aries or Mars" / Cuti Prinnios **House VI** Lates XIII	arb. Ch/Ea, Choad/Eashadh	13. Eadon,	**House I** from 0.00 to 13.20 / **Ram** Southern lunar node	1. Ashvini, "The Horselike"
Lates XIV Ram	arb. G, Gort, Gart	14. Garmuin	13.20 to 26.40 / Ram, Venus	2. Bharani, "The Life-bearer"
Taurus: Sciatos Ander, "The Winged Bull" / Giamoni Prinnios **House VII** Lates XV	insci. U, Ur;	15. Fedelma	26.40 to 10.00 / Bull, Sun	3. Krittika "The Cutter"
Lates XVI Taurus	insci. N, Nuin, Nion	16. Nemain	10.00 to 23.20 / Taurus, Moon	4. Rohini, "The Red"
Gemini: Roudiosuccoi, "The Red Pigs" / Simiuisoni Prinnios **House VIII** Lates XVII	ruidzûig T, Tinne	17. Tea	**House III** 23.20 in Taurus to 6.40 in Gemini / Mars	5. Mrigashirsha, "The Deer head"

Names of the Gaelic constellations and Gallic (initial equinox in autumn) and their houses:	In-cusps and out-cusps with their constellations:	Medb's 27 handmaids and maidens (after the Irish tales):	Star chart (according to Vedic astrology) with astral houses, degrees and planets:	Vedic Lunar Mansions with the 27 daughters of Daksha and companions of Soma (the Moon God):
Lates XVIII Gémeaux	ruidzûig Ng, Ngetal	18. Cneisgel	6.40 to 20.00 Gemini Northern lunar node	6. Ardra "The Fresh"
Cancer: Uillos, "Horse" / Equi Prinnios **House IX** Lates XIX	iùl. E, Eadha, Eodha	19. Eile	**House IV** 20.00 to 3.20 / Cancer, Jupiter	7. Punarvasu "The Bright Renewal"
Lates XX Cancer	iùl. E	20. Emer et Er,	3.20 to 16.40 Cancer, Saturn	8. Pushya "The Nurse"
Lates XXI Cancer	iùl. F (V), Fearn	21. Findabair	16.40 to 30 Cancer, Mercury	9. Ashlesha "The Embracer"
Lion: Aga, "The Deer" / Elembiui Prinnios **House X** Lates XXII	og C, Coll	22. Collach	**House V** From 0–13 to 20.00 / Leo Southern lunar node	10. Magha "The Great"
Lates XXIII Leo	og St (Sd), Straif	23. Sláine ní Seren	13.20 to 26.40 Leo Venus	11. Purva Phalguni "The First Red"
Virgo: Ecco | Esoxs / Edrinni Prinnios **House XI** Lates XXIV	ech Ioho, Idho, Iubhar	24. Caer Ibormeith	**Maison VI** From 26.40 in Leo to 10.00 in Virgo / Sun	12. Uttara Phalguni "The Last Red"
Lates XXV	ech S, Saille	25. Sadb	10.00 to 23.20 Virgo, Moon	13. Hasta "The Hand"
Libra: Indouelicon / Cantli Prinnios **House XII** Lates XXVI	ind Q, Quert	26. Coinchend	**Maison VII** From 23.20 in Virgo to 6.40 in Scales / Mars	14. Chitra "The Bright"

Names of the Gaelic constellations and Gallic (initial equinox in autumn) and their houses:	In-cusps and out-cusps with their constellations:	Medb's 27 handmaids and maidens (after the Irish tales):	Star chart (according to Vedic astrology) with astral houses, degrees and planets:	Vedic Lunar Mansions with the 27 daughters of Daksha and companions of Soma (the Moon God):
Lates XXVII	ind R, Ruis	27. Réid	6.40 to 20.00 Scales, Northern lunar node	15. Swati "The Sword or Independence"

Astrology and the Lunar Mansions

"Nine small white hands.... And nine mothers.... Nine Korrigans dancing with flowers in her hair and in robes of white wool around the fountain in the light of the full moon."— *Barzhaz Breizh*, "The Bardic Lore of Brittany"

Why the number nine? Simply because this figure is three times three and is symbolic of Nemain,[9] the goddess of the novena period. Also, nine gives an even tripling breakdown of the mansions: 3 × 9 = 27. Therefore, there is a potential allocation of 9 signs for each of the lunar mansions of Emain Macha.

The royal palace of Emain Macha[10] had three large main halls. The first hall, Craobh Ruadh (< Roudia Crobas), "The Red Bough," had nine rooms. This is where the king and his attendant hero slept and feasted. It is described as a circular structure made of yew (iogh < iuocos, "goodly, auspicious, clearly, strongly") and having plated bronze walls. The king's bedroom was at the center of it and had a silver ceiling supported by columns of gold-plated bronze. Around the fortress of Emain Macha, there was the battle field aptly called, "the Plain of Macha." The severed heads of fallen warriors from after the battle were prosaically called "the hazelnuts of Macha." The second largest hall, Craobh Derg,[11] was the royal treasure room in which were contained the war trophies and spoils of war. In the third hall, Teite Brecc,[12] were kept the weapons and battle gear of the heroes, because it was agreed by all that no one came to the banquet armed. The name is reminiscent of Briccos, "the speckled, the trout" (and punning with Brictillos, "the mackerel," Bricta or Bricstia, "magic").

Another famous building mentioned in the Irish cycles was the Hostel of Airtheach.[13] Brann regularly visits this hostel which was located on an island to the west of Ireland and which was surrounded by the plain of Magh Airtchech. Also mentioned is Da Derga's Hostel,[14] which was a hospital for wounded warriors. And finally, the tales also relate of the destruction of the Hostel of Bron Mac Bruin. Bron, from the Old Celtic name Bronnos means, "lame." Bron (< Bronna/Bronda) generally given as meaning "breasts or chest," sounds similar to the Welsh name of the goddess Brannwen, "the white Raven-hen," who was also called Bronnwen, "of the white breasts."

Other Legendary Buildings

Buchat's Hostel

The Rennes Dindshenchas (section 113) mentions that Odras was a Hospitaller of Buasach (< bouosacos), the cow-chief of Cormac hua Cuind, and owner of the House of Care. In Buchat's Hostel, or Bruidhean Buchat Buasaich, was found a cauldron that was always hot. Therefore, the men of Leinster referred to Buchat (< bucatos, "public crier") as "the cauldron of generosity." In the Irish tongue, a buasach, was a man who had many cows.

Tech Duinn

Tech Duinn, "the house of Donn, the dark," which was the inn of the dead, was located beyond the waves on an island in the ocean to the southwest of Ireland. The Irish cycles attribute to each house a geographical orientation and a cosmological meaning that hint at their position in time and space.

GEOGRAPHY OF THE LEGENDARY MANSIONS:

(1) North East (Ulster):
(2) East: Bruigh na Boinne (< Brugden Bouendas), "the Hostel of the Boyne," is located at the site of New Grange. Other designations: Tara, Rath Gráinne (< Rate Greinas), Tech Cormaic, or Teite Corbmac (< Tegos Corbomaqi). Cormac was father of Gráinne.
(3) South East (Leinster): Bruidne Dá Derga (< Brugden Deuos Dergos), Da Derga's Hostel or Caer Feddwid (< Qataira Uedduidogli), "Fortress of Twilight-appearance."
(4) South: Temair Luchra (Tumera Lucaras), "the Hill of Luchra," the Tara of the South at Luachra's South Rath; Other designation: Baile Lughaide (< Lugu Balion), "the domain of Lugh."
(5) South West (Munster): Tech Duinn (< Tegos Donni), "the house of Donn."
(6) West: Emain Abhlach; other designation: Airtheach or Airgtech (< Aeritegia) "the house of Care."
(7) Northwest (Connacht): Rath Cruachan (< Rate Cruccon), "Rath of the Slope," the stronghold of Ailill and Medb. Other designation: Bruidhean Buchat Buasaich (<) or Buchat's Hostel.
(8) North: Emain Macha (< Emniou Magosias), "Twin City of the Plain," with its three large halls.

The Sidh of Cruachan (< Sidos Cruccon)

The Lunar Mansions in Sections of three Novenas: Qatairai Emniou Magosias, the three halls of the Palace of the Twin City of the Plains.

I—QATAIRA ROUDAS CROBAS
(PALACE OF THE RED BRANCH, INCLUDING ITS NINE HALLS):

(1) Almha (livestock)
(2) Achall (elevation)

(3) Badb (combat)
(4) Uathach and Scathach (monstrous, the omen, the pretext)
(5) Mugain or Mumain (concealed, graceful)
(6) Fethan (denial, challenge)
(7) Odras (invincibility)
(8) Oonagh (reunion, strength, fatigue, thirst)
(9) Eibhir (oblivion)

II—Qataira Dergas Crobas
(Palace of the Red Branch, including its nine halls):

(10) Lochu (fault, error, balanced)
(11) Lebarcham (eloquent, resonant sound)
(12) Daireann, Dairine (of young girls, rage, madness)
(13) Eadon (fervor, ardor)
(14) Garmuin (responsiveness to calls)
(15) Fedelma (clairvoyance)
(16) Nemain (hostile, enemy)
(17) Tea (support cover)
(18) Cneisgel (gasoline, quintessence)

III—Tegia Brecca Tectas (House of Motley Property, including the following nine houses):

(19) Eile (striping, breath)
(20) Er or Emer (back, behind, sadness)
(21) Findabair (ghostly)
(22) Collach (auspicious omen)
(23) Slaine ní Seren (health, star)
(24) Caer Ibormeith (beauty, goodness)
(25) Sadb (peace, peace, peace)
(26) Coinchend (intelligence, knowledge, wisdom)
(27) Reid (travel, availability).

Let's note that the first of the three halls is noisy and rowdy, the second is dark and quiet while the third is bright and joyful.

The 27 Cusps According to Taliesin's Cad Goddeu

(1) U. Uernos, "alder tree." "The alder trees, the head of the line, formed the van."
(2) S. Salixs, "willow." "The willows and quicken trees came late to the army."
(3) B. Brinio, "plum tree." "Plum-trees, that are scarce, unlonged for of men."
(4) M. Mespilos > Nespila, "medlar." "The elaborate meddler-trees, true objects of contention."
(5) A. Acuilentos > Apilentos (cf. Latin aculentum "wild rose,") or Acuilenton > Apilenton, "wild rose"; Broica/Uroica, "heather, wild rose." "The prickly rose-bushes against a host of giants."

(6) S. Subitocrobios, "raspberry." "The raspberry brake did what is better failed for the security of life."
(7) G. Gabromelxos, "privet." "Privet and woodbine and ivy at the front of the battle."
(8) G. Gortia, "furze." "Furze, like ivy went to the combat."
(9) C. Carasos, "cherry tree." "The cherry-tree was provoked."
(10) B. Betus, "birch." "The birch, notwithstanding his high mind, was late before he was arrayed."
(11) C > Ch > X. Cista (Greek cf. Khistos), "laburnum." "Not because of his cowardice, but on account of his greatness. The laburnum held in mind, that your wild nature was foreign."
(12) P. Pados, "pine tree." "Pine-trees at the doorstep of the chair of disputation were greatly exalted in the presence of kings. Morawg and Morydd were made prosperous in pines."
(13) L. Lemos, "elm tree." "The elm with his retinue did not go aside a foot less he would fight the center, and the flanks, and the rear."
(14) C. Coslos, cosla, cuslos, "hazel tree." "Hazel-trees, it was judged, that ample was thy mental exertion."
(15) G. Gabromelxos, "privet bush.""The privet, happy his lot, the bull of battle, the lord of the world."
(16) C. Colenos, "holly bush." "Holly, it was tinted with green, he was the hero."
(17) S. (sp/sq,'s' mutating into 'h') > H. Spetes, or Acinarios, "hawthorn." "The hawthorn, surrounded by prickles, with pain at his hand."
(18) C. Critacos, crennos, "aspen." "The aspen-wood has been topped, it was topped in battle."
(19) R. Ratis, "fern." V/F: (B/U) Roica: "heather." "The fern that was plundered."
(20) G. Genista, banatlos, "broom." "The broom, in the van of the army, in the trenches he was hurt."
(21) A. Actina, "gorse bush." "The gorse did not do well, notwithstanding let it overspread."
(22) B/U > V/F, Uroica, broica, heather. "The heath was victorious, keeping off on all sides. The common people were charmed, during time proceeding of the men."
(23) D. Deruos, "oak." "The oak, quickly moving, before him, tremble heaven and earth. A valiant door-keeper against an enemy, his name is considered. The blue-bells combined, and caused a consternation. In rejecting, were rejected, others, that were perforated."
(24) P. Periarios, pesiarios, "pear tree." "Pear-trees, the best intruders in time conflict of the plain."
(25) A. Abassia, "chestnut tree." "A very wrathful wood, the chestnut is bashful, the opponent of happiness, the jet has become black, the mountain has become crooked, the woods have become a kiln, existing formerly in the great seas since was heard the shout."
(26) B. Betua, "birch tree." "The tops of the birch covered us with leaves, and transformed us, and changed our faded state."

(27) E. Ercus, "oak tree (in general)." "The oak, quickly moving, before him, tremble heaven and earth. A valiant door-keeper against an enemy, his name is considered."

Proposed Model for the Gallic Lunar Mansions

(1) A. Argantoreta (the silver wheel)
(2) Â. Andarta (great she-bear)
(3) B. Belisama (most bright)
(4) C. Catubodua (battle crow)
(5) D. Diuona (lunar)
(6) Đ. Đirona (star-like)
(7) E. Elitiuai Matres (the visionaries)
(8) Ê. Epona (the mare)
(9) G. Glanis (the pure)
(10) I. Ialona (of the grove)
(11) Î. Icouellauna (excellent water)
(12) L. Loucena Uirodaxtis (lightning turning one)
(13) M. Mogontia (the powerful)
(14) N. Nemetona (the sanctuary)
(15) O. Onniona (the ash)
(16) Ô. Oadianai/Osdianai?
(17) P. Pendusa (the final); Parga (the slope)
(18) Q. Quadriiai < Quetruaduai/Petruaduai (the four ways)
(19) PH. Phernouinexai < Bernouinexai (naiads of the outflow)
(20) R. Rosmerta (providence)
(21) S. Suliuia (well colored)
(22) T. Tangonai Matres (patch-mender mothers)
(23) TH. Tiana/Thiana (kind, trim)
(24) U. Uacalinexai/Baccalinexai (naiads of the vintagers)
(25) Û. Uroica (heather)
(26) X. Xandrumanexa (hundred oars naiads)
(27) XS. Xsulsigiai (the hypnotic ones)

X

Signs of the Zodiac

"'What better plan could we carry out' said he, 'than to go and attack yonder man who is checking and holding back the four great provinces of Ireland and to bring back with us his head in triumph to Ailill and Medb. Though we have done many wrongs and injuries to Ailill and to Medb, we shall obtain peace thereby if that man fall by us.' That is the plan they decided on. And they came forward to the place where Cú Chulainn was, and when they came, they did not grant him fair play or single combat but all twelve of them attacked him straightaway. However Cú Chulainn fell upon them and forthwith struck off their twelve heads. And he planted twelve stones for them in the ground and put a head of each one of them on its stone and also put Ferchú Loingsech's head on it's stone. So that the spot where Ferchú Loingsech left his head is called Cinnit Ferchon that is, Cennáit Ferchon *the Headplace of Ferchú*."—*Book of Leinster–Táin Bó Cualnge*, translated by Cecile O'Rahilly, p. 209

Gallic Drachma of the Tectosages (from 12 to 52 BC) depicting a sun wheel with moon crescents and cosmic symbols such as bean-shaped globes and axe. The axe as an astronomical symbol lends itself to a few crafty puns such as: seruo, "vagabond, planet," serro, "axe," and amsero, "time age." Author's drawing after a photograph from Laurent Fabre numismate.

The Head Place of Ferchú (Cennáit Ferchon < Qendotia Uiroconos)—the Zodiacal Belt

As recalled by Diodorus of Siculus in the 1st century BCE, the Druids practiced mysteries and created symbols that codified their knowledge into abstract images.

> The Gauls are terrifying in aspect and their voices are deep and altogether harsh; when they meet together they converse with few words and in riddles, hinting darkly at things for the most part and using one word when they mean another; and they like to talk in superlatives, to the end that they may extol themselves and depreciate all other men. They are also boasters and threateners and are fond of pompous language, and yet they have sharp wits and are not without cleverness at learning. Among them are also to be found lyric poets whom they call Bards. These men sing to the accompaniment of instruments which are like lyres, and their songs may be either of praise or of obloquy. Philosophers, as we may call them, and men learned in religious affairs are unusually honoured among them and are called by them Druids. The Gauls likewise make use of diviners, accounting them worthy of high approbation, and these men foretell the future by means of the flight or cries of birds and of the slaughter of sacred animals, and they have all the multitude subservient to them.[1]

Therefore, as Diodorus writes, the Druids said one thing while meaning another. This is an important passage if we are to understand the mechanics of wordplay in the arts of divination. Further on in his *History*, Diodorus explains the importance of letters and writing used by the Gallic Druids.

> They (the Gauls) invite strangers to their feasts, and do not enquire until after the meal who they are and of what things they stand in need. And it is their custom, even during the course of the meal, to seize upon any trivial matter as an occasion for keen disputation and then to challenge one another to single combat, without any regard for their lives; for the belief of Pythagoras prevails among them, that the souls of men are immortal and that after a prescribed number of years they commence upon a new life, the soul entering into another body. Consequently, we are told, at the funerals of their dead some cast letters upon the pyre which they have written to their deceased kinsmen, as if the dead would be able to read these letters.[2]

They were most certainly the undisputed masters of the graphic arts; and this expertise nowhere else shines more than in the numismatic arts. If we should want to know the precise nomenclature and terminology of Druidical astrology, we will have to look elsewhere.

If we are to rely on the data collected from the *Book of Ballymote*, up until the late medieval Irish times, Celtic names for the zodiacal signs were still maintained. But then again, these names are significantly different from those found on the Coligny plates dating from late Gallic Antiquity. Obviously, much of this difference is not only due to cultural differences but can also be explained by the way copyist monks tended to gloss over pagan content, there seeking to conform the material to their Orientalizing Christian views. Needless to say that this revisionist approach will greatly obscure the older cosmological system. In time, the original Irish astrological scheme will be quickly abandoned and forgotten in favor of the current Greco-Roman models.

Luckily, thanks to the comparative linguistic and mythological approaches, it is now possible to uncover the real McCoy lying under centuries of overlays. This chapter presents the proposed names for the zodiacal constellations of the ancient Gaulish and late medieval Old Irish versions.

Gallic gold stater depicting astronomical symbols. Author's drawing.

The Twelve Signs of the Gallic Zodiac

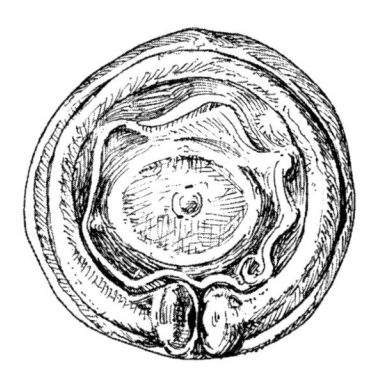

Gold Stater depicting a torque and a solar eye surrounded by a halo. Author's drawing from a photograph by D. Bertuzzi, in *Dossiers Archéologie et sciences des origines*, p. 58.

I—Libra: Cantli Prinnios, "Constellation of the loop of the ring." Cantlos, "looping," connoting Cantalon, "memorial pillar."

The Greeks called this constellation Zygos, for "yoked (zygon "yoke")," that is, the claws of the scorpion. The Romans saw it as a scale and named it Libra next to Virgo which marked the autumnal equinox. In Vedic astrology, it was also called the scale as Tula. The Celts of Antiquity, who represented Libra as a ring or a memorial pillar in former times, saw it as the antlers of a deer. But again, the word Cantlos carried several meanings such as: "looping, buckling," and/or "chant or setting of a ring." Cantalon or Cantlon means both, "ceremony with songs," and "memorial pillar," while Cantla means "lesson." Therefore, this Gallic zodiacal sign was imagined as a ring loop representing the annual cycle. As the sun reflected on water at sunset, a twinkling light shaft seemed to mirror a pillar on its surface. Here, the ring or wheel is mounted on a pillar; an image which served to mark the end of the sun's daily path. In short, the motif of the sun ring and the pillar allegorically served as markers for the cycle's end.

Cyclops character holding a mace and a torque all in representation of the constellation of Ophiuchus (Ophiuchus), which marked the beginning of the Celtic Zodiac. Coinage of the Catalauni kept at the Bibliothèque Nationale de Paris. Author's drawing after a photograph by Blanchet.

II—Scorpio: Samoni Prinnios, "Constellation of the sower rally," and Samonios, "the Sower."

According to a Greek mythological theme, the scorpion Skorpios (Scorpio) was instrumental in resolving the dispute between the goddess Artemis and the god Orion. This image was also shared by the Indians known as Vrscika, "the scorpion," in Sanskrit.

The Celts, unlike their southern Mediterranean neighbors, did not imagine this sign as a scorpion. In fact, they imagined it as a sower throwing the seeds for the oncoming year as it was called Samonos. The name for the sower hinted at Samoindon which literally meant "summer's end, that is," late summer." The Old Celtic name for summer was Samos. The term Samon hinted at many other meanings since it stood for "seed," or "meeting, assembly, reunion." This vocabulary illustrates just what the feasts of Samhain were, New Year celebrations. Also taken figuratively was the term Samo which expressed quietness, calm, balance, firmness and continuity. The Constellation of the Scorpion, along with that of the Serpent, served to indicate the beginning of the new zodiacal cycle.

III—Sagittarius: Dumanni Prinnios, "Constellation of darkening, nebulous," and connoting Dumannios, "of the dark horse, the dark man."

The Greeks formerly associated this constellation with the satyr Krotos, inventor of the bow and son of the god Pan and of the Charite muse Eupheme. It was later associated with the centaur Chiron. The Indians called it Dhanus, "the bow." The name Dumannios for the month of December and its corresponding constellation also connotes Dunomannos, meaning "the horse man," that is, the centaur. This period was also called the time of fumigations and the name hints at dumacos which meant foggy, overcast and nebulous since it is the darkest time of the year. In the old Roman pre–Julian calendar (700 BCE), February (from februarius, februare, "to purify") was the last month of the year. When Julius Caesar became pontifex maximus (high-priest), he fixed the calendar by taking out the intercalary months. Therefore, for the Gauls, December probably marked the beginning of purification through fire and smoke. Moreover, the prefix du-, meaning "dark, black, evil," combined with the root word mann-os/mand-, for "small horse" is a direct pun with dumacos, "darkened, foggy." Mannos also puns with mana, "thought, intelligence," and manda, "residence," and manos, man, human." It was therefore a time of darkening, of retreat and reflection, symbolized as a black horse.

Gallic gold stater depicting two sun or moon beams along with two rays emanating from Venus. From the collection of the Bibliothèque Nationale de Paris. Author's drawing after a photograph by Blanchet.

X: Signs of the Zodiac

IV—Capricorn: Riuri Prinnios, "Constellation of freezing, of frost." Riuros, "frozen," is in wordplay with Riuoros, "radiant, beaming," and connoting Ariurocon, "before the water bucket," that is, before the water pot, Aquarius. The plural of riuo, for "ray," is riuones. The riuones are therefore the seven cosmic rays.

Capricorn comes from the Latin Capricornus, a compound name coined from capra, "goat," and cornus, "horn." The Capricorn mythical beast was the equivalent of the Greek aegocerus. This fabulous half-goat, half-fish beast most likely refers to large scaled fish, probably a sturgeon. The Indian name Makara also designates a sea monster. In Vedic astrology, the makara, is either described as a Capricorn, half stag, half fish, a dolphin or a crocodile. This mythical beast is probably a garbled reminiscence of the original Black Sea Sturgeon. On one of the panels of the Gundestrup Cauldron is depicted a boy riding what seems to be a dolphin but looks rather like a large sturgeon. Likewise, the image of the down-pouring water pot could also be a mythologized reminder of the flooding of the Black Sea by the higher waters of the Mediterranean Sea (circa 5600 BCE).

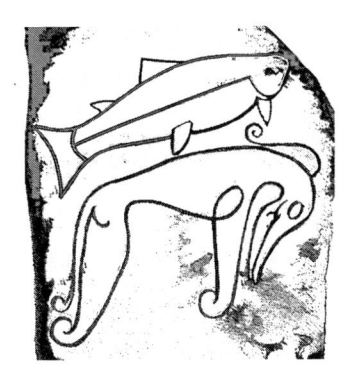

Left: Pictish stele of Barflat, Scotland, depicting a salmon and a dolphin. Dating from the fourth or fifth century CE. From a pencil drawing by J. Stuart in *Symbol Stones of Scotland*, Aberdeen, 1856.
Right: Currency of the Helvetii depicting an ibex, Bibliothèque Nationale de Paris. Author's drawing after a photograph by Blanchet.

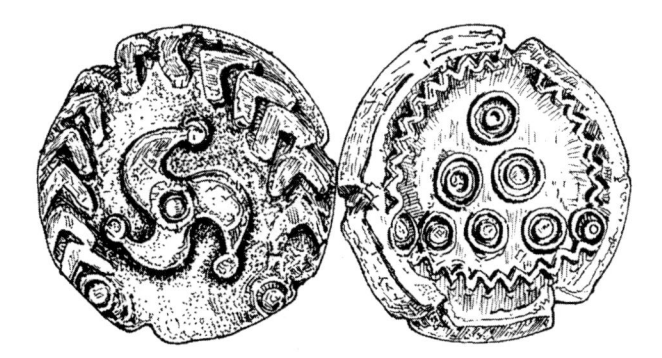

Celtic gold stater of the Belgians with graphic representations of a Triskelion, zigzag patterns in the form of waves, and the eight main stars of Aquarius. From the Rhine Valley, Germany, 1st century BCE. Author's drawing from a photograph at the Money Museum, Hadlaubstrasse, Zürich, Switzerland, collection.

V—Aquarius: Anaganti Prinnios, "Constellation of inaction, or of the calamitous." Anacantios, "calamitous," hints at Anaxs or Anappon, a "goblet, cup or pot."

This term also suggests the name of an official agent in the form of anacontios, a "cup-bearer, pot bearer," or again, a "water boy." The representation of a cup-bearer, pouring his pot in a pool in which swam a large fish was common to both Classical and Vedic astrology. Here, the large fish is for the constellation of the southern fish (Piscis Austrinus) which the Celts saw as a salmon. The Vedic Indians also entertained the idea of a pot as Kumbha, the "pot." The Greeks called this constellation Hydrochoos, which meant the "water-pourer," and the Romans called it Aquarius, the "water carrier or cup-bearer." Aquarius was identified to Ganymede, the cup-bearer of Zeus. And in Celtic bardic wordplay, this sign stands for Ancena or Ncena, "dire necessity, fatality or violent coercion." And again, in standard poetic formulation, Ana gantas, stood for "pond of the geese."

The Ophidian headed ram is the classical symbol for this sign. Gallic coin representing a head with a torque, lightning bolt and a coiled snake. From the collection of the Bibliothèque Nationale de Paris. Author's drawing after a photograph by Blanchet.

VI—Pisces: Ogroni Prinnios, "Constellation of coolness, the cold-blooded." Ogronoi, "fishes, snakes, amphibians, cold-blooded animals."

The constellation of the Fishes (Ichtyes in Greek and Pisces in Latin) commemorates the myth where Aphrodite and her child Ichthus were turned into fish and pursued by the malicious Typhon, the Titan of smoke and winds, in the waters of the Euphrates. This theme of the fish was also present in Vedic astrology and known as Mīna, "the fish." Along with ogronos, some of the Old Celtic names for snake or ophidian were: anguis and nadralis or natralis. The Celtic terms ogros and ogris both refer to cold.

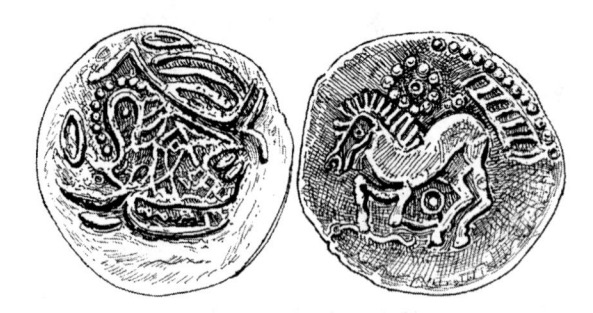

Celtic Tetradrachm of the Danube Valley from the 2nd or 1st century BCE. Left: the head of Aries, right: a horse (Pegasus) topped by the Northern Crown and below it, the sun disk. The rake symbol represents the constellation of the Boar (Little Dipper). Drawing by the author.

X: Signs of the Zodiac

VII—Aries: Cuti Prinnios, "Constellation of Aries." Cutios/Qutios/Putios, "the ram."

The adjective cuti-os/-a/-on, means "fiery, fervent or ardent," when not "sneaky, hypocritical." The name cutios, for "ram," puns with cutis, "skin, leather," as for a pouch or a leather purse. The Greeks called the constellation of Aries, Krios. The Latin name Aries should not be confused with the Greek name for the god since it was Mars in Latin. The Vedic name for this constellation was Mesa, the "ram."

Left: Bull, detail from the Gundestrup Cauldron, 1st century BCE. Author's drawing from a photograph by E. Lessing, National Museum of Copenhagen.
Right: Coinage from southern Gaul. Representation of a bull with the inscription Massalihto (or perhaps Massalieton "Massalia"). Bibliothèque Nationale de Paris. Author's drawing after a photograph by Blanchet.

VIII—Taurus: Giamoni Prinnios, "Constellation of shoots, germinating." Giamonos, "germinator"; connoting gammos, "cattle or deer buck," and/or gamminos, "steer."

The Greeks imagined this constellation as a white bull, an aspect of Zeus in association with the goddess Europa. Its Greek name was Tauros Kretaios, "the retan Bull." The Indians called it Vṛṣ abha, also for "bull." The Gallic phrasing for Taurus was Giamos or Giiemos, which should not be confused with the Gallic form gemos, which is from geimos or giamos, and which coalesces with giamos for "winter." Thus, the true meaning of this month, and astrological sign, was giiemo > giamo which meant "germination."

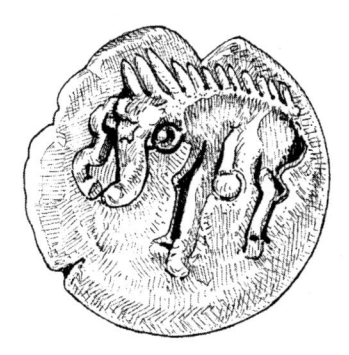

Left: Boar with the stars of the Septentrion. Drawing by the author from a photograph at the Bibliothèque Nationale de Paris.
Right: Apollonian Head (Cepheus) flanked by a wild boar (Little Dipper). Author's drawing after a photograph by Blanchet.

IX—Gemini: Simiuisonni Prinnios, "Constellation of the spirited breezes." Simiuisunoi, "worthy and lighthearted," connoting Semiuesses, small and lively, spirited, vivacious pigs. The Latin term Gemini was borrowed from the Greek Didymoi, the "twins," being the Dioscuri, Castor and Pollux. The Sanskrit term Mithuna was also for "twins."

The first element of the term, *simis* or *semis* means "light, lighthearted or reckless." The second element can also be taken for a pun on uisunos, meaning "worthy, excellent," which is the name for the dawn goddess prosaically called Uisuna or Uesuna, "the Worthy."

The eagle riding a horse supported by an acrobat warrior. Gold coin from the 3rd or 2nd centuries BCE of the Unelle tribe of Armorica bearing the label EXC. Author's drawing after a photograph from the Cabinet des Médailles de Paris collection.

X—Cancer: Equi Prinnios, "balanced, adjusted constellation or Constellation of the horse." Ecuos/Epos < Equos, "horse."

Ecuos, from the Old Celtic root word aecuos, meant "equalized and balanced." Again, in poetic wordplay, this puns with equos/epos, for "horse." Thus, for the Celts, the crab motif, called Karkinos in Greek, Cancer in Latin and Karkata in Sanskrit, was actually under the sign of the horse. This designation also shows up as Du-mannos, "the dark pony," for the Gallic Sagittarius, as well as Ech, "horse" for Virgo, in the Old Irish *Book of Ballymote*. In Classical astrology, the crab was found in association with the goddess Hera. And, in other Greek fables, from an earlier period perhaps, this constellation was under the sign of the Asini, the asses of Dionysus.

Toward the end of the La Tène period (2nd and 1st centuries BCE), the Greco-Roman lion replaced the Celtic doe or fawn symbol for this constellation.

A lion pursued by a snake. Coin from the Bibliothèque Nationale de Paris. Author's drawing after a photograph by Blanchet.

XI—Leo: Elembiuii Prinnios, "Constellation of the fawn." Elembos, "fawn."

According to legend, the constellation of Leo was so called by the Greeks in remembrance of the Nemean lion that Hercules had to overcome during one of his twelve labors. In Vedic astrology, this sign was also called the Lion as Simha. Therefore, the Celtic representation of the deer, doe or fawn, for this constellation seems to be very ancient. In former times, the deer motif was used in Indo-European cosmology to name the combined constellations of Libra and Scorpio. The lion symbol belonged to the Greek and Anatolian cultures and was not familiar to the continental Celts.

XII—Virgo: Edrini Prinnios, "Constellation of the judge" (in wordplay with Aedrinios, "heat wave"). Edrinos, "judge, arbitrator, referee," connoting, Andera, "maiden, girl, young woman."

The Maiden, or Virgo, was called Parthenos, Dike, Demeter, Tyche Thespia, Kore, or Persephone, in Greek, and Fortuna in Latin. These were just some of the many names of the Goddess under her youthful aspects. In the myths, she was depicted holding a sheaf of corn or a wheat stalk. The star Spica of Virgo is symbolized by a spike of wheat. In Sanskrit, the maid or virgin was called Kanya, literally meaning "daughter." The Celts, called her Dera or Andera or Ogia Magula, "the young maiden." In this situation, Gaulish astrology seems to have preferred the image of a wise man in place of a maiden for this sign.

The Twelve Signs of the Zodiac in the Irish Ogham

The Old Irish names of the Oghams are rendered in Old Celtic in order to restore all of their original meanings, connotations, and cryptic meanings.

Ind.

Libra: Indouelicon, "the ring, or the ultimate circle," and Indamia, "the maid." Cantos, "ring"; Gallic sign: Cantli Prinnios.

The sign of Libra is here replaced by the antler of a roe buck, or a deer buck. The antlers belonged to the horned god Cernunnos, lord of animals, and serpent bearer. Cernundos was the Old Celtic name for Ophiuchus which covered both constellations of Libra (Antlers) and Ophiuchus (overlapping Scorpio).

Cusp of entry: Qerta, "crab-apple," qertocos, "crab-apple tree";
Bird sign: Qarca < carca, "hen"; animal sign: qrumis, "worm, maggot";
Hidden meaning: qert-os/-a/-on, "turned, rolled, twisted"; qernio, "victory."
Out-cusp: Rudioscaua/ruscia, "elder tree";
Bird sign: Rucinatis, "rook"; animal sign: ructu, "pig";
Figuratively: Rusca, "hive bark"; ruscon, "basket, beehive"; rudi-os/-a/-on, "rough."
House I: Indon, "end result"; [losses, costs, waste]; planets: Venus and the Southern lunar node as an aspect of Mars.

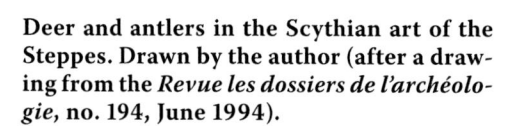

Deer and antlers in the Scythian art of the Steppes. Drawn by the author (after a drawing from the *Revue les dossiers de l'archéologie*, no. 194, June 1994).

Lii./Ln.

Scorpio: Liathag < leitacos, "salmon-trout, young salmon," if not Lingonis, "jumper, dashing dancer." Siltarios or Samonios, "the sower"; Gallic sign: Samoni Prinnios.

The theme of the sower for this sign was common to both the continental Gauls and the insular Gaels or Scots. In the Ogham, the Scorpio logo is drawn in the shape of a compass, an instrument of choice for graphic designers, cartographers and astrologers.

In-cusp: Alamios, "Scottish pine";
Bird sign: Alauda, "lark"; animal sign: alcis, "red deer, elk";
Hidden meaning: Alamos, "herd, livestock, cattle, capital, wealth"; alabis/alanis, "beautiful."
Out-cusp: Betua, "birch";
Bird sign: Boduos, "crow"; animal sign: baedos/bagios, "boar";
Hidden meaning: Bitu/bitus, "world, the living world"; bit-os/-a/-on, "immortal, eternal."
House II: Lingmen, "on scene, starting point"; [birth, origin, commencement, start]; Planets: Mars and the Northern lunar node as an aspect of Saturn.

R-Viros, a stater of the Nervis where the letters form a bird rebus. Author's drawing after a photograph by Blanchet from the Bibliothèque Nationale de Paris.

Rii.

Sagittarius: Bogdariios, "the archer"; Gallic sign: Dumanni Prinnios; Rii, that is, rii-os/-a/-on, "free"; rigi-os/-a/-on, "royal, pertaining to the king"; Ridir < rediarios "rider, cavalier, knight."

The logo for *rii* is drawn like a rake and sometimes as a wing or a fork. This symbols also appears on Celtic coinage and is at times drawn the shape of three lines which either represent a horse's mane, an eagle's wing or the crest of a boar.

Stater bearing a stylized boar and the North Star (Polaris) drawn as a cross-mark. Author's drawing after a photograph by Blanchet from the Bibliothèque Nationale de Paris.

In-cusp: Squiats, "hawthorn";

Bird sign: Sciatos, "duck," or scrauo, "black-headed gull," and screua/scriua, "skua gull"; animal sign: scobarnocos, "hare";

Hidden meaning: Scetac-os/-a/-on, "inciting to offence, scheming"; sceito/sceta / scetis, "wing, fin"; scito/scitos, "fatigue";

Out-cusp: mUinia, "bramble or vine";

Bird sign: Mesalcos, "blackbird"; animal sign: mugnos, "salmon (mythical)"; Morimoccos, "porpoise";

Hidden meaning: Muinos/moinos, "treasure"; muinon, "the blessing"; muncis, "cloud."

House III: Artigatiom, "plowing"; [life, livelihood, work]; Planet: Jupiter.

Lu.

Capricorn: Lucius/lugius, "pike," formerly attiluis, "sturgeon," and connoting luamos, "pilot," or lugos, "crow"; Gallic sign: Riuri Prinnios;

The man holding an adze and a knife on the Pictish Stone seems to be a person of authority The "F"-shaped symbol could also be taken for a measuring tool, a cross-staff or Jacob's staff, that is, a surveyor's tool, a gnomon, when not an astrolabe.

Above: Artist's rendition of an old book engraving depicting a browser using a cross-staff or Jacob's staff. *Middle*: Detail from a Pictish stele representing a man of authority holding an adze and a knife along with astral symbols. *Right*: Detail from the Bayeux tapestry showing a ship carpenter using an adze.

In-cusp: Petios/qetios, "opulus";
Bird sign: Pincio/pinciu, "finch"; animal sign: peigno < pencinio, "salmon";
Hidden meaning: Petitt-os/-a/on, "small"; petiia/pettiia/pettia, "room";
Out-cusp: Phagos> phogos/bagos, "beech," or spidna, "mackerel currant";
Bird sign: Sparuo, "sparrow"; animal sign: phrucnios < sprocnios, "horse";
Hidden meaning: Phland-os/-a/-on < bland-os/-a/-on, "nice"; phindon, "end."
House IV: Eluetia, "abundance (of goods)"; [fraternal relations, friendly and social]; Planet: Saturn.

Fii.

Boy riding a sea animal (porpoise or giant sturgeon). This may be an early representation of Moritasgos, the young Belenos, and Romanized as the "Apollo of the Sea." Detail from the Gundestrup Cauldron, 1st century BCE. Author's drawing after a photograph by E. Lessing from the National Museum of Copenhagen.

Aquarius: Udesciocos, "watery, aqueous," or Uisucios/Uiseceos, "the crow"; Gallic sign: Anaganti Prinnios.

On a quarter stater of the Gallic Leuques tribe is figured a warrior whose arms have turned into flapping wings. Could it be the god Lugus metamorphosed into a raven? Let's not forget that the constellation of the Raven is not far from that of Aquarius. This anthropomorphic image very well illustrates the idea of fluidity as that of a figure with winged arms moving like waves or gusts of wind. It parallels the Classical water-bearer motif pouring a large amphora at arm's length into the mouth of a large fish. This bird-man moves through air as the bird flies.

Coin depicting the metamorphosis of Lugus (or Lugos) into a bird along with the directional arrow of solar progression. Quarter stater of the Leuques from around the 3rd or 2nd century BCE. Author's drawing after a photograph by D. Hollard from the Bibliothèque Nationale de France, Paris.

In-cusp: Onna, "ash"; acstino/ocstino, "gorse";
Bird sign: Olerca/olerica/alarca, "swan"; animal sign: ouios "sheep," ouica "sheep," ognos, "lamb";
Hidden meaning: Onna > ona/ono, "river, stream," ona, "shame."
Out-cusp: Lusis, "rowan";
Bird sign: Lugos/luogos, "crow"; animal sign: Lucius/lugius, "pike";
Hidden meaning: Lussoios < luxsoios, "burning"; luuios, "guide, leader, chief"; Luutos, "dwarf."
House V: Uindobios, "happiness, bliss"; {**maternal relationships, happiness**}; Planet: Saturn.

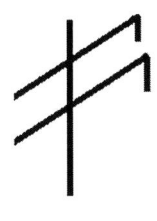

Ict.

Pisces: Escoi, "fishes"; Gallic sign: Ogroni Prinnios.
The Irish symbol for the constellation of Pisces is almost identical to that of classical astrology. The abbreviation ict. is probably an attempt to reconcile the Latin icthus, Greek ixthús, "fish (punning with ictus, "sudden shock, suffering, heartbeat and pulse measurement)," with the Celtic escos/iscos, for "fish," or escate, "fish," to the collective mode.
In-cusp: Xoiton, "thicket";
Bird sign: Cauacos/cauocos, "jackdaw," or couixs, "cuckoo"; animal sign: Cu, "dog," cunthos, "hound dog";
Hidden meaning: Xaimon, "homeland, ethnic home"; xodoni-os/-a/-on, "chthonic, earth"; xsulsigiactos, "hypnotism";
Out cusp: Daruos, "oak";
Bird sign: Druuos, driuolos, "wren"; animal sign: damatos, "sheep";
Hidden meaning: Derb-os/-a/-on, derb-os/-a/-on, "sure and certain, proven"; deruiis, "being certain, truthful"; dirouedon > deruedon, "end";
House VI: extincón, "abundance, waxing"; {**offspring, brood, children**}; Planet: Jupiter.

Arb.

Aries: Aruos, Aruios, "attacking"; Aros, the god Ares, "Mars," in Old Celtic; Gallic sign: Cutii Prinnios, cutios > qutios, "ram."
The abbreviation arb, implies ploughing, rauo, "to plough"; aruon, eruon, "furrow,

plowed field or land." Arb also connotes arbos, orbos, "heir"; arbio, orbio, "heirloom"; arbion, orbion, "heritage."

In-cusp: Taranos, "green oak";

Bird sign: Tarascala, "thrush, song thrush"; animal sign: tarandos, "reindeer";

Hidden meaning: Tarannos < tanaros, "thunder"; taranautos, "storm"; torindos, "spark anvil"; torina/torinna, "flour."

Out-cusp: Gortia, "ivy";

Bird sign: Gansa, "wild goose"; garannos, "crane"; animal sign: gabro, gabros, "goat";

Hidden meaning: Gortos > gartos, "plot, fenced garden"; gorton/gortion, "croft, closed garden"; gortus > gurtus, "heat."

House VII: Aruos, "striker"; {**opposition, diseases and obstacles**}; Planet: Mars.

Insci.

Taurus: Insciatos, "winged," or Sciatos Ander, "winged bovine"; Gallic sign: Giamoni Prinnios; Taruos, "bull."

This strange graphic symbol also appears on a Gallic stater of the Remi along with a depiction of a deer or horse on the tail side of the coin. It is a stylized udder or heart in the shape of a head. In this case, the abbreviation insci < insqiia/eniscuia, "speech, discourse," seems to connote eneqos, eneco, "face (of a person)."

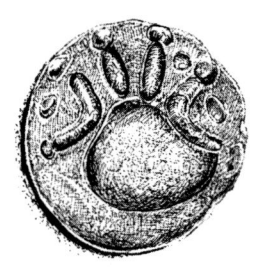

Left: Beef heart, udder or head? Quarter stater of the Remi, Seine-et-Marne. Author's drawing after a photograph from the *New Atlas of Gallic Coins*. *Right:* Gold stater with a stylized ox head. Author's drawings after a photograph by D. Bertuzzi.

In-cusp: Uroica, "heather, wild rose";

Bird sign: Udarocrago, "corncrake"; animal sign: uros > urus, "bison, ure-ox, aurochs," and/or urleo, "large wild cat, lynx, leopard";

Hidden meaning: Ur/uron, "fire"; ura, "grave"; uracia, "unmarried woman, spinster"; uraccaia, "spark, flash"; ur-os/-a/-on, "pure."

Out-cusp: Uernos, "alder";

Bird sign: uailennos > uoilennos, "gull, seagull"; animal sign: uerbis < uerba/uerua, "cow"; uetsis > uisis, "(young) sow, sow," and/or ualos/uolcos, "wolf";

Hidden meaning: Uernon/bernon, "marsh, swamp"; uernon, "field, property, property value"; uern-os/-a/-on, "good"; uirona, "sincerity"; uroniia, "truth."

House VIII: Insqiiate/eniscuiate, "speeches, discourses"; {**Partnerships, marital relations**}; Planet: Venus.

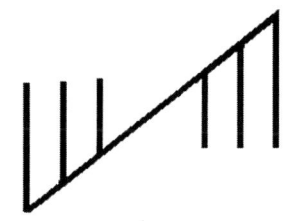

Ruidzuig/ruidsuig.

Cock-headed character represented with a house (constellation), a ladder (sky), a winged bull (Taurus) and a griffon (winds). Engraved stone from the Isle of Wight. Redrawn after a drawing from John Lindsay in the *Origins of Astrology*, London, Muller, 1971.

Gemini: Roudiosuccoi, "red hogs"; Gallic sign: Simiuisoni Prinnios; Semiuesses, "lively pigs."

The symbol for Gemini is made up of a doubled rake such as the one for Sagittarius. It may be the stylization of a boar's mane or the crest. This being, that there were three rays on the sun god's crown. Also note that these two constellations are perfectly opposed.

Silver coin with opposing wolves. Bibliothèque Nationale de Paris. Author's drawing after a photograph by Blanchet.

In-cusp: Tennos, "holly";
Bird sign: Trosdis > trodis, "starling"; animal sign: trucos/tretios, "boar";
Hidden meaning: Tannis, "glowing, the hue of fire"; tepnia > tennia, "(wood) fire"; ten-os/-a/-on, "strict, severe."
Out-cusp: 'nGaitalis < in-caitalis, "water reed";
Bird sign: Engnaca, "hooded crow"; animal sign: ancoracos > ancoragos, "old salmon";
Hidden meaning: Anguinon, "serpent's egg, fossil sea urchin test, cosmic egg"; ancos, "servant"; ncu < ancu < anco < ancouo, "inevitability"; encouo, "death (personified)."

House IX: Roudios, "ruin, fall (from prestige or eminence)"; {**death, destruction, annihilation**}; Planet: Mercury and Counter-Earth.

Iul.

Cancer: Uillos, "horse"; Gallic sign: Equi Prinnios; Equos, "horse."

This sign is designed as to suggest a prancing horse or a man raising his arms to heaven. Horse-shaped abstractions and stylizations are very often found in Gallic numismatic art.

In-cusp: Elto, eltos, "poplar";

Bird sign: eruros/eror, "eagle"; animal sign: epos/eqos, "horse";

Hidden meaning: aecu-os/-a/-on > equ-os/-a/-on, "equalized, compensated, adjusted, balanced"; aecos, "resident"; ecu, "cattle";

Out-cusp: Salixs, "willow";

Bird sign: Sebacos, "hawk"; animal sign: sidos, "deer";

Hidden meaning: Saulios/sauelios/saulos/saualis, "sun"; suligu, "harmony"; Sulis, "eye"; sulisma, "look, demeanor, good look," name of the solar goddess;

House X: Uilia, "honesty, will"; {**Dharma, the law of good order of the world and of his own nature**}; Planet: Moon.

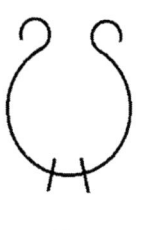

Og.

Left: **Macha of the red tresses, the Irish mare goddess and an equivalent to the Gallic Epona.**

Leo: Aga "doe"; Elembos, "fawn"; Elembiui Prinnios;

The symbol for Leo, which is substantially the same as that of Greek astrology, accentuates the shape of the lyre. Vega, the alpha star of Lyra, is one of the brightest stars of the summer sky. It is at its peak between May and September. We also find the same symbol on Gallic coinage along with horse representations.

Silver Tetradrachm with horse and lyre representations. Author's drawing after a photograph by D. Bertuzzi in *Dossiers Archéologie et sciences des origines*, **p. 59.**

In-cusp: Coslos, "hazel";

Bird sign: Caliacos/calliacos, "cock"; animal sign: cattos, "cat";

Hidden meaning: Cala, "stone"; cailos/coilos/coelios, "omen, auspicious, favorable"; coilu, "auspices"; cailiacos/coiliacos, "omen, soothsayer."

Out-cusp: Sdragenos < dragenos, "barberry";

Bird sign: Ðragena> draena/drasina/drascina, "thrush"; animal sign: dragenocos, "hedgehog";

Hidden meaning: dir < sdir < ðira < sðira, "star"; ðireula, "astronomy"; ðunios/dunios < donios < xdonios, "human being, man."

House XI: Agtate/actate, "acts, facts, actions, and decisions for action"; {**actions, rewards, karma**}; Planet: Sun.

Ech.

Virgo: Ecco, the "country priest"; Gallic sign: Edrini Prinnios; Edrinos, "judge, arbitrator."

It is ironic that the sign for Virgo is represented here by the symbol of a penis. Needless to mention that this surprising representation does lend itself to several interpretations, that are: a fish shaped symbol or a drawing of a woman wearing a hooded cloak, if not, the penis of a horse. Also, three sun strokes are depicted at the top of the symbol. In Celtic art, strokes are often drawn around orbs or over the heads of animals and characters.

In-cusp: Iuos/iburos, "yew";

Bird sign: Iar > giar < iaro, "cock, gallinaceous, domestic fowl"; animal sign: iorcellos < iorcos, "deer"; and/or, isoxs/esoxs, "pike";

Left: **Gallic stater depicting a woman-headed horse along with a representation of the annual cycle of the moon. Note the praying figure with the mare. Priests were often depicted with arms raised. Author's drawing after a photograph from the Bibliothèque Nationale de Paris.**
Right: **The Irish Gaelic Zodiacal Circle.**

Hidden meaning: iuos/-a/-on, "good, propitious, valid, stout, reddish"; iuer < iuuer, "spry, fresh, swift"; iueriu < iuueriu, "vitality, vigor, freshness, fertility";

Out-cusp: Nertos, "myrtle";

Bird sign: Naudauica/nauscua, "snipe"; animal sign: natris/naðris, "snake";

Hidden meaning: nertos, "strength"; nertacos, "vigorous"; nariia, "discreet bounties, bountiful discreetness";

House XII: Ecuodecs, "perfectly fair"; {**gains, profits, possessions**}; Planet: Mercury.

XI

Planetary Yokes and Cosmic Forces

"Who will measure Uffern?
How thick its veil?
How wide its mouth?
What the size of its stones?
Or the tops of its whirling trees?
Who bends them so crooked?
Or what fumes may be about their stems?"
   —*The Red Book of Hergest XXIII, Taliesin's First Address*

The Tarascan severed heads. Author's drawing after a photograph from the British Museum, London.

"**W**ho will measure Uffern?" This question can be asked otherwise: how do we measure the depths of sky? Here Uffern[1] refers to the Underworld, literally the Christian Inferno seen as an abysmal void. Ever since the earliest stages of astronomical science and astrological art, measuring distances between the constellations of the ecliptic was an impossible task. Thus, the question was reduced to its simplest solution: either the constellations formed equal houses or that they were at distance from each other. In order to visualize a working model, the Druid-astronomers imagined the astral houses in a vast garden domain surrounded by the trees of the forest. As we have seen in the previous chapters, the empty spaces on the zodiacal belt between constellations were marked by trees seen as markers. The Greeks and Romans saw these markers as cusps or horns. And then, what were the distances between the planets, their sizes, their conjunctions (meetings), their astral features, aspects or their cosmic powers? Again, how did the ancient astrologers consider all of these questions?

As we have seen, the little we know concerning the mechanisms of the astrological system of the Druids was given by the Classical authors. This information is by far less than what can be gleaned from the Irish and Welsh texts. In addition, these cosmological fragments, gleaned here and there in the old Classical and Medieval texts, are not only difficult to access but the keys to unlock their meaning are not given by these authors. It is nevertheless possible, from the collected data, to restore the broken pot with its missing pieces.

Yokes and Forces in Astrology

According to the ancient astrological scheme, the yokes of the planetary or cosmic forces do not hold when under influence of the giant planets such as Jupiter and Saturn which exert beneficial or malevolent forces on the other planets. Mars and Mercury were considered active while Venus was considered passive. Nevertheless, a measure of deterrence was envisioned. When lightning is fired by Mars in the vicinity of Jupiter and Saturn, then the movements of other celestial bodies are set in motion. It was imagined that these flashes, seen as heavenly lights, were caused by comets in that they were believed to be the cause of lightning. Their frequency is unpredictable and can only be foreseen through meticulous observation maintained over long periods of time. Since it is difficult to distinguish a comet from a meteorite, their passages could only be predicted because of their constant elliptical orbits around the sun. And again, they vary in shape and appearance, so much so that the ancient astrologers simply classified them in the general category of wandering or erratic stars.

It is from the outer zones of the solar system, after their passage into Jupiter's orbit, that they are disturbed in their revolutions, to the point as to deviate from their usual course. Another argument for the allocation of evil qualities given to erratic stars was because of their alleged destructive properties. That is, they ignite, become inflamed and lose some of their mass as they approach the sun. In light of this, comets differed from meteors in that they have elliptical or hyperbolic orbits. Only comets run on a periodic elliptical orbit. The average frequency of comets is of thirty-five to fifty years. For example, Haley's comet visits us every seventy-five years.

Concerning the influence of comets and planet Saturn exerted on the other stars, Seneca in *Natural Questions* wrote the following lines:

> So much is certain; two authors, Epigenes and Apollonius of Myndus, the latter highly skilled in casting horoscopes, who say that they studied among the Chaldeans, are at variance in their accounts. The latter asserts that comets are placed by the Chaldeans among the number of the wandering stars (i.e. planets), and that their orbits have been determined. Epigenes, on the contrary, asserts that the Chaldeans have ascertained nothing regarding comets, which are thought by them to be fires produced by a kind of eddy of violently rotating air.
>
> In the first place, if it like you, let us set down the views of the last-mentioned author and refute them. He supposes that the planet Saturn has, most influence in determining all motions of the heavenly bodies. When it presses upon the constellations next Mars, or crosses to the neighborhood of the moon, or encounters the rays of the sun, being naturally cold and windy, it contracts and masses the atmosphere at more than one place. By and by, if Saturn absorb all the sun s rays, there is thunder and lightning. If he has Mars in agreement, the lightning is forked. Moreover, he continues, forked and sheet lightning contain different materials. Evaporation from water or other moisture produces only gleams that threaten but stop short of striking. The hotter and drier exhalation of the earth forges the bolts of forked lightning. Beam meteors and torches, which differ from one another only in size, are produced in this same way. When any ball of air what we call a whirlwind encloses moist earthy matter, wherever it rushes it presents the appearance of an extended line of fire, which lasts just so long as the mass of air remains, which carries within it the supply of moist earthy matter.[2]

The Welsh Bard Taliesin, in *The Spoils of Taliesin*, is in agreement with Seneca's views on comets: "Mal rot tanhwydin dros eluyd. Mal ton teithiawc llwyfenyd. [Like the wheeling of a fiery meteor over the earth. Like a wave that governs Llwyvenydd]."[3] Or, in the author's literal translation: "As the wheel of the sun of fire over the country./As the wave that governs Llwyvenydd."[4]

On the Cosmic Forces

In traditional astrology, the word "strength," stands for power, force, and energy, including all other aspects or qualities of a star or planet. In the enumeration of the heavenly bodies, the numeral quality of the strength of a planet falls in a given order. This order of the planets varies according to the different astrological traditions. In Classical and Vedic astrology, signs are credited as having good or evil qualities. The Old Celtic names for these allotments were the following: mata, "beneficial, good," and anmata, "non-beneficial, not good." Some of the ancient schools of astrology favored a rule based on the qualities of the sun, while others on the moon, and still others on Jupiter. These ranking orders were undoubtedly referred to as rectus in Old Celtic (rectuarios, "regulator"). Thus, according to the accepted order, a number is assigned to each planet. In some traditions, the moon was the first regulator. Accordingly, in Vedic astrology the lunar nodes were added to this scheme. This ranking significantly changes the allotted cosmic forces. From the list found in the *Book of Ballymote*, we suspect that the Old Irish also considered the nodes as planets.

The ancient Greeks classified the planets in two categories: one assigned for the criteria of astronomy and the other for the considerations of astrology. Let's not forget that the point of view of ancient sky observation was strictly geocentric. However, this did not exclude later speculations on a possible heliocentric order.

Order of the Planets Given by the Greek Astronomers

1. Moon; 2. Mercury; 3. Venus; 4. Sun; 5. Mars; 6. Jupiter; 7. Saturn.

Greek Astrological Order:

1. Sun; 2. Moon; 3. Saturn; 4. Jupiter; 5. Mars; 6. Venus; 7. Mercury.

Greek Ptolemaic Order of Late Alexandria:

1. Moon; 2. Sun; 3. Mercury; 4. Venus; 5. Mars; 6. Jupiter; 7. Saturn.

Roman Mithraic Order:

1. Saturn; 2. Sun; 3. Moon; 4. Jupiter; 5. Mars; 6. Venus; 7. Mercury.

The Vedic Astrological Ranking Along with Cosmic Strengths and Aspects:

1. Surya, Sun: uniqueness, foundation, spirit generally evil;
2. Chandra, Moon: duality, balance, thinking, generally beneficial;
3. Kuja, Mars: energy, action will; slightest evil;
4. Budha, Mercury: order, balance, reason, generally beneficial;
5. Brihaspati or Guru, Jupiter: law, education, intellect greatly beneficial;
6. Shukra, Venus: harmony, beauty, intuition, slight benefit;
7. Shani, Saturn: control, purpose, wisdom, great evil;
8. Rahu, the North Node Moon: duality, great dispersion, return, greater evil;
9. Ketu South Node, Moon: tripling, trinity, creation, release, slighter evil.

Order of the Planets According to the IRISH List (*Book of Ballymote*) Along with Their Inherent Meaning:

1. Gealac, Moon: Gelaca, "clear, milky white";
2. Goac, Mars: Coccos, "red";
3. Grian, Sun: Greina, "light, radiant";
4. Tuct, Jupiter Tectos, "sent, emissary";
5. L(u)ct, Mercury: Luctos, "troop, party, light";
6. Rii, Venus, Riia/Reiia > Ria/Reia, "free";
7. Milni, Saturn: Melnos, "slow, lazy, sluggish, indolent";
8. Ear, Tail: South Lunar Node: Ersa Ambeios, "dragon's tail";
9. (c)Ean, Head: North Node Moon: Qennos Ambeios, "dragon's head."

However, we should not conclude that this old medieval Irish order was subsequently the typical common Celtic ranking for the planets. Although we do not absolutely know for sure what the generally admitted order for the planets was at the time of the ancient Druids. It is nevertheless possible to propose a hypothetical sequel from the list of deities given by Julius Caesar in his *War Commentaries*.

Proposal for a Gallic Ranking After Caesar's Roman Interpretation:

1. Moon? 2. Mercury; 3. Sun; 4. Mars; 5. Jupiter; 6. Venus; 7. Saturn?

Please note that Caesar does not give the godly equivalents for the Moon and Saturn. In addition, when comparing this list with that of the medieval Welsh texts, we understand that there is no overall consensus for the previous lists.

List of Planets According to the Medieval Bardic Tradition of Taliesin:

(1) Sun; (2) Moon; (3) Mars; (4) Mercury; (5) Venus; (6) Jupiter; (7) Saturn.

Nevertheless, some constants do emerge when comparing these lists:

- Sun and Moon are usually given in the first position;
- The two luminaries are usually followed by Mars, Mercury and Jupiter;
- Venus is constantly given in sixth position;
- Saturn generally ends the list;
- The lunar nodes are also listed at the end of the Indian and Irish lists.

Acuity of the Planets—Ogiomu Seruoretlanom

From the cosmic drama scripted in the myths, we know that many of the deities and heroes acted as heavenly bodies. And thanks to these myths, we can guess what role these actors played.... That is, what were their relationships and interactions? What follows is a rundown and working model for an astrological system of planetary yokes and strengths for Celtic astrological themes.

Since the Old Celtic lexicon is rich with astronomical vocabulary, finding the Classical and Vedic parallels is made easier. For example, the Sanskrit word *yoga*, for "yoke" (from Proto-Germanic yukam), is found not only in Latin as iugum, Greek, zygon, and in Old Celtic, iugon. They all derive from the Proto-Indo-European root yugóm. From this root also derived the terms for conjunction, from Latin *coniunctio*, which were also found in Sanskrit as *kuyoga*, and in Old Celtic as *cumiugon*, thus the Old Irish *cuing*. The conjunction of two luminaries or heavenly bodies was called amba in Sanskrit and ambo in Old Celtic. Other cognates are the Sanskrit bala, "force," and Celtic bala, "charge, weight." This Sanskrit word was used as follows to name many astronomical concepts: Amsa Bala, force due to the Earth's longitude; Chara Bala, force due to nature; Sthira Bala, force due to the presence of one or more planets in an astrological sign. And the name Sanskrit bala, for "strength, power, power," had many Celtic equivalents: briga, "power"; gala, "force, power, strength of mind"; nertos, "force, might"; sego, "prevalent force or might"; stertis, "strength and resilience," and ualos, "harmful force, overpowering strength."

Early Vedic astrologers believed that each of the forces emanated from a cosmic ray called Marici in Sanskrit. The Marici rays were sent by the Maruts as a light particles, a sun or moon ray, originally emanating from the stars of the Big Dipper. The Old Celtic name for these cosmic rays was most likely *riuones*, the plural of riuo, "ray," thus punning with *reuos/riuos*, "frost." We have seen in a previous chapter that the Gallic constellation of Capricorn was called Riuros. The Old Gallic term for a cosmic ray was probably riuo-albiios, while the name for a light beam was most likely touindo or touindedo (feminine case). The Moon, as goddess of sovereignty, reflected light beams in a greater number than the other heavenly bodies. These were thought to affect the mind. Therefore, the expression moon-stricken or moonstruck, implying, "to be stricken by madness or dazed with romantic sentiment." The Sanskrit term Rasi, which also means a sign (of the Zodiac) has no Celtic equivalent. The term Prinnios, for "tree, out-branching," was the usual Gallic denomination for a "zodiacal constellation, zodiacal period, or sign."

Sanskrit Terminology for the Yokes and Strengths in Vedic Astrology:

Rasi Bala, "strength of evidence";

Rasi Dasa, "prevalence period of astral signs";

Rasi Vriddhi, "gain or increase of a sign";

Rasi Hrasa, "debilitation, reduction or collapse of a sign."

When comparing these Sanskrit expressions with those of the Gaulish *Coligny Calendar* we get:

Ogiomu, "sharp constellation";

Tratus, "time lapse of a zodiacal sign";

Loudextio/Loudixtio, "astronomical rising, ascent"; Prinnios Loudextio "ascending constellation";

Lagiato, "fall, descent (of a constellation)"; Prinnios Lagiato, "falling, descending constellation."

Here are the following strengths of the various planets according to the Irish list (note that each score gives the power of a planetary yoke):

Moon plus the lunar nodes: 1 + 8 = 9; Mars: 2; Sun: 3; Jupiter: 4; Mercury: 5; Venus and Saturn: 6 and 7.

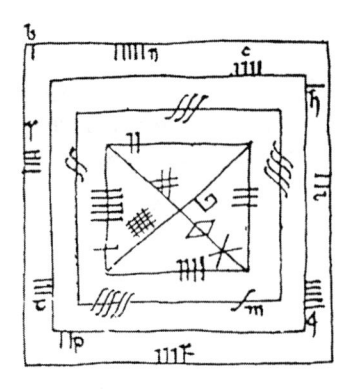

Magical square or divining table with the positions of the Ogham cusps. The central section corresponds to the Moon Grid.

The Irish Model

Moon

Yoke: Iugon Gelacai, "yoke of the Moon," gala, "(moral) might, bravery, storm";
Strength: Oinos, "one, one"; ointu, "unit, cohesion";
Planetary ruler: Medb < Medua, "drunkenness."
Mystical sense: Meda, "balance, measure"; mana, "thinking mind"; mênmania, "thought"; mentio, "thought"; mena, "desire"; mentos, "project"; manda, "residence."
Zodiac: Cancer; Uillos, "horse," mandos, "pony."

South lunar node

Yoke: Iugon Ersa-Ambeios, "yoke of the dragon's tail";
Strength: Oxtu, "eight"; oxtonoxs, "week";
Planetary ruler: Cermait < cermatis, the "sorb"; also referred to as "the honey mouthed";
Mystical sense: Ersacos, "tail, behind, appendix"; comarios, "the opposite hand"; cormogon, "profit"; comarta, "comparison, comparative impression";
Zodiac: Libra; in conjunction with the South Node as an aspect of Mercury.

North lunar node

Yoke: Iugon Qennos-Ambeios, "the yoke of the dragon's head";
Strength: Nouen, "nine";
Planetary ruer: Bodb Derg < Dergos Boduos, the "red crow";
Mystical sense: Derca, "aspect"; dercsma, "(sense of) vision"; dercsmen, "(faculty of) vision"; qacria, "vortex, spiral"; qernio, "victory";
Zodiac: Scorpio: North Node, an aspect of Mars.

Mars

Yoke: Iugon Cocci, "yoke of the red";
Strength: Duo > uo, "two";
Planetary ruler: Ogma < Ogmios, "mystical champion," or Cumal < Camulos, "dynamic";
Mystical sense: Aedon, "fervor, zeal"; auilla/euilla, "will";
Astrological signs: Aries; Aros, "Ares/Mars"; Scorpio; Siltarios/Samonios, "the sower."

Sun

Yoke: Greinai Iugon, "the yoke of the beaming one";
Strength: Tris, "three";
Planetary rulers: Bile < Belios, "clear"; Aonghus Mac Óg < Oinogustios Ogios Maqos, "the first choice young son," and Greine < Greina, "sunny, the Sun Goddess";
Mystical sense: Grendmen, "advance progress"; anauo, "harmony"; anatios, "spirit"; anatmon, "soul";
Zodiac: Leo; Aga, "doe."

Jupiter

Yoke: Tecti Iugon, "the yoke of the envoy";

Strength: Qeteor, "four";

Planetary ruler: Dagda < Dagodeuos, "good god"; Eochaidh < Iuocatuos, "good or strong warrior," or the "yew fighter"; Ruadh Rofessa < Roudios Roueosos, "the red great knowledge";

Mystical sense: Tecto/tectu, "possession, custody"; tectos, "traveler, envoy, messenger"; carantia, "friendship"; lutu, "passion"; qeisla, "intelligence, thinking, understanding"; uercantlo, "education, instruction";

Astrological signs: Sagittarius; Bogdariios, "the archer"; Pisces; Escoi, "the fish."

Mercury

Yoke: Lucti Iugon, "yoke of the burden";

Strength: Quenque > Qenqe, "five";

Planetary ruler: Lugh < Lugus, "splendid";

Mystical sense: Luctos/luxtos, "part, burden, charge, bunch, party, people"; Condo/comdo, "understanding, intelligence, meaning";

Astrological Signs: Virgo; Ecco, the "country priest"; Gemini; Roudiosuccoi, "the red pigs."

Venus

Yoke: Riiai Iugon, "yoke of the free";

Strength: Suexs, "six";

Planetary ruler: Brigid/Brigit < Brigantia, "nobility"; or Dana/Danu < Daua, "impetuous, vehement";

Mystical sense: Briga, "value, power, might, insolence"; brigantiia, "lofty, moral elevation, greatness of the soul"; cainieto, "beauty"; cerda, "art"; coimo, "love, kindness"; comruto, "emotion"; etanna, "poetry";

Astrological signs: Taurus; Sciatos Ander, "the winged ox"; Libra; Indouelicon, "the ring or the ultimate circle."

Saturn

Yoke: Melni Iugon;

Strength: Sextan, "seven";

Planetary ruler: Nuada < Nodons, "the angler"; Bress < Brestos, "broken, impetuous, split, cracked"; or, Bretsos, "beautiful."

Mystical sense: Ancommen, "loss of memory, amnesia"; amaro, "sorrow, grief"; ancauos, "death"; ancena, "hard necessity, violent coercion, violence"; cassia, "violent passion"; dilegnis/delegnis, dits > dis, "annihilation, destruction";

Astrological signs: Capricorn: Attiluis, "sturgeon"; Riuri Prinnios Aquarius: Udesciocos, "aqueous," or Uisucios /Uiseceos, "raven."

The Breton Series

Le Druide et l'enfant [The Druid and the Child], also called in French, *Les séries* [The Series], is a Breton children's song from the *Barzaz Breiz* collected and edited by

Hersart Villemarqué. It offers an interesting and rare view on continental British numerology. Through its symbolism, it is possible to understand what the yokes and astrological strengths could have been for the Druid-astrologers. After closer examination, this enigmatic riddle, long considered to be nothing but a simple nursery rhyme, is far from being naive. According to Hersart the Villemarqué, wet nurses of Lower Brittany used this repetitive ancient versification to put children to sleep. Most certainly Villemarqué went for the most archaic version of the song leaving out those that seemed to have suffered the most Christianizing censorship. Also noticed by the literary minded were the embellishments made by the genius of the poet's pen. Villemarqué just wanted it to be as it was in the earlier days. Many accused him of having invented these verses from scratch, while others cursed him for having transformed a Breton ditty into a kind of pseudo-Druidic prayer. Whatever the case, these rhymes were much older than anyone wanted to admit and in these verses were hidden esoteric teachings that went way beyond any retrospective critical appraisal. And to quote Jean Cocteau, who came to the defense of Villemarqué, the alleged author of the *Barzaz Breizh*, "he was too much of a poet to be despised so!"

AR RANNOU (SERIES)

1. No series (but the number one);
   Red,[5] the course only;
   Ankon, death, ann Anken tad, father of sorrow[6];
   Nothing before, nothing more.

2. Two bulls yoked to a shell[7]
   Pulling, they will expire.
   Ponder the wonder!

3. Three parts worldwide.[8]
   Three beginnings and three ends[9]
   For man as for oak.
   Three kingdoms for Marzin[10];
   Full-color fruits of honey along with happy flowers.
   And children's laughter!

4. Four grindstones,
   Whetstones of Marzin
   That sharpen poor swords.[11]

5. Five girdles of the earth,[12]
   Five ages in the periods of time.[13]
   Five rocks on our sister.[14]

6. Six little children made of wax,
   Sustained by the energy of the moon.
   If you ignore this, I know.
   Six (medicinal) herbs in the small cauldron,[15]
   Drink that mixes (Körrig) the dwarf,[16]
   His little finger in his mouth.

7. Seven suns and seven moons,
    Seven planets along with the Hen,[17]
    Seven elements with the flour of the air.[18]

8. Eight winds that blow,
    Eight fires with Tantad, the Great Fire[19]
    In May on the Mount of Battle.
    Eight heifers as white foam,
    Grazing on the deep island,[20]
    The eight white heifers of the Lady.[21]

9. Nine small hands on the area's table,
    Near the tower of Lezarmeur,[22]
    and nine mothers who greatly mourn,
    Nine goblins (korrigans) who dance[23]
    With flowers in her hair and dresses of wool,
    Around the moonlit fountain.
    The boar-sow and her nine piglets,
    At the door of their lair,
    Growling and burrowing,
    Burrowing and growling.
    Small ones, small ones, small ones, hasten to the apple-tree!
    The old boar will give you a lesson.

10. Ten enemy ships
    we saw coming from Nantes[24]:
    Woe to you, woe to you people of Vannes![25]

11. Eleven armed priests from Vannes,
    With their broken swords;
    And their bloody robes;
    And their hazel crutches[26];
    Three hundred more than they, the eleven!

12. Twelve months and twelve signs, the penultimate,
    Sagittarius delivers his arrow, armed with a dart,
    The twelve signs are at war.[27]
    Beautiful cow, black cow with the white forehead,
    Out of the forest of Spoils[28];
    In his chest is the sting of the arrow;
    His blood is flowing,
    She bellows, head up.
    The trumpet sounds with fire and thunder,
    Rain and wind, thunder and fire;
    Nothing, nothing more, and no more series!

DECRYPTION OF THE STRENGTHS AND PLANETARY YOKES
FROM THE BRETON SERIES OF THE *BARZAZ BREIZH*

1. Capricorn (330°–360°):
   Yoke: Red (< reida, "race," reidos, "runner"); Tad an Anken (< Tatis Ancenas "father of the hard necessity");
   Planet: Saturn; strength: 7.
2. Aquarius (300°–330°):
   Yoke: two oxen yoked to a shell (the sky vault);
   Planet: Saturn; strength: 7.
3. Fish (270°–300°):
   Yoke: the three worlds, three beginnings and ends, the three kingdoms of Marzin (Merlin);
   Planet: Jupiter; strength: 6.
4. Aries (240°–270°):
   Yoke: the four whetstones of Marzin (Merlin);
   Planet: Mars; strength: 3.
5. Taurus (210°–240°):
   Yoke: the five girdles of the earth, five ages in the length of time; five stones on our sister (Earth);
   Planet: Venus; strength: 5.
6. Gemini (180°–210°):
   Yoke: six grandchildren, the energy of the moon, herbs, small pot (the cauldron of Cerridwen, the constellation of Crater), and the drink that mixes the dwarf (Corros);
   Planet: Mercury; strength: 4.
7. Cancer (150°–180°):
   Yoke: seven stars (plus the sun and moon with the five planets) with the Hen (an asterism of the Pleiades), the seven elements along with the flour of the air (bracis, "flour"; cobrextio, "fog, mist"; brectu/brextu/bricto, "magic"; = "quintessence");
   Planet: Moon; strength: 2.
8. Leo (120°–150°):
   Yoke: the eight winds, the eight fires along with Tantad (< tepnedo < tepneto, "fire"; Belotepnion, "bonfire"), the Great Fire, the eight white heifers of the Lady (Moon?).
   Planet: Sun; strength: 1.
9. Virgo (90°–120°):
   Yoke: nine small hands, nine mothers and nine goblins (< corrigena, "gnome"), the sow, its nine piglets and the old boar (baedd coed < baeðos caiti, "the solitary woodland boar"; constellation of Pegasus);
   Planet: Mercury; strength: 4.
10. (60°–90°):
    Yoke: ten enemy ships (lestr < Lenster, "ship," the constellation of Navis, the Ship);
    Planet: Venus; strength: 5.

11. Scorpio (30°–60°):
    Yoke: eleven armed monks with their dull swords and their broken hazelwood crosiers (more than three hundred and eleven priests);
    Planet: Mars; strength: 3.
12. Sagittarius (0°–30°):
    Yoke: twelve months and twelve zodiacal signs, the penultimate, Sagittarius delivers his arrow, the beautiful cow, the black cow with the white forehead out of the forest of Spoils (that were, trees, cusps of the zodiacal constellations);
    Planet: Jupiter; strength: 6.

Geoffrey of Monmouth (ca. 1100–ca. 1155), in his *Historia Regum Britanniae* (*History of the Kings of Britain*),[29] there exposed Merlin's prognostics and cosmological visions there painting a highly symbolic and prosaic picture of the relationship of the planets, the constellations, and their many conjunctions:

1. The stars shall turn their faces away from them (those mortal men) and shall quit their usual tracks across the sky.
2. In the wrath of the stars, crops shall wither and the rain from the vault of heaven shall be withheld.
3. Roots and branches (the constellar cusps) shall exchange places and the novelty of this shall seem a miracle.
4. The shining sun shall be visible to those who see it.
   The planet Mercury from Arcadia shall change its shield and the helmet of Mars shall call to Venus.
   The helmet of Mars shall cast its shadow; the fury of Mercury shall pass the bounds. Iron Orion shall draw his naked sword.
   Oceanic Apollo shall whip the clouds.
   Jupiter shall emerge from his established bounds and Venus shall abandon her salutary tracks.
   The Star of Saturn shall rush forth in lead-colored (rain?) and with a crooked sickle shall kill mortals.
   The twice six houses of the stars shall weep that their hosts jump their tracks.
   The Twins shall depart from their usual embrace and shall call the bowl to the water-bearer.
   The scales of Libra shall swing free until Aries shall place his crooked horns under the balance.
   The tail of Scorpio shall ferment lightning and Cancer shall contend with the sun. Virgo shall rise on the back of Sagittarius and shall forget her virginal flowers.
5. The chariot of the Moon shall disturb the Zodiac and the Pleiades shall burst into tears.
   None shall return to their appointed course, but Adriana (Arianrhod, the Northern Crown) behind a closed door shall seek refuge in her causeways. (The occultation of Corona Borealis at the gateway of the underworld in Taurus)
   At a stroke of the wand the winds shall rush forth and the dust of Uentu(rum?) shall blow on us again.
   (The Moon, travelling at night in the spring in his chariot by its passage in the Hyades in Taurus causes rain. The Hyades, "the rainy fairies," were precisely the Greek nymphs of rain.)
6. The winds shall collide with a dire thunderclap and their blast shall echo among the stars.

To conclude, the gold plates of the Clandon Barrow Lozenge, found in 1882 near Stonehenge (Maiden Castle, in the area of Dorchester), are very similar in detail and graphic layout to the Ogham Square depicted in the *Book of Ballymote*. It is relatively easy, starting from the Irish and Indian examples, to configure the Stonehenge grid or Clandon Barrow Lozenge in order to calculate the forces and yokes for a working Celtic astrological chart.

SIGNIFICATORS AND ASPECTS OF THE PLANETARY RULERS
(the first significator is in parentheses):

BRIGA (strong), more or less beneficial or slightly beneficial:
(1) Moon; (2) Mars; (3) Sun.
MATA (auspicious), or beneficial:
(1) Jupiter; (2) Mercury; (3) Venus.
ANMATA (harmful), or not auspicious, evil:
(1) Caput Draconis (Dragon's Head); (2) Cauda Draconis (Dragon's Tail); (3) Saturn.
LAGUS (vile), or greatly evil:
(1) Counter-Earth; (2) The Postern, the black moon in conjunction with Taurus (?); (3) Uranus (?).

Prior to modern times, Uranus was not a known planet. It was perceived as one of the epiphanies of Mercury since it appeared and disappeared at whim. Was not Mercury (the Celtic Lug) the messenger of the gods? Also, it is not certain whether if the ancient Celts knew the astrological concept of the Dark Moon either. However, the mention of a door occulting the Northern Crown and obscuring the Moon clearly hints at a dark spot in Taurus which was only known by the ancient astronomers.

The plural form of "yokes" in old Celtic was Iuga. The Yugas are combinations or planetary conjunctions that occur in the signs of the Zodiac in Vedic astrology. The significator is a measure of power or strength given to each of these yokes according to the combinations and conjunctions of the planets entering the astral house. Also, the significator indicates the strength given to the yoke when the sun enters or leaves an astral or lunar mansion. For a house, the first cusp is the "ascendant," and the second cusp is the "descendant." In this case the ruling master of the sign or house is seen as the host. Once again, it is the aspect of the time period which tells us if the house is auspicious or inauspicious (unlucky). The significator defines any marker, good or bad, on the qualities or aspects attributed to the house ruler.

To the best of our knowledge, for the interpretation of astral themes, Druid-astrologers could sometimes have recourse to the astral houses of the solar Zodiac while sometimes could resort to the lunar mansions.

Combinations and Planetary Conjunctions

In astrological terms, conjunctions (Gaelic cuing, "yoke, bond, obligation"; Old Celtic comiugon, "conjunction") are defined as links between signs and their various aspects. A meaning or significator is given to the various possibilities of planetary encounters and combinations. Therefore, the significator varies according to the planetary conjunctions. For example, when two or three planets are found in the same sign or house during the sun's passage, the significator varies according to the planets therein. The sun, in the presence of a host or house master, can then be under good or bad auspices. That is, he finds himself in good or bad company. For some planets are granted beneficial qualities and for others, evil ones. Thus, the masters of different signs also have their strengths and qualities. As for the houses, the masters number twelve. Since

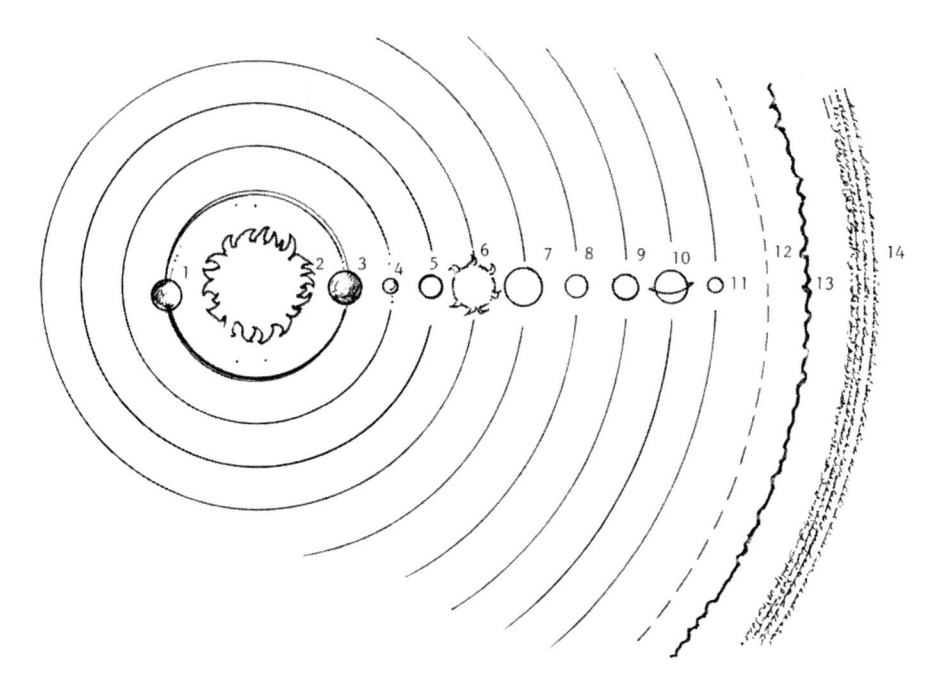

Representation of the solar system as imagined by the astronomers of Antiquity. 1—Anti-Earth (hidden from sight); **2**—Sun (luminary); **3**—Earth (sphere); **4**—Moon (phasing luminary); **5**—Mercury (fast wandering star); **6**—Venus (luminary, morning star); **7**—Venus (evening star); **8**—Mars (wandering star emitting cosmic rays); **9**—Jupiter (wandering star emitting fire bolts); **10**—Saturn (slow wandering star); **11**—Uranus (cloaked, an aspect of Mercury); **12**—The region of the fixed stars and the invisible world; **13**—The Empyrean; **14**—The heavenly ring of fire.

that there are only seven planets, each house cannot have its own planet. Some planets are doubled in order to accommodate the remaining five houses. Nevertheless, try to imagine the number of possible conjunctions and yokes. It would be a bit long to go through all the combinations, a much too complicated and tedious exercise, so let us just retain the qualities given to the astral planets and houses (according to the Old Irish order as found in the *Book of Ballymote*).

Old Irish Order for the Planets

1—MOON: The Moon, as queen of heaven, has the greatest cosmic force. If we are to calculate its position in the order of importance, the following calculation yields: Moon: 1 + lunar nodes: 8 = 9. To wit, nine, as triple of three, for the Triune Goddess, the three matrons or fate fairies.

2—MARS: Mars as the god of war brings opposition. This planet is under the sign of duality and thus takes the power of 2.

3—SUN: The Sun takes the cosmic force of 3. Its symbol is traditionally represented by the symbol of the three rays called Tribann Breton.

4—JUPITER: Jupiter's cosmic force is of 4, thus the doubling of 2. Being the king of the gods, he is the king of warriors under the command of Mars.

5—MERCURY: Mercury takes the cosmic force of 5. This figure is emblematic of the cosmic wheel with the four spokes and hub. The wheel also represents inner space including the center along with the four directions.

6—VENUS: Venus takes the strength of 6, doubling its tripling. This number is in association with the three fairies.

7—SATURN: Saturn, in connection with the agrarian world, takes on the cosmic force of 7. This figure shows the different dimensions of the world: the 4 directions, top, middle and bottom. This figure is also in association with the seven stars of the North and the seven Pleiades.

8—LUNAR NODES: The lunar nodes each have the strength of eight. The north lunar node, the Dragon's head, is considered beneficial or favorable while the south node is evil and unfavorable.

THE COSMIC RULERS

1—MOON: The Moon is ruled by the great heavenly Queen Mother. It has many surnames in the different Celtic cultures and languages. In Gaul, she was known as Matrona, the matron, the mother of gods and mortals. Some of her other Gallic names were: Diuonna, "bright water," Epona, "the equine," and Rosmerta, "providence." In Ireland, her many names were: Medb, "drunkenness," Macha, "the plain," and Morrigu, "the great queen," among others, her British names included: Rhiannon, "the majestic," and Arianrod, "the silver wheel." Queen Medb, along with her little companion sunny Ailill, is the allegory of Sovereignty and the Dominion of the earthly world.

2—MARS: Mars is the lord of war and of the heavenly hosts. He is a very ancient pan-Celtic, proto-Celtic or Italo-Celtic deity and was also highly regarded in ancient Lazio. The Gauls and Gaels identified him under the same name, Ogmios in Gaul and Ogma in Ireland. As it was generally proposed, the name does not come from the Greek ogmos, "furrow, straight line," but the Celtic Ogmios, "(mystic) champion, magic hero." In Gaul, he had several nicknames including: Albiorix "king of the world," Camulos, "active servant or warrior," Caturix, "the king of battle," Corotiacos, "the circular," Lenos, "the influx, the profusion," Loucetios, "bright one," Mullo, "heap, pile of loot," Nabelcos, "the cloudy," Nodens/Nodons, "the angler, line fisherman," and Olloudios, "the totalitarian." Nodens had the same name in Ireland, Wales and Brittany with the following forms: Nuada, Nudd or Llud and Nuz.

3—SUN: Apollo had several names in the different Celtic languages. In Gaul, he was called Maponos, "the son," Grannos, "the radiant," and Belenos, "the brilliant." In Ireland, he was called Mac Òc, "the young son," and Aongus/Oengus, "the first choice." The Welsh knew him as Gwalhaved, "the summer hawk," or Gwalchmei, "the hawk of May," or Galahad, French Gauvin, in the Arthurian tales.

4—JUPITER: Taranis, the Gaulish Jupiter, was called "the amazing," or Uxellimos, "the supreme." The Irish called him Dagda, "the good God," Rofessa Ruadh, "the red to the great wisdom," or Donn, "the tan or dark Lord." In Welsh mythology, he was referred to as Brân, "the raven."

5—MERCURY: Mercury was called Lugos or Lugus, if not Lugios, in Gaul. He was a very ancient pan-Celtic deity and his name is also found in Celtiberian, Irish, and Welsh texts as well. Regional variants of the name are declined as such: Lug or Lugh, in Ireland and Lleu in Wales. Among his many Gallic epicleses the following names are found: Artaios, "the bear-keeper," Cissonios, "the charioteer," Gebrinios, "the frost," Moccos, "the pig or boar," and Uisucios, "the crafty."

6—VENUS: Minerva in Gaul also had several names, these included: Belisama, "the very clear," Brigindo, "of nobility, of sublimity," and Nantosuelta, "flittering in the valley." In Ireland, she had many names: Brigit (or Brigantia in the British Isles), "of nobility," Etaine, "poetry," and Boann, "the ultimate cow or the white cow."

7—SATURN: The Gallic Saturn was Toutatis or Teutatis, which Julius Caesar in his *Gallic Wars Commentaries* called Dis Pater, who was the father-god of the people. In Ireland, he went under the name of Bress, "the cleft, the split."

8—THE LUNAR NODES: Cauda Draconis, the Dragon's Tail, the South node (descending); the Moon under the influence of Venus. Caput Draconis, the Dragon's Head, North node (ascending); The Moon under the influence of Saturn.

Irish Zodiacal and Planetary Cosmic Forces

Please note that the numbers correspond to the values of cosmic forces in a given zodiacal sign or house.

Libra, Venus: 6 Scorpio, Mars: 2 Sagittarius, Jupiter: 4	Capricorn, Saturn: 7 Aquarius, Saturn: 7 Pisces, Jupiter: 4
Aries, Mars: 2 Taurus, Venus: 6 Gemini, Mercury: 5	Cancer, Moon: 1 Leo, Sun: 2 Virgo, Mercury: 5

XII

Themes and Predictions

"The world's profit (is) small, the heat of the sun is lost.
The Druid will prophesy what has been will be.
Sky of Geirionydd, I would go with thee gloomy like the evening,
in the recesses of the mountain."
 —The Praise of Lludd the Great, *The Book of Taliesin LII*

A Hibernian Druid astrologer sitting on a bull skin divining from the fedha, "wood," cusps, on a shamanic drum called a bodhran in Gaelic. Drawing by the author.

Divining by the Stars

According to Caesar, the Gallic nation is entirely given over to religious practices and this includes magic and divination. Others such as W. A. McDevitte and W. S. Bohn (1869), have translated this passage as meaning: "The nation of all the Gauls is extremely devoted to superstitious rites." Or again, in *War Commentaries, Book VI,* verses 14 to 16, that: "The Gallic nation is entirely given over to religious practices...." We also know through Caesar, "that the druids had lengthy discussions on the stars and their movement and on the dimensions of the world and of the earth, on nature, and on the power of the immortal gods...." This power possessed by the immortal Celtic gods was described by the other ancient peoples, their neighbors, the Teutons, the Romans, and the Greeks in very similar terms. The qualities of their celestial abodes, the planets, also differed little.

Cicero (106 BCE–43 BCE), in *De Divinatione,* "On Divination," reported that he had a hearing with the famous Aeduan Gallic Druid, Diuiciacos[1] (or Diviciacus/Divitiac), who spoke on many topics. According to Diuiciacos, the Druids were very careful observers of nature as a whole. Nor is the practice of divination disregarded even among uncivilized tribes, if indeed there are Druids in Gaul—and there are, for I knew one of them myself, Divitiacus, the Aeduan, your guest and eulogist. He claimed to have that knowledge of nature which the Greeks call "physiologia," and he used to make predictions, sometimes by means of augury and sometimes by means of conjecture.[2]

Another classical writer, the Greek historian Plutarchus (Ploútarkhos, ca. 46 CE–120 CE), writes in *Morals, Of Fate,* the role of divining practices on the island of Ogygia. Ogygia was said to be located "five days to the West of Great Britain." Therefore, Ogygia was the Greek name for the land of the Ogygoi (Greek Ogygos, a mythical ruler of the sea at the time of the Deluge), that were, the Scots or Gaels of Ireland.

> For they affirm the nature of the island (of Ogygia) and the mildness of the air which environs it to be admirable; and that there have been some persons who, intending to depart thence, have been hindered by the Divinity or Genius of the place showing himself to them, as to his familiar friends and acquaintance, not only in dreams and exterior signs, but also visibly appearing to them by the means of familiar spirits discoursing and conversing with them. For they say, that Saturn himself is personally there, lying asleep in the deep cave of a hollow rock, shining like fine gold, Jupiter having prepared sleep instead of fetters and shackles to keep him from stirring; but that there are on the top of this rock certain birds, which fly down and carry him ambrosia; that the whole island is filled with an admirable fragrancy and perfume, which is spread all over it, arising from this cave, as from an odoriferous fountain; that these Daemons serve and minister to Saturn, having been his courtiers and nearest attendants when he held the empire and exercised regal authority over men and Gods; and that having the science of divining future occurrences, they of themselves foretell many things; but the greatest and of the highest importance, when they return from assisting Saturn, and reveal his dreams; for whatever Jupiter premeditates, Saturn dreams; but his awakenings are Titanical passions or perturbations of the soul in him, which sleep altogether controls, in order that the royal and divine nature may be pure and uncontaminated in itself. This stranger then, having been brought thither, and there serving the God in repose and at his ease, attained to as great skill in astrology as it is possible for anyone to do that has made the greatest progress in geometry; as for the rest of philosophy, having given himself to that which is called natural, he was seized with an extraordinary desire and longing to visit and see the great island; for so they call the continent inhabited by us.[3]

Again, Plutarch gives us the key to unlock the mysteries of divination by the astrologers of Antiquity along with the role played by the planets Jupiter and Saturn in the formulation of predictions. That is, Jupiter was the ruler of the daytime sky while Saturn is one of the night sky. Those questions which were blurred by the light of the day found their answer in the serenity of the star speckled night. This mythological and cosmic theme involving planetary gods survived into the late medieval days in Irish and Welsh literature. The following passage was taken from the *Historia Regum Britanniae*, or "History of the Kings of Britain," by Geoffrey of Monmouth. This excerpt is from the chapter entitled "The prophecies of Merlin":

> The planet Mercury from Arcadia shall change its shield and the helmet of Mars shall call to Venus. The helmet of Mars shall cast its shadow; the fury of Mercury shall pass the bounds. Iron Orion shall draw his naked sword. Oceanic Apollo shall whip the clouds. Jupiter shall emerge from his established bounds and Venus shall abandon her salutary tracks. The Star of Saturn shall rush forth in lead-colored (rain?) and with a crooked sickle shall kill mortals.[4]

An exegesis of this passage gives us a glimpse on the planets behavior. It is therefore possible to better understand the occult meanings of the strengths and roles granted to each of these planetary gods by the British Celts.

The planets are in a good position when they are in their given houses. Things get complicated when they come in conjunction with other planets. As we have previously seen, some conjunctions, or yokes, are then considered beneficial while others are baleful.

(1) Jupiter, the wise judge, projects cosmic fire into the aether which are perceived as thought forms by mortals in their dreams. Jupiter's borders are defined by the length of the day: starting from dawn to dusk. It is flanked by the two manifestations of Venus (the Dawn Goddess): the Morning Star and the Evening Star.

(2) Saturn, the soothsayer, captures the cosmic rays (thought forms of dream and imagination) thrown by Jupiter and send them down to Earth at the humans who then experience violent passions.

(3) Mercury, can shield himself from the rays sent by Jupiter and with the help of Venus, ensure peace and livelihood.

(4) Mars possesses a war helmet that casts a shadow (obscuring sunlight) over the Earth. He can throw cosmic rays at humans in the form of thunder bolts or flashes. Mars can not only provoke wars but can also be a strong protector.

(5) Apollo, the brilliant sun youth, rides is in the clouds on his Sun Chariot driven by Venus.

(6) Saturn, lord of the Underworld and of agriculture, carries a long scythe with which, like the Grim Reaper, he mows down mortals. The scythe is also found in the *Book of Ballymote* as an astrological symbol for the planet Saturn.

(7) The Moon is not mentioned in this passage. In general, however, it is linked to the psyche and the mind.

> But we now once again turn our discourse to Fate, as it is an energy. For concerning this it is that there are so many natural, moral, and logical questions. Having therefore already in some sort sufficiently defined what it is, we are now in the next place to say something of its quality, although it may seem absurd to many. I say then that Fate, though comprehending as it were in a circle the infinity of all those things which are and have been from infinite times and shall be to infinite ages, is not in itself infinite, but determinate and finite; for neither law, reason, nor any other divine thins: can be infinite. And this you will the better understand, if you consider the total revolution and the A whole time in which the revolutions of the eight circles (that is. of the eight spheres of the fixed stars, sun, moon, and five planets), having (as Timaeus says) finished their course, return to one and the same point, being measured by the circle of the same, which

goes always after one manner. For in this order, which is finite and determinate, shall all things (which, as well in heaven as in earth, consist by necessity from above) be reduced to the same situation, and restored again to their first beginning. Wherefore the habitude of heaven alone, being thus ordained in all things, as well in regard of itself as of the earth and all terrestrial matters, shall again (after long revolutions) one day return; and those things that in order follow after, and being linked together in a continuity are maintained in their course, shall be present, every one of them by necessity bringing what is its own.[5]

Calculating the Strengths of the Planetary Conjunctions

The yokes take grip at the conjunction of planets entering a house. The strength of the yoke's grip results in the combined planetary forces acting on the house ruler. Since these house-rulers are hosts to the celestial gods seen as planetary rulers, these forces have an effect on the activities of the gods as well as on the fate of men. The numerical values given to the planets and the strengths of their yokes do not necessarily translate into a scale of increasing values. Given that force one is given to the moon, this does not mean that this planet is weak or at the bottom of the scale in importance, but rather that it takes precedence and is first in line. As we have seen, queen Medb takes advantage over her king, Ailill, and his warriors. The term briga, "force," indicates that the yoke is strong and powerful. Briga can also be of good or bad influence. In general, it is considered more or less neutral or beneficial that is, auspicious. The term mata defines a yoke having a non-overpowering good influence. It is therefore beneficial or auspicious. The term anmata indicates an inauspicious yoke or simply indicating that it is not beneficial. The higher the power of the yoke, the more it is harmful, and then it is considered vile, baleful, that is to say *lagus* in ancient Celtic.

BRIGA (strong), more or less beneficial or slightly beneficial: (1) Moon; (2) Mars; (3) Sun.
MATA (good), beneficial: (1) Jupiter; (2) Mercury; (3) Venus.
ANMATA or Lagus (bad) non-beneficial, vile, and baleful: (1) Saturn.

Planetary Conjunctions and Significators

Planet	*MATA (auspicious)* or beneficial	*BRIGA (strong, powerful)* less or slightly beneficial	*ANMATA (bad or non-auspicious)* or *LAGUS (vile, malefic or baleful)*
Moon	Venus and Mars	Jupiter, Sun and Mercury	Saturn
Mars	Jupiter, Mercury and Venus	Moon and Sun	Saturn
Sun	Jupiter, Mercury, Venus	Moon, Mars	Saturn
Jupiter	Mercury and Venus	Moon, Mars and Sun	Saturn
Mercury	Jupiter and Venus	Moon, Mars and Sun	Saturn
Venus	Jupiter and Mercury	Moon, Mars and Sun	Saturn
Saturn			Moon, Mars, Sun, Jupiter, Venus and Mercury

Planetary Forces (Book of Ballymote, Ireland)

Moon: 1 + 8 = 9;
Mars: 2;
Sun: 3;
Jupiter: 4;
Mercury: 5;
Venus: 6;
Saturn: 7.

Numerical Value of the Yokes

One: Initial, the unit, the monad, the sovereign entity.

Two: duality, opposition, the conflict, opposing ends.

Three: top, middle and bottom, completion, reciprocity, increased.

Four: space, the 4 directions, closing, protection.

Five: man, measurement, movement, change.

Six: duplication of three (3 to the superlative or tripling).

Seven: wisdom, the stars (planets and stars of the Pleiades and of the North), the seven fairies, the seven sages, the seven rulers.

Eight: the duplication of four (number 4 on the increase, to the superlative, to the power of 4).

Nine: the tripling of three (number 3 on the increase, to the superlative, to the power of three).

Ten: the sacred (the duplication of five), and according to Pythagoras, decad ten represents the entire universe since the first four numbers are contained in the decan: 1 (the centre point), 2 (the straight line), 3 (the triangular plan, triangulation), and 4 (space, square); thus, ten is the guiding principle of life, both earthly and divine.

Eleven: infinity, the mirror of number 1. While number one represents the point or the essential unity, number 11 represents infinity without ever being complete: 11-22-44-88, etc....

Twelve: this number is the product of three (divine spirit), 4 (earthly body), and 5 (man). The sum of 3, 4, and 5, which, like 7 gives symbolical consistency to a series of odd numbers.

Thirteen represents closure, completion of a cycle, buckling of a twelve period cycle, that is, the 13th embolismic moon.

According to the Pythagorean Greek philosopher Philolaus (circa 430 BCE), number 1, the monad, symbolizes the point, dash or dot; 2, the duad, two lines; 3, the triad, three lines, a triangle; 4, the tetrad, four lines, a box, a rectangle, a volume; 5, the pentad, grades and colors; 6, hexad, the soul; 7, the heptad, the mind, health and light; 8, the ogdoad, love, friendship, cunning and intellectualization; 9, the ennead, failure, shortcoming, man; and 10, the decad, perfection.

Significators and Strengths

Zodiacal Sign, Houses and Planet	Significator and Strength

Cancer, House X, Moon:	briga 1+ Mars, briga 2 = force 3, slightly beneficial;
	briga 1+ Sun, briga 3 = force 4, slightly beneficial;
	briga 1 + Jupiter, briga 4 = force, 5 beneficial;
	briga 1+ Mercury, mata 5 = force 6, beneficial;
	briga 1+ Venus, mata 6 = force 7, beneficial;
	briga 1+ Saturn, anmata 7 = force 8, baleful;

Scorpio, House II; Taurus, House VIII; Mars:	briga 2 + Moon, briga 1 = force 3, slightly beneficial;
	briga 2 + Sun, briga 3 = force 5, slightly beneficial;
	briga 2 + Jupiter, mata 4 = force 6, beneficial;
	briga 2 + Mercury, mata 5 = force 7, beneficial;
	briga 2 + Venus, mata 6 = force 8, beneficial;
	briga 2 + Saturn, anmata 7 = force 9, baleful;

Leo, House XI, Sun:	briga 3 + Moon, briga 1 = force 4, slightly beneficial;
	briga 3 + Mars, briga 2 = 5, slightly beneficial;
	briga 3 + Jupiter, mata 4 = 7, beneficial;
	briga 3 + Mercury mata 5 = force 8, beneficial;
	briga 3 + Venus, mata 6 = force 9, beneficial;
	briga 3 + Saturn, anmata 7 = force 10, baleful;

Sagittarius, House III; Pisces, House VI; Jupiter:	mata 4 + Moon, briga 1 = force 5, slightly beneficial;
	mata 4 + Mars briga 2 = force 6, slightly beneficial;
	mata 4 + Sun, briga 3 = force 7, slightly beneficial;
	mata 4 + Mercury, mata 5 = force 9, beneficial;
	mata 4 + Venus, mata 6 = force 10, beneficial;
	mata 4 + Saturn, anmata 7 = force 11, baleful;

Gemini, House IX; Virgo, House XII; Mercury:	mata 5 + Moon, briga 1 = force 6, slightly beneficial;
	mata 5 + Mars briga 2 = force 7, slightly beneficial;
	mata 5 + Sun, briga 3 = force 8, slightly beneficial;
	mata 5 + Jupiter mata 4 = force 9, beneficial;
	mata 5 + Venus, mata 6 = force 11, beneficial;
	mata 5 + Saturn, anmata 7 = force 12, baleful;

Libra, House I; Taurus, House VIII; Venus:	mata 6 + Moon, briga 1 = force 7, slightly beneficial;
	mata 6 + Mars, briga 2= force 8, slightly beneficial;
	mata 6 + Sun, briga 3= force 9, slightly beneficial;
	mata 6 + Jupiter, mata 4= force 10, beneficial;
	mata 6 + Mercury, mata 5= force 11, beneficial;
	mata 6 + Saturn, anamata 7= force 13, baleful;

Zodiacal Sign, Houses and Planet	Significator and Strength
Capricorn, House IV; Aquarius, House V; Saturn:	anmata 7 + Moon, briga 1= force 8, baleful; anmata 7 + Mars, briga 2= force 9, baleful; anmata 7 + Sun, briga 3= force 10, baleful; anmata 7 + Jupiter, mata 4= force 11, baleful; anmata 7 + Mercury, mata 5= force 12, baleful; anmata 7 + Venus mata 6= force 13, baleful.

The Astral Theme

In order to make a prognostic or interpretation, it is important to consider several aspects before developing a theme (or natal chart). The astral theme for a specific event or for the birth of a person is not only given through the meaning from the astrological sign itself, but also from the cusps of entry and exit of the sun in a given house. We must also consider the symbolic meanings given to the houses and the planets present in the subject's natal chart. Further themes or aspects can also come from other sources such as the lunar mansions and their zodiacal symbols. This being said, a zodiacal sign and its house can yield much information through their cusps and their tree, animal and bird signs. Messenger birds are found in the trees (= constellation cusps) and zodiacal animals are found at their foot roaming in the astral domain. Zodiacal signs and houses can also be aspected by the passing of a comet or a meteor, which also negatively color the interpretation.

The chart is graphically drawn from four parallel lines intersecting four other lines in order to form a grid. The arrows indicate the four directions marked by the two equinoxes and the two solstices. According to this graph, House I starts in Libra because the old Celts did not consider the vernal point of Aries as the initial zodiacal marker. The autumnal point was therefore the starting point. This was also the case for the older Zodiacs such as the early Greek and Vedic models. This archaic trait, however, does not contradict the other elements of the Celtic astrological system which differed little from the other classical Greek, Roman or Vedic Zodiacs.

XIII

Medical Astrology

"I am steel; I am a druid.
I am an artificer; I am a scientific one.
I am a serpent; I am love; I will indulge in feasting."
—*Book of Taliesin III, Buarch Beird* [The Fold of the Bards]

A Druid mistletoe picker with bow and sickle. Small horns at the top of the head indicate the sacredness of this character. Gallic statue from Mont-Saint-Jean, Sarthe, France. Author's drawing after a photograph from the Musée d'Archéologie Nationale, St-Germain-en-Laye, France.

Druidical Medicine

As boasted the Welsh poet, Taliesin, the Druid-physician is the steel of his scalpel, a snake of medicine, a scientist and a physician. More compelling still, are the incredible feats described in the various myths. Astounding acts of medicine are recorded in the stories surrounding the Irish god of medicine where Dian Cécht is evoked in the famed *Battle of Mag Tuired*. The medical achievements described in these myths are worthy of Space-Age science.

> Núadu's hand was cut off in that battle—Sreng mac Sengainn struck it from him. So with Crédne the brazier helping him, Dian Cécht the physician put on him a silver hand that moved as well as any other hand. Now Núadu was being treated, and Dían Cécht put a silver hand on him which had the movement of any other hand. But his son Míach did not like that. He went to the hand and said "joint to joint of it, and sinew to sinew"; and he healed it in nine days and nights. The first three days he carried it against his side, and it became covered with skin. The second three days he carried it against his chest. The third three days he would cast white wisps of black bulrushes after they had been blackened in a fire.[1]

From Antiquity to the Renaissance period, the practice of medicine necessarily included concepts of astrology. Since the task was to restore health through the balance of vital functions, medicine resorted to the elements of nature. Were not the Druids the sovereign masters of the elements? The main elements available to the Druid physician were the basic five: water, earth, air and fire.

Insofar as medical practice required a body of knowledge that was not within the reach of anybody, medicine was jealously guarded by the elite members of the Druidical class. The ancient Greek physicians turned to the gods Apollo and Asclepios for guidance and the ill and wounded were treated in healing centers called asclepia. Medical treatment was then under the patronage of the goddesses Panacea and Hygea. In India, Ayurvedic medicine was also guarded by a priestly caste called the Brahmin. The etymologies of the Old Celtic name Dru Uidiia is an exact match to the Sanskrit Dhru Vidya, both for, "firm knowledge." In a world where there was no separation between the sacred and the profane, gods would communicate with mortals in their sleep and in meditation. Man, the mortal creature, was not only made in the image of the gods, but was also a macrocosm and a microcosm of the world.

And, medicine was the art and the science aimed at attaining the balance between the great and the small. In Welsh bardic thought, the Manred (< mino-redo "small course"/mino-redia "tiny space") was in reference to the activities of the microcosm. This quest for balance was attained through the exercise of mind, body and soul. Wisdom and technical know-how went hand in hand. In this order of things, the medical act was also structured according to a tripartite ranking: (1) psychological and mental healing; (2) physical healing and surgery; (3) herbal and natural healing.

The Indo-European Tri-Functional Medical Doctrine

Priestly level: incantatory medicine, spells and formulas;	Warriors' Level: surgery and physical medicine;	Craftsmen's level: herbal and natural medicine.

In short, medical doctrine was the intellectual matter of high-level Druids. As the name recalls, were not Druids "very knowledgeable" in all domains? Another related term was Suuides, which meant, "well knowledgeable," and both names, were used to qualify astute scholars. And as pointed out by the French Celtic scholars Guyonvarc'h and Le Roux,[2] medicine was practiced solely by the members of the Druid class. Therefore, doctors of medicine had to be educated as Druids provided they followed the right curriculum. Thus, medical education was given to future physicians by the Druids.

Also note that in Antiquity, medicine was mostly empirical. Logically, the Druid-physician was an empirical healer. The practices of midwifery and herbal medicine were also important elements of popular medicine for everyday life. Celtic medical practice, as a legal doctrine, was most evidently under the patronage of the gods.

Iolo Morgawg and the Book of the Fferyllt *(Virgil)*

During the Middle Ages, magical powers were attributed to Vergil who was seen as one of the great thaumaturgists of Antiquity. In one of the old Welsh manuscripts, as Morgannwg claimed, a medical book used by the witch Cerridwen was mentioned. The oldest passage is found in the *Hanes Taliesin*, "The History of Taliesin," and was later picked-up by Iolo Morganwg in the late 18th or early 19th centuries.

> Now Caridwen his mother thought that he was not likely to be admitted among men of noble birth, by reason of his ugliness, unless he had some exalted merits or knowledge. For it was in the beginning of Arthur's time and of the Round Table. So she resolved according to the arts of the books of the Fferyllt, to boil a cauldron of Inspiration and Science for her son, that his reception might be honorable because of his knowledge of the mysteries of the future state of the world. Then she began to boil the cauldron, which from the beginning of its boiling might not cease to boil for a year and a day, until three blessed drops were obtained of the grace of Inspiration.

Although it is doubtful that such a book by Virgil ever existed, manuscript copies handed down through oral lore did surely exist.

Levels Within the Druidic Order

A specialization of the Druidic order was that of the Veledes (< ueledos, f. ueleda); ueles/uilis, the file or the filid). Doctors were called leagioi (or sing. Leagios/lepagios) in ancient Celtic. In Antiquity, occupations and professional work was shared by the household couple. Therefore, the Leagia, the doctor's wife, was far from being just a passive observer and was often responsible for the maintenance and order of the family clinic. The term Leagiaxto, which means, "one who prescribes or prescriber," covers everything that surrounded medical practice of the ancient Celts. The name lepagios designated the formulator, that is, the diagnostician, the prescriber and caster of spells and formulas. At this level, they were not only general practitioners but also petty surgeons and practitioners of diverse professions such as those of ophthalmology, trepanation, emergency treatment, toxicology and herbalism.

For the clerics' specialization, that of the *vates* (Old Irish fáid > fáith < uatis, f. uatissa), the medical practitioner was the uatis-leagios, the physician's clerk. Better regarded than today's nurses, he was the doctor's assistant and prescriber. Another actor of the field was the *dedgobaro, dedgobara*, the cup-bearer, the specialist and carrier of liquids.

Because of his degree of expertise in toxic products and antidotes, he was an associate of doctors and physicians at the level of clerks (uatis or ueletos).

Since the druidical philosophy focused on two distinct doctrines of faith, that of monism and that dualism, it was just a matter of time before a conflict should arise between the two doctrinal positions. Nevertheless, it was generally agreed upon that there was interdependency between the physical and the psychic realms. Therefore, any diagnosis could be supported using physical auscultation and psychological observation. Treatment could also be performed using psychological reinforcement and mystic chanting. Or in the words of one of my informants, the Breton neo–Druid Alain Le Goff[3]:

> In the druidical tradition, healing is especially psychosomatic in that, it is more often:
> 1—a reconciliation with the patient himself (removal of blockages and inhibitions or body ailments);
> 2—the patient's reconciliation with others: (restoration of disrupted human and environmental relationships);
> 3—and finally, restoration of the patient's relationship with the mystical and the divine and removal of hidden pathologies (making peace with oneself in balance with the physical).

Hence, the adjuvant or activating principle of will, thus the axiom of Sophocles: "Heaven ne'er helps the men who will not act."

Aspects of Druidical Medicine

I—Medical Discipline:	II—Techniques and Approaches:
Parapsychology and disorders of the soul	Mantic spells and incantations, meditation and self-control
Psychology, character, types, moods and temperaments	Adjuvant will and sleep restoration
Diseases	Diagnostics and appropriate treatment
Medical Astrology	Cosmic energy, solar rays and moon beams, both restorative and debilitating
Herbalism and apothecary	Potions, ointments, poultices and balms
Hygienism	Prevention and Hygiene ; healing by the elements (water, earth, fire and air), and spa treatments, the vital importance of water
Anatomy	Surgery

The Ancient Physicians of Ireland

> Dían Cécht did not like that cure. He hurled a sword at the crown of his son's head and cut his skin to the flesh. The young man healed it by means of his skill. He struck him again and cut his flesh until he reached the bone. The young man healed it by the same means. He struck the third blow and reached the membrane of his brain. The young man healed this too by the same means. Then he struck the fourth blow and cut out the brain, so that Míach died; and Dían Cécht said that no physician could heal him of that blow.[4]

The Irish Apollo was undoubtedly Oengus/Aongus, if not Bile. As god and patron of medicine, he also bore the nickname Diancecht.[5] This Druid-physician god had two sons,

Miach[6] and Oirmiach[7] and a daughter called Airmed.[8] According to the Indo-European triple order of social functions: "Oengus is patron of incantatory and priestly medicine; Diancecht is patron of bloody medicine or surgery; Miach, Oirmiach and Airmed are the patrons of minor surgery, natural medicine and herbalism." Medicine in general is under the medicine-god Belenos, the Celtic Apollo of Ceasar's list. The Gaelic Aonghus or the Gallic Belenos had two aspects:

(1) Aonghus (< Oinogustios, "the first choice") or Belenos, "the brilliant"; brightness, everything that is heavenly, beautiful, young and healthy;
(2) Diancecht (< Diuanno Cextis, "the brutal grasp"; or Grannos, "beaming"; medical procedure, everything that is physiological, bodily and intervening.

In short, it always follows this logic: Aonghus or Belenos represents the principles of sacred or incantatory medicine; and Diancecht or Grannos, represents the principles of bloody surgical medicine. In addition, the herbalist Druids were masters in the botanical science of herbs and in the art of preparing medicinal concoctions. Since they had quite a sense of humor, they also played metaphorical jokes and crafty puns. An episode from *The Dialogue of two Sages* easily comes to mind. Here, four young apprentices, puzzled at the meaning of plant names, began to question themselves accordingly:

> Nede then left, and his three brothers were with him, namely Lugaid, Cairpre, and Cruttine. On the path, they stumbled on a rod of digitalis. One of them said: Why is this called digitalis? As they did not know, they returned home and were a month with Eochaid. Then, they were set to resume their journey. On the way, they found reed. One of them said: Why is this called reed? As they did not know, they returned again to their tutor. There, they spent another month. Afterwards, they journeyed on and on the way, they found a sanicle plant. As they did not know why it was called sanicle, they returned home and were with Eochaid another month.[9]

As the story goes, answer to the mystery is actually found in the names of the plants themselves. To truly understand the hidden implications, one must turn to the original Gaelic names. Digitalis, or digitalis purpurea, was called lus-nam-ban-sith, "the fairy grass," when not, lus-a'-bhalgair, "fox grass." The sith element in the name is a variant of sidh, or sid in Old Irish, which is derived from the Old Celtic sidos, which means, "peace, abode," and which was one of the names for the Other World seen as the earthly residences of the gods or fairies. Another one of these Irish names is bolgan beic (< bolganon beccon) for, "small belly." In Scotland, it is called an-lus-mos, the "great plant." The Welsh call it nienyg ellyllon, the "fairy glove." But again, in Old Celtic, digitalis was called spiona and purple foxglove was called baccharis.

The Gaelic name for reed is cuilc. Another name for reed was n'getal (< ena-caitalis), "swamp grass, reed." The Old Celtic words for reed, depending on the variety, were colcis, corisos, and lisca or caitalis sesca. The name cuilc (< colcis), lends itself to interesting word plays such as: golg, cuilg, "of masculine aspect, virile, manly" (Old Celtic, golga, "straw beard"). Straw beard was traditionally used by young aspiring bards as a disguise during examinations or again to mock their old masters.

The Irish and Scottish Gaelic name for sanicle is coille bodan (Old Celtic, boddos caldi) which literally meant "wood penis." Along with its well-recognized haemostatic qualities, this plant was also known to have the same property as the bois bande or Dominican Mama Juana (mamajuana) plant, the viagra of the Caribbean. No one could have missed the implied cynicism of the pun surrounding fiodh < fidh (< uidus), "wood," fios < fis (< uesos < ueidtos) "knowledge, science, understanding," and dru, "firm, hard."

Confusion remains surrounding the Old Celtic name samolos. It is unclear whether it is the same as the Latin samolus for brook-weed and water pimpernel if not, shamrock, samole, pasque flower or maybe Dane's blood, and chickweed?

Gallic Empirical Medicine

Medicine played an important part in the Celtic world. In Gaul and Britain there were renowned healing centers such as Vichy and Bath. Archaeological digs have also unearthed artifacts such as medical kits, surgical instruments and remedy vials.

As we have seen, for all other matters of science and healing, it went without saying that incantatory magic and psychic medicine came under the supervision of the Druids. The last known of the Gallic empirical physicians was Marcellus of Bordeaux. His Gallo-Roman name was Marcellus Empiricus and he was born the 4th century CE in the vicinity of Bordeaux. In his treatise entitled *De Medicamentis*,[10] he gives a short list of all sorts of remedies and healing spells. This type of medicine, closer to that of the Druids than to that of Hippocrates, largely relies on the power of speech for the process of healing. It was therefore a psychological technique of appeasing comparable to the mantras of Indian Ayur Vedic medicine. And as rightfully noted by Clement of Alexandria (Stobe, Stromata I, XV): "Pythagoras was an auditor with the Galatians and the Brahmins." To quote Pythagoras: "the world is born of thought, not of time."

Healing Spells from Marcellus of Bordeaux

exscicom acrisos	To counter cold congestion "Cold congestion, go away!"
tetunc resonco bregan gresso	The evacuation of dust in the eye "I swear away this lowly particle of suffering!"
in mon dercomarcos axatison	To treat swelling or irritation of the eye "This conjunctivitis in me, remove it!"
rica rica soro	To treat a sty "Cut, cut out (this liquid)!"
Curia curia cassaria surôbri	To treat a sty "Cure, cure this sty of severe pain!"
vigaria gassaria	To treat a sty "Force this sty out (from my eye)"
argidam margidam sturgidam	To counter tooth sores "Kill this nagging neuralgia"
crisi crasi cancrasi	To soothe throat aches "Surround and shrivel it with drying!"
heilen prosaggeri vome si polla nabuliet onodieni iden eliton	To clear the throat "In hope that this ointment will reach and evacuate all the liquid at this moment!"
Xsi exsu cricon exsu criglion Aisus scrisumio velor exsu cricon exsu crilau.	To clear the throat "So Flee, mucus! Aisus, I want to spit! Flee, flee, (and so flee) throat ache!"

The Microcosm and the Macrocosm in Man

As masters of the elements, the Druids had mastery over all ancient natural sciences. In some of his poems, the bard Taliesin evokes the realms of the macrocosm and the microcosm along with the notion of the fundamental elements and sub-elements. In order to have a better general understanding of this cosmological order, the following is the traditional Irish classification:

The macrocosm:	The microcosm:
Talam < talamu), the earth;	Colàind < colanis), the body;
Muir < mori), the sea;	Fuil < uolisa), blood;
Cloch < clocca), stone;	Cnaim < cnama, bones;
Nel < neblioi, clouds;	Imradud < ambiradeto, the brain or cerebellum, thought, reflection;
Gaeth < goita (also auentos), Wind;	Anal < anatla, breath, respiration;
Grian < greina, beaming (also sauelios, sonnos), the sun;	Dréch < dricsma, the face;
Dee < dé (< deuoi), the gods;	Anam < anatmon, the soul, vital breath.

THE ZODIACAL SIGNS WHICH GOVERN THE BODY PARTS IN GRECO-ROMAN CLASSICAL ASTROLOGY

Aries: the head and the organs, etc.
Taurus: the neck and throat, etc.
Gemini: the shoulders, arms and lungs, etc.
Cancer: the digestive system and chest, etc.
Lion: the heart and the spine, etc.
Virgo: the stomach, intestines, etc.
Libra: the lower back, kidneys and bladder, etc.
Scorpio: the genitals and the rectum, etc.
Sagittarius: hips and thighs, etc.
Capricorn: knees and legs, etc.
Aquarius: ankles, etc.
Pisces: feet, etc.

THE ELEMENTS AND BODY PARTS IN THE IRISH TRADITION

Cneas (Old Celtic, Cicon), the flesh; talamh < talamu, the earth;
Fuil < ulasnos/uolisa, blood; uisce < udescio/udesca; aqa (Gaulish, aba/aua), water: mori, the sea;
Cnámh < cnama/astcornon; cloch < cloca, stone, phonolith; caletia, hardness, stone, bone;
Inchinn < eniqennos, the brain; aer < auer, air, nebeloi, the clouds;
Aghaidh < eneqos/eneco/aneco (Gaulish, anipos, dricsma), face; Aedh < Aedis fire, sun.

Irish and Indian Cosmologies Compared

Earth: Talamh < talamu; deity, Tailtiu < Talantio, "the deified earth"; (Prthivi-pati, master of the Earth in India);

Fire: Tine < tepneton, also ur, aedis; toirneach < tanaros, lightning; deity, Aedh < Aedus the morning sun (the fire god Agni in India);

Water: uisce < udescio, also aqa/aba/aua; mori, the sea; deity, Lir < Lero, the lord of the waves and the sea (AP-pati, Ap, "water," the lord of water in India);

Air: Aer < auer, wind, or auentos, auella; deity, Aoife < Esuia, "the (divine) breath," or Esuuia, "the terrible"; (Vayu the god of wind in India);

Ether: Nemh < namos, nemos, sky; geal < gleua, bright (leuxsita, light); (Akasha in India)

Lugh < Lugos (brightness, splendor) or Loucetios (bright) or Diuanno (the light that illuminates), the god of light, the universal essence, a source containing all the qualities of the elements above.

Northwest (Air) **MELDONO** (lymph)	Northeast (Earth) **MALACNON** (fluid/bile)
Master: Findias < Uindia, "of the white;" Uscias / Uiscias < Udescios, "the watery;" or Arias < Arios / Ariats, "the free man, the land owner, the land lord;" Uindiassos, "the splendid one, white one."	Master: Gorias < Goria, "of the warm, the hot;" Esrus, Esras < Esdrios / Esdratis, "he who has means, who has the way;" Urus < Uros, the pure, "original, fresh;" or Urias < Urios, "the pure;" Goriassos, "the hot one."
Southwest (Water) **UOLIA** (blood)	Sud-Est (Fire) **BULACA** (swelling/phlegm)
Master: Murias < Moria, "of the sea;" Semias > Semios / Semiatis, "the flitty, fluttering, vivacious, dashing;" Moriassos, "of the sea."	Master: Falias < Ualia, "of the strong, the mighty;" Marouesos, "of great knowledge;" or Morias < Morios / Moriatos, "of the sea;" also Fios / Fessus < Uesos, "knowing, knowledgeable;" Ualiassos, "the strong, the worthy."

Galiones—The Humors

Since there are four basic elements, it was speculated that in druidical medicine, there were four basic humors (Old Celtic, galiones). The humors were seen as organic liquids that maintain bodily functions. When one of these fluids is disturbed, discomfort or illness occurs. Humors, as body fluids, can be affected by the other elements. For example, Earth has the qualities of hardness as with bones, rocks and stones and causes coagulation and clot. Bile is a yellowish and greenish liquid and is associated with the earth. Fire causes fever and other burning and boiling sensations. The word phlegm comes from Medieval Latin phlegma which was borrowed from the Greek phlegma meaning, "inflammation," (phlegein, "to burn"). Phlegm is associated with fire. The air element causes gas, bloating and rashes. Lymph is a whitish, yellowish liquid that is traditionally associated with water in Greece. In Irish cosmology, it is blood that was associated with water and sea.

Humors and Elements

(Main qualities: moisture, heat, cold, drying)
Fire: Phlegm (hot and dry)
Earth: Bile (hot and dry—cold and wet)
Water: Blood (cold or hot and humid)
Air: Lymph (dry and hot—cold and wet)

Tempers and Emotions

Tempers, or Temperaments (Dantoues), are related to moods, elements and parts of the body associated with the zodiacal signs. Temperaments are inborn and are influenced by emotions and moods. Temperaments are personality types. Emotions or sadness or joy, arise from energy centers in the body content. Other emotions, such as emulation and human and divine love, are also considered. Love, carantia or coima in Celtic (Kama in Sanskrit), is a quality of the soul arising from the principle of desire, auilla. The gods also have personalities. As conceptualized, there were two types of love: divine and human.

TEMPERS MAY BE FORMULATED IN CELTIC AS FOLLOWS:

Uoliacos, "sanguine," characterized by robustness, high resolution and cheerfulness;
Meldonacos, "lymphatic," lack of physical or mental energy, weakness;
Malacnicos, "bilious," the spleen is prone to irritability and melancholy, inclination to anger;
Bulacos, "phlegmatic," showing a slow, phlegmatic temperament and impassive.

Emotions are of two types: *brugno*, "sadness," or *amaro*, "sorrow," and *lauenia*, or *ualetia*, "joy." In Old Celtic, divine joy was referred to as *deualis lauenia* and human joy was called *dunia lauenia*. The word for longing or mental aspiration was *aueidos* (> auedos, also spelled eueidos).

Druid with a mistletoe crown. The mistletoe-shaped lobes represent the character's psychic and mystical powers. A Gaulish carved menhir of the La Tène period. Author's drawing after a photograph of a reproduction kept at the Musée des antiquités nationales, now called the Musée d'archéologie nationale.

Oghamic Herbal Medicine

> After that, Míach was buried by Dían Cécht, and three hundred and sixty-five herbs grew through the grave, corresponding to the number of his joints and sinews. Then Airmed spread her cloak and uprooted those herbs according to their properties. Dían Cécht came to her and mixed the herbs, so that no one knows their proper healing qualities unless the Holy Spirit taught them afterwards. And Dían Cécht said, "Though Míach no longer lives, Airmed shall remain."—*Cath Maige Tuired* [The Second Battle of Mag Tured], translated by Elizabeth A. Gray, p. 33

In the *Book of Ballymote*, there is this line which describes an Ogham series inserted into a snake-shaped waving line reading: "Natar fa fercecni, 'the snake in man of power,' which is usually translated as: nathair Fraoch, the 'snake in the heath.'" The Celtic etymology for this Old Irish line goes as follows:

Natar, Old Irish for nathir, modern Irish, nathair, from the Old Celtic root natrix > Natris/naðris/natro, "snake," (cf. Welsh, neidr; Breton naer);

Fa < uare < uo -are, "on"; Fa < fo < uo, "under";

Fercecni, compound noun, fer/fir < uiros, "man," and cect-ni (elision of "t"), Irish ceacht "power, cycle of science, instruction, lesson," from the Old Celtic, cacto "power"; Fercec(t) < Uirocacetinos, "man of power." It is most likely a variant of the name Fercerdne/Fercertne, "master of art," if not, the Gaelic name for the mythic serpent.

Creeping ivy is also called athair lus in Gaelic, which literally stands for, "snake grass," since it creeps and undulates on the ground.

The Ader Ogham "under the power of Man"	Translation of the symbols
[ogham snake figure]	**Ida/Idho/Iodha/Ioho/Iubhar:** icuris, "liver;" ilion, "intestine;" imbilon/embilon, "navel;" **Eadha /Edadh:** eniqendos/enipennos, "brain, grey matter;" **Ur:** ulnia/olnia, "elbow;" **On/Ohn:** odbos/oðbos, "thigh;" omaca, "neck;" ordlaca, "thumb;" ordiga > ordiclos > orticlos, "big toe;" **Ailm:** ades, "foot;" aredurnon, "wrist;" astis/ostis, "bone;" ausia, "ear;" **Ruis:** roscon, "eye;" rousmen > rumen, "teat;" raton, "phallus, penis;" **Straif/Draighean:** stilnon, "eye;" **Ngetal/Gilcach:** enguina > engina, "finger nail;" **Gort:** garra < sgarra, "leg;" garris, "calf;" glunos, "knee;" **Mediu/Min /Muin:** monio, "neck;" moina, "hand;" mâtos, "thumb;" **Quert:** qendos/pennos, "head;" qacria / pacria, "chakra;" **Sail/Saile:** sulis, "eye;" selga < spelga, "spleen;" **Coll:** calona, "heart;" callia, "testicle;" cûlos, "rear end, bottom;" **Fearn:** uerailia, "eye brow;" uerba,"pimple;" **Tin/Tine /Tinne /Teine:** tuta, "vulva, vagina;" toibos,"side;" taros, "belly;" **Nin/Nion/Nuin:** neibo > nebo, "vital energy;" negsa > nexsa/nessa, "injury;" **Dur /Duir:** drica,"physiognomy;" driccos, "face;" drigo, "hair;" drumbos/drommen, "back;" dossos, "arm;" **Luis:** lama, "hand;" luston/loston, "extremity, end;" letsto > letos, "thigh;" louno, "kidney;" **Huath:** uaitis/uétis, "vein;" uaddos/uaitos < ueisdos, "blood;" uéda/uida, "face;" scamantos, "lung;" scéda/sceidos, "shoulder;" **Beth:** bistis < bidsis/bistion,"finger;" buta, "penis;" buðdu > bussu, "mouth;" bragans, "throat;" brusnia > brunnia, "chest."

Gallic Medicinal Plants

Gallo-Roman culture retained a rich repertoire of Celtic names for medicinal plants which passed into the modern French language. It is a miracle that, despite the slow assimilation of the Gallic-speaking elite and erasure of the pre–Christian religion and traditions, so much of the culture survived in the provincial dialects. In order to show this, we have collected a thorough list of the Gallic names for the medicinal herbs.

Gallic Herbal Pharmacopia

Abolos/abulos/opulos, "rowan," used as an astringent, diuretic, emmenagogue (also spelled emmenagog), anti-haemorrhagic, laxative and anti-scorbutic. Used to stimulate blood flow in the pelvic and uterus area in order to stimulate menstruation and treat diarrhoea.

Alos/alus, "comfrey, donkey ear"; It was, according to Pedanios Dioscorides (1st century, b. ca. 40 CE, d. 90 CE), prescribed against the spitting of blood and piles or hemorrhoids. A medicinal plant used to treat diseases of the chest, hemoptysis and consumption.

Baditis, "(white) lily"; Marcellus of Bordeaux recommended to crush the root. In Antiquity, a concoction was made from the root to turn children into eunuchs. Antispasmodic and sedative plant. Used to treat leucorrhoea, nervousness, rosacea, and cough and sleep problems.

Banatlos/genista, ginesta, "broom, English broom," cardiotonic, diuretic, depurative, vasoconstrictor. Slow heart rate good for abscesses, liver, edema, albuminuria, rheumatism, and gout.

Belenountia, "hen-bane"; vaticinatory plant that causes hallucinations in high doses and having para sympatholytic effects. Indicated for digestive problems.

Beliocandos or beliucandos, "yarrow"; a plant antiseptic, vulnerary, tonic, diuretic, emmenagogue, haemostatic, astringent, carminative, healing, antispasmodic, digestive, anti-inflammatory, appetizer, sedative. Used in the treatment of menopause, rheumatism, varicose veins, cellulite, acne, cracking, scabies, sores, digestive disorders, liver and biliary disorders, premenstrual breast pain, hemorrhoids and circulatory disorders.

Betilolen or betidolen, "great burdock"; used as a depurative, diaphoretic, anti-rheumatic, its root contains an active ingredient with effects are identical to those of penicillin. It is a natural antibiotic, an astringent, antiseptic, and a diuretic antiseborrheic. It was also used to deal with abscesses, carbuncles, gout, rheumatism, boils, sores, acne, eczema, hair loss and hemorrhoids.

Blutthagion or bluthagia, "marigold"; an anti-rheumatic, repellent and detoxifying antidote. It was mainly used to treat rheumatism.

Bricumos, "mugwort"; used to cure epilepsy, nervous problems (St. Vitus' Dance or Sydenham's chorea) and hysteria or problems of the female reproductive organs.

Bugio, "sage"; antibacterial, antioxidant, antiseptic, antispasmodic, antiperspirant, antiviral, astringent, cholagogue (agent that stimulates the gallbladder promoting bile flow), digestive, emmenagogue, febrifuge, estrogenic, stimulant, stomachic and is used as a general tonic for the treatment of amenorrhea, angina, ulcers, arthritis, catarrh (inflammation of mucous with emission of mucus), menstrual pain, muscle pain, gingivitis, gout, influenza, herpes, impetigo, indigestion, gastrointestinal infection, respiratory infections, laryngitis, sore throat, loss of appetite, bad breath, problems related to menopause, osteoporosis, pharyngitis, wounds and colds.

Calliomarcos, "colts-foot"; as its name indicates, colts-foot has expectorant, anti-inflammatory and antispasmodic properties. It was used as a cure for colds, bronchitis, coughs and asthma. Its leaves were used a poultice on wounds.

Calocatanos, "poppy"; as a cough remedy, a soothing, emollient, astringent, antitussive, vulnerary, anti-diarrheal, anti-hemorrhagic and anti-inflammatory agent. Heals burns, skin problems, stomach ailments, sore throat, sprains, and ulcers, inflammation of the mouth, bruises, sprains and wounds.

Corna, "agrimony, poppy agrimony"; anti-inflammatory, vulnerary, diuretic, astringent, resolvent. Used to treat wounds, obesity, migraine, fractures, sprains, diarrhea, diabetes, bruises, the sore throat, hoarseness.

Deximon < texsimon, "clematis Aristolochia"; Aristolochia has been used for centuries in Europe to provoke birth; consumed on a regular basis, its aristolochic acid (carboxylic acid) has toxic effects that can cause major kidney failure and cancer of the kidneys.

Douco or duco, "danewort"; as a purgative, resolvent and sudorific; to treat constipation, sprains, bruises, swelling and cough.

Ercinon, "gerrymander"; recommended for digestive disorders, speeds recovery and eliminates fatigue, has vulnerary properties. It was used to treat wounds and stomach ulcers. Its flowers have a bitter stimulating effect that were used as an antiseptic, diuretic and for the treatment of liver diseases, anaemia and painful menstruation.

Exacon, "centaury"; not to be confused with the great knapweed. It heals intestinal atony along with constipation or diarrhea, lack of appetite, stomach cramps, hyper-acidity, bloating through anxiety and stress as well as urticarial skin irritations and dyspepsia. It is also a good stimulant for liver function and a general tonic prescribed for recovery. It was generally used to treat discomfort of the abdominal glands, anemia and overwork.

Gelasonen, "milkweed, Asclepias, cotton, cotton grass"; used as an expectorant, depurative, with emetic and laxative properties; prescribed to treat bronchitis, flu and fever.

Gigaros, "arum, draconcule, serpentaria"; it is thought to be a good alexiteric, as a preservative against contagious and infectious diseases, the effects of poison in general and as an antidote in treating snake bites and dogs rabies.

Gilaros, "thyme"; used as a tonic, anthelmintic, diuretic, antispasmodic, stomachic, stimulant for breathing, a vasodilator and an expectorant. Treats influenza, whooping cough, dry cough, bronchitis, dyspepsia, flatulence, asthenia, asthma, emphysema, anxiety. A physical asthenia treatment for respiratory asphyxia, nosebleeds, upset stomach and enteritis.

Glaston/glastron, "woad"; a dye and medicinal plant used against infections and fast healing action.

Iubaron/iubaros, "black hellebore, Lenten rose (helleborus orientalis), melampode (helleborus niger, also called black hellebore christe herbe, and Christmas rose)"; poisonous plant that should be used with great caution. Rhizome powder has sternutatory properties (causing sneezing). Helleborine acts as a drastic narcotic, emetic and emmenagogue.

Lagonon, "false hellebore, Indian poke, Indian hellebore, green false hellebore, veratrum viride"; it acts on the cardiovascular and respiratory system, renal system, the skeletal muscles and smooth muscles, the nervous system and thermal control, the skin and mucus, it behaves as a repellent, anesthetic and sternutatory.

Laguna/lagina, "white hellebore, false hellebore, white veratrum"; its root contains violent antispasmodic, emetic and cathartic substances.

Merioitoimorion < meriseimorion, "melissa"; antispasmodic qualities, carminative, choleretic and of stomachic, also taken as a tonic, appetizer, digestive and sedative, bactericidal, and is also used to treat tinnitus, insect bites, insomnia, loss of appetite, asthma, indigestion, dizziness, anemia, respiratory infections, lack of appetite, migraine.

Mulicandos/beliocandos, "yarrow"; (see Beliocandos).

Ninatis < nenadis, "nettle"; used as an hematinic, antidiabetic, astringent, depurative, diuretic, galactogogues, hemostatic, repulsive, dietary, hepatoprotective and is used to treat anemia, ulcer, diabetes, diarrhea, enuresis, bleeding nose, swelling, skin problems, rheumatism, sciatica, leucorrhoea, menopause, insect bites, bleeding, psoriasis and hives.

Oualoida < oualidia < oualoiða < obalða, "chamomile"; was used as an antispasmodic, tonic, sedative, vermifuge, emmenagogue, stomachic, febrifuge, healing analgesic, cholagogue, antiseptic, treats rheumatism, gout, lung disease, stomach spasms, flatulence, neuralgia, ulcers, intestinal parasites, sluggish digestive, inflammation of the skin, painful menstruation, acne, headaches, arthritis and allergies.

Ousoubem < usubes/usubis/eugubis, "laurel chamaedaphne, periwinkle, oleander, broom"; according to Pliny (Natural History, Book XXI), "a dose of periwinkle or chamaedaphneis is given on a spoon crushed dry mixed in water for treating dropsy and it very quickly discharges the liquid. Cooked in ashes and sprinkled with wine, it dissolves tumors. Its juice is a cure for ear infection. As a suppository, this plant is believed to be very good against diarrhea (little periwinkle plant)."

Pempedula or pimpedula, "cinquefoil"; it was used to treat hemorrhoids and diarrhea.

Pones, "mugwort"; was used as an antispasmodic and once was given to treat the beginnings of epileptic disorders and chorea.

Ratis, "fern"; the male plant is excellent against parasites and as a detergent. It is also effective in the treatment of internal parasites, gout, rheumatism and wounds.

Rhoda < rodora, from Latin rodarum, Gallo-Roman, rodaron, "meadowsweet, mead wort, filipendula ulmaria"; plant used as a diuretic, anti-rheumatic and sudorific. In folk remedy, it was used against colds, flu symptoms and general pains. A good source of salicylic acid, the active agent aspirin. For these properties, it was recently found as a good treatment against obesity and cellulite.

Salicos/salixs, "willow"; salicylic acid is extracted from it. It is used as an antineuralgic, antispasmodic, sedative of the genitals, nervous sedative, antipyretic and digestive tonic. It can also relieve rheumatic neuralgia, headaches, menstrual pain, feverish conditions, anxiety, insomnia and psychological disorders such as neurasthenia.

Sappos/sappouidus, "balsam"; pine gum was used as antiscorbutic, as an antiseptic in wounds and poultices for burns.

Scobies, "elder"; used as a diuretic, anti-rheumatic, against sweating. It is also an anti-inflammatory, astringent, anti-hemorrhagic, anti-neuralgic, and laxative and is used to treat rheumatism, skin diseases, conjunctivitis, colds, flu, urinary tract infection, hemorrhoids, arteriosclerosis, constipation, neuralgia and nosebleeds.

Scubulon/scobilo, "black nightshade"; a toxic plant formerly used internally as a sedative or for calming nervous pain. It is nowadays rarely used, and only externally, against skin problems such as acne, seborrhea, bruises and abscesses.

Sistameor < sestamora, "wild fennel"; plant used as an appetizer. It is a galactagogic, sedative, vermifuge, stomachic, diuretic, tonic digestive, laxative, and expectorant. It was used for gum treatment and for its antitoxic, emmenagogue and antispasmodic qualities. It therefore treated lack of appetite, bloating, intestinal parasites, urinary calculi, flatulence, dyspepsia, and sluggishness of the digestive tract, milk insufficiency in young mothers, lung diseases, gums, fatigue, cough and hoarseness, among other ailments.

Sapana, "chickweed"; a plant with vulnerary, diuretic and tonic effects. It was used to treat hemorrhoids, bruises and anemia.

Suibitis, "ivy"; a medicinal plant used to calm cough and soothe bronchitis.

Tarbelodathion < taruotabation/taruotebation, "broad-leaf plantain"; herb that cures many ailments. Contains aucubine which accelerates elimination in the kidneys and has antimicrobial properties and apigenin which is an anti-inflammatory. A leaf poultice is effective against boils and its mucilage inhibit appetite and activate the intestinal transit.

Taurucs/taruxs, "gladiolus"; a dye and medicinal plant. Gladiolus is used to purify the body. Slightly laxative and diuretic, it stimulates the production of urine and bile, and its purifying properties also treat chronic skin conditions such as acne and eczema. It is also used to relieve constipation, gastric, biliary and liver disorders.

Thona/tona, "greater celandine"; celandine is a poisonous plant that can cause hepatitis. Its latex was traditionally used as an ointment applied on warts since its latex is caustic and is potentially antiviral. This is the reason why it was also called wart grass or wart spurge.

Titumen, "wormwood to a rod"; (see Pones).

Uela, "mustard wormseed, erysimum cheirantoides, false flax"; its seeds act in the bile ducts as an antispasmodic and its leaves have expectorant properties that can soothe coughs and infections of the larynx.

Uelaron, "hedge mustard"; an herb that contains sulphur compounds that are beneficial for asthmatics and for people with sore throats. It also has diuretic and stomachic effects.

Uettonica > bettonica > betonica, "betony"; when used internally in large doses, it acts as a purgative and emetic. In external application as a vinous decoction, it gives good results on infected wounds and varicose ulcers.

Uisumaros, "clover"; used to prevent endometrial cancer in women and limit prostate cancer in men. It can prevent heart disease and is used to alleviate hot flushes. Its procured heat stimulates blood circulation, lowers cholesterol and improves breast health. It is also used to help prevent osteoporosis and reduce the development of benign prostatic hyperplasia.

Uitu, "willow scrub"; (see Salicos).

Medicinal Herbs in the Ogham

> "Lusogam .i. ainm secip nach iosa do ga(ba)il ar in fidh a tindscanfa, ut est, braisech ar beiti, 7rl." [For the herbs Ogham one must take the name of a choice plant, then take the first letter of the name in association with the corresponding letter ut est (this being) that braisech (or praiseach), "kale," precedes beiti, "birch," for "b" and so forth.]— George Calder, *Auraicept na n-Éces*, p. 299

The key for the order of medicinal plants in the Ogham is provided by the *Auraicept na n-Éces*, or "scholars' Primer." That is, the usual tree names are replaced with the closest medicinal herb name beginning with the same initial letter.

Cusps and Medicinal Plants in Astrology

(Classification of medicinal plants according to the Ogham ranking)

Libra (Venus):

1st cusp: Q- Querta, "apple";

Qertocos/certocos, "crab-apple tree or wild apple tree";

Anatomy: qacria/pacria, "circle"; cf. Sanskrit, chakra.

2nd cusp: R- Rudioscaua/ruscia, "elder";

Ratis, "fern"; rodaron, "meadow-sweet spiraea or meadow-sweet";

Anatomy: rousmen > rumen, "breast"; raton, "phallus"; lingam in Sanskrit.

Scorpio (Mars):

1st cusp: A- Alamios, "pine";

Aballinca, "alpine medlar"; Aballos, "apple tree"; abassia, "hazel tree";

Anatomy: ades, "feet"; astis/ostis, "bones."

Second cusp: B- Betua, "birch";

Belenountia, "henbane"; a derivative of the proper name Belenos; a psychotropic drug which in high doses is a narcotic that can cause hallucinations; also called beliocandos, "achillea millefolium," and betilolen, "burdock"; bugio, "sage";

Anatomy : bistis < bidsis/bistion, "finger"; buta, "penis."

XIII: Medical Astrology

Sagittarius (Jupiter):
    1st cusp: H < SC/SP (XQ/XP) Squiats, "hawthorn";
    Scalos, "thistle"; scobies, "elder," or scobilo/scubulon, "black nightshade";
    Anatomy: scamantos, "lung"; scéda/sceidos, "shoulder."
    2nd cusp: M- mUinia, "bramble or vine";
    Merioitoimorion, "melissa";
    Anatomy: monio, "neck"; moina, "hand."

Capricorn (Saturn):
    1st cusp: P-(IA), Petios/qetios, "opulus";
    Pempedula, "cinquefoil"; ponem, "common wormwood"; pados, "pine";
        Periarios/pesiarios, "pear tree";
    Anatomy: pennos/qendos, "head."
    2nd cusp: PH (UI)–Phagos > phogos/bagos, "beech"; or spidna, "mackerel
        currant"; Phrinio/brinio, "plum tree";
    Anatomy: srocna/procna < sprocna, "nostrils."

Aquarius (Saturn):
    1st cusp: O- Onna, "ash"; acstino/ocstino, "gorse";
    Odocos, "dwarf elder, danewort"; olloiacetos, "cure-all, mistletoe";
    Anatomy: odbos/oðbos, "hip"; ordiga > ordiclos > orticlos, "toe."
    2nd cusp: L- Luis/lusis, "rowan";
    Lagonon, "false hellebore, hellebore, white hellebore";
    Anatomy: Louno, "kidneys"; letsto > letos, "hip."
    Pisces (Jupiter):
    1st cusp: X(EA)- Xoiton, "copse, thicket";
    Ximalos, "hops";
    Anatomy: cudis/croccena, croccina, "skin, derm."
    2nd cusp: D- Daruos, "oak";
    Ducone, "dwarf elder";
    Anatomy: drumbos/drømmen, "back"; dossos, "arms."

Aries (March):
    1st cusp: T- Taranos, "green oak tree";
    TH(OI)- Thona, "celandine";
    Anatomy: tengato/tabaton/tauaton, "tongue."
    2nd cusp: G- Gortia, "ivy";
    Gilaros, "thyme";
    Anatomy: garra < sgarra, "leg"; garris, "calf"; glunos, "knee."

Taurus (Venus):
    1st cusp: U- Uroica, "heather";
    Usubes, "halo broom"; oualoida, "chamomile";
    Anatomy: ulnia/olnia, "elbow."
    2nd cusp: V (U)- Uernos, "alder";
    Uerbenaca, "verbena"; uettonica/bettonica, "betony"; uidion, "mistletoe";
        Uisumarus, "clover";
    Anatomy: uerailia, "eyebrow"; uenso, "hair"; uétis, "nerve."

Gemini (Mercury):
> 1st cusp: T- tennos, "holly";
> Taruotebation, "plantain"; literally, "bull's tongue";
> Anatomy: toibos, "flank"; taro, "belly."
> 2nd cusp: 'N (NC>NG)- 'nGaitalis < incaitalis, "reed"[11];
> 'Ngaitalis/corisos, "reed";
> Anatomy: enguina > engina, "finger nail."

Cancer (Moon):
> 1st cusp: E- Elto/eltos, "poplar";
> Ercinon, "germander"; exacon, "centaury";
> Anatomy: eniqendos/enipennos, "brain, cerebelum."
> 2nd cusp: S- Salics, "willow";
> Salixs, "willow"; sapana, "scarlet pimpernel"; sappos/sapouidus, "fir"; Sistrameor, "wild fennel"; suibitis, "ivy";
> Anatomy: sulis/stilnon, "eye"; selga "spleen."

Lion (Sun):
> 1st cusp: C- Coslos, "hazel";
> Canabos, "hemp"; calliomarcos, "coltsfoot," lit., "horse's testicles"; corna, "argemone poppy";
> Anatomy: calona, "heart"; callia, "testicle"; culos, "behind, bottom, buttocks."
> 2nd cusp: Đ (SD/ST)–Sdragenos < ðragenos, "barberry";
> Đraginos/sdraginos, "blackthorn";
> Anatomy: dilon, "nipple."

Virgo (Mercury):
> 1st cusp: I- Iuos/iburos, "yew";
> Ioubaron, "a variety of hellebore"; iuos, "yew";
> Anatomy: icuris, "liver"; ilium, "intestine, gut"; imbilon/embilon, "navel."
> 2nd cusp: N- Nertos, "myrtle";
> Ninatis/nenadis, "nettle";
> Anatomy: neibo > nebo, "vital energy."

Gallic coinage depicting a knight brandishing a spear. Drawing by the author.

Appendix

Additional Data and Celtic Nomenclature

Woodcut, author unknown. Taken from "The Atmosphere" written by Camille Flammarion for *Popular Meteorology* in 1888. An astronomer looks through the vault of the sky hoping to understand the workings of the Cosmos. The original contained the caption: "A medieval missionary claims that he has found the meeting point between heaven and earth…"

Astronomical Data

Planetary Revolutions

- Moon: 27.32166 days per revolution around Earth;
- Moon: 29.53058 days for the duration of one lunar cycle;
- Sun: 365.24221 days for one tropical solar year (turn of the zodiac);
- Mercury: 87.96858 days for its revolution around the Sun;
- Venus: 224.70068 days for its revolution around the Sun;
- Mars: 686.98044 days for its revolution around the Sun;
- Jupiter: 11.86222 years for one complete turnaround of the zodiac;
- Saturn: 29.45776 years for one complete turnaround of the zodiac;
- Uranus: 84.01312 years for one complete turnaround of the zodiac;
- Neptune: 164.79334 years for one complete turnaround of the zodiac;
- Pluto: 248.40299 years for one complete turnaround of the zodiac.

Duration of the Planetary Cycles

- Moon: 19.00011 years, lunation (mean average time for one lunar phase) on the same zodiacal degree for one Metonic cycle;
- Sun: 33.00004 years, for the return to the same zodiacal position, same time of the day;
- Mercury: 78.99494 years, for the return to the same position, same day;
- Venus: 7.99863 years, for the return to the same position, same day;
- Mars: 78.99224 years, for the return to the same position, same day;
- Jupiter: 82.99465 years, for the return to the same position, same day;
- Saturn: 58.95719 years, for the return to the same position, same day;
- Uranus: 83.94768 years, for the return to the same position, same day;
- Neptune: 163.95529 years, for the return to the same position, same day;
- Pluto: 247 years + one degree, for the return to the same position, same day.

Positions of the Sun and Moon in the Zodiac

Sun in:	FM in:	LQ in:	NM in:	FQ in:
Libra	Aries	Cancer	Libra	Capricorn
Scorpio	Taurus	Leo	Scorpio	Aquarius
Sagittarius	Gemini	Virgo	Sagittarius	Pisces
Capricorn	Cancer	Libra	Capricorn	Aries
Aquarius	Leo	Scorpio	Aquarius	Taurus
Pisces	Virgo	Sagittarius	Pisces	Gemini
Aries	Libra	Capricorn	Aries	Cancer
Taurus	Scorpio	Aquarius	Taurus	Leo
Gemini	Sagittarius	Pisces	Gemini	Virgo

Sun in:	FM in:	LQ in:	NM in:	FQ in:
Cancer	Capricorn	Aries	Cancer	Libra
Leo	Aquarius	Taurus	Leo	Scorpio
Virgo	Pisces	Gemini	Virgo	Sagittarius
FM = Full Moon; LQ = Last Quarter; NM = New Moon; FQ = First Quarter.				

The Wandering Stars, the Planets in Gaelic Irish

Grian, the Sun;
Gealach, the gleaming one, the Moon;
Mercuir, the sun-faced one, Mercury;
Uenir, the bright one, Venus;
Mhàirt, the red one, Mars;
Joib, the fiery one, Jupiter;
Grian, the shining one;
Gealach, the silver one.

Old Celtic Astronomical Lexicon

Anacronyms for the abbreviations: Brt, "Brythonic or P-Celtic"; Gdl, "Goidelic or Q-Celtic"; OClt, "Old-Celtic."

Acmos, "Acme," also Uertomu, strength taken by a planet or luminary in Astrology.

Aedus, a small constellation found at the intersection of the Milky Way and ecliptic at the boundary of Taurus and Gemini. It is made up of the stars grouped around Tejat Prior, Tejat Poster and M 35, an open star cluster visible to the naked eye (see Sianas).

Albiio/albis, "the Universe, the Cosmos."

Albiiorixs, "King of the Cosmos," the Chronocrator, also called Cernunnos, "the Horned-One."

Ambis, "the Dragon," the constellation of Draco. The name dragon is also in relation to the lunar nodes Cauda and Caput Draconis.

Anaganti Prinnios, the constellation of Aquarius, the Water-bearer (January\February), for both the constellation and the zodiacal sign. Anagatios, stands for, "inactive," a pun with Anacantios, "calamitous."

Andarta, the constellation of Ursa Major, the Great Bear, and The Great Dipper (also called Eburos OClt).

Andecrundion, "Counter-Earth," opposite Earth behind the Sun, a mystical and mythical plane seen as the Earth's opposite and counted as a planet (Latin Anti-Terra, Greek, Antichthon)

Angnatos Magosias, "The Stranger of the Plain" (of Macha), the star Canopus, a star of the first magnitude in the constellation of Argo. Is not visible north of the 37° latitude, can only be seen in Celtiberia, hence the term "stranger, unknown person."

Anguinon, "the cosmic egg"; or serpent's egg, from which emerged the Cosmos; also Ogos Nadiras.

Areculon, "backwards movement"; retrograde motion of a heavenly body such as Saturn.

Aremedion, lit., "before the middle," entering a zodiacal house, the first cusp, or Mid Heaven.

Argantoreta, the constellation of Corona Borealis, the Northern Crown, word for word, "silver wheel," also a lunar asterism.

Artaios, "the Bear Keeper," the star Arcturus, in Bootes, from Artos, "the bear (a nickname of Arthur)." It is one of the spiritual realms sometimes counted as an extra planet.

Artulla, "the little she-bear," the constellation of Ursa Minor, one of the names of the Little Dipper.

Belca Uindas Boucas, "the track of the white cow," the Galaxy, the Milky Way, from Boann < Bo-Uinda, the Irish Cow goddess.

Belisama/Belesame, "brilliant"; the moon as a goddess.

Bledios, "the Wolf," the constellation of Lupus, Brt.

Boudios, "the victorious," also Boduos, "crow," one of the alternate names of Lugus, Latin, Mercury, and a cognate of the Sanskrit Buddhi.

Brigiomu, literally, "in force, at the summit"; an astronomical term followed by the name of a constellation, it indicates that the Sun is in a constellation.

Cantli Prinnios, the constellation of Libra, Scale (September\October), a constellation and astral sign. It has the meaning of "songs," as a thanksgiving celebration after the time of harvests. In connotation, it can be taken to stand for "cycle-settling" (cantos, "ring").

Carbantos/Carbantos Diuoni, "the Moon's chariot," it carries the moon over land during night time.

Carpantos/Carbantos Sonni, "the Sun's chariot," it carries the Sun over land during day time.

Carpidaros < Caibré/Cairpré, "the carpenter," beta Leporis of the Lepus constellation; also referred to as Cattos Qendos/Pennos, "the cat's head."

Cattos, "the Cat," the Hyades star group, a cluster of Taurus; Cattosira, the Cat-star, the alpha star of the Hyades.

Cnabetiosira or Cnabetica Sira, w. for w., "long-haired star," comet.

Cnouai Uidias, "the nuts of knowledge," a small cluster of bright stars found in the Milky Way by Sagittarius at the southern intersection of the ecliptic and not far from another bright region referred to as the "Well of Segais."

Coiluater, "divining agent," astronomer/astrologer.

Comiugon > cuing, "conjunction," meeting or passing of two or more celestial bodies at the same degree of the Zodiac.

Corsos Maqos/Mapos, "the dwarfish son," the alpha Leporis star in the constellation of Lepus.

Coscorâdios > Cuscraid, "peace thinking one," gamma Leporis in the Hare constellation.

Crundnion > Cruinne, "rotund, globe," the Globe, the World, the Earth (astronomy).

Cunomaros, "the great dog," or Cunocobarios, "the dog of assistance, helper dog," Canis Major and the star Sirius.

Cuti Prinnios, "the ram," the constellation of Aries, (March/April), a constellation and an astral sign. It stands for "fiery." A pun with Cutios/Putios, "Ram."

Danua < Danu, "of boons, gifts," an old name for the constellation of Cassiopeia.

Diaremedion, lit., "out of the middle"; the sun exiting an astral house, the second cusp, or Mid Heaven.

Dira/ðira, (see also sdira, sira), "star."

Direula/ðireula, (see also sireula), "astronomy."

Dirio/ðirio, "constellation."

Dironos, adj. ðiron-os\-a\-on, (see also sdironos, sironos\-a\-on), "starry."

Diuon, the Moon's astronomical name, it stands for "luminary."

Donnotaruos, "the tan bull"; the alpha star of Taurus, alpha Tauri, Aldebaran.

Dregia/Ðregia, lit., "tracing," a meteor.

Druuios, "wren"; the Wren star, Alpha Draconis, the former Pole Star.

Dumanni Prinnios, "darkening, dusky," and connoting dumannos, "dark man, dark ponny"; the constellation of Sagittarius, the Archer (November\December), taken as a constellation and an astral sign. These are the years' darkest moments.

Eburos, "boar" punning with "yew"; the Big Dipper.

Elembiui Prinnios, "of arbitration" and connotes "hot flux"; the constellation of Virgo, the Maiden (August/September), a constellation and a zodiacal sign. Also spelled Aedrinios and Aedurinios.

Epos Leruos, "Horse of Lir"; a late British name for the constellation of Pegasus.

Equi Prinnios, "adjusted, equalized," punning with Equos/Epos, "horse"; the constellation of Cancer, the Crab (June/July). Both a constellation and a zodiacal sign

Equos or Aecuos, the ecliptic ("adjusted balance"), the ecliptic bisects Cancer evenly, therefore, Equos, the horse is taken as the symbol for the ecliptic.

Esus, "holy lord"; the star Vega.

Exito, "exit"; exit of a heavenly body from an astral house or constellation.

Garannai, "the cranes"; the Pleiades, a star cluster of Taurus.

Giamoni Prinnios, the bull, the constellation of Taurus.

Giamonios < Giiemonios, "of sprouts, shoots"; moon of April/May, from April (or of early May, if after the Ciallosbuis leap-month).

Giamos/giemos < gemos, "winter"; connoting "shoots," for vegetative.

Giiemorotlio > geamhradh, "shoots-cycle"; dark half-year (autumn + winter-time) or vegetative period.

Greinatarostami, "Sun standing," Gdl; summer solstice, the solstice in general.

Grenna > Greina/Granna > grian, "beaming"; feminine adjective used as a periphrasis in the Goidelic dialects to name the Sun.

Grisgaconai, "those as pebbles," Gdl; a Goidelic periphrasis for the Pleiades.

Iatus > àth, "ford"; in Old Celtic astronomy, was seen as a point on the equator where the ecliptic crosses.

Iatus Brassalios > hi Breasal, "the ford of the bulky"; the southern point of crossing on the ecliptic and equator; a mythical place called Land of Breasal < Brassalis, the King of the summer world, situated to the South.

Iatus Ualcias, "ford of the wolf"; the northern point marked by the bisection of the equator by the ecliptic; a mythical location of the Other-world or Underworld, ruled by wolves and evil.

In, ini, inis, abbreviations in the Coligny Calendar for innisma, inisma, "isolation"; a meteorological note meaning, "hazy, covered, cloudy screen."

Iu-os/-a/-on, adj. "good, fine," a meteorological note meaning "very distinct"; and punning with iuos, "yew."

Labaron, "insignia, emblem, banner"; the zodiacal wheel, and a distinguishing mark of the druidic world order (dema < dedma).

Lag., abbreviation of Laget.

Laget, "it lowers, it sets down, it descends."

Lagiato, "descent of a heavenly body, of a constellation, waning of the Moon."

Lat., abbreviation of Lates.

Latis, "a nycthemer (night + day), a calendar day."

Lostos Ambios, "the dragon's tail"; Cauda Draconis, the descending southern lunar node.

Lostos Crucas, "the scorpion's tail"; the stars of the Scorpion's stinger, sub-constellation of Scorpio, the stars Sco or Shaula, and Lesath.

Lostos Nadiras, "the serpent's tail"; Cauda Serpentis, a sub-constellation of Serpens Ophiucus.

Leucar-os/-a/-on, "very light emitting, light beaming"; NB: a Brythonic periphrasis for the moon, whence, logra < lloer in Welsh.

Lisson Danuas > Llys Don, "the palace of Danu"; the constellation of Cassiopeia.

Lodex., abbreviation of Loudextio.

Loud., abb. of Loudet.

Loudet, "raises, gets up."

Loudextio, "ascending"; waxing of the moon, ascent of a constellation.

Lucotios, "the mouse"; the present Pole Star, Polaris, the alpha star of Ursa Minor.

Luctos/Luxtos/Louxtos > luct, "war party, organized troop, military unit"; also Loucetios, "light giving," planet Mercury.

Lugos, "bird, raven"; a probable name for planet Mercury.

Luminaries index: Sun—Sonna (f.n.), Sonnos (m.n.), Sauelia /Saualis/ Saulo (f.n.) Sauelios/Saulios/Saulos (m.n.), Grannos (m.n. OClt), Greina (f.n. Gdl); Moon—Diuon (n.n.), Eidsciia (f.n. Gdl) Luxsna, Lugra < Leucara (f.n.).

Luxna, the moon's most usual name.

M., abb. of Mens.

Manutera > muintir, "household"; a zodiacal House.

Maron Nauson, "the great ship"; the Constellation of Argos or Navis.

Mat., abb. of Mata.

Mata, "good as complete," code for even months.

Mat D., abb. for Matu Diuon.

Mat N., abb. for Matu Nabelcon.

Matrai, "mothers"; the stars of Eridanus.

Matrona, "matron"; Achernar, the alpha star of Eridanus.

Matu Diuon, "quite clear (light emitting)," as on the full moon.

Matu Nabelco, "quite cloudy, overcast."

Additional Data and Celtic Nomenclature

Medianoxs, "mid-night."

Medionemesos, "mid heaven"; abbreviated as MC, for Medium coeli, in Latin.

Melnos > meln, "sluggish, slow"; planet Saturn.

Mens/Mins, "month"; pl. nominative: menses, a lunar month as opposed to a solar month.

Mid Samonios, "middle of the November month"; the abbreviation MIDX Mens in dueixtionu was followed by Samonios to indicate where the autumn embolismic month was introduced.

Midiuon/Mediuon, "half moon"; the quarter moon.

MIDX., abb. of Mens in dueixtionu for "month in duplication," the name of the autumn leap-month.

MM, abb. of Menses, the plural for mens, "month."

Mogus Retas > Mog Ruith, "servant-boy of the wheel"; a mythological or legendary Irish master astrologer.

N., abb. of Nabelcos, for "cloudy."

Namos/Nemos, "sky, heaven, ether"; singular genitive, nemesos, the sky in general, heaven's vault.

Nebelca, "nebulous"; Latin, Nebulae, nebulous star clusters.

Nebelcos, "nebulous"; an alias of Lugus as god of Meteorology; the Celtic continental name of Manamann or Manawydan.

Nebladoarecanacto > Neldoracht, "cloud divination"; in Goidelic.

Nebladoarecania, "cloud divining," for meteorological prediction and astrology under covered skies.

Neinon, "zenith"; the point of the celestial sphere that is directly opposite to the nadir and is vertically above the observer.

Nemetolatis, "holy day": fifth or sixth day of the month after the full moon, starting the novena, nine day period; a day of rest, gatherings and reunion.

Noiolatis, "novena"; a nine days period in the month.

Noxs/nouxs < noxts, pl. nominative, noctes, genitive, noxtos, "night."

Nucturos Uosiros, "nocturnal and sluggish"; a periphrasis for Saturn seen as the loiterer of wandering stars; also Melnos.

Ociomu/Ogiomu, "clear visibility (of a constellation)."

Ogambios < Ogmios > Ogma (Gaelic)/Euydd (Welsh), Constellation of Hercules.

Ogos Nadiras, "the serpent's egg"; Scutum, Scutum Sobiescianum, Sobieski's Shield; also Anguinon.

Ogroni Prinnios, "constellation of the cold-blooded"; the Fish, Pisces.

Ogronios, "of the cold, cold blooded (animals)"; moon of February/March, month starting from the February full moon.

Oxtucomoctioi, "Eight magical powers"; a system of astrological prediction using a Venusian cycle of eight years seen as sources of energy the other planets are subjected to.

Oxtureuiai, "eight phases"; the eight principle phases of the Moon.

Oxturotlio > oxturotio, "eight cycles"; the eight cycles of Venus.

Pennos/Qendos Ambios, "the dragon's head"; Caput Draconis, the ascending northern lunar node.

Pennos/Qendos Balori, "Balor's head"; Caput Medusa a sub-constellation of Perseus.

Pennos/Qendos Nadiras, "the serpent's head"; Caput Serpentis, a sub-constellation of Serpens Ophiucus.

Planet index: Mercury, Lugos (?) (J. Monard, R. Reznikov), Loucetios or Luxtos (Ballymote); Venus, Reiia, Reia, Ria (J. Monard) Epona (?), Uasnia, (Ushas the Vedic Aurora, R. Reznikov); Earth, Crundion (Gruinne in Gaelic), Bitu; Mars, Toutatis-Cocidios (?) (J. Monard), Segomo or Roudionos/Roudiobos (R. Reznikov), Cocidios (Ballymote); Jupiter, Taranis (?) (J. Monard), Tectos (Ballymote); Saturn, Nucturos, Uosiros (J. Monard), Melnos (*Book of Ballymote*); Uranus (?): probably Cenos (?), Counter-Earth, Andecrundion.

Posdedortonis, "epact, w. for w., post computation"; singular accusative, posdedortonin.

Prennos, "tree"; for a cusp, a mathematical point marked by the House's ascendant; also uidus in Goidelic.

Prin., abb. of Prinnios.

Prinnios, "branching"; a zodiacal constellation, a zodiacal period.

Prinniacto/prinniaxto, astrology by the Zodiac.

Quimon, "lustre"; a period of five days, from quinquimon an archaic word, Latin, quinquennium.

Raco, "before, in first position"; Raco Prennos, or Raco Uidus, the first cusp of a House."

Ramaca Reta or Reta Ramacas, "rowing wheel" or "wheel of rowing"; a divining wheel; a periphrasis for the Zodiac.

Reiia/Riia > Rii, "free"; Venus as a Planet.

Rendu, "star, a stellar body."

Rendunemos > rindneam, lit. "star heaven," the constellations as a whole.

Rendureidsmen > rindreim > rianreim, lit. "star order, course," a constellation.

Reta Greinas, "the sun wheel," Gdl, the Zodiac.

Reta Sauelias, Reta Suléos, "the sun wheel," the Zodiac.

Retios > Reith, Aries, the Ram stars.

Reui, "luminary"; usually the Moon (cf. Sanskrit "Ravi").

Reuia, "lunation"; a period averaging 29 days, 12 hours, elapsing between two successive full moons.

Riuo > riodh, a ray, a beam of light.

Riuri Prinnios, the Goat, Capricorn.

Riuros, December/January, from December FM, w. for w.: "frost."

Rotlio, "cycle"; the semestrial cycle.

Sagilias, Uabero or Rino Sagilias, "the well of generosity" or Uabero Conlanias, "the well of plenitude"; a very bright region of the Milky Way intersecting the ecliptic in the constellation of Sagittarius at the southern hemisphere; also, there is another area called Uabero Sianas, "the well of binding," which intersects the ecliptic in the north, at the boundary of Taurus and Gemini. This is where the star Aedus > Aedh is found.

Saitlon < setlon, "age"; a thirty years cycle; a solar cycle of thirty years.

Samoni Prinnios, "constellation of the sower, of reunion"; the zodiacal constellation of Scorpio.

Samonios: October/November, from October FM, w. for w., "of the meeting, of the sower"; in connotation, Samoindon, "summer's end."

Samos, "summer."

Santara Mens/mins, "leap-month," w. for w., "month set aside."

Saueliamos, Suliamos, "sundial, gnomon."

Sauelios, the Sun's most usual name.

Segomos, "the vanquisher, the winner"; an alias of the Gallic Mars, Aries.

Sembros, "the trefoil, clover"; a three star formation of Aquarius, see Uisumaros.

Semiuisoni Prinnios, "the constellation of the frisky"; the constellation of the Twins, Gemini.

Semiuisonios, Simiuisonios, "of dashing breezes"; the month of May/June, starting from the May full moon.

Semorotlio, "seeds cycle"; the clear half-year made up of springtime and summertime.

Sentio, "path"; orbit of a luminary, mainly of the sun from which Setantios > Setanta, or Cuculantios > Cuchulainn was named; see also, uxsentio.

Seruoretla or Seruonta Retla, "wandering star"; a planet.

Seruoretla Acmos, seruoretlacmos, "acme of a planet"; zenith of a planet's orbit.

Sexten Cosloi Uidias, "the seven hazels of knowledge"; a euphemism for the stars of Sagittarius found by the Milky Way.

Sextendirio, "the constellation of seven, the Septentrion"; the Little Bear or Little Dipper.

Sianas, Sionas, "the binding"; also called Uabero Sianas, "the well of binding"; a star cluster called M 35 in a sub-constellation of Gemini (Aedus OClt) intersecting the ecliptic in the north at the boundary of Taurus and Gemini.

Smertus, "the sword"; the star Deneb, alpha Cygni.

Sonna/sonnos, "the sun (in astronomy)."

Sonnau-os/-a/-on, adj. "sunny"; aspect of the sun, solar.

Sonnauos mens/mins, "the solar month"; as opposed to a lunar month.

Sonnocinxs, "the sun's march"; the solar year, the ecliptic (sing. genitive, sonnocingos, the Zodiac; pl. nominative, sonnocinges, the sun's course).

Sonnotarostami, "sun standing"; a euphemism for the summer solstice.

Stars index: **A**—Aldebaran: Donnotaruos; Andromeda: Uiradectis (?); Aquila/Eagle: Erur; Aquarius/Water-Bearer: Duprosopos; Aries/Ram: Putios/Cutios; Auriga/Coachman: Agomaros Couinnarios; **B**—Bootes/Cattleman: Boucolios; Bow in Canis Major: Boggos; **C**—Capricornius/Goat: Riuri Prinios, Capella: Gabros; Cassiopea: Letsto Donni, Chair: Sedlon; Centaurus/Centaur: Marcodunios; Cepheus: Sadro (?); Cetus/Whale: Beldua; Canis Major/Great Hound: Maros Cu; Canis Minor/Little Hound: Colignos; Cancer/Crab: Equi Prinnios; Columba/Dove: Eglecopala; Coma Berenices/Berenice's Fleece: Etannas Ualtos (?); Corona Australis/Southern Crown: Dexsiuon Aestion; Corona Borealis/Northern Crown: Argantoreta; Crater/Mixing Bowl: Parios/Qarios; Corvus/Raven: Brannos; Cygnus/Swan: Alarcos; **D**—Delphinus/Dolphin: Morimoccos; Draco/Dragon: Ambis; **E**—Equuleus/Pony: Mannos; Eridanus: Bodincos; **F**—Fomalhaut/Salmon: Encinio; **G**—Gemini/Twins: Semiuisoni Prinnios, Emni; **H**—Hawk: Sebacos; Hercules: Ogmios; Hyades/Cat Star: Cattos; Hydra: Eiscanguis, Abonna Eiscanguios; **L**—Leo/Lion: Elembiui Prinnios, Leuo; Lepus/Hare: Scobarnocos; Libra/Scale: Cantli Prinnios, Mantala; Lupus/Wolf: Bledios; Lyra/Lyre: Talannos; **M**—Medusa

Caput/Head of the Medusa: Pennos Balori; **O**—Ophiuchus: Nadiroberos (?), Esculape: Diuannocextis, Orion: Selgarios; **P**—Pegasus: Cauaromarcos, Etnosos Epos; Perseus: Londoandeslucos; Piscis Australis/Southern Fish: Dexsiuos Eiscos; Pisces/Fishes: Ogroni Prinnios, Eiscoi; Puppis/Ship: Nauson; **S**—Scorpio/Scorpion: Samoni Prinnios, Sgorpiu; Serpens/Snake: Nadira, Serpentis Caput/Snakes Head: (Q)-Pennos Nadiras, Serpentis Cauda/Snake's Tail: Lostos Nadiras; Sagitta/Arrow: Beru, Cesta; Sagittarius/Archer: Dumanni Prinnios, Uarcustos; **T**—Taurus/Bull: Giamoni Prinnios, Taruos; Triangulum/Triangle Trigenacos; **U**—Ursa Major/Great Bear: Eburos, Dipper: Andarta; Ursa Minor/Little Bear: Sextendirio, Artulla; **V**—Virgo/Maiden: Edrini Prinnios, Magula.

Stolos, "retreat, military retreat"; retrograde, contrary direction to that of the general motion of similar bodies; see areculon.

Suelcu Reuias, > Resholly, "bright period"; moon light, the bright period around the full moon.

Sutrebos, "welfare"; beginning of autumn, Indian summer; the solar month of October.

Talabaranos > Talhearn, "choleric face"; a legendary or mythical Welsh master of stars, a bard, an astrologer and a diviner.

Talouaro/Talouero, Gallic, Talaro, "borderline, side of a field"; seen as the limit or border of a constellation.

Tarabarra, "the wishing bars"; or Wheel of Fortune, the Zodiacal Wheel (Kalachakra in Sanskrit).

Taruos Trigannianom, "the bull with the three cranes"; Aldebaran, alpha star of the Pleiades and the Pleiadean group as a whole; punning with Taruos Tricaranos, "the three horned bull."

Tasgopeilas Reta, "performing thought wheel"; a divining wheel, the Zodiac.

Tectos > tect, "messenger, envoy"; planet Jupiter.

Temelé, "darkness, pitch dark night."

Tricoros, "three circles"; a triskelion, triskele; symbol for the triune order, the trinity or trimurti, a druidical cosmic or stellar insignia.

Trigenacos, "triangle"; the constellation of Triangulum, the "triangle" in Latin, also Tricoros, the Triskelion. The three stars of Trienacos were: Sulaxsus/Eulaxsos > Eolas, "knowledge," Uesos > Fios/Fius, "knowing," and Uocomarcos > Fochmarc, "inquiry."

Trinux., abb. of trinuxtio.

Trinuxtio, "predominance," (pl. nominative, trinuxtiones (followed with a name of a zodiacal period) has the meaning of: its opening by entry of the Sun therein.

Tritios, Tritios Prennos, or Tritios Uidus, the third cusp, the point of exit from a constellation; see exito.

Uasnia, "dawn"; the planet Venus as the Morning Star.

Uesara/uestnos/uesenteinon, "springtime."

Uidus/uidon, "tree"; a zodiacal cusp; also Prennos in Brythonic.

Uiliasamiacto/uiliasamiaxto, "wishful interpretation"; a divining technique.

Uindosenos > Fintan, "the white elder"; a mythical druid-seer, the Irish name given to Fomalhaut, the alpha star of Pisces Austrinus, the Southern Fish.

Uisumaros, "the trefoil, clover"; the trefoil formation of Aquarius; see Sembros.

Uogemos, "autumn, fall"; please note that the Goidelic synonym was Cengiamos, w. for w., "sub-winter."

Uonidion, "setting"; setting of a luminary.

Uosutrebos, dog days, w. for w.: "lower welfare"; the solar month of July.

Uxellos > Ochill (Gaelic), "lofty, high, prominent"; the constellation of Aquila.

Uxsentio, "high path"; a heavenly body's highest orbit; path of a heavenly body through the Milky Way.

Chapter Notes

Introduction
1. From Claude Ptolemy's chart.

Chapter I
1. Harald Meller in *National Geographic Magazine*, 2004.
2. *Rig Veda* I—Asya Vâmasya, v. 48.
3. Sûrya-siddahânta, p. 2, quoted by Richard L. Thompson in *Vedic Cosmology*, p. 22.
4. Lucian, *Of Astrology*, Book XXXVI, vs. 411–412)
5. Antiquity, Vol 1, pp. 31–41.
6. Kugler (I) Erg. 2, 207; Gossmann, quoted from Jack Lindsay in *Origins of Astrology*, p. 54.
7. *Rig Veda* I, 140–164.
8. *Rig Veda* I, 155.
9. Aelian, *Various History, of Some Astronomers, and of the Great Year, along with Meton's Pillars*, Book X, chap. VII.
10. All quotes on the Hittite tablets are from *Le Combat pour l'immortalité. Héritage indo-européen dans la mythologie anatolienne*, "The struggle for immortality in Anatolian mythology" by Emilia Masson, chap. 2, *Les trois mondes des Hittites* "The Three Worlds of the Hittites," p. 187–223, author's translation from French.
11. From Emilia Masson, *Le Combat pour l'immortalité—Héritage indo-européen dans la mythologie anatolienne*, pp. 187–223.
12. Zoroaster, Avesta, Chapter 19, verse 42, translated into English by James Darmesteter, from *The Avesta*, 1898.
13. Reference for this Chaldean chart is given by Jack Lindsey in *Origins of Astrology*, 1971, p. 69.
14. Black, J.A., Cunningham, G., Fluckiger-Hawker, E, Robson, E., and Zólyomi, G., *Emmerkar and the Lord of Aratta*, The Electronic Text Corpus of Sumerian Literature (http://www-etcsl.orient.ox.ac.uk/), Oxford 1998; verses 499–514.
15. Jack Lindsay, *Origins of Astrology*, 1971.

Chapter II
1. Just < Iustus in Latin, from PIE root *yewes-, "law," with cognates, the Avestic yaozda, "to make ritually pure," and the Celtic auentos, "right, just."
2. Nobly born, that was called Arya in Sanskrit for "land-owner," Altus in Latin and Celts in Old Celtic, both meaning "lofty."
3. Dharma, from PIE root *dhe-, *dh-mā, "status testimony"; by its dialectal variant Pali dhamma (cf. old Indian dhaman-, "law, housing, troop, multitude, crowd, etc.," Avestan Persian daman, "site, creature"; Old Celtic dedma, Gaulish, dema "statute"); dharma (dharmán- "holder," or dhárman-, "supports"). It is of the same root by the mutation of the initial consonant of d shifting to f (d > f-) as the Latin firmus, "firm, solid, resistant."
4. The ritual nectar, Soma in Sanskrit, Haoma in Avestic, Ambrosia in Greek and Medus in Celtic. Varenne, Jean, *Zarathustra et la tradition mazdéenne*, p. 23–35.
5. J. Arthur de Gobineau, *Histoire de Perses*, pp. 36–37.
6. Flamens and Brahmans, priestly oblation carriers; flamines in Latin, brahmana in Sanskrit, both from I.E. roots *blagmena or *beromena for the Proto-Italo-Celts.
7. Tocharian, from Greek Tokharoi (< Tacaros, "chiefly"), were most likely Proto-Celts of mixed Illyrian Cimmerian stock as shown by the Old Chinese name Xiemmer. The Iranian speaking Scythians called themselves Skolots, and were referred to as the Sakas in the Vedas.
8. David Frawley, letter, April 25, 2000.
9. A cultural and historical society review which continues the *Antaios Journal* founded in 1959 by Mircea Eliade and Ernst Jünger. Quoted from: Centro Studi La Runa, Archivio di storia, letteratura, tradizione, filosofia: http://www.centrostudilaruna.it/haudryreligion.html.
10. Aristotle, *The History of Animals*, Book VI, and Chapter 35, translated by D'Arcy Wentworth Thompson.
11. Riuros, literally "cold feeling, intense frost"; riuo, "frost," riuo, "ray, stylized ray"; implying riu-ros, "great ray."
12. Cat Stars, an old name of the Pleiades which should not be confused with a small constellation between Hydra (the water snake) and Antlia (the pump) created by the French astronomer Lalande in 1799.
13. The Greeks saw the Small Bear as a Boar. In Greek myths, Hercules slew the Erymanthian Boar. The boar or pig, since both animals were often confused by the ancient Celts.
14. Cath Pagug, literally "the cat in absentia," is

mentioned in the Welsh *Trioedd Ynys Prydein, Triad 26*, in the Paniarth *16 MS* and in the Llyfr Gwyn Rhydderch.

15. *Rig Veda*, Visvakarma, 10. 82, 1.
16. *Rig Veda*, Purusha, 10, 13.
17. Zoroaster, *Avesta, Greater Bundahishn*, Chapter XXXV, translated by Behramgore Tehmuras Anklesaria, lines 38 to 40.

Chapter III

1. In *Revue d'études anciennes*, 1902, p. 115, quote from Hutin, Serge. Histoire de l'astrologie. p. 105.
2. Pomponius Mela, a Roman geographer born in Tingentera small town in Baetica, and active to 43 CE.
3. Flavius Magnus Aurelius Cassidorus born about 490 CE in Squillace, Calabria, and died in 583.
4. Dromichætes < Dromicatus "fighter of the ridge, of the back."
5. Diceneus / Dicineus, the Latin spelling of the Greek version Dikaineos which was most likely borrowed from the Celtic name *Dicanios "reciter"; verb dicanō "to recite."
6. According to Jornandes, the Belagines were natural law texts given to the Gets by the philosopher Diceneus. Again, the name is best explained through a Celtic etymon: Belagines < Belogenio, "of luminous origins"; belo- clear, luminous + suffix –genos/-a/-on, for an "idea of origin, coming from something," + suffix –io, "idea of abstraction."
7. Pausanias, *Description of Greece*, Book I, Attica, chapter I, author's English translation from French.
8. Abaris < Abaris "the water," or Abare-os/-a/-on, Abaros/-a, adj. "quibbling," Abaron, "matter."
9. Peter Berresford Ellis, *Dictionary of Celtic Mythology* (Astrology) p. 35.
10. Berresford Ellis, "Our Druid Cousins, Meet the Brahmins of Ancient Europe, the High Caste of Celtic Society," *Hinduism Today*, February 2000.
11. Strabo, the Greek geographer born in Amasea in Pontus in 64 BCE and died in 24 CE.
12. Plutarch, in *Moralia* on Ogygia, p. 191.
13. Plutarch's *Moralia, Concerning the Face Which Appears in the Orb of the Moon*, vol. XII, section 26.
14. Plutarch, in *Moralia*, p. 191.
15. Ailill < Alpillis, "the elf, elfin, dwarf (nature) spirit."
16. *The second battle of Mag Tured*, v. 76, p 66, author's translation from Christian J. Guyonvarc'h's French translation.
17. Oengus Céile Dé, *Saltair na Rann*; Whitley Stokes, *Saltair na Rann, A Collection of Early Middle Irish Poems*. Oxford, 1883; quoted from the Introduction, viii.
18. *Saltair na Rann, The Creation of the Universe*, a 10th century manuscript translated by Eleanor Hull, 1912.
19. Sanas Cormaic, "Cormac's Glossary," Whitley Stokes edition, translated by John O'Donovan, Irish Archaeological and Celtic Society, Calcutta, 1868.
20. Jim Tester in *History of Western Astrology*, p. 10.
21. Julius Caesar in *De Bello Gallico, "The Gallic Wars," Campaign Against the Suevi*, Book VI, chap. 14.
22. That was mainly the Sidh of Ailill and Medb < Sidos Alpilleios Ac Meduas in Old Celtic.
23. The science of the stars in ancient Celtic, according to modern etymologists, was: *ðireula > *sireula (P-Celtic) or * retlaeulaxta > reuleolacht, "science of the stars"), adj. *retlaeulac-os/-a/-on (> reuleolach, "astrology or astronomy"). The etymologies for "astrologer" could have been: *sireulacoi (P-Celtic) and *retlodruuides for the Irish Gaelic real-druidh. Another class of sky diviners was the néladoir < * nabeltarios, the "cloud-diviner" or "augur."
24. Fege Find > feige Fion, from uecos, "(religious) obligation, moral debt"; uecos/ begos, "bent, curved"; ueicos, "community house"; uega, "fabric, linnen, canvas." Fege Find is usually translated as, "circle of Finn," but in the astrological context, I would opt for, "common house," or "hotel." Fionn < Finn < Find < Uindos, "White, splendid"; in the *Battle of Cath Fionntragh*, for "strand or track of Fionn."
25. Daire Donn < Darius, "the tumultuous"; Donn, from Donnos, "lord, chief, brown, tan."
26. *Upanishads*, Third Adhyaya, verse 26.
27. Magh Elta < Magos Eltonon, "the poplar grove field"; from elto, "poplar," in wordplay with elata, "ability," if not, eltina, "hatchet."
28. Monard, J., "Notice sur les Coelbrenni," unpublished monograph, 1994 or 1995?

Chapter IV

1. Fomoiri < Uomorioi "submarine"; grotesque and violent gods, who came from beyond the waves in the area of Try island.
2. Balor < Baloros / Belaros, "luminescent"; the Fomori lord of doom and grand-father of the Irish god Lugh.
3. Brig Leith or Bri Liath < Letio Briga, "the court of height, value or power"; Leita Briga, "grey, damp or wet height, etc.," in Old Irish. Mide mag / mide magh < medio magos, "middle plain," Leita Briga Mediomagos, the "grey fortress of the central plain)."
4. Aobh or Aebh < Aibo, *Aiba, «good-looking, pretty face "); Aoife < Aiua, "of age;" Arbha < Arba, "heiress."
5. Astakavarga, from ashta "eight" and kavarga "acme," the eight paroxysms or acmes of Vedic astrology; yielding *oxtuacmoi, if we were to coin an Old Celtic parallel.
6. Tech Duinn < *tegos "house" and Donni, genitive of Donnos "dun, brown"; Donn was the Irish god of the dead who resided in the Gaelic Elysian Fields to the south-west of Ireland.
7. Fer Cherdne < Uirocerdinios, "copper-smith, man of art, artist, craftsman,"
8. Blathnat < Blatanata, "flower girl"; Blathnath, whose name recalls the lunar year, Bliadhna < bledṇis.
9. Cu Roi < Cu Redias, "dog of the plain."
10. Setanta < Sentonos, "whoever goes, roaming"; feel, "driveway, path, way"; sentio/sintio, "path way"; Setantoi, "the distant ones," a small tribe of the Brigantes Nation on Merseyside of Lancashire.
11. Sulis Minerva/Sulevia < Suleuia < * Suliuia, or in Latin form, Sulevia and inscribed on a monument as Sulis Minerva.
12. Diodorus Siculus, *Library of History*, Book V, Verse 30, p. 177.

13. Sigla 5, *Book of Ballymote*.
14. Heôsphoros, that is to say Eosphoros < Phosphoros or Phaesphoros, "the bearer of Dawn," and Hesperos, "the vesperal."

Chapter V

1. Taliesin in Canu y Byd Mawr, "Song of the Great World." Myv. Arch. v. i. p. 25.
2. *The Barddas of Iolo Morganwg*, Vol. I., ed. by J. Williams Ab Ithel, 1862.
3. Adriana is a subtle play on words with the Latinized Greek Ariadna < Ariana and Brythonic Arianrod > Argantoreta, "the silver wheel." The silver wheel as a symbol for the lunar orb called Arianrod in Welsh, "the silver wheel." Allegedly an old goddess called Medua Argantoretas that is, Medb (in wordplay with medu / medus "mead").
4. *The Mabinogion* by Lady Charlotte Guest, p. 421.
5. Math < Matus, "bear"; Lord of Gwynedd was regarded as the god of increasing wealth.
6. Dylan Eil Ton < Tuliionos Tondas, "the rising tide of the wave."
7. Llew Llaw Gyffes < Lugus Lama Uadas, "Lugus of the long hand."
8. Gwydion < Uidions, "knowing"; the druid god, he has complete knowledge of the World's History.
9. Gwynfyd < Uindobitu, literally "the splendid word," seen as a world of white light, a paradise realm; Gaelic, Tír na nÓg, "land of youth," or Mag Mell, "land of delight."
10. Annwn < Andumnon, "non-world," a kind of cold hell similar to the Tartarus.
11. Uentu(rum?) < Uinturion, "height," punning with Uentos > Auentos, "wind." Uinturion, was the Gallic name of Mount Ventoux or Sainte-Victoire which was seen as the place of origin of the south winds. In most Indo-European traditions, different Winds numbered from four to eight and sometimes twelve. Therefore, the Uinturion was one of the mountains from which the winds blew.
12. Joseph Monard, in a letter dated January 28, 2004.
13. Indeed, wandering stars were planets, the Old Celtic plural names to designate fixed stars were: dirai < sdirai / stirai < sirai, "stars," or retlai, "stars."

Chapter VI

1. *Ranna an Aeir*, Edinburgh, National Library of Scotland, The National Library of Ireland, microfilm copy n. 307, p. 452.
2. *Ptolemy's Almagest*, Translated and annotated by G.J. Toomer with a foreword by Owen Gingerich, Princeton University Press, 1998.
3. The etymology for Starn is Sdironos, from the Old Celtic root *Ðironos, "the stellar" as for Nemanach, it derives from *Nemonacos, "the heavenly."
4. See also the chapter on astronomy.
5. Quoted from Book I, chapter VI, and pp. 342–343 in *Aristotle, Meteorology* (Meteorological), Book I, Chapter VI, Comets, Opinions and explanations of Anaxagoras, Democritus, Hippocrates of Ceos and Aeschylus. Refutations of these misconceptions, verses 3 and 6. The Works of Aristotle, translated into English under the editorship of D. Ross, M.A., Hon. LL.D. (Edin.), provost of Oriel College, honorary fellow of Merton College, fellow of the British Academy, Volume III, Meteorologica by E. W. Webster, Oxford at the Clarendon Press 1931.
6. Seneca Book XVII, p. 290 and *Seneca, Book VII, Natural Questions, Which Treats of Comets*, verse 17. *Physical Science in the Time of Nero*, Quaestiones Naturales of Seneca, translated by John Clarke, The MacMillan and Co. Of Canada, Ltd., Toronto, 1910.
7. Bealach na bó finne < Belca uindas bouccas, "crossing the white cow."
8. Slighe bhainneach < Banniaca slegeta, "the Milky Way."
9. Slighe chlann Uisnich < Slegeta qlandion Uxonaci, "the way of the son of Uisnech."
10. Hynt Gwydion < Senton Uidionos, "Gwydion's pathway," or Caer Gwydion < Qataira Uidionos, "Gwydion's enclosure."
11. Llwybr Llaethog < *(m)lactocos leispros, "Milky track," cf. Latin, circulus lacteus/ lacteus via, the "Milky Way"; Hent an neñvou < Senton nemeson, "pathway to heaven," or Hent ar Stered < Senton sdiratiom, "path of the stars."
12. Gilvaethwy < * Golouatis, "light emitting one, emanating from the light."
13. Uisneach < Usonacia, "that of the most lofty."
14. Usnach/Usnagh/Uisliu < Uxonacos, the "very high one."
15. Ebhla < Eblana, "free space."
16. Cathbad < Catubatuos, "fighting killer."
17. Bile Medba < bilion Meduas, "the (sacred) tree of Medb," if not, Bile Bith < Bitubilion, "the World tree."
18. Cei < Ceaiios, "the epiphany, the appearance, the presence."
19. Manilus, *Astronomica, Book V*, 118–130; Loeb pp. 307–309. Marcus Manilius was a Roman astrologer of the 1st century CE and author of the *Astronomica* or *Astronomicon libri V*.
20. Artehe, Artahe, is the Latinized translation of Ataxei, dative of Artaxa, a Pyrenaean variant of Artaio (feminine goddess) and not of Artaios (masculine god). VSLM = votum soluens libens merito, for "accomplishing willingly a vow as merited (J. Monard 1994)."
21. Llys Don < Lettos Danonas, "the court of Don."
22. Da Chich Anand < Cicoi Anende Duo, or in English, "the Paps of Anu," or "two breasts of Ana."
23. Beli/Bile > Belios, "clear," punning with Bilios, "tree."
24. Telyn < Talanon, "the little harp"; Telyn Arthur < Talanon Aretorii, "Arthur's little harp."
25. Uaithne < Uatina, "harmony."
26. The etymologies of these names are equally revealing: Gol-trade < Golos "tears"; Suan-trade < Suomno, "sleep"; Gen-trade < Genos < Gesnos, "smile." The radical trade > tradh in these names means shaft, spear-shaft in Old Irish, from the Celtic root tragla (cf. Latin tragula), "javelin."
27. Oisin < Uxouinos, "fawn."
28. Steredenn ar C'hi < Sðira Conos, the "dog star."
29. Reul na Madra < Retla Maddi, "the dog star."
30. This name suggests both "yew" and "clear," with Iuchar (< Iuocaros, "clear friend, friend of yew"), of a similar formation.

Chapter VII

1. Ogyrven < Gogyrven < *adgrauano, "with material, with writing, with letters," grauo, "a letter in an inscription", grauon "writing";
2. Awen < auentia, "rightfulness, truthfulness, justice"; 2. Auentia, "moral elevation," connoting "(divine) inspiration, mental inspiration;" the name of the muse of the bards and poets.
3. George Calder, *Auraicept na n-Éces: The Scholar's Primer*. Edinburgh: John Grant, 1917.
4. Claude Sterckx, *Manuel élémentaire pour servir à l'étude de la civilisation celtique*, Université Libre de Bruxelles, p. 59–60.
5. Joseph Monard, *Notice sur les Oghams* (monograph), 1994.
6. Joseph Monard, *Notice sur les Ogham*, unpublished monograph, 1994.

Chapter VIII

1. George Henderson, *Fled Bricrend: The Feast of Bricriu*, Chapter VIII, verses 54–55, p. 69–71. Published for the Irish Text Society by D. Nutt, London, 1899.
2. Yayati, the king of the gods of the lunar dynasty and son of Nahusha to whom he succeeded. His two wives came from two lunar lines: that of Ushanas or Shukra through his son Yadu and that of Sharmishtha, daughter of Vrisha-Parvan, by his son Puru. Yayati is also considered as the author of the *Rig Veda* (RV. ix, 101, 4–6). He is comparable to the Irish god-king Eochaid (Eochaid Ollathair > Iuocatuos Olloater, "good/strong warrior all-father").
3. Madhavi, daughter of Yayati belonging to the race of Madhu or Yadu and identified with the goddess Durga or to one of Matri watching over Skanda (MBh). She is identifiable to the Irish queen Medb or Meadb.
4. Compare the Sanskrit Madhavi and the old Celtic Medðua both meaning "drunkenness, intoxication through mead."
5. Dumézil, *Myth and Epic II*. p. 341.
6. George Henderson, *Fled Bricrend*, Chapter I, verses 1, 4, p. 2–3.
7. *The Story of Mac Datho's Pig*, quotes from paragraphs 1 and 7; Rudolf Thurneysen, Dublin, Ireland, 1935, reprinted in 2004.
8. Saptârishayah or Saptarsayah, that is, the "seven wise men," of the north or the seven stars of the Little Dipper which were described in Vedic literature as the incarnation of sacred science. In the older mythology, they constitute a group apart from the other spiritual entities along with the Devas and Asuras, gods and demons, Devayoni, demigods, Atipurusa, while the heroes and Martas, mere mortals. Therefore, they all had the empowerment of religious authority. In the Vedic tradition, when it is written, "Rishi said," then it implies that it is sacred and that "it has the force of law." The seven Rishis or sages were seen as the early deified saints of Vedic religion. They were named as follows: Gotama, Bharadvaja, Vishva—Mitra, Jamadagni Vasishtha, Kasyapa and Atri. And, according to other sources, they were called: Marici Atri, Angiras, Pulaha, Kratu, Pulastya and Vasishtha. These were the primordial sages of the first Manvantara. The names Manvantaras (the secondary or avatars of Manu) subsequently were: Pracetas or Daksha, Bhrigu and Narada. They were created by Manu Svayambhuva in order to generate the souls of the gods and humans.

Each of the seven sages had an abode placed in the stars of the Little Dipper and represented one of the Chakras of the spiritual body. The Chakras, as glands, had a physical reality and thus secreted the seven vital essences of the human body. The name Rishi is from the Proto-Indo-Aryan root *dRsh which meant "see, under, perceive (psychologically)," for "seer," or "soothsayer." This term is similar to the Old Persian erešiš "mystical" and perhaps the old Irish Arsan, for "wise." The Vedic tradition has three categories, often four and seven: the Devarshis the Brahmarshis and Rajarshis. These four categories were: the Maharshis the Paramarshis, and the Srutarshis Kandarshis. And this included the seven previously listed.

The Rishis were also associated with the moon, the cosmic zodiacal circle and the seven rays of light beaming from the seven northern stars of Ursa Minor.
9. Mantera < Mandera, "household, the family, dwellers under one roof"; The household, or manutera, traditionally included the wife, family, foster children and domestics.
10. Mynogeni > Manogenoi, "breed of man," the descendants of the ancestor Belomaros, Manos for the old Celts.
11. Elizabeth A. Gray, *Do Cath Muighe Tuireadh ann so, Second Battle of the Great Plain of the Mounds*, p. 55.
12. The etymologies for these names are as follows: Moronoe < *Maronia "One of great (aptitude)"; along with a thresome: Gliten < *Glitina "clayish," Gliton / Glitona < Glitona "of the pasture," Tyronoe < *Turonia "swelling," Thiton and Thiten < *Tittana / Tettana "the tit, nipple," punning with *Tittona "revengeful."
13. Seven Cailleach: Cailleach (< Cailiaca, "prophetess"), Cailleach Bolus (< Bolussas, "of apples"), Cailleach Corca Duibhne (< Crocnos Dubnis, "red abyss") Caileach Bui (< Bodia, "walleye"), Cailleach Beara (> Beriia, "flat plateau") and Cailleach Beinne Bhric (< Bennia Brica, "mountain top").
14. Tea (< Tega, "support, coverage"), Fás (< Uassa, "servant"), Fíal (< Uilia "willingness, honesty"), Líben (< Libana "mountain stone") Odba (< Odbia "hip" / Odbatia, "fascination"), and Scota (< Scotta, "flower").
15. In reference to the secrets of the stone door, that is, the eastern gate through which the sun passes the horizon. The stone door is actually the sun's gate. Which was probably called Duron saulii or Sauelii duoron Greinas in Old Celtic. Or in poetic phrasing: Duoron Salicos, "the willow door." Much more than a silly pun, the willow, alder and elm, were at the top of the list of trees in Taliesin's *Cad Godeu*, the "Battle of trees." Therefore, *Duoron Greinas* was another subtle wordplay with Grannos, "the sun god" (whose name literally means, "shining and bearded") and Greinos, "sunny and bright." Greina was also the name of the Goidelic sun, seen as the sun goddess. Quartz was seen as the solar stone and was called Greinoclocca. The prophet was called Doarelabaros (doare-, "start" + labaros, "talking"). Thus the pun: duoron, "door," and duorolabaron, "door sign." The Labaron, the sun symbol, was also called Subuton, the Old Celtic name for the Sanskrit Swastika. As in India, this symbol was incorporated on objects, masonry and doors in order to attract good luck.

16. Tethra < Tetras, "sea," in wordplay with teptarios, "fugitive deserter," tetorios, the male crow. The crow found on battlefields was the allegory of war. Tethra Formori was a king killed during the First Battle of Mag Tured and whose sword was reused by Ogma. He was regarded as a god of the sea and his wife, much like the Morrigan, was a "spirit of death."
17. Retrograde motion is the apparent backward movement of a planet as observed from Earth. Our Earth seems to pass forward because of its faster orbit when it is in opposition with certain stars. The sun and moon are never in retrograde motion. The word "rapid," refers to these heavenly bodies: Moon, Sun, Mercury, Mars and Venus.
18. Aedh < Aedus "ardent," one of the names of the morning sun as a divinity.
19. Ruad Rofessa > Roudios Rouesos, "the red of great knowledge."
20. Bodb Dearg > Dergos Boduos, "red crow," if not Dercos, "eye."
21. Rodrubán > Ro-dru-bona, "very strong foundation."
22. Nuada > Nodons, "the angler, fisherman."
23. Dechtire > Dexsitera, "right-wing," a goddess seen as the right hand of the gods.
24. Cuchulainn < Cuculantios, a hero and demigod son of Lugh whose name means, "dog of Culann (< Coslanos)."
25. Camal < *Camulos, "dynamic."
26. The doormen of Tara: Camal < *Camulos, "dynamic," and twin Gamal < *Gemelos, "the good, straightness, iron (fetter), chain."

Chapter IX

1. Nakshatras, this Sanskrit term generally refers to a bright heavenly body, sometimes the sun, a star, a star cluster or an asterism, a constellation through which the moon passes or when a planet is present in a lunar mansion. Lunar mansions, numbering 27 (or periodically 28), include: 1. Shravishtha or Dhanishtha; 2. Shata—Bhishaj; 3. Purva-Bhadrapada; 4. Uttara-bhñbhadrapada; 5. Revati; 6. Ashvini; 7. Bharani; 8. Krittika; 9. Rohini or Brahmi; 10. Mriga-shiras or Agrahayani; 11. Ardra; 12. Punarvasu or Yamakau; 13. Pushya or Sidhya; 14. Ashlesha; 15. Magha; 16. Purva-phaguni; 17. Uttara-phñphaguni; 18. Hasta; 19. Citra; 20. Svati; 21. Visakha or Radha; 22. Anuradha; 23. Jyeshtha; 24. Mulla; 25. Purvashadha; 26. Uttarashñadha; 27. Abhijit; 28. Shravana. In other versions, Revati, Uttara- Phalguni, Uttara-Bhadrapada and Uttara-Shadha dhruvani are seen as "fixed" and none movable. In the Vedas, the Nakshatras were considered to be the abodes of the gods and of the pious dead when not the companions of the daughters of Daksha.
2. Alexandra David-Neel, *L'Inde où j'ai vécu* [The India Where I Lived], p. 200.
3. Tithi is a full moon day, that is, a day and a night and a 30th of a complete lunar cycle of twenty-seven and so solar days. A tithi is measured in two fortnights, each forming a light and a dark half. The beneficial tithis are: Nanda, Bhadra, Vijaya and Purna.
4. George Calder, *Auraicept na n-Éces*, p. 287.
5. George Calder, *Auraicept na n-Éces*, p. 277.
6. George Calder, *Auraicept na n-Éces*, p. 293.

7. "The Raid of Cooley Cows," *Book of Leinster—Táin Bó Cualnge*, p.143.
8. "The Raid of Cooley Cows," *Book of Leinster—Táin Bó Cualnge*, p.175.
9. That is, Nemain < Namantia, "the hostile," which meant Noiolatis, "the ninth day" of the novena in the calendar. The name is from nametos, naumetos, noumetos, for "ninth," and connoting nametos, nemetos, "holy."
10. Emain Macha < Emania Magosias, "the twin (city) of the plain."
11. Craobh Derg < Derga Crobas, "the red leg," dergos punning with dercos, "eye."
12. Teite Brecc < Brecca Tectas, "the colorfully stained property," or Brecta Tegia "the spotted house."
13. Airtheach/Airgthech < Aericotegia, "house of care."
14. Da Derga < Dergos Deuos, "the red god," and Bron-Bherg < Brugno Bargii, "worry of the unable or disabled."

Chapter X

1. Diodorus Siculus, *Library of History*, Book V, verse 28, p.173.
2. Diodorus Siculus, *Library of History*, verse 31, p. 179.

Chapter XI

1. Uffern < Inferno, "hell," in Latin; Celtic designation: Annwn < Andumnon "the non-world, the underworld."
2. Seneca, *The Natural Questions, Causes of Comets*, Book VII, 3–4, p. 274–276, translated by John Clark, MacMillan and Co., Limited, London, 1910.
3. Taliesin, Llyfr *Taliesin XXXVII*, "Book of Taliesin XXXVII," Yspeil Taliessin, "The Spoils of Taliesin, a song to Urien"; translated by W. F. Skene in 1858.
4. Llwyvenydd < Lemania, "the elm-grove."
5. Red < Redia, "course"; usually translated as "necessity", should be written Anken < Ancena. This is one of the important traditional concepts of Druidism also found in *The Barddas* of Morganwg, in wordplay with Ancu, "fatality," found implicitly in Ogham as: 'NC/U' > NG/V' for NCU < 'Ncu < Ancu.
6. Ankon, Ankou, "death"; Ancauos / Ancouos, "death inevitable downfall"; Ancouo > Ancu, "death personified," also Dis < Dits, "death, dissolution, the inevitable decline"; thus the folkloric Breton character, Tad ann Anken < Tatis Ancena, "the father of grief, sorrow and pain, a late version of the Gallic Dits Ater or Belios; who according to Caesar was the Father of death in Gaul.
7. "Two bulls yoked to a shell," this because the ancient Gauls imagined the world as consisting of two bowls, one inverted and the other to the place. This sphere was powered by two oxen and turned on a shaft or an axis (axis mundi). The Ox was taken as a symbol of the days of the world divided into dark and light periods. A similar pattern is found in the Vedic texts.
8. "Three parts in the world"; these being, the upper world, the middle world, and the underworld.
9. "Three beginnings and three purposes"; that is, a beginning for each world and a birth for every

man, and a beginning for each of the three components of being: body, mind, soul / spirit.

10. Marzin < Moridunios > Merlin, "the seaman, the sailor."

11. "Four grinding stones"; which are the four summits, which were: Artuana Alba, "the hard top as stone," the winter solstice; Elaris Alba "the lively summit," the spring equinox; Eruina Alba, "the agrarian summit," the summer solstice; and Eluetias Alba, "the autumn summit, fall, the autumnal equinox." "The whetstones of Marzin that sharpen dull swords!" This grouping of four suggests the four material realms: mineral, vegetable, animal, and human, but then in the context of the stones, these strongly suggest the four directions and the four seasonal solar stations. Finally, an allusion to the four elements is also very likely. In light of these insights, the sword represents the will, courage, purpose, and direction. In druidical symbolism, the sword is one of the four sacred objects from the cities of the North and is the allegorical symbol for the north wind. This is the infallible sword that gives death ('Ncu, Dis) and that belongs to the god-king Nudonos / Nodons and that comes from the mythical city of Finias (Uindia, "the white"). This was a small bronze ceremonial sword.

12. "Five girdles of the earth"; that are the five climatic zones.

13. "Five ages in the period of time"; that are the four ages in addition to the middle age.

14. "Five stones on our sister"; being the markers of the cardinal points seen as macro-cosmic land Chakras (the material world) on the deified earth seen as the mother goddess. In Celtic philosophy, Chakras were seen as pebbles (caliuoi).

15. "Six herbs in a small pot"; which were the six traditional herbs of Saint John's day.

16. "Potion blended by the dwarf"; that is, mead (< Medu / Medus), the Ambrosia or Soma of the Celts.

17. "Seven suns and seven moons, seven planets counting the Hen"; this being, the multiplication of seven in order to express time and space: the seven directions, East, South, West, North, and the above, middle ground, bottom, etc... Yar < Iara, "hen"; Yarig Wenn he c'chec'h Evned < Uinda iara (Canti) Esias suexs aunate, "the white chick and the six birds (or chicks)"; a euphemism for the asterism of the Pleiades in Taurus.

18. "Seven elements along with the flour of the air"; that are, the four main elements: earth, fire, water, air, and ether, the flour of the air also connotes the three states of being: thinking, individuality, and free will.

19. Great Fire, in Breton: Tan-Tad < Tepneton, "fire"; Belotepnion, "bright fire, bonfire," that were the May fires, Christianized as the fires of St. John.

20. "The deep island"; that is, Dubnon or Dumnon, "the low world, the earthly plane, the material world."

21. "The eight white heifers of the Lady"; in reference to the eight convents of the Druid priestesses of the Isle of Sein or Sena off the coast of Brittany.

22. Lezarmeur < Lethoaremori, "the seaside court or palace enclosure by the sea."

23. "Nine Korrigans who dance," that is, korrigan, from corrigenoi, "the dwarf people."

24. Nantes < Nantiacon, "the valley field"; the capital city of Nantes (Namnetes, "people of the Valley") in Brittany.

25. Vannes < Uindana, "the white, the dazzling, the splendid," the capital of the Veneti (Uenetoi / Uenetes, "the federated, the beautiful and beloved").

26. "And hazel crosiers"; a euphemism for the pilgrim's staff or crook of bishops. Coll < cosla, "hazel," in the Ogham. It is traditionally associated with divination and in this context, is an omen to the treachery and repression to come.

27. The Constellation of Sagittarius, Dumanni Prinnios, which in Celtic literally stands for: Dumannios, "darkening," and Prinnios, "tree branching, and having the technical meaning of "constellation."

28. The twelve signs of the zodiac, in reference to Taliesin's Cad Godeu < Catu Uiduion, "the battle of trees," a euphemism for the phonetic classification of letters.

29. Geoffrey of Monmouth, *History of the Kings of Britain*, translated from Latin by Norma Lorre Goodrich, 1987; French translation by Laurence Mathey-Maille, p. 173.

Chapter XII

1. Divitiac < Diviciacus < Diuiciacos, "the theologian," a Gallic druid met by Caesar, he bore the title of Vergobret for the capital city of the Aedui. He was a moderator of the Roman party against the Swabian Germans of Ariovistus, and he travelled to Rome in 60 BCE to gain the support of the Senate after the defeat of the Aeduan battle of Magetobriga.

2. Cicero, *De Divinatione*, "On Divination," Book I. v. 41, p. 323.

3. Plutarch, *Moralia*, from the face that appears on the Moon, Ogygia is an island far out at sea, p. 991.

4. Geoffrey of Monmouth, *History of the Kings of Britain*, p. 173.

5. Plutarch's *Morals, of Fate*, 3, p. 294–295.

Chapter XIII

1. *Cath Maige Tuired*, "The Second Battle of Mag Tuired," translated by Elizabeth A. Gray, verse 11, p. 1.

2. Christian Guyonvarc'h and Françoise Le Roux, *La civilization celtique*, p. 139.

3. Alain Le Goff, *La Médecine des Celtes*, Ialon, p. 15.

4. *Cath Maige Tuired*, "The Second Battle of Mag Tuired," translated by Elizabeth A. Gray, verse 34.

5. Diancecht < Danuuiacaceto, "the powerful grip."

6. Miach > Miacos, "bushel."

7. Oirmiach > Aremiacos, "great bushel."

8. Airmed < Aremedto, "assessment, good measure."

9. *Dialogue of the Two Sages*, translated and commented by Christian-J. Guyonvarc'h, p. 72.

10. Marcellus of Bordeaux, *De medicamentis liber*; a famous Gallic empirical doctor who was nicknamed, "of Bordeaux," since he was born there in the middle of the fourth century.

11. The ng consonant is most often used in initial position and marks the elision of an unstressed vowel. According to the Meriam-Webster dictionary: "*a*: the use of a speech form that lacks a final or initial sound which a variant speech form has (as *'s* instead of *is* in *there's*); *b*: the omission of an unstressed vowel or syllable in a verse to achieve a uniform metrical pattern."

Bibliography

Manuscript Sources

Annals of Ireland (the Four Masters): CELT: Corpus of Electronic Texts: University College, Cork, Ireland; Dublin, Royal Irish Academy, MS 1220.

Book of Ballymote: M.S. compiled about the year 1391; Library of the Royal Irish Academy, Dublin.

Cath Maige Tuired: The Second Battle of Mag Tuired, translated by Elizabeth A. Gray; CELT: Corpus of Electronic Texts: a project of University College, Cork College Road, Cork, Ireland—http://www.ucc.ie/celt (2003).

Cauldron of Poesy: Henry, P.L. "The Cauldron of Poesy." *Studica Celtica* #14/15, 1979/1980; Legal codex H.3.18, dated to c. 1500 CE.

The Feast of Bricriu, An Eearly Gaelic Saga Transcribed from Older MSS. Into the Book of The Dun Cow, by Moelmuiri Mac Mic Cuinn Na M-Bocht of the Community of the Culdees at Clonmacnois, with conclusion from Gaelic MS. XL. Edinburgh Advocates' Library, Edited with translation, introduction, and notes by George Henderson, Published for the Irish texts Society by David Nutt, 270 and 271 Strand, London, 1899.

Guyonvarc'h, Christian-J., and Françoise Le Roux. "Lebor Gabàla Érenn," *Textes Mythologiques Irlandais*, vol. 1. Rennes: Ogam—Celticum, 1980.

Irish Texts Society. *Astronomical and Medical*, a Latin version of an Arabic treatise by Messahalah or Mascha Allah a Jewish astronomer of Alexandria, who flourished shortly before 800 AD. MS B II 1.

Llyfr Taliesin, The Book of Taliesin, Peniarth MS 2. National Library of Wales. The manuscript of the book was copied by a single scribe, probably in Glamorgan, dating to the beginning of the 14th century.

Scél Mucci Mic Dathó, from the *Book of Leinster*, translated after Rudolf Thurneysen's edition by Angela Grant, 2009. Celtic Studies, Kestrel's Nest; URL: http://kestrels-nest.org.uk/celtic/translations/smmd.html.

Scela Mucce Meic Datho, edited by Rudolf Thurneysen, Dublin Institute for Advanced Studies, Dublin, 1935–39.

General Bibliography

Aristotle, *The History of Animals*, translated by D'Arcy Wentworth Thompson, John Bell Publisher, London, 1907. Online edition, University of Chicago. http://penelope.uchicago.edu/aristotle/histanimals6.html.

Astronomy of the Ancients. Edited by Kenneth Brecher and Michael Feirtag, The Massachusetts Institute of Technology Press, Cambridge, Mass., 1981.

Bain, Robert. *The Clans and Tartans of Scotland*. Fontana/Collins, Glasgow and London, 1988.

Barbault, André. *Connaissance de L'Astrologie*. Editions du Seuil, Paris, 1975.

Berresford Ellis, Peter. *Dictionary of Celtic Myhtology*, Constable, London UK, 1992.

———. *A Dictionary of Irish Mythology*, Oxford University Press, Oxford, UK, 1991.

———. "The Fabrication of 'Celtic' Astrology," previously published in *The Astrological Journal* vol. 39, no. 4 (1997), C.U.R.A., Centre Universitaire de Recherche en Astrologie, edited by Pierre Guinard, Paris, 2001. http://cura.free.fr/xv/13ellis2.html.

Bianucci, Piero. *Étoile par Étoile, guide touristique de l'univers*. Bordas, Paris, 1988.

Bliss, Edgar. *Astrologie Gauloise*. (Set of cards), Éditions Gendre, Paris.

Bloch, Raymond. *La divination dans l'Antiquité*. Presses Universitaires de France, Paris, 1984.

Brooke Ballard, Juliet. *The Hidden Laws of Earth*. A. R. E. Press, Virginia Beach, U.S.A., 1979.

Caesar's War Commentaries. Translated by John Warrington, J. M. Dent & Sons Ltd, London, 1953.

Calder, George. *Auraicept na n-Éces*, J. Grant Publisher, Edinburgh, 1917.

Carnac, Carol. *L'Astrologie Celtique*. Ed. Primeur/Sand, 1986.

Chadwick, Nora K. *Celtic Britain.* Newcastle Publishing Co., Inc. California, 1989.

Cicero. *De Divinatione.* English translation by W. A. Falconer, Loeb Classical Library, Harvard University Press, Cambridge, Mass., vol. XX, 1923.

Cormac's Glossary, translated by John O'Donoyan and edited by Whitely Stokes, Irish Archaeological and Celtic Society, Calcutta, 1868.

Couderc, Paul. *Histoire de l'astrologie classique,* Presses universitaires de France, Paris 1945.

Curcio, Michele. *Dictionnaire de L'Astrologie.* Casterman, Belgique, 1976.

Darmesteter, James. *The Avesta, Vendidad,* Translated by from *Sacred Books of the East,* The Christian Literature Company, New York, 1898.

De Callatay, Vincent. *Atlas du ciel.* Albert de Visscher/Marcel Broquet, Bruxelles, 1986.

De Vries, Jan. *La Religion des Celtes.* (Keltische Religion), French translation by L. Jospin, Payot, Paris, 1975.

Dictionnaire des mythologies et religions des sociétés traditionnelles et du monde antique. Directed by Yves Bonnefoy, published by the Centre National des Lettres, Flammarion.

Dottin, Georges. *La Langue Gauloise—Grammaire, textes et glossaire.* Collection pour l'étude des antiquités nationales, Paris, 1918.

Duhaime, Pierre. *System in the World History of Cosmic Doctrines of Plato of Copernicus,* editor A. Herman, vol. 2, Paris, 1913.

Dumézil, Georges. *Mythes et dieux des Indoeuropéens.* Flammarion, 1992.

Eliade, Mircea. *Myth And Reality.* Harper Torchbooks, New York, 1963.

Ellis Davidson, H. R. *Scandinavian Mythology.* Paul Hamlyn (The Hamlyn Publishing Group Ltd.), London, 1969.

Enmerkar and the Lord of Aratta, The Electronic Text Corpus of Sumerian Literature, University of Oxford, UK, 2002. http://etcsl.orinst.ox.ac.uk/section1/tr1823.htm.

Evans, David Ellis. *Gaulish Personal Names, A Study of Some Continental Celtic Formations.* Oxford Clarendon, 1967.

Evert Hopman, Ellen. *A Druid's Herbal for The Sacred Year.* Destiny Books Rochester, Vermont, 1995.

Faucouneau, Jean. "Qui inventa les constellations?" *Actualité de l'histoire mystérieuse,* No 9, nov. 1994.

Frawley, David. *The Astrology of The Seers.* A comprehensive Guide to Vedic Astrology, Motilal Banarsidass Publishers, Delhi, India, 1996.

_____. *The Myth of the Aryan Invasion of India.* Voice of India, New Delhi, 1995.

_____. *Vedic Origins of the Zodiac, The Hymns of Dirghatamas in the Rig Veda,* Archaeology Online, 2005. http://archaeologyonline.net/artifacts/origins-zodiac.

Fuzeau-Braesch, Suzel. *L'Astrologie.* Presses Universitaires de France, Paris, 1989.

Geoffry of Monmouth. *Histories of the Kings of Britain,* translation by Sebastian Evans, Temple Classics edition, J.M. Dent and Co., London, 1904.

Giraud, Daniel. *Métaphysique de l'astrologie.* Henri Veyrier, Paris, 1988.

Gobineau, J. Arthur de. *Histoire des Perses.* Henri Plon Impimeur-Éditeur, Paris, 1869.

Goodrich, Norma Lorre. *Medieval Myths.* Meridian, Penguin Books USA Inc., NY, 1994.

_____. *Merlin.* Perennial Library, Harper & Row, Publishers, NY, 1988.

"Greater Bundahishn: Introduction." Translation by Behramgore Tehmuras Anklesaria, digital edition by Joseph H. Peterson, 2002. http://www.avesta.org/mp/grb27.htm

Grenier, Albert. *Les Gaulois.* Payot, Paris, 1994.

Guyonvarc'h, Christian J., and Françoise Le Roux. *La Civilisation Celtique.* Payot, Paris, 1995.

Hamburg, Michael. *Astronomy Made Simple.* Doubleday, New York, 1993.

Harper, Douglas. *The Online Etymology Dictionary,* 2001–2014. http://www.etymonline.com/index.php.

Haudry, Jean, *General characteristics of Indo-European Religion,* vol. 1: *The Heavens and the Earth, The Indo-Europeans,* Lyon, Institut d'Etudes Indo-Européennes, 1994; Centro Studi La Runa, Archivio di storia, letteratura, tradizione, filosofia. http://www.centrostudilaruna.it/haudryreligion.html.

_____. *General characteristics of Indo-European religion,* The New Antaios Journal, Online edition by Einar on August 22, 2011. http://www.new-antaios.net/2011/08/general-characteristics-of-indo-european-religion-dr-jean-haudry/

_____. *La Religion cosmique des Indo-Européens,* Milano / Paris: Archè; Les Belles Lettres; collection Études Indo-Européennes (dirigée par Jean Varenne), 1987.

Hull, Eleanor. *The Poem-Book of the Gael,* Printed by Ballantyne, Hanson & Co. Uallantyne Press, Edinburgh, 1912.

Hutin, Serge. *Histoire de l'astrologie. Science ou superstition?* Marabout Université, Belgique, 1970.

Ialon, Clairière. *Revue d'études druidiques de la Kredenn Geltiek Hollvedel,* Nos. 1, 2, 3, 4, 5, 6, 7, 8, 9, 10, 11.

Jordanes, *The Origin and Deeds of the Goths,* translated by Charles C. Mierow, Princeton University Press, 1908.

Le Goff, Alain, *La Médecine des Celtes,* Ialon semestriel, Page 15, Numéro 15 [Belotennia 3872].

Le Roux, Françoise, et Guyonvarc'h, Christian-J. *Les Druides.* Editions Ouest-France Université, Rennes, 1986.

The Library of History of Diodorus Siculus, published in Vol. III, of the Loeb Classical Library edition, 1939.

Lindsay, Jack. *Origins of Astrology*. Frederick Muller, London, 1971.

Lucian of Samosata. *Of Astrology*, Translation by William Tooke, F.R.S., Longman, Hurst, Rees, Orme, and Brown, Publishers, London, 1820.

MacBain, Alexander. *An Etymological Dictionary of the Gaelic Language*. Gairm Publications, Glasgow, Scotland, 1982.

Masson, Emilia. *Le Combat pour l'immortalité*. Héritage Indo-Européen dans la mythologie Anatolienne, Presses universitaires de France, Paris, 1991.

Matthews, John. *Taliesin, Shamanism and The Bardic Mysteries In Britain and Ireland*. The Aquarian Press, 1991.

Mauduit, J.A. *L'Épopée des Celtes*. Editions Robert Laffont, Paris, 1973.

"Momies gauloises." *La Recherche*, No. 314, novembre 1998.

Monard, Joseph. *About the Coligny Calendar*. Privately published, 1996.

_____. *Découpage saisonnier de l'année celtique*. Privately published, 1996.

_____. *Éléments divers d'astronomie pour l'élaboration d'un almanach*. Privately published, 1996.

_____. *Glossaire trilingue celtique-français-anglais*. Privately published, 1994.

_____. Letters to the author from 1994 to 1999.

_____. *Notice sur les Coelbren*. Privately published, 1996.

_____. *Notice sur les Oghams*. Privately published, 1995.

_____. *Origines, structure et contenu du druidisme antique*. Privately published, 1997.

_____. *Vocabulaire des triades de Iolo Morgannwg*. Privately published, 1993.

Nash, D.W. *Taliesin, or, The bards and Druids of Britain: a translation of the remains of the earliest Welsh bards, and an examination of the bardic mysteries*, mss. attributed to Siom Kent, John Russel Smith, London, 1858.

Neve, Peter. *Across the Anatolian Plateau: Readings in the Archaeology of Ancient Turkey*. Edited by David C. Hopkins. American School of Oriental Research, Boston, 2000.

O'Flaherty, Wendy. *Hindu Myths*. Penguin Classics, London, 1975.

Ordos. *Mythes, mystères et légendes de la tradition celtique*. Etudes anciennes. Parentés Indoeuropéennes des nombres. No. 1, mai 1994.

Paterson, Helena. *The Handbook of Celtic Astrology*. Llewellyn Publications, St. Paul, Minnesota, 1995.

Pennick, Nigel. *The Secret Lore of Runes and Other Ancient Alphabets*. Rider, London, 1991.

Plutarch's Morals, translated by William W. Goodavin, with an introduction by Ralph Waldo Emerson. Vol. v., Little, Brown, and Company, Boston, 1878.

The Poem Book of the Gael, translations from Irish Gaelic Poetry into English Prose and Verse, selected and edited by Eleanor Hull, Chatto and Windus, London, 1912.

Raman, Bangalore Venkata. *Ashtakavarga System of Prediction*. IBH Prakashana, Bangalore, India, 1981.

_____. *L'Astrologie des maîtres Hindous*. Éd. Claire Vigne, 1995.

_____. *Astrology for Beginners*. IBH Prakashana, Bangalore, India, 1976.

_____. *Studies in Jaimini Astrology*, Sagar Publications New Delhi, India, 1975.

Renfrew, Colin. *Archeology and Language, The Puzzle of Indo-European Origins*. Jonathan Cape Ltd, London, 1987.

Reznikov, Raimonde. *Les Celtes et le druidisme, Racines de la Tradition occidentale*. Éditions Dangles, St-Jean-De-Braye (France), 1994.

The Rig Vedas, Selected, translated and annotated by Wendy Doniger O'Flaherty. London: Penguin Classics, 1981.

"Les Scythes. Guerriers nomades au contact des brillantes civilisations grecques, perse et chinoise." *Les dossiers d'archéologie*. No. 194, juin 1994.

Sjoestedt, Marie-Louise. *Dieux et Héros des Celtes*. Rennes: Terre de brume Editions, 1993.

Skene, William Forbes. *The Four Ancient Books of Wales, Black book of Carmarthen, Book of Haneirin, Book of Taliesin, Red book of Hergest, containing the Cymric poems attributed to the bards of the sixth century*. Oxford University, 1858.

Stanley, Thomas. *Claudius Aelianus His Various History*. Printed for Thomas Basset at the George, in Fleet-Street, near Cliffords-Inne, London, 1660.

Sullivan, Rosenda. *Readings for the Golden Echo, The Iliad, The Odyssey, Morte D'Arthur*. W. H. Sadlier, Inc., NY, 1963.

Tester, Jim. *A History of Western Astrology*. Ballantine Books, New York, 1987.

Thompson, Richard L. *Vedic Cosmography ans Astronomy*, Bhaktivedanta Book Trust, Alachua, Fl, 1996.

Tucker, William J. *Ptolemaic Astrology*. 1962, French translation by Janine Reigner, L'astrologie de Ptolémée. Payot, Paris, 1981.

Upanishads. *The Sacred Writings of the World's Great Religions*, Selected and edited by S.E. Frost, Jr. McGraw Hill Book Company. New York, 1975.

"Le vrai visage des Celtes." *L'Archéologue*, No. 3, février 1994.

Index

Abaris 46, 240
Aelian 24, 239
Ailill 46–47, 68, 135–36, 138, 144, 149, 156–57, 165, 169, 201, 206, 240
air, element 142, 180, 189, 196–97, 204, 211, 213, 216–17, 218, 244
Airmed 214, 219, 244
Airtheach 164, 243
Alharva Veda 18
Almagest (Ptolemy) 96, 241
Almanac 9, 69, 95
Amairgen/Amorgen 140–41, 143
Andarta 96, 109, 168, 229, 236
Andromeda 28, 30, 95–96, 108, 112, 235
Antiearth 147, 149, 200, 229, 234
Aongus/Aonghus/Oengus 14, 68, 149, 201, 213–14, 240
Apollo 14, 36, 40, 69, 89, 107, 110, 180, 198, 201, 205, 211, 213–14
Apollonian 61, 68, 125, 175
Apollonius of Myndus 100, 189
April 12, 39, 40, 70–71, 231
Aquarius 11, 12, 26–28, 30, 36–38, 41, 49, 54, 57, 78, 82, 98, 104, 115, 125, 128, 130, 145, 152, 161–62, 173–74, 180, 194, 197, 202, 209, 216, 225, 228–29, 235–36
Aquila 20, 35, 96, 98, 114, 125, 235, 237
Aratus 18, 24, 28, 29
Arcturus 58, 96, 102, 110, 113, 137, 139, 143, 145, 230
Argantoreta 114, 168, 230, 235, 241
Arianrhod 87, 114, 198
Aries 88, 104, 128, 141, 144, 146, 152, 162, 174–75, 181, 193, 197–98, 202, 209, 216, 225, 228
Artaios 58, 96, 102–3, 109–10, 113, 137, 145, 148, 202, 230, 241
Artemis 18, 36, 109, 172
Atharva Veda 18, 24

Arthur 58, 97, 109, 111, 113, 115–16, 158, 212, 230, 241
Ashtakavarga 63, 76
Asia Minor 18, 24–25, 27–28
aspect 149, 188–90, 199, 209
astral house 64, 76–77, 134, 139–43, 149–50, 155, 160–64, 188, 199, 231
astral theme 76, 95, 115, 199, 209
astrological ogham 52, 79
Asura 21, 27, 40, 242
August 12, 55, 72, 231
Augustus 100–1
Auraicept na n-Éces (George Calder) 59–60, 120–22, 224, 157, 242
Auriga 28, 30, 108, 113, 235
Awen 119, 149, 242
Ayana 18
Ayurvedic medicine 6, 211

Badb/Badba 138, 156, 158–59, 161, 166
banshee 160
Barddas (John Williams) 13, 58, 87, 96, 241
Barzaz Breizh 63, 154, 195, 197
Battle of Mag Tuired, Second Battle of Mag Tuired 21, 89, 211, 219, 243–44
Belenos 14, 116, 140, 149, 180, 201, 214
Beli Mawr 14, 68, 102, 105, 110, 193, 241
Belisama 148, 168, 202, 230
Belos/Belios 105, 193, 241, 243
Berresford Ellis, Peter 45–47, 49, 135, 240, 245
Betelgueuse 20
Beth-Luis-Nion letter 10
Bhagavata Purana 135
Bilé 68, 105, 110, 193, 241
Black Book of Carmarthen 17
Boann 107, 111, 202, 230
Boar Star 20, 41
Book of Ballymote 42, 49–50, 54, 59–61, 80–81, 89, 90–92, 122, 170, 176, 189–190, 198, 200, 205, 207, 219, 234, 241

Book of Leinster (Cecile O'Rahilly) 137, 169, 343
Bootes 96, 108, 113, 137, 143, 230, 135
Brahman 7, 14, 33
Brahmanas 18, 24, 239
Branwen 11, 164
Bricriu 135–36, 242
Britain 13, 69, 77, 98, 143, 156, 198, 204–5, 215, 244
Bronze Age 20, 24–26, 47

Cad Godeu 66, 111, 242, 244
Caesar, Julius 13, 46, 51, 100–1, 105, 172, 191, 204, 243–44
Calder, George 157, 224, 242–43
Cancer 11–12, 26–27, 30, 35–38, 42, 50, 54, 57, 79, 83–84, 88, 107, 129, 131, 141, 146, 152, 163, 176, 184, 193, 197–98, 202, 208, 216, 221, 224, 226, 228–29, 231, 235
Canis Major 40–41, 88, 115, 117, 230, 235
Canis Minor 40, 115, 117, 235
Capella 98, 113, 235
Capricorn 216, 225, 228
Cassiopeia 96, 98, 102, 108, 110, 132, 136, 231
Cat star 41, 106, 235, 239
Cathbad 125
Celtiberia 50, 202, 122, 229
Cepheus 108, 110, 175, 235
Cetus 96, 115, 147, 235
Chaldean 13, 21–22, 27, 30, 39, 47, 189, 239
Ciallosbuis Sonnocingos 11, 70, 231
circumpolar stars 18, 108
clotting month 11; *see also* intercalary month
Cocteau, Jean 195
Coelbren 58, 122, 132, 240
Coligny Calendar 10–11, 38–39, 41–43, 49, 54, 70–71, 124, 170, 192, 232
Coma Berenices 98, 113, 235
comet 100–1, 188–89, 241, 243
conjunction 30, 77, 85, 97, 98,

249

100, 104, 141, 199, 200, 205–6, 230
Corona Borealis 114, 198, 230, 235
Corvus 50, 118, 235
cosmic force 187–89, 202
cosmic ray 40, 58, 90, 137, 150, 173, 191–92, 200, 205
Crater 50, 98, 118, 125, 197, 235
Cuchulainn 68, 76–77, 124–25, 150, 159, 235, 243
cusp 51, 59, 64, 78, 119, 123–24, 126, 130–31, 139–40, 166, 188, 192, 198, 203, 209, 224

Danu 14, 68, 110, 194, 231–32
Danube 13, 18–19, 32, 45, 174
Dawn Goddess 19, 176, 205, 239
December 10, 12, 71, 172, 231, 234
De Divinatione (Cicero) 204, 244
De Medicamentis (Marcellus of Bordeaux) 215, 244
Delphinus 96, 114, 235
Dendera 18, 23
Dian Cécht 211, 213, 219
Die Kosmologie der Babylonier (Peter Jensen) 22
digitalis/digitalis purpurea 214
Dis Pater 105, 202
Diviciacus 51, 204, 244
Diuon, mon 70, 91, 150, 231, 232
Don, Dôn 14, 68, 88, 97–98, 102, 109–10, 232, 241
Donn 76, 105, 165, 240
Doom, tablets of 25–26
Draco 65, 96, 108, 124, 229
Draconis 18, 73, 144–45, 148, 199, 202, 229, 231–33, 235
druid 50–52, 61, 64, 76, 78, 81, 102, 108, 112, 122, 125, 139, 141–42, 154–55, 158, 169–70, 188, 190, 194–95, 199, 203–4, 210, 211–16, 218, 236, 240–41, 244
druidess 138–39, 157, 244
Duextionu 11, 70, 233
Dumézil, Georges 8, 21, 135, 242

Early Civilization and Literacy in Europe (Harald Haarmann) 19
earth, element 64, 123, 142, 153, 181, 211, 213, 216–18
Egypt 5, 20, 22–23, 47, 48, 100
elements 216–17
Emain Abhlach 165
Emain Macha 164
empirical medicine
Engonasin 20, 96
Eochaid 14, 53, 135, 138, 148, 194, 214, 242
Equuleus 115

Eridanus 115
Etaine/Etana 145, 149, 158–59, 202
Exodus 18–19

February 12, 39–40, 58, 71, 113, 118, 172, 229, 233
Fege Fin 61, 240
Ferchertne 62, 219
fidh 140, 215, 224
file/filidh 81, 212
Finn 61, 137
fire, element 2, 33, 36, 41–42, 51, 56, 63–65, 71, 81, 90, 100, 107, 123–24, 132, 141–42, 151, 172, 182–83, 189, 196–97, 200, 205, 211, 213, 216–17, 244
fixed star 87, 96, 99, 100, 200, 205, 241
Fled Bricrend 135–36, 242
forfedha 64, 76, 123
Fourier, Joseph 18
Frawley, David 1, 6, 18, 21, 24, 27–28, 35, 239, 246

Gallic War Commentaries (Caesar) 14, 51, 92, 122, 190, 202, 204, 240, 245
Gaul 80, 170, 172, 175, 178, 201–2, 204, 215, 243
Gaulish astrology 177
Gemini 10–12, 26–28, 30, 36–39, 42, 50, 54, 57, 79, 83, 99, 107, 113, 125, 129, 131, 141, 146, 152, 162–63, 176, 183, 194, 197, 202, 208, 216, 226, 228–29, 234–35
Getae 13, 45
gnomon 179, 235
Grannos 14, 91, 147, 149, 201, 214, 232, 242
Graves, Robert 7, 9, 10–12
Great Bear 20, 109, 229, 236
Great Wain 18
Greece 3, 5, 22, 25, 29, 47, 84, 113, 139, 218, 240
Greek Zodiac 22–23, 30
Gregory, Lady Augusta 124
Greina 90, 91, 147, 165, 190, 193, 216, 231, 234, 242
Gundestrup Cauldron 24, 33, 37, 40–43, 89, 103, 106–8, 116, 121, 155, 173, 175, 180
Guton Uxellimon 13, 14, 201
Guyonvarc'h, C. and Leroux, F. 112, 212, 240, 244
Gwenhwyfar 11
Gwydion 44, 68, 88, 97, 101–2, 241

Halley's Comet 101
Hallstatt 20
Haudry, Jean 34, 246
herbal medicine 219
Hercules 20, 96, 111, 177, 233, 235, 239
Hesiodus 160
hidden planet 149

Hipparchus 17, 18, 24
Hittite 1, 5, 19, 24–27, 32, 34, 38–39, 41–43, 239
house 6, 20, 63, 126, 135, 139–47, 149, 150–51, 155–56, 160, 166, 188, 198–200, 205, 208–9
humor 217–18
Hyades 28, 35, 41–42, 105–6, 198, 230, 235
Hydra 50, 87, 99, 118, 235, 239

Ialon 244, 246–47
Ireland 59, 61, 63, 68, 89, 102, 105, 107, 110, 112, 115–16, 120, 122, 136–37, 143, 156, 158–60, 164–65, 169, 201–2, 240
Iron Age 20

Jensen, Peter 22
July 11–12, 43, 54, 70, 72, 84, 101, 141, 231, 237
June 12, 72, 118, 141, 231, 235
Jupiter 80, 90–93, 103, 127–28, 142–43, 145, 146–48, 150–52, 160–63, 179, 181, 188–94, 197–209, 225, 228–29, 234, 236

Kallisto 20
key sounds, keys of knowledge, Eochra esci 58, 60
Khrysaor 20
Krittika 18, 24, 139, 162, 243
Kurgan 32, 35

Ladon 20
La Tène 20, 101, 176, 218
leap month 11; *see also* clotting month; intercalary month
Le Goff, Alain 213, 244, 247
Leo 11–12, 18, 24, 26, 30, 35–36, 38–39, 43, 50, 54, 57, 79, 83, 108, 116, 129, 131, 147, 153, 163, 177, 184, 193, 197, 202, 208, 216, 226, 228–29, 234, 235
Leo Major 28
Lepus 26, 96, 117, 230, 235
Libra 6, 11–12, 26–28, 30, 35–39, 49, 54–55, 57, 77–78, 96, 103, 125–26, 130, 140, 142, 144, 151, 160, 163, 171, 177, 193–94, 198, 202, 208–9, 216, 224, 228–30, 235
Library of History 80, 240
Lir 68, 105, 159, 217, 231
Llyr 68, 97–99, 112
Loka 13, 52, 93
Lugh 48, 57, 83, 89, 124, 139, 165, 194, 202, 217, 240, 243
lunar dynasty 68, 149, 242
lunar mansion 10, 131, 155, 157, 159–65, 168, 199, 209, 243
lunar node 26, 72, 148, 163–64, 177–78, 189–93, 200–2, 229, 232–33

Index

Lupus 39, 98, 118, 125, 230, 235
Lyra 97, 108, 111, 184, 235

Macalister, R.A. Stewart 13, 52
Mac Cuileannain, Cormac 46
Mac Datho 136–37, 242
Macedonia 18, 23, 29, 45
MacFirbis, Duald 13
Macha 14, 117, 125, 138, 158, 164–65, 184, 201, 229, 243
macrocosm 33, 61, 63, 75, 92, 211, 216
Magha 18, 243
Magi 13, 47
Maine 68, 125, 137–38, 144–49, 156
Manannan mac Lir 89, 105, 157
Manred 211
March 12, 39, 70–71, 97, 99, 225, 231, 233, 235
Markale, Jean 110
Mars 14, 28, 36, 38, 49, 56–57, 71, 86–87, 89–93, 103, 127–28, 142–43, 145–47, 149, 150–52, 161–63, 175, 177–78, 181–82, 188–93, 197–2, 205–7, 224, 228–29, 234
Mathematici 13
May 39, 41, 71, 103, 113, 144, 184, 196, 201, 231, 235, 244
Maya Danava 21, 22
Medb/Medba 46, 63, 68, 74, 102–3, 115, 135–38, 144–47, 149, 155–61, 165, 169, 193, 201, 206, 240
medicinal plants, astrology 224
medicinal plants, herbs 220, 224
Medium Coeli, mid heaven 141, 230
Mercury 205, 207
Merlin 49, 73, 87–89, 110, 197–98, 205, 244
meteor 6, 96, 99, 100, 188–89, 209, 231
Metonic cycle 11, 24, 228
Miach 211, 213–14, 219, 244
microcosm 33, 63, 92, 211, 216
Milky Way 26, 39, 99–102, 107, 111–13, 125, 136, 229–30, 234–35, 237, 241
Mog Ruith 21, 61, 233
Monard, Joseph 14, 63, 70, 89, 91, 110, 115, 122, 124, 133, 234
moon god 135, 160, 162–64
moon goddess 70, 74, 135, 156
moon grid 74, 123, 192
Morals (Plutarch) 46–47, 52, 204, 247
Morann Mac Main 157
Morrigan 14, 138, 156, 159, 243

naked eye astronomy 9, 13, 25, 86, 91, 229
Nakshatra 46, 135, 155–56, 160, 243
NASA 87
Natural Questions (Seneca) 189, 241
Navis 98, 197, 232
Nebra disc 20, 24, 41
North Node 72–73, 90, 127, 145, 190, 193, 202
North Star 52, 93–94, 102, 179
November 12, 41, 70–71, 144, 231

October 11–12, 70, 72, 144, 230
Oengus 213, 240
O'Flaherty, Roderick 13
Ogham 51–52, 54, 58–64, 76, 78–81, 120–24, 126, 130–31, 157, 177, 192, 198, 219, 224; medicinal herbs 219, 224
Ogma 14, 55, 60, 77, 120, 243
Ogygia 13, 204
Oirmiach 214, 219
Ophiuchus 35, 37, 39, 81, 96, 108, 114, 171, 177, 236
The Origin and Deeds of the Goths (Jordanes) 13
Orion 18, 20, 115

Parsons, William, Lord Rosse 109
Pegasus 95–96, 99, 108, 112, 174, 197, 231, 236
Perseus 28, 30, 110, 113, 234, 236
Phaenomena 24, 29
Phenomenons and Prognostics 18
Philolaus 207
Pisces 11–12, 24–28, 30, 36–38, 41, 49, 54, 57, 59, 78, 82, 104, 162, 174, 181, 216, 228
Pisces Austrini 115
planetary cycle 11
planetary ruler 142, 199, 206, 142
planisphere 18–19, 23
Pleiades 20, 24, 28, 30, 41, 98, 105, 138–39, 197–98, 201, 207, 231, 236
Pluto 87, 143, 228
Pole Star 18, 102–3, 231
prenn 63, 140
Prophecies of Merlin 87
Puppis 236

Qendos 219, 225–26, 230, 233–34
Qendos Balori/Balor's Head 234
Quimon 234

Rath Cruachan 135, 143, 165
reed 12, 38, 42, 58, 65, 79, 83, 124, 129, 131, 183, 214, 226

Rennes Dindshenchas 165
Reznikov, Raimonde 234
Rig Veda 19, 23, 31, 42, 59, 120, 156, 242
Rishis 3, 13, 40, 47, 51, 242
Rome 3, 40, 101, 113, 117–18

Sagitta 19, 98, 104, 113, 198, 236
Sagittarius 11–12, 26–28, 30, 35–39, 41, 49, 54, 57, 78, 82, 102, 216, 225, 228–231, 234–236
St. Patrick 122
sanicle 214
Santarana 11; *see also* Ciallosbuis Sonnocingos
Sarianidi, Viktor 20
Saturn 28, 47, 49, 87, 89, 91–93, 120, 127–28, 142–43, 145–46, 148, 149–52, 161, 163, 178, 180–81, 188–92, 194, 197–2, 204–5, 206–9, 225, 228, 230, 233–34
Scorpio 26, 36–39, 49, 54–55, 57, 78, 81, 103, 108, 125, 127, 130, 145, 151, 160–61, 172, 177–78, 193, 198, 202, 208, 216, 224, 228–29, 232, 234, 236
Scythian 1, 33–34, 59–60, 120, 178, 239
The Secret Languages of Ireland 52
seed sounds 119
September 12, 40, 55, 72, 113, 184, 230–31
Shannon 107, 118, 159
shooting star 100
sideral month 10, 155
sideral year 10
Sidh 13, 52, 125, 141, 158, 159–60, 165, 214, 240; *see also* Loka, Sidos
Sidos 37, 52, 55, 103, 129, 165, 184, 214, 240
significator 77, 81, 142, 144–47, 151–53, 199, 206, 208–9
Sirius 18, 77, 117–18, 230
Snake star, Serpens 96, 114, 219, 232, 234, 236
solar grid, sun grid 75, 77, 123
Sophocles 213
South Node 72–73, 127, 144, 190, 193, 201–2
Sterckx, Claude 122, 242
Stone Age 9, 109
The Story of Mac Datho's pig, Thurneysen, Rudolf 136
Sumer 5, 28, 30, 32, 39, 42, 47, 239
Sumerian Zodiac 30
sun 10–11, 24, 30, 39, 42, 47, 49, 52, 54, 65, 67–68, 70, 74–78, 81, 89, 91–93, 107, 123–24, 205, 236, 242–43
sun god 22, 26, 34, 61
sun goddess 61, 69, 77

Supreme Being 13; *see also* Guton Uxellimon
Sword star, Smertus 20, 96, 235

Tain Bo Cualgne 106, 137, 156, 169, 243
Taliesin 46, 48, 66, 87, 91–92, 96, 98–99, 105, 111, 119, 131, 140, 166, 189, 191, 211–12, 216, 241
Taurus 216, 225, 228
Tech Duinn 165, 240
tempers, temperaments 218
Theodosius 105
Theon 14
Three Cranes, Trigaranai 37, 41, 56, 104–5, 236
Tom Thumb 10
tree calendar 12
Triangulum 98, 112, 236

Upanishads 62–63, 240
Uranus 87, 89–90, 143, 146, 151, 199–0, 228, 234
Ursa Major 18–20, 35, 108–9, 113, 229, 236
Ursa Minor 99, 102, 109, 137, 230, 232, 236, 242

vagabon star 13, 91, 169
vate 63, 212
Vedanta 40
Vedic Zodiac 38, 41, 59, 77, 209
Venus 67–68, 84–87, 89–94, 106, 127–28, 143–48, 151, 188, 190–92, 194, 198–99, 200–2, 205–9, 228–9, 233–34, 236, 339
Venus pentagram 84–85
Villemarqué, Hersart 195

Virgil 212
Virgo 216, 226, 228

wandering star 86–87, 90–92, 99–100, 189, 200, 229, 233, 241
water, element 55–56, 64, 74, 82, 104, 123, 128, 142, 180, 211, 213, 216–18
Wheel God 21
White Goddess 11
White Lady 11

yoke 76–77, 142, 188, 191–92, 195, 197–99, 200, 205–7

zodiacal chart 38, 57, 76, 115
zodiacal house 87, 143, 151, 230, 232